MASTERPLOTS
FIFTEEN-VOLUME
COMBINED EDITION

Volume Five
Essa-Grea

MASTERPLOTS

15-Volume Combined Edition
FIFTEEN HUNDRED AND TEN
Plot-Stories and Essay-Reviews
from the
WORLD'S FINE LITERATURE

Edited by
FRANK N. MAGILL

Story Editor
DAYTON KOHLER

VOLUME FIVE — ESSA-GREA

SALEM PRESS
INCORPORATED
NEW YORK

This work also appears under the title of

MASTERPIECES OF WORLD LITERATURE IN DIGEST FORM

ESSAYS OF ELIA and LAST ESSAYS OF ELIA

Type of work: Essays
Author: Charles Lamb (1775-1834)
First published: 1823 and 1833

Among modern platitudes at least half true is the assertion that conversation is a lost art. Certainly more than half true is a similar statement: that the art of the personal essay as practiced by Charles Lamb in *The Essays of Elia* is an art that few modern writers practice. Both conversation and the personal essay—as might be pointed out by persons who lived at other stages of our culture—depend on periods of quiet, periods of boredom, and finally mental action that is various and witty, the display of riches that have been laid up in periods of quiet and refined in periods of apparent boredom. The personal essay, at any rate, can be only the product of a person who has followed from his youth onward the dictum of Dr. Samuel Johnson and read five hours a day and who, in his middle years, takes delight in displaying, sometimes with mock modesty, the fruits of silent study. Lamb's essays are, at any rate, a kind of conversation with the unhurried reader; and the reader's part, though mute, is essential. He must be a "good listener"; he must be patient and allot to Lamb time enough to play with a thought as well as to develop it; he must award a smile to the poor "jokes" that mingle with the good ones told by Elia; he must be able to follow the quick alternations of mood that appear in such essays as "The South-Sea House," "Dream-Children," and "The Superannuated Man." He must be willing to be irresponsibly playful along with the author who is, at a particular moment, writing "A Dissertation on Roast Pig" or "A Chapter on Ears."

For these reasons it is obvious that the old-style personal essay, as written by Lamb and his great contemporary William Hazlitt, is a form of writing to which hasty readers, readers for information, will continue to remain indiffer-ent. Such readers read essays as they attend lectures. They wish to be informed about a topic on which, it is supposed, the speaker is an expert. Or they hope to be given a new set of ideas; and they scan these ideas energetically to see whether the lecturer is unsound on crucial issues. Lamb demands no such attention; indeed, he suffers from it. Lamb does not write to convey ideas or facts or convictions even though his essays are full of all these. But his ideas are mostly playful, as in "Sanity of True Genius"; he aims not to persuade the reader of the truth of a concept but chiefly to provide temporary entertainment by presenting a startling assertion. And though his essays abound in facts about old houses and old relatives and old clerks, they are not facts that "prove" anything; they simply stand as reminders of mileposts along which "Elia" (Lamb's pen name) has passed in his journey—mileposts of which it is amusing to speak. Finally, Elia-Lamb is not without convictions, but they are not ideas that command attention because they belong to the abstract level of philosophy. The true, the beautiful, and the good do not exist in Lamb's essays and demand our assent or denial. Lamb's mind seizes little portions of truth that turn up in the daily round. In his world virtue is not a system; it is a fleeting deed or a glance of affection detected in a parlor, over a game of whist. Nor is beauty an intellectual entity; it is, at the most, a hundred tiny little impressions recorded during a summer stroll and now shared with us.

By such perceptions we can come to understand what Lamb's essays offer to us. Originally written for the *London Magazine,* the essays survive their first appearance in a modest but insistent way. Weightier writing of the time—Coleridge's essays, for example, which were not conversations but lectures and "final" philosophical pronouncements, and similar writings—survive in the "complete works" and become the subject of graduate study. Lamb's essays continue to speak to a small but faithful company of readers who are more drawn by a tone, a sensibility delicate and yet robust, hinting rather than explicit. (Some of this company are probably readers of Jane Austen also, whose ideas may fade but whose perceptions of truth are deathless.)

Doubtless the conditions of Lamb's life, once they are known, add to the interest of the essays. That Lamb had a stammer and could not find a way to complete his education, that he worked through a hundred folios of bookkeeping for the East India Company, that violence and insanity threatened the good cheer of his life, that "Dream-Children" was written by a man condemned to solitary life, that "Old China" speaks of luxury that Lamb himself could never possess, that many essays explore old books that Lamb haunted bookstalls to buy—all such knowledge adds to our response to the blend of whimsy, outright jest, and fleeting sentiment in the essays.

This blend was Lamb's own. But it is not without its models in language and form, as Lamb would be ready to admit. It might be said that Lamb's literary tastes caused him to leap backward more than a century. He ignored the essays of Addison and Steele and even more those of Dr. Samuel Johnson; these were writers who tended toward public address, public instruction, and public betterment, whatever they treated. Lamb, who sought an audience of friends rather than a cluster of worshipful inferiors, turned to such seventeenth-century masters as Sir Thomas Browne and Robert Burton, men who wrote before English prose had taken on a cold, instructing, and regular form. Sir Thomas Browne said, "I love to lose myself in O Altitudos"; and in such spirit does Lamb love to pursue the small ecstasies of his daily life: the middle-class jaunts, the excitements of the card-table, and the thrills of inexpensive theatrical attendance. "T'is all mine, none mine," wrote Robert Burton of his disorderly masterpiece, *The Anatomy of Melancholy,* that vast tissue of quotation and opinionated comment. So might Lamb say; whatever he treats, there are ancient echoes. In these echoes sound the quaint, crabbed spirits of Browne and Burton, and the more generous and still more undisciplined natures of Elizabethan dramatists who, though "minor," were one and all great to Lamb, one of their first "discoverers."

No analysis or digest can suggest to the reader the charm of the *Essays of Elia* or the *Last Essays.* They must, if we may use a word-play that would please Lamb, not be *di*gested but digested, and that again and again.

ESTHER WATERS

Type of work: Novel
Author: George Moore (1852-1933)
Type of plot: Naturalism
Time of plot: Late nineteenth century
Locale: England
First published: 1894

Principal characters:
ESTHER WATERS, a servant girl
WILLIAM LATCH, her betrayer
MRS. BARFIELD, her mistress
SARAH TUCKER, her enemy
JACKIE, her son
FRED PARSONS, her betrothed
MISS RICE, her employer

Critique:

Esther Waters is a landmark in the development of realism in English fiction. The story of Esther and her struggle against almost insurmountable odds shows the influence of Balzac and Zola. Between Richardson's *Pamela* and Moore's *Esther Waters* there is a dividing line of a completely new theory of art as well as a division of time in the history of the novel.

The Story:

The first person Esther Waters met when she arrived at Woodview was William Latch, the son of the cook under whose direction Esther was to work. William was the bane of his mother's life, for he was like his dead father, a gambler. Mrs. Latch had hoped that William would become a delivery boy and leave Woodview, but William was determined to go into service for Mr. and Mrs. Barfield, the owners of Woodview, in order to observe their racing stable.

The position as kitchenmaid at Woodview was a godsend to Esther, for her stepfather, claiming that he had too many mouths to feed, had forced her to leave home. The workhouse might have been her only refuge if she had not secured a position with the Barfields. But in spite of her efforts to do her work well, it was hard for her to get along with the other servants. Mrs. Latch seemed to go out of her way to make life unpleasant for Esther, and the maids teased her because she was religious. Among the servants, William was at first her only champion, and she was grateful to him. Then Esther found an unexpected friend in her mistress, Mrs. Barfield. She, too, was deeply religious, and she invited Esther to join the services she held in her room each Sunday morning. Learning that Esther could not read, Mrs. Barfield tried to teach her. To Esther, Mrs. Barfield seemed a friend as well as an employer.

Mrs. Barfield's interest made Esther's life easier for a time. William continued to pay her special attention, to the anguish of Sarah Tucker, another of the maids. After a servant's ball in celebration of the victory of one of the Woodview horses, William took Esther out to some wheat stacks and seduced her after telling her that they would be married as soon as he had enough money. By the following morning Esther had convinced herself that she had been betrayed, and she refused to speak to William. He tried to reason with her, telling her that he loved her and they would be married soon, but she would not listen. Tiring at last of her sulking, he turned to Miss Peggy Barfield, a cousin of his master, and after a few weeks eloped with her.

Three months later Esther realized that she was pregnant. Strangely, the servant girls who had been her former tormentors became kind and sympathetic, and their kindness made her feel even more ashamed of her wickedness. In spite of her sympathy, Mrs. Barfield had to send Esther away, for she had become a bad example for the other girls.

There was no place for her to go but to her home. There she found her mother also pregnant and her stepfather more cruel than ever. But he tolerated her as long as she paid her rent and gave him money to buy beer. At last Esther knew that she would have to leave before all her savings were used up and there would be nothing left for her baby.

She took lodgings close to the hospital where she was to be confined. After her son, Jackie, was born, she was filled with a happiness she had never known before, but her joy was lessened when she learned that her mother had died in childbirth, just a few days after Esther's baby was born. Soon afterward Esther's stepfather and the other children went to Australia; with their going Esther felt that she was really alone in the world.

For Esther the next few years were terrible ones. Sometimes she worked seventeen and eighteen hours a day. Once she had to go to the workhouse. Her greatest grief was the need to leave her child in someone's care while she worked, for Jackie was her whole life. When he was six years old, Esther found work with Miss Rice, a writer whose home was a haven to Esther. Miss Rice knew Esther's story and tried to make the girl's life easier for her.

One day Esther met Fred Parsons, a colorless man, but honest, dependable, and religious. When Esther told him her story, he readily forgave her. She took Fred to see Jackie, and the man and the boy were fast friends from the first meeting. Esther and Fred planned to be married as soon as Miss Rice could get another servant, for Esther would not leave her mistress uncared-for. One evening, while on an errand for Miss Rice, Esther unexpectedly met William Latch, who told her that Peggy had left him. When he learned that Esther had borne his child, he pleaded to come back to her, and hinted that it was her Christian duty to Jackie to give the boy his rightful father. Esther knew that she would be better off with Fred, as would Jackie, for William had become a tavern keeper and a bookie. But Jackie met his father and loved him instantly. For his sake Esther and William were married.

At first William made money. Jackie was put in a good school, and Esther had two servants to wait on her. But there were days of anxious waiting to hear the results of a race. Often William had thousands of pounds to cover if the favorite won. After a time he began to lose heavily. It was against the law to accept bets at the tavern, and William was in constant danger of being reported to the police. Fred Parsons came to warn Esther to leave William, to tell her that the tavern was to be raided, but Esther refused to desert her husband. Then Sarah Tucker came to the tavern to ask for help after she had stolen a silver plate from her employer. The police found her there. Later, when the tavern was raided, William's fine was heavy. Business began to dwindle, and Esther and William had lean times.

After William became tubercular, the dampness and fog of the race tracks only made him cough more, and at last he had to go to the hospital. There the doctors told him that he must go to Egypt for his health. He and Esther gambled all their money on a single race, and lost. Esther tried to be cheerful for William's sake, but when he died a few days later she wished that she had died with him. She had no money and no place to go. Her only blessing was that Jackie was big enough to take care of himself.

Esther went back to Woodview. Only Mrs. Barfield was left, and she was poor. Most of the land had gone to pay racing debts. But Esther would have stayed with Mrs. Barfield without wages, for she had never forgotten her old friend's kindness. Jackie enlisted in the army and went to Woodview to tell his mother goodbye. With pride she introduced him to Mrs. Barfield. She knew that her sin had been redeemed and that she would never have to be ashamed again. She had given her country a fine soldier. Few women could do more.

ETHAN FROME

Type of work: Novel
Author: Edith Wharton (1862-1937)
Type of plot: Domestic tragedy
Time of plot: Late nineteenth century
Locale: Starkfield, Massachusetts
First published: 1911

Principal characters:

ETHAN FROME, a New England farmer
ZENOBIA FROME (ZEENA), his wife
MATTIE SILVER, Zeena's cousin

Critique:

Although not considered representative of Edith Wharton's works, *Ethan Frome* is probably the best and most popular of her novels. Told in less than two hundred pages, it is a tragic story of three peoples' wasted lives: Ethan Frome; Zeena, his wife; and young Mattie Silver, Zeena's cousin. Through the flash-back technique, Edith Wharton permits us to glimpse the fate of Ethan Frome at the beginning, but we must wait until the end of the book to see how that fate is brought about. Although we know that the story is to have an unhappy ending, the author's crushing use of irony makes the conclusion come as a surprise.

The Story:

Ethan Frome was twenty-eight years old when he married Zenobia Pierce, a distant cousin who nursed his sick mother during her last illness. It was a wedding without love. Zenobia, called Zeena, had no home of her own, and Ethan was lonely. So they were married. But Zeena's talkativeness, which had been pleasing to Ethan during his mother's illness, quickly subsided, and within a year of their marriage Zeena developed the sickliness which was to plague her husband all her life. Ethan became increasingly dissatisfied with his life. He was an intelligent and ambitious young man who had hoped to become an engineer or a chemist. But he soon found himself chained to a wife he detested and a farm he could not sell.

The arrival of Mattie Silver brightened the gloomy house considerably. Mattie, Zeena's cousin, had come to Starkfield partly because she had no other place to go and partly because Zeena felt in need of a companion around the house. Ethan saw in Mattie's goodness and beauty every fine quality that Zeena lacked.

When Zeena suggested that Ethan help Mattie find a husband, he began to realize how much he himself was attracted to the girl. When he went to a church social to bring Mattie home and saw her dancing with the son of a rich Irish grocer, he realized that he was jealous of his rival and in love with Mattie. On his way home with her, Ethan felt his love for Mattie more than ever, for on that occasion as on others, she flattered him by asking him questions on astronomy. His dreams of happiness were short-lived however, for when he reached home Zeena was her nagging, sour self. The contrast between Zeena and Mattie impressed him more and more.

One day Ethan returned from his morning's work to find Zeena dressed in her traveling clothes. She was going to visit a new doctor in nearby Bettsbridge. Ordinarily Ethan would have objected to the journey because of the expensive remedies which Zeena was in the habit of buying on her trips to town. But on that occasion he was overjoyed at the news of Zeena's proposed departure, for he realized that he and Mattie would have the house to themselves overnight.

With Zeena out of the way, Ethan again became a changed man. Later in the evening, before supper, Ethan and Mattie sat quietly before the fire, just as Ethan imagined happily married couples would do. During supper the cat broke Zeena's favorite pickle dish, which Mattie had used to brighten up the table. In spite of the accident, they spent the rest of the evening happily. They talked about going sledding together, and Ethan told shyly—and perhaps wistfully—that he had seen Ruth Varnum and Ned Hale, a young engaged couple, stealing a kiss earlier in the evening.

In the morning Ethan was happy, but not because of anything out of the ordinary the night before. In fact, when he went to bed, he remembered sadly that he had not so much as touched Mattie's fingertips or looked into her eyes. He was happy because he could imagine what a wonderful life he could have if he were married to Mattie. He got glue to mend the pickle dish, but Zeena's unexpected return prevented him from repairing it. His spirits were further dampened when Zeena told him that the Bettsbridge doctor considered her quite sick. He had advised her to get a girl to relieve her of all household duties, a stronger girl than Mattie. She had already engaged the new girl. Ethan was dumbfounded by this development. In her insistence that Mattie be sent away Zeena gave the first real hint that she may have been aware of gossip about her husband and Mattie.

When Ethan told Mattie of Zeena's decision, the girl was as crestfallen as Ethan. Zeena interrupted their lamentations, however, by coming downstairs for something to eat. After supper she required stomach powders to relieve a case of heartburn. In getting the powders, which she had hidden in a spot supposedly unknown to Mattie, Zeena discovered the broken pickle dish, which had been carefully reassembled in order to give the appearance of being unbroken. Having detected the deception and learned that Mattie was responsible for the broken dish, Zeena called Mattie insulting names and showed plainly that the girl would be sent away at the earliest possible moment.

Faced with the certainty of Mattie's departure, Ethan thought of running away with her. But his poverty, as well as his sense of responsibility to Zeena, offered no solution to his problem, only greater despair. On the morning Mattie was to leave Starkfield, Ethan, against the wishes of his wife, insisted on driving Mattie to the station. The thought of parting was unbearable to both. They decided to take the sleigh ride that Ethan had promised Mattie the night before. Down the hill they went, narrowly missing a large elm tree at the bottom. Mattie, who had told Ethan that she would rather die than leave him, begged until Ethan agreed to take her down the hill a second time and run the sled into the elm at the bottom of the slope. But they failed to hit the tree with force sufficient to kill them. The death they sought became a living death, for in the accident Mattie suffered a permanent spine injury and Ethan an incurable lameness. The person who received Mattie into her home, who waited on her, and who cooked for Ethan was—Zeena.

ETHICS

Type of work: Philosophy
Author: Benedictus de Spinoza (1632-1677)
First published: 1677

The complete Latin title of Spinoza's masterpiece is *Ethica ordine geometrico demonstrata.* A geometric demonstration of ethics is a novelty in the history of thought, but this work is famous not because of, but in spite of, its novelty of method. The principal advantage of the method is that it reveals Spinoza's thought as clearly as possible, and although the demonstrations may not satisfy critics who concern themselves only with definitions and logical form, they have a strong persuasive force upon those who, already committed to the love of the good and of God, need clarity and structure in their thoughts.

Spinoza begins with definitions, proceeds to axioms (unproved but obviously acceptable), and then to propositions and demonstrations. Obviously, if one must find fault with Spinoza's argument, any place is vulnerable, for one can quarrel about the definitions, doubt the truth of the axioms, or question the validity of the demonstrations. But in order to reject the book it would be necessary to question the integrity and wisdom of Spinoza's spirit, and that would be not only difficult but impertinent to do.

It has long been regarded an error in philosophy to attempt to deduce what men ought to do from a study of what men do, but what Spinoza attempts is a deduction of what men ought to do from a study of what must be, according to his definitions and axioms. The primary criticism of his method, then, is not that he errs—although most critics find errors in Spinoza—but that he tries to use logical means to derive ethical truths. The criticism depends, of course, on the assumption that ethical truths are either matters of fact, not of logic, or else that they are not truths at all but, for example, emotive expressions.

Spinoza begins the *Ethics* with defini-

tions of "cause," "finite," "substance," "attribute," "mode," "free," "eternity," and "God," the latter term being defined to mean "Being absolutely infinite, that is to say, substance consisting of infinite attributes, each one of which expresses eternal and infinite essence." To understand this definition one must relate it to the definitions of the terms within it —such as "substance," "finite," and "attribute"—but one must also resist the temptation to identify the term, so defined, with any conventionally used term. Spinoza's God is quite different from anyone else's God, at least in conception. The point of the definition is that what Spinoza means by "God" is whatever is "conceived through itself" (is substance), has no limit to its essential characteristics (has infinite attributes), and maintains its character eternally. As one might suspect, the definition of "God" is crucial.

The axioms contain such logical and semantical truths as "I. Everything which is, is either in itself or in another"; "II. That which cannot be conceived through another must be conceived through itself"; "VI. A true idea must agree with that of which it is the idea," and "VII. The essence of that thing which can be conceived as not existing does not involve existence." At first the axioms may be puzzling, but they are not as extraordinary as they seem. The last axiom, for example, number VII, means only that anything which can be thought of as not existing does not by its nature *have* to exist.

The propositions begin as directly implied by the definitions: "I. Substance is by its nature prior to its modifications" follows from the definitions of "substance" and "mode," and "II. Two substances having different attributes have nothing in common with one another" is another consequence of the definition of "substance." As the propositions increase, the proofs become longer, making reference not only to definitions but also to previous propositions and their corollaries. For those interested in technical philosophy the proofs are intriguing even when they are unconvincing, but for others they are unnecessary; the important thing is to get at Spinoza's central idea.

Proposition XI is important in preparing the way for Spinoza's main contention: "XI. God or substance consisting of infinite attributes, each one of which expresses eternal and infinite essence, necessarily exists." Although one may be tempted to seize upon this proposition as an instrument to use against atheists, it is necessary to remember that the term "God" is a technical term for Spinoza and has little, if anything, to do with the object of religious worship.

Proposition XIV soon follows with the startling claim that "Besides God no substance can be nor can be conceived." A corollary of this proposition is the idea that God is one; that is, everything that exists, all of nature, is God. Individual things do not by their natures exist, but only through God's action; and God is not only the cause of their existence but also of their natures. (XXIV, XXV.) We might expect, consequently, that a great deal of the universe is contingent; that is, it depends upon something other than itself and need not be as it is. But Spinoza argues in Proposition XXIX that "In Nature, there is nothing contingent, but all things are determined from the necessity of the divine nature to exist and act in a certain manner." Consequently, man's will is not free but necessary. (XXXII.) This was one of the ideas that made Spinoza unpopular with both Jews and Christians.

Having used Part One of the *Ethics* to develop the conception of God, Spinoza goes on in Part Two, after presenting further definitions and axioms, to explain the nature and origin of mind. Here again Spinoza concludes that "In the mind there is no absolute or free will

. . ." (XLVIII.) In this section he also. develops the idea that God is a thinking and extended being.

In Part Three, "On the Origin and Nature of the Emotions," Spinoza argues that emotions are confused ideas. "Our mind acts at times and at times suffers," he contends in Proposition I of Part Three; "in so far as it has adequate ideas, it necessarily acts; and in so far as it has inadequate ideas, it necessarily suffers." Perhaps it is well to note that Spinoza defines "emotion" as any modification of the body "by which the power of acting of the body itself is increased, diminished, helped, or hindered, together with the ideas of these modifications."

By this time in his book Spinoza has created the idea that God, as both thinking and extended substance, is such that all nature is both thinking and extended (since everything that is must be part of God). Another way of putting it is that everything that exists does so both as body and as idea. Thus, the human being exists as both body and idea. If, then, the human being, as idea, does not adequately comprehend the modifications of the human body, the mind suffers.

In Part Four, "Of Human Bondage; or of the Strength of the Emotions," Spinoza defines the good as "that which we certainly know is useful to us," and in a series of propositions he develops the idea that each person necessarily desires what he considers to be good, that in striving to preserve his being a man acquires virtue, and that the desire to be happy and to live well involves desiring to act, to live, "that is to say, actually to exist." In this attempt to relate man's freedom to his will to act and in the identification of the good with the striving toward existence, Spinoza anticipated much of the more significant work of the twentieth-century Existentialists.

In Proposition XXVIII of Part IV, Spinoza writes that "The highest good of the mind is the knowledge of God, and the highest virtue of the mind is to know God." This claim has been prepared for by previous propositions relating the good to what is desired, the desire to action, action to being, and being to God. Because of the intricacy of Spinoza's argument it becomes possible for him to argue that to seek being, to seek the good, to use reason, and to seek God are one and the same. To use reason involves coming to have adequate ideas, having adequate ideas involves knowing the nature of things, knowing the nature of things involves knowing God.

Although it might seem that Spinoza's philosophy, for all its references to God, is egoistic in that this crucial phase of his argument depends upon the claim that each man seeks to preserve his own being, a full examination of Part IV will show that Spinoza manages to transcend the egoistic base of action by arguing that to serve the self best one uses reason; but to use reason is to seek an adequate idea of God and, consequently, to seek what is good for all men. In fact, Spinoza specifically states that whatever causes men to live in harmony with one another is profitable and good, and that whatever brings discord is evil.

The highest happiness or blessedness of man, according to Spinoza, is "the peace of mind which springs from the intuitive knowledge of God." This conclusion is certainly consistent with Spinoza's ideas that man's good consists in escaping from the human bondage of the passions, that to escape from the passions is to understand the causes that affect the self, that to understand the causes involves action, and that action leads to God.

When man through rational action comes to determine himself, he participates in the essence of all being; he becomes so at one with God that he possesses an intellectual love of God, which is man's blessedness and virtue. The eternal is known only by the eternal; hence, in knowing God, man makes himself eternal—not in any finite or individual way, but as part of God's being.

Divested of its formal trappings and of those respects in which philosophic imagination outruns credibility—for example, the claim that everything is both thought and extension—Spinoza's philosophy of ethics tells the reader that happiness consists in understanding the causes of things. It might be argued that this idea, so familiar in philosophy, puts more simply than any other concept the kind of faith that makes a man a philosopher. But to understand the causes of things is, as Spinoza concludes, "as difficult as it is rare."

EUGENE ARAM

Type of work: Novel
Author: Edward George Earle Bulwer-Lytton (1803-1873)
Type of plot: Mystery romance
Time of plot: Mid-eighteenth century
Locale: England
First published: 1832

Principal characters:
ROWLAND LESTER, an English gentleman
MADELINE, his daughter
ELLINOR, another daughter
WALTER LESTER, a nephew
HOUSEMAN, a rogue
EUGENE ARAM, a scholar

Critique:

The history of the crime and trial of Eugene Aram had fascinated English writers long before Bulwer-Lytton wrote his novel on the subject. In an introduction to his book he comments on the popularity of the story and deplores that he is not a greater writer so that he could better handle the intriguing tale. The novel attempts to show that a man of good character can, under the influence of poverty and hunger, of desire and mental confusion, commit a serious crime. The novel has qualities which link it to both *Crime and Punishment* and the Doctor Faustus legend.

The Story:

When Geoffrey Lester, a roving and dissipated man, ran away from his wife and only son, his brother, Rowland Lester, took the forsaken family into his own home at Grassdale. Soon both brothers' wives died, and kindly old Rowland took over the responsibility of rearing not only his two daughters, Madeline and Ellinor, but also his young nephew, Walter. As the children grew up, Walter fell in love with Madeline, but his love was not returned. It was Ellinor who idealized her cousin as a perfect young man.

One day a stranger came to Grassdale, a crude, ugly man who was to affect all their lives. Madeline and Ellinor, startled by the man while they were out walking, fled to the house of Eugene Aram, a young recluse and scholar whom they knew slightly. Aram did his best to make the two sisters comfortable and went to secure a carriage to take them home. During his absence the stranger came to the cottage and asked if Eugene Aram were in. He was sent away. That night he appeared again at the cottage. Aram recognized him as a man named Houseman, whom he had known under dreadful circumstances years before.

Aram, in spite of his solitary preoccupation with science and philosophy, began to visit the Lester family. Before long it was obvious to Walter that Madeline and Aram were falling in love, and Walter begged Rowland to let him go away for a while. Rowland, sensing his nephew's feelings, allowed him to go. Before he left, Walter had a long talk with Madeline and warned her to consider well her fondness for Aram, who he felt would not make her happy. Madeline took his advice as an insult to her intelligence, and the anger which she showed went far to dispel the love Walter had felt for her.

Walter and Bunting, a servant, set out for London. Old Rowland had given Walter several letters of introduction to his friends there and had advised the boy to learn what he could about the fortunes of his lost father. From an old friend of his uncle, Walter learned that Geoffrey Lester had been to India, had returned, and under the name of Clarke had gone to

1119

Yorkshire to collect a legacy left him by a friend he had known in India. Walter and Bunting started for Yorkshire to trace Geoffrey's whereabouts.

Meanwhile Houseman reappeared in Grassdale and again bothered Aram. In times past Houseman had been connected with Aram in a way which Aram did not wish to have announced to the world. Houseman, Aram knew, was involved in robbery and worse, but he was not in a position to expose the man. Houseman promised to leave the country if Aram would settle a yearly allowance on Houseman's daughter, the only person in the world whom he loved or who loved him. Aram went to London, where he was able to raise the sum demanded by Houseman. When he returned to Grassdale, Aram thought that he was rid of Houseman forever.

In Yorkshire Walter learned that his father had been seen last in the village of Knaresborough. On the way there he and Bunting met Houseman, whom Walter recognized as a man who had robbed him on a previous occasion. Bunting recognized him as a man who had been in Grassdale. Houseman, having learned that his daughter was dying, was hastening to Knaresborough, where she lay on her deathbed. As his horse had gone lame, Houseman begged Walter to lend him his, and Walter, despite Bunting's objections, was so moved by the man's story that he did so.

When they arrived at Knaresborough, the two travelers learned that Houseman had arrived in time to hold his daughter in his arms before she died. Walter also learned more of his father, who under the name of Clarke had come to the town years before. He had also, Walter was told, stolen some jewels and run up bills in all the shops of the town before he had mysteriously disappeared. An inquest had been held after Clarke's disappearance, and the last two men who had seen him had been tried, but released for lack of evidence. With surprise and horror Walter heard that these two men were House-

man and Eugene Aram.

Walter went immediately to see Houseman, whom he found almost mad over the death of his child. He was unable to answer Walter's questions. Then came word of the discovery of a body that had been buried about the time Clarke had disappeared. Walter forced Houseman to go with him to the newly opened grave and demanded to know if those were the bones of his father. Houseman said that the bones were not those of Clarke, that Clarke had been killed and his body buried in a cave. He said that he and Aram had planned to rob Clarke, but that in the struggle Aram had killed Clarke. The remains of Clarke were uncovered in the place Houseman had described. Walter prepared to return home with the news that Madeline's lover was a murderer.

Meanwhile Rowland had given his permission to the marriage of Madeline and Aram, and had come to love his prospective son-in-law almost as much as he loved his daughter. Walter's arrival with his terrible news threw the household into despair. Aram, arrested for the crime, denied his guilt. Madeline wasted away with grief over the affair, and old Rowland could barely make himself see the reasons which made his nephew bring his charge against Aram.

As the day of the trial drew near, Madeline grew weaker and weaker. Walter realized that whether Aram was found guilty or not guilty, there was no place for him in England. If Aram was judged not guilty, Walter could never ask forgiveness, especially as he would always doubt the judgment. If Aram was found guilty, Walter could not face his family and Madeline again.

At last the day of the trial arrived. Madeline, convinced of Aram's innocence, went dressed in the clothes she had hoped to wear at her wedding. Houseman was called as a witness by the prosecution. Aram defended himself by pointing out the lack of evidence and the contradiction between his own life and the life of a man who could commit such a crime. Houseman's testimony, he said, could not be counted, as Houseman was known as a thief and robber. But the jury, in accordance with the judge's statement that it was often possible for a man who had led an exemplary life to commit a crime, brought in a verdict of guilty.

As she returned home from the court, Madeline died, broken-hearted. In jail Aram still maintained his innocence. Walter, in great mental turmoil over the decision of the court, was disturbed by fears that Aram might not be guilty and that he had caused both the death of his cousin and Aram without reason. Granted permission to visit Aram in jail, Walter pleaded with the prisoner to tell him the truth. Aram promised to leave a letter which Walter could read after the execution.

Walter awaited with anxiety the day of the execution. When it was over, he opened the letter and read Aram's confession of guilt. Aram tried to justify his deed. He had robbed so that he would have money to continue scientific studies which he thought would be of great benefit to mankind. The murder had been the accidental killing of a worthless rogue who had run away from his family, a liar and a thief. Aram thought it only right that such a man should be robbed, even killed, if the money gained went to the betterment of mankind. He had not known that Clarke had really been Geoffrey Lester, uncle of the woman he later planned to marry. Walter was astonished at a mind, so brilliant in so many respects, which could draw such false conclusions.

Walter kept the letter a secret. Knowing the grief he had caused, he left the home of his uncle and cousin and lived for many years abroad. On his return he went secretly to Grassdale. There Bunting recognized his old master, showed him old Rowland's grave, and gave him directions to the place where Ellinor lived. After a time Walter and Ellinor married and lived a happy life which served to compensate for all the grief the family had known in the past.

EUGENE ONEGIN

Type of work: Poem
Author: Alexander Pushkin (1799-1837)
Type of plot: Impressionistic romance
Time of plot: Nineteenth century
Locale: Russia
First published: 1833

Principal characters:
EUGENE ONEGIN, a Russian dandy
VLADIMIR LENSKY, his friend
TATYANA LARIN, in love with Eugene
OLGA, her sister

Critique:

The outstanding character in this narrative poem is Tatyana, often called the first in the long line of Russian heroines; indeed, *Eugene Onegin* as a whole must be regarded as a kind of fountainhead for the illustrious group of nineteenth-century Russian novels. Pushkin's conception of his theme is romantic and his treatment often lyrical. There are in the poem many autobiographical elements, particularly in the resemblance between Eugene and Pushkin himself. The Soviet regime has continued to set a high value on Pushkin's work. The poem was dramatized as an opera by Tschaikowsky.

The Story:

Eugene Onegin was brought up in the aristocratic tradition. Although he had little classical background, he had a flashing wit and he was well-read in economics. He had become an accomplished man of the world by the time he reached young manhood. In fact, he had been so successful in love and so accustomed to the social life of Moscow that he habitually felt a supreme boredom with life. Even the ballet had lately failed to hold his attention.

Eugene's father had led the usual life. He gave balls regularly and tried his best to keep up his social position by borrowing recklessly. Just as he was declared a bankrupt, Eugene received word that his uncle was dying. Since he was the heir, he left in haste to attend the dying man. Grumbling meanwhile at the call of duty,

he was thankful to be coming into an inheritance.

His uncle, however, died before he arrived. After the relatives had departed Eugene settled down to enjoy his uncle's handsome country estate. The cool woods and the fertile fields charmed him at first, but after two days of country life his old boredom returned. He soon acquired a reputation as an eccentric. If neighbors called, Eugene found himself obliged to leave on an urgent errand. After a while the neighbors left him to himself.

Vladimir Lensky remained his friend. At eighteen Vladimir was still romantic and filled with illusions of life and love. He had been in Germany, where he was much influenced by Kant and Schiller. In Russia his German temperament set him apart. He and Eugene became more and more intimate.

The Larins had two daughters, Olga and Tatyana. Olga was pretty and popular, and although she was the younger, she was the leader in their group. Tatyana was reserved and withdrawn, but a discerning observer would have seen her real beauty. She made no effort to join in the country life. Olga had been long betrothed to Vladimir; the family despaired of a marriage for Tatyana.

On Vladimir's invitation Eugene reluctantly agreed to pay a visit to the Larins. When the family heard that the two men were coming, they immediately thought of Eugene as a suitor for Tatyana. But Eugene was greatly bored with his visit. The refreshments were too ample and too rustic, and the talk was heavy and dull. He paid little attention to Tatyana.

After he left, Tatyana was much disturbed. Having fallen deeply in love, she had no arts to lead Eugene on. After confiding in her dull-witted nurse, she wrote Eugene a passionate, revealing love letter. She wrote in French, for she could not write Russian grammatically.

Eugene, stirred by her letter, paid another visit to the Larins and found Tatyana in a secluded garden. He told her the brutal truth. He was not a good man for a husband, for he had had too much experience with women and too many disillusionments. Life with him would not be at all worthy of Tatyana. The girl, making no protest, suffered in silence.

On his lonely estate Eugene lived the life of an anchorite. He bathed every morning in a stream, read, walked and rode in the countryside, and slept soundly nights. Only Vladimir called occasionally.

That winter the Larins celebrated Tatyana's name-day. When Vladimir represented the gathering as only a small family affair, Eugene consented to go. He felt betrayed when he found the guests numerous, the food heavy, and the ball obligatory. For revenge, he danced too much with Olga, preventing Vladimir from enjoying his fiancée's company. Vladimir became jealously angry and challenged Eugene to a duel. Through stubbornness Eugene accepted the challenge.

Before the duel Vladimir went to see Olga. His purpose was to reproach her for her behavior, but Olga, as cheerful and affectionate as ever, acted as if nothing had happened. More light-hearted but somewhat puzzled, Vladimir prepared to meet Eugene on the dueling ground.

When the two friends met, Eugene shot Vladimir through the heart. Remorseful at last, Eugene left his estate to wander by himself. Olga soon afterward married an army man and left home.

In spite of the scandal, Tatyana still loved Eugene. She visited his house and made friends with his old housekeeper. She sat in his study reading his books and pondering his marginal notes. Eugene had been especially fond of *Don Juan* and other cynical works, and his notes revealed much about his selfishness and disillusionment. Tatyana, who had hitherto read very little, learned much bitterness from his books and came to know more of Eugene.

At home Tatyana's mother did not know what to do. The girl seemed to have no interest in suitors and had refused several proposals. On the advice of relatives the mother decided to take Tatyana to Moscow, where there were more eligible men. They were to visit a cousin for a season in hopes that Tatyana would become betrothed.

From her younger cousins Tatyana learned to do her hair stylishly and to act more urbanely in society. At a ball a famous general, a prince, was attracted to Tatyana. In spite of the fact that he was big and fat she accepted his proposal.

After more than two years of wandering, Eugene returned to Moscow. Still indifferent to life, he decided to attend a fashionable ball, simply to escape from boredom for a few hours. He was warmly greeted by his host, whom he had known well in former times. While the prince was reproaching him for his long absence, Eugene could not keep from staring at a queenly woman who dominated the gathering. She looked familiar. When he asked the prince about her, he was astounded to learn that she was Tatyana, his host's wife.

The changed Tatyana showed no traces of the shy rustic girl who had written so revealingly of her love. Eugene, much attracted to her, frequently went to her house, but he never received more than a cool reception and a distant hand to kiss.

Finally Eugene began to write her letters in which he expressed his hopeless longing. Still Tatyana gave no sign. All that winter Eugene kept to his gloomy room, reading and musing. At last, in desperation, he called on Tatyana unannounced and surprised her rereading his letters.

Tatyana refused to give in to his importunate declarations. Why had he scorned the country girl and why did he now pursue the married woman? She would rather listen to his brutal rejection than to new pleadings. She had once been in love with Eugene and would gladly have been his wife; perhaps she was still in love with him. Perhaps she had been wrong in listening to her mother, who had been insistent that she marry the prince. But now she was married, and she would remain faithful to her husband until she died.

EUGÉNIE GRANDET

Type of work: Novel
Author: Honoré de Balzac (1799-1850)
Type of plot: Naturalism
Time of plot: Early nineteenth century
Locale: Saumur, France
First published: 1833

Principal characters:
MONSIEUR GRANDET, a miser
EUGÉNIE, his daughter
CHARLES GRANDET, his nephew
MONSIEUR DE GRASSINS, a banker
MONSIEUR CRUCHOT, a notary

Critique:

Eugénie Grandet is one of the best of Balzac's novels. His use of realistic detail, so cumbersome and boring in many of his works, is restricted here to what is actually needed. Primarily the book is a character sketch of a loathsome miser whose greed has warped his own life and made the lives of his wife and daughter miserable. The story is told simply and concisely. Its tragedy lies in the fact that Eugénie is doomed to a lonely and loveless life. In any event, she and Grandet are two of Balzac's most successful creations.

The Story:

In the French town of Saumur, old Grandet was a prominent personality, and the story of his rise to fortune was known throughout the district. He was a master cooper who had married the daughter of a prosperous wood merchant. When the new French Republic offered for sale the church property in Saumur, Grandet used his savings and his wife's dowry to buy an old abbey, a fine vineyard, and several farms. Under the Consulate he became mayor and grew still more wealthy. In 1806 he inherited three fortunes from his wife's mother, her grandfather, and her grandmother. By this time he owned the abbey, a hundred acres of vineyard, thirteen farms, and the house in which he lived. In 1811 he bought the nearby estate of an impoverished nobleman.

He was known for his miserliness, but he was respected for the same reason. His manners were simple, his table was meager, but his speech and gestures were the law of the countryside. His household consisted of his wife, his daughter, Eugénie, and a servant, Nanon. Old Grandet had reduced his wife almost to slavery, using her as a screen for his devious financial dealings. Nanon, who did all of the housework, was gaunt and ugly but of great strength. She was devoted to her master because he had taken her in after everyone else had refused to hire her because of her appearance. On each birthday Eugénie received a gold piece from her father and a winter and a summer dress from her mother. Each New Year's Day Grandet would ask to see the coins and would gloat over their yellow brightness.

He begrudged his family everything except the bare necessities of life. Every day he would carefully measure and dole out the food for the household—a few lumps of sugar, several pieces of butter, a loaf of bread. He forbade the lighting of fires in the rooms before the middle of November. His family, like his tenants, lived under the austere circumstances he imposed upon them.

The townspeople wondered whom Eugénie would marry. There were two rivals for her hand. One of them, M. Cruchot, was the son of the local notary. The other, M. de Grassins, was the son of the local banker. On Eugénie's birthday, in the year 1819, both called at the

Grandet home. During the evening there was an unexpected knock at the door, and in came Charles Grandet, the miser's nephew. Charles' father had amassed a fortune in Paris, and Charles himself, dressed in the most fashionable Parisian manner, was an example of Parisian customs and habits for these awkward, gawking provincials whom he tried to impress with his superior airs.

Eugénie outdid herself in an effort to make the visitor welcome, even defying her father in the matter of heat, candlelight, and other luxuries for Charles. Grandet was polite enough to his nephew that evening, as he read a letter Charles had brought from his father. In it Grandet's brother announced he had lost his fortune, that he was about to commit suicide, and that he entrusted Charles to his brother's care. The young man was quite unaware of what his father had written, and when informed next day of his father's failure and suicide, he burst into tears and remained in his room for several days. Finally he wrote to a friend in Paris and asked him to dispose of his property and pay his debts. To Eugénie, her mother, and Nanon, he gave little trinkets. Grandet looked at them greedily and said he would have them appraised. He informed his wife and daughter that he intended to turn the young man out as soon as his father's affairs were settled.

Charles felt there was a stain on his honor. Grandet felt so too, especially since he and his late brother had the same family name. In consultation with the local banker, M. de Grassins, he arranged a plan whereby he could save the family reputation without, at the same time, spending a penny. M. de Grassins went to Paris to act for Grandet. He did not return, but lived a life of pleasure in the capital.

In the meantime, Eugénie fell in love with Charles. Sympathizing with his penniless state, she decided to give him her hoard of coins so that he could go to the Indies and make his fortune. The two young people pledged everlasting love to each other, and Charles left Saumur.

On the following New Year's Day, Grandet asked to see Eugénie's money. Her mother, who knew her daughter's secret, kept silent. In spite of Eugénie's denials, Grandet guessed what she had done with the gold. He ordered her to keep to her room, and he would have nothing to do with either her or her mother. Rumors began to arise in the town. The notary, M. Cruchot, told Grandet that if his wife died, there would have to be a division of the property—if Eugénie insisted on it. The village whispered that Mme. Grandet was dying of a broken heart and the maltreatment of her husband. Realizing that he might lose a part of his fortune, Grandet relented and forgave them both. When his wife died, he tricked Eugénie into signing over to him her share of the property.

Five years passed, with no word from Charles to brighten Eugénie's drab existence. In 1827, when Grandet was eighty-two years old, he was stricken with paralysis. He died urging Eugénie to take care of his money.

Eugénie lived with old Nanon, still waiting for Charles to return. One day a letter came. Charles no longer wished to marry her. Instead, he hoped to marry the daughter of a titled nobleman and secure by royal ordinance his father-in-law's title and coat of arms. Eugénie released Charles, but M. de Grassins hurried to Charles and told him that his father's creditors had not been satisfied. Until they were, his fiancée's family would not allow a marriage. Learning of his predicament, Eugénie herself paid the debt, and Charles was married.

Eugénie continued to live alone. The routine of the house was exactly what it had been while Grandet lived. Suitors came again. Young de Grassins was now in disgrace because of the loose life his father was living in Paris, but M. Cruchot, who had risen to a high post in the provincial government, continued to press his suit. At last Eugénie agreed to marry him, providing he did not demand the prerogatives of marriage, for she would be his wife in name only. They were married only a short time before M. Cruchot died. To her own property Eugénie added his. Nanon herself had married and she and her husband stayed with Eugénie. Convinced that Nanon was her only friend, the young widow resigned herself to a lonely life. She lived as she had always lived in the bare old house. She had great wealth, but, lacking everything else in life, she was indifferent to it.

THE EUNUCH

Type of work: Drama
Author: Terence (Publius Terentius Afer, c. 190-159 B. C.)
Type of plot: Comedy of intrigue
Time of plot: Fourth century B. C.
Locale: Athens
First presented: 161 B. C.

Principal characters:

PHAEDRIA, a young Athenian in love with Thais
THAIS, a courtesan
THRASO, a soldier and rival of Phaedria
PARMENO, Phaedria's slave
CHAEREA, Phaedria's younger brother, in love with Pamphila
PAMPHILA, a slave girl
CHREMES, Pamphila's brother

Critique:

In antiquity, this was the most famous and popular of Terence's plays. Tradition has it that it was once produced twice in one day. Like most Roman drama, it had its origins in the plays of Greek dramatists, and borrowings from the works of Menander are apparent. In this play we find that Terence tried to depart from some of the traditional conventions of the Roman drama. Most Roman comedies contained the insolent parasite, the rascally slave, and the braggart warrior. These characters are present in name in *The Eunuch,* but Terence worked over his figures until they are somewhat different from the conventional portrayals. The slave is an honest and well-meaning fellow, lacking in the usual insolence. The warrior, an Athenian captain, is a fool, but he strives to be a wit, so that he is more than a boaster about deeds which he may or may not have accomplished.

The Story:

Phaedria, a young Athenian of good family, was disturbed because he had been excluded from the house of Thais, a courtesan. He was also perturbed because of the love he felt for the woman. Phaedria's slave, anxious to help his master, advised that Phaedria retire to the country for a time and try to forget her. Parmeno, the slave, really believed the woman was wicked and that his master

would be better off without her. As master and slave stood before Thais' house, which was next to Phaedria's father's residence, the courtesan herself came out to explain why she had refused to admit the young man. She explained that Thraso, a warrior, had purchased a slave who had formerly belonged to her mother. Thais believed that the slave, a young girl, was actually a free citizen of Athens. In order to get a good name in Athens, to which city she had recently come, Thais hoped to learn the girl's identity and restore her to her family. Thais had to humor the captain in order to get possession of the slave girl.

Phaedria believed Thais and promised to go away into the country for two days, so that she could work on the captain with her charms and get possession of the girl. Before he left, Phaedria gave Parmeno orders to go into his father's house and get the two slaves whom he had purchased for Thais. One of the slaves was an Ethiopian girl, the other a eunuch; Thais wanted a eunuch because royalty preferred them.

On his way to get the slaves for Thais, Parmeno met Phaedria's younger brother, Chaerea, who had seen the slave girl Thais wanted and had fallen in love with her. Chaerea persuaded Parmeno to introduce him into Thais' household in place of the eunuch, and the exchange was made. In the meantime Thraso's parasite had brought the slave girl to Thais' house as a present to the courtesan from the warrior. He also bade Thais meet his master for dinner.

Thais and some of her maids went to Thraso's house as he had requested. While they were gone, Chaerea, in the person of the eunuch, was entrusted with the care of Pamphila, the slave girl. He sent her to be bathed by other slaves. When she was returned, he was so overcome by her charms, aided by a picture of Jupiter's rape of Danaë, that he raped the girl. Ashamed at what he had done, he fled.

While Thais was gone, Pamphila's brother Chremes came to the house at the request of Thais. Told that she was not at home, he went in search of her at Thraso's residence. Thraso, thinking Chremes a rival for Thais' affections, behaved boorishly. Disgusted, Thais took her leave, after telling Chremes to meet her shortly thereafter at her own house.

Phaedria, in the meantime, had left for the country, but, overcome by his affection for Thais, he turned back. Arriving at his father's house, he was met by one of Thais' maids, who told him that the eunuch had raped Pamphila. Phaedria, swearing that such things could not happen, found the eunuch dressed in his brother's clothing. The maid, upon seeing the eunuch, realized that the guilty man was not the eunuch but Phaedria's brother. The brother, meanwhile, had gone off to a dinner with some friends. He was both sorry and glad for his deed; most of all, he wanted to marry the girl.

Thais returned, distressed and angry when she heard what had happened. Her anger was cut short by the arrival of Chremes, who thought that Pamphila was his sister, stolen in infancy. To make sure, he went off to get the nurse who had been in charge of his sister. Before he could leave, however, he had to chase off Thraso, who had arrived with a band of servants to reclaim the slave he had

given to Thais.

Chaerea returned and confessed his actions to Thais. When she accused him of doing the deed to spite her, a courtesan, he demurred, swearing that he had raped the girl because he loved her overmuch. He still claimed that he wanted to marry her. Chremes returned with the nurse, who quickly identified Pamphila as Chremes' long-lost sister, a free citizen of the city, a member of a good family, and a fine wife for Chaerea, if the lad could get his father's consent.

While they were conferring, Thais' maid resolved to have her own revenge on Parmeno, Phaedria's slave. She told Parmeno that Chaerea had been seized and that he was about to be mutilated, as was the customary treatment of rapists in ancient Athens. Parmeno ran to Laches, the father of Phaedria and Chaerea, to get the older man's help.

When Laches learned the true facts, he was quite willing to permit a marriage between his younger son and the girl whom he had dishonored. More than that, the father became reconciled to his older son's love for the courtesan, since she had proved herself in her efforts to restore the slave to freedom and her proper position in life. He agreed to look after the courtesan's welfare and to permit his older son to live with her. This plan made Phaedria and Thais very happy, for they truly loved one another.

When Thraso returned for one last attempt to regain the favor of the courtesan, Phaedria threatened to kill him if he appeared in that street again. But Thraso's parasite suggested to Phaedria and Thais that they keep the braggart for entertainment. The parasite pointed out that Thraso was very foolish, had a lot of money, and could be kept dangling a long time by the courtesan without ever receiving any of her favors. Phaedria, seeing the humor of the situation, agreed to the terms. The warrior, not realizing he was to be made a fool, was so happy with the arrangement that he promised to

behave himself and to be more generous
than ever with the parasite who had got
him into the silly situation.

EUPHUES AND HIS ENGLAND

Type of work: Novel
Author: John Lyly (c. 1554-1606)
Type of plot: Didactic romance
Time of plot: 1579-1580
Locale: England
First published: 1580

Principal characters:
EUPHUES, a young gentleman of Athens
PHILAUTUS, a young gentleman of Naples, Euphues' friend
CAMILLA, a young maiden of England
LADY FLAVIA, a lady of England
SURIUS, an English nobleman
FIDUS, an elderly Englishman
FRANCES, a young English girl, Lady Flavia's niece

Critique:

This sequel to *Euphues,* which deals less directly with morals and more openly with the psychology of love, is in some ways an improvement over the first book. Although there is the same dependency on classical sources, such as Pliny and Erasmus, for examples to illustrate truths and for the truths themselves, this work has a better, more coherent plot and depends less on the use of letters from one character to another as a narrative method. The style is, if anything, more graceful and delicate than that in the earlier narrative. Some passages might well please the more fastidious modern reader, and certainly most of the book pleased the Elizabethan reader. Perhaps the most pleased was Queen Elizabeth, since much of the book is taken up with praise of England, Englishmen, and the queen herself. Also of interest to Lyly's contemporaries, undoubtedly, were the extensive and often penetrating passages on the many facets of love. Much sound advice is freely given among the characters, and the events in the plot serve to support the wisdom embodied in action and character.

The Story:

As they had previously planned, Euphues and Philautus embarked from Athens for England. During the two-month voyage Euphues offered Philautus considerable counsel on how to behave while in the strange country, and cautioned him especially about his penchant for falling too easily in love. To illustrate his point, Euphues told the tale of young Callimachus, who learned through bitter experience the perils of travel. Euphues closed his discourse with a description of the island to which they sailed.

Upon their arrival, the two young men encountered Fidus, an old man who kept bees. After telling them of the folly of discussing the queen, about whom they had asked, Fidus illustrated for them the principles of a sensible monarchy by describing his colony of bees, with its queen, workers, and drones. Upon the urging of Philautus, he also told them of his own unhappy experience when he fell in love with a young maiden who loved another man and who died of grief after her lover was killed in a distant land. This experience had led Fidus to retire to beekeeping in a secluded area near Dover.

Leaving the old gentleman with thanks for his hospitality and his story, Euphues and Philautus proceeded toward London. The trip was largely taken up with another warning by Euphues to Philautus about the dangers of love, advice given in spite of the Italian's vehement denials of any such weakness.

Soon the two strangers arrived in London, where they were welcomed because of their wit and address. Admitted into court circles, they were delighted with English virtue and charm. Philautus' eye soon fell upon Camilla, a young maiden not of high birth but of great beauty and virtue. He fell immediately, and hopelessly, in love. After a heated debate with himself about his plight, Philautus was discovered by Euphues, who began praising English women for their beauty and virtue. Philautus stopped his friend and accused him of being in love. The two young men quarreled, and Euphues moved to new lodgings.

At a masque, Philautus revealed his affection to Camilla, who received his overtures coldly. After further rebuffs, he went to an Italian sorcerer in search of a charm to win his beloved. The sorcerer told Philautus that stories of such spells of love, about which he told many popular tales, were all false and that only God, who made the human heart, could govern its inclinations. He advised Philautus to write to his love of his devotion.

The young Italian did so several times, one letter being secretly transported to Camilla in the hollowed-out core of a pomegranate and her reply returned in a volume of Petrarch. Camilla still refused his love, however, and soon she refused to answer his letters. During his pursuit of Camilla, which took place mostly at the house of Lady Flavia, his hostess introduced Philautus to Frances, a girl who was almost as beautiful as Camilla and quite as witty and virtuous. She engaged with him in several debates about love and looked with considerably more favor upon the young Italian.

Philautus, finally convinced of the hopelessness of his love for Camilla, who was also courted by Surius, a young English nobleman, began to feel strongly the loss of his friendship with Euphues. After an exchange of letters, in which Philautus begged his former friend's pardon, the two young men were reunited.

At a party given by Lady Flavia, Camilla and Surius, Frances and Philautus, and Lady Flavia and an old friend engaged in a three-sided debate which Euphues judged. Wisely taking the middle ground, he declared that virtue and honor must be part of love for both the man and the woman, and he praised that higher love which is above lust. At the party Philautus discovered that he was very fond of Frances, and Camilla realized that she loved Surius.

While Philautus wooed Frances in the country, Euphues remained in London to study the court and English ways. Before long, however, he was called back to Athens by urgent business. From his home Euphues wrote his *Euphues' Glass for Europe*, in which he praised at some length English life, the English court, and, especially, the English sovereign, whose beauty, chastity, and wisdom Euphues declared to be perfect.

In a letter from Philautus, Euphues learned of his friend's plan to marry Frances, of Camilla's marriage to Surius, and of the good wishes of his English friends. Euphues replied with a long letter containing counsel for his friend concerning the management of a marriage. Then the wise Athenian retired to a distant mountain for study and meditation.

EUPHUES, THE ANATOMY OF WIT

Type of work: Novel
Author: John Lyly (c. 1554-1606)
Type of plot: Didactic romance
Time of plot: Sixteenth century
Locale: Naples and Athens
First published: 1579

Principal characters:
  EUPHUES, a young gentleman of Athens
  PHILAUTUS, a nobleman of Naples, his friend
  DON FERARDO, a governor of Naples
  LUCILLA, his daughter, engaged to Philautus
  LIVIA, her friend
  EUBULUS, an old gentleman of Naples

Critique:

Unquestionably the greatest contribution of Lyly's romance to the development of the English novel was the style of the writing. Although the "euphuistic" style, characterized by numerous similes, the use of countless examples taken from nature and mythology, frequent rhetorical questions, balanced sentence construction, and alliteration, had appeared earlier in English prose, no one before Lyly had used it so skillfully or with such persistence. As always, Lyly's intention was to refine the manners of an era that realized its need for delicacy and sophistication. There is, in addition, a strong strain of moralistic didacticism in *Euphues*, which was also written to oppose Italian influences in the court of Queen Elizabeth. Athens is generally accepted to have been, in Lyly's mind, a symbol of Oxford University; and he addressed a brief epilogue to the "Gentlemen Scholars of Oxford." What little plot there is in *Euphues* is probably based on some of Lyly's own experiences during his college days, but the story is less important for its own sake than as a vehicle for ornately written digressions, so that its essential purpose, the development of a graceful and ornate prose style, is undeniably well achieved. That the Elizabethan age welcomed such a development is shown by the fact that the extreme popularity of *Euphues* gave the name that still clings to the kind of writing which Lyly perfected.

The Story:

Euphues, a young gentleman of Athens, was graced by nature with great personal beauty and by fortune with a large patrimony, but he used his brilliant wit to enjoy the pleasures of wickedness rather than the honors of virtue. In his search for new experiences the young man went to Naples, a city famed for loose living. There he found many eager to encourage a waste of time and talent, but he was ever cautious, trusting no one and taking none for a friend. Thus he escaped real harm from the company of idle youths with whom he associated.

An elderly gentleman of Naples, Eubulus, one day approached Euphues and admonished the young man for his easy ways, warning him of the evil results that were sure to follow and urging him to be merry with modesty and reserve. In a witty reply Euphues rebuffed the old man's counsel and told him that his pious urgings only resulted from his withered old age. So in spite of the sage warning, Euphues remained in Naples, and after two months there he met a pleasing young man named Philautus, whom he determined to make his only and eternal friend. Philautus, impressed by the charm of Euphues, readily agreed to be his firm friend forever. Their friendship grew, and the two young men soon became inseparable.

Philautus had long before earned the affection and trust of Don Ferardo, a

1133

prominent official of Naples, and had fallen in love with his beautiful daughter Lucilla. While Don Ferardo was on a trip to Naples, Philautus took his friend with him to visit Lucilla and a group of her friends. After dinner Euphues was given the task of entertaining the company with an extemporaneous discourse on love. He declared that one should love another for his mind, not for his appearance. When the conversation turned to a discussion of constancy, Lucilla asserted that her sex was wholly fickle. Euphues began to dispute her, but, suddenly struck by Lucilla's beauty and confused by his feelings, he broke off his speech and quickly left.

Lucilla discovered that she was attracted to the young Athenian. After weighing the respective claims of Euphues and Philautus on her affections, she convinced herself that it would not be wrong to abandon Philautus for Euphues; however, she decided to pretend to each that he was her only love. Euphues, meanwhile, had persuaded himself that Lucilla must be his in spite of Philautus: friendship must give way before love. In order to deceive his friend, Euphues pretended to be in love with Livia, Lucilla's friend. Philautus was overjoyed and promised to help him win Livia.

The two young men went immediately to the house of Don Ferardo. While Philautus was attending the governor, who had finally completed arrangements for his daughter's marriage to the young man, Euphues and Lucilla engaged in a subtle debate about love and finally declared their passion for each other. When Don Ferardo told his daughter of his plans for her marriage to Philautus, she told him of her love for Euphues.

Philautus, betrayed at once by both his friend and his beloved, blamed now one and now the other. He wrote a scathing letter to Euphues, saying that they were friends no longer and that he hoped Euphues would soon be in his own unhappy situation, for Lucilla, having proved untrue, might be faithless again. Euphues replied in a taunting letter that deception in love is natural. He expressed confidence that Lucilla would be faithful to him forever.

After what had happened, however, it was impossible for Euphues to visit Lucilla while her father was at home. During her lover's absence she fell in love again, this time with Curio, a gentleman who possessed neither wealth nor wit. When Euphues at last went to apologize for being away so long, Lucilla replied curtly that she had hoped his absence would be longer. Admitting that her new lover was inferior to both Philautus and Euphues, she supposed God was punishing her for her fickleness. Although she realized that her life was likely to be unhappy, a fate she had earned, she did not hesitate to scorn Euphues. Don Ferardo argued that it was her filial duty to give up the worthless Curio. When she refused, her father died of grief not long after.

Having renewed his friendship with Philautus before departing from Naples, Euphues left with his friend a written discourse against the folly of love. Saying that love, although it started with pleasure, ended in destruction and grief, he urged his friend to forget passion and to turn his attention toward more serious pursuits.

After returning to Athens, where he engaged in long hours of study, Euphues wrote a treatise on the proper way to rear a child. With the weakness of his own upbringing in mind, since it had not steered him away from the shoals of sloth and wickedness, he urged that a young man should be legitimately born and should be brought up under the influence of three major forces: nature, reason, and use. In this manner the young man would be educated in the ways of virtue as well as in the customs of use.

Euphues wrote many other letters and treatises: in one he urged the gentlemen scholars of Athens to study with the laws of God in mind; in another he debated with an atheist and converted him to godliness; a letter to Philautus encouraged him to abandon his dissolute life in Naples; in a letter to Eubulus, Euphues thanked the old man for his good advice and told him of his return to righteousness; another letter to Philautus expressed regret at the death of Lucilla and at the irreligious character of her life; two letters to a pair of young men told them to accept their destiny and to live virtuously; in response to a letter in which Livia told of her intention to be virtuous, Euphues praised her and told her of Philautus' possible visit to Athens.

EVAN HARRINGTON

Type of work: Novel
Author: George Meredith (1828-1909)
Type of plot: Social satire
Time of plot: Nineteenth century
Locale: England
First published: 1861

Principal characters:
EVAN HARRINGTON, a tailor's son
HARRIET COGGLESBY,
CAROLINE STRIKE, and
LOUISA, THE COUNTESS DE SALDAR, Evan's sisters
ROSE JOCELYN, an heiress
FERDINAND LAXLEY, Evan's rival

Critique:

That a common tradesman can vindicate himself in the presence of the upper classes is the theme of this novel. How the Countess de Saldar contrives to uphold the honor of her brother and sisters provides the plot. Although the plot is handicapped by complications often difficult to follow, the novel is, aside from Meredith's intricate method and involved style, rich in social satire, smoothly maneuvered to reach its climax, and ironically amusing in its consistent characterizations. Evan Harrington is no mere social climber; he is more or less a symbol of the refinement latent in his own class as opposed to upper-class vulgarity. In the novel Meredith drew heavily on his own family background and experience. Melchisedec Harrington was drawn from his own grandfather, a tailor, and Evan's sisters are the writer's three aunts, thinly disguised.

The Story:

Melchisedec Harrington was a tailor with the bearing and manners of a great nobleman. When he died, his neighbors spoke fondly of him and wondered what his son, who was in Portugal, would do. His widow knew that the great Mel, as he was called, had left debts amounting to more than four thousand pounds, which Evan would want to repay. The boy was to go to Mr. Goren in London to learn the tailor's trade.

There had been three daughters in the tailor's household, each of whom had married so well that they had thenceforth cut themselves apart from their father, a common tradesman. Harriet had married a brewer, Andrew Cogglesby; Caroline had married Major Strike, and Louisa had become the Countess de Saldar. The countess decided that her brother Evan must also marry well, and she tried to ally him with Rose Jocelyn, who had money of her own.

When Mrs. Harrington told Evan about old Mel's debts, the son consented to go to London and learn his trade from Mr. Goren; not even the countess' entreaties and assurances that Rose loved him could dissuade him from his course. Setting out for London on foot, he met Jack Raikes, an old school friend. They went to the Green Dragon Inn, where they joined a group of men at dinner. Old Tom Cogglesby, brother of Andrew, the brewer, presided. Among those present were Harry Jocelyn, Rose's brother, and Ferdinand Laxley, his friend. Evan and Jack got into a drunken brawl involving much name calling and many threats. The gentlemen present scoffed at Evan's choice of trade. Laxley challenged Evan to a duel, but on learning that Evan was the son of a tailor he haughtily declined to fight a common tradesman.

The day after the tavern brawl, while watching a cricket match on the green, Evan met Rose Jocelyn and her party, which included the Countess de Saldar. He was prevailed upon to visit the

Jocelyns at Beckley Court before he went to London. As he rode along beside Rose, one of the men with whom he had quarreled the night before pointed him out as a tailor. At Beckley Court the countess was able to persuade Harry Jocelyn that Evan was not the tailor but that Jack Raikes was. Still, Laxley demanded that Evan deny his trade and fight the duel as a gentleman or else acknowledge it.

Laxley was one of Rose's suitors. Resenting Evan, he continually challenged him to admit he was not a real gentleman. Since claiming that he was a gentleman would mean a duel with Laxley, Evan resolved to leave Beckley Court.

The countess, fearing to see all her plans ruined, prevailed upon Evan to seek the advice of his relatives. Harriet, Caroline, and Andrew were also visiting at Beckley Court; Evan's predicament concerned all of them. Andrew offered the young man a position in his brewery.

Glorying in her position, Rose encouraged her admirers to outrace each other in an amateur steeplechase, the prize to be her handkerchief. Evan won the prize but was injured when thrown from his horse.

There was a rumor in Lymport that at the age of sixteen the Countess de Saldar tried to run off with a certain George Uploft. Melchisedec allegedly had chased the pair down and ended the romance. When Uploft appeared at Beckley Court, the countess brazenly defied him to recall her background. At dinner the conversation swung to old Mel, and during the last anecdote, which involved Mel's oldest daughter, Caroline swooned and was taken from the room, but not before Uploft recognized her as Mel's daughter.

Although confined to bed because of his injury, Evan was still determined to leave Beckley Court. The masquerade he was playing, pretending to be one of the upper class when he was actually a tailor's son, was too much for him. That evening, seeing Rose in the garden, he followed her

to claim the handkerchief which he had won. When he revealed his love, and she responded, he promised himself that he would disclose his base origin to her on the morrow.

The next day Evan told Rose the facts about himself. She admitted that she already knew his story and loved him in spite of it, and she promised to fight her family for the right to marry him. She also asked him to accept employment as her Uncle Melville's secretary.

Awaiting Evan's arrival in London, Mr. Goren learned from Jack Raikes that Evan was loitering at Beckley Court. Mr. Goren wrote a complaint to Mrs. Harrington, who proceeded at once to Beckley Court. Stopping overnight at the Green Dragon Inn, she met the obstreperous Tom Cogglesby and tamed him with her efficiency and good sense. Since both were going to Beckley Court, they traveled together the next day. Tom was on his way, he said, to help a tailor marry a gentlewoman.

The social involvements at Beckley Court grew more tense. Laxley was blamed for an outrageous blunder in revealing the whereabouts of a runaway wife whom Lady Jocelyn had befriended, and he was sent away. The Countess de Saldar had a triumphant moment. Mrs. Harrington conducted herself with finesse in the midst of a difficult situation.

But the Harringtons had been publicly exposed as the family of the tailor Melchisedec. Evan, fearing that he had lost Rose, discovered that his sister, the Countess de Saldar, was responsible for the anonymous letter Laxley was supposed to have written. Failing in his entreaties to convince his sister to confess the truth to Lady Jocelyn, Evan decided to take the blame for Laxley's dismissal. After declaring his guilt to Lady Jocelyn, he wrote also to Laxley. Evan decided beforehand that if Laxley challenged him to a duel he would refuse the challenge.

Juliana, Rose's cousin and a plain-looking crippled girl, was in love with Evan and had always been loyal to him. From the beginning she had known the facts about his background. When the question of his infamous deception involving Laxley arose, Juliana refused to believe ill of Evan.

On the day of Evan's departure from Beckley Court, Rose came to him and asked him if he had been responsible for Laxley's humiliation. Feeling that if she truly loved him she would not need to ask, he refused to explain. Laxley arrived and took possession of Rose. A note from Juliana told Evan that she believed in him.

In Mr. Goren's shop Evan prepared to follow his trade. The Cogglesbys, receiving Juliana as a guest in their home, set out to win Evan's heart for the invalid girl. But Evan still pined for Rose, who cut him cruelly when she met him on the street.

When Andrew's brewery went bankrupt and he lost all his property, the three sisters, who had been living in the Cogglesby house, were forced to go to their mother in Lymport. At Evan's request, Lady Jocelyn had taken Juliana, in poor health, back to Beckley Court.

Juliana inherited Beckley Court upon the death of her grandmother. Just before she died, her malady being incurable, Juliana wrote to Rose and revealed Evan's innocence. She also wrote a will leaving her estate to Evan. Meanwhile Rose, engaged to Laxley, felt herself bound by promise to Evan and sent for him to release her before she could marry his rival. Evan did so with no show of self-sacrifice. Later Rose learned that Evan, rejecting Juliana's bequest, had returned Beckley Court to Lady Jocelyn.

Everyone had become indebted to Evan for his generosity; he himself had simply tried to make everyone happy. Lady Jocelyn and Rose went to Lymport to thank him. There Rose, speaking with Evan alone, asked him why he had blackened his name to her. No longer compelled to pretend anything about himself, Evan rose manfully to the occasion. When he declared his love, Rose accepted him. Old Tom Cogglesby, delighted, offered to give Evan an income.

The sisters went back to their former ways of life. Mrs. Harrington became Tom Cogglesby's housekeeper.

EVANGELINE

Type of work: Poem
Author: Henry Wadsworth Longfellow (1807-1882)
Type of plot: Pastoral romance
Time of plot: Mid-eighteenth century
Locale: French Canada and the United States
First published: 1847

Principal characters:
EVANGELINE BELLEFONTAINE
GABRIEL LAJEUNESSE, her betrothed
BASIL LAJEUNESSE, Gabriel's father
BENEDICT BELLEFONTAINE, Evangeline's father

Critique:

The note of gentleness on which *Evangeline, A Tale of Acadie* begins never falters throughout the poem. The description of a kindly, contented people, who accept their exile as God's will, is followed by an account of Evangeline's wanderings and her patience through a lifetime of disappointment. Force and drama exist only in distilled forms, but the freshness, music, and poetic imagery of *Evangeline* give it wide popularity.

The Story:

In the Acadian province, in the village of Grand-Pré, lived a peaceful farming people who were undisturbed by the wars between the French and British. In a land where there was enough for all, there was no covetousness and no envy, and every man lived at peace with his neighbor. Benedict Bellefontaine had his farm somewhat apart from the village. His daughter, Evangeline, directed her father's household. Although she had many suitors, she favored only one, Gabriel Lajeunesse, the son of Basil, the village blacksmith. Their fathers were friends, and the children had grown up together.

One fall day, while Benedict rested by the fire and Evangeline sat at her spinning wheel, Basil brought word that the men of the village were to meet at the church the next day. They were to be told the plans of the English, whose ships were riding at anchor in the harbor.

That night Benedict and Basil signed the wedding contract which would unite the wedding contract which would unite their children. Then, while their fathers played draughts, Evangeline and Gabriel whispered in the darkening room until it was time to say goodnight.

The next morning everyone, including the folk from the outlying districts, came to the village to hear the announcement the English commander was to make. Everybody wore holiday dress, as if the occasion were one for celebration. At the Bellefontaine farm there was especial joy, for with a feast and dancing the family and its guests were celebrating the betrothal of Gabriel and Evangeline. In the afternoon the church bell rang, summoning the men to the church. When they filed in, they were followed by the guard from the ship. Outside the women stood, waiting.

The news the English commander had for the little community was a crushing blow. By order of the king, their land, houses, and cattle were forfeited to the crown, and the entire population of Grand-Pré was to be transported. The men were to consider themselves his prisoners.

The tragic news spread quickly through the village, and to the farm where Evangeline was awaiting Benedict's return. At sunset she started toward the church, on her way comforting the downcast women she met. Outside she called Gabriel's name, but there was no answer from the church where the men were imprisoned.

The men were held prisoners for five days. On the fifth, the women brought their household goods to the shore to be loaded in boats, and late that afternoon the men were led out of the church by their guards. Evangeline, standing at the side of the road, watched them coming toward her. She was able to comfort Gabriel with the assurance that their love would keep them from harm, but for her father she could do nothing. In the five days he had aged greatly.

Basil and his son were put on separate ships. Evangeline remained on the beach with Benedict. That night the villagers of Grand-Pré watched their homes go up in flames, and listened to their animals bellowing as the barns burned. Turning from the sight, Evangeline saw that her father had fallen dead. She dropped in a swoon upon his breast and lay there until morning; then with the aid of Father Felician, the village priest, the Acadians buried Benedict Bellefontaine by the shore. That day Evangeline sailed with the other exiles.

The scattered exiles from Grand-Pré wandered far over the face of North America in search of their friends and families. Sometimes Evangeline lingered for a while in a town, but always she was driven on by her longing for Gabriel. Looking at unmarked graves, she imagined they might contain her lover. Sometimes she heard rumors of his whereabouts; sometimes she spoke with people who had actually seen and known him, but always long ago. The notary's son, Baptiste Leblanc, followed her faithfully and loyally through her years of searching, but she would have no one but Gabriel for a husband.

Finally a band of exiles rowed down the Mississippi, bound for Louisiana, where they hoped to find some of their kinsmen. Evangeline and Father Felician were among them, Evangeline heartened because she felt she was nearing Gabriel at last. Then in the heat of the noonday, the voyagers pulled their craft to shore and lay down to sleep behind some bushes. While they slumbered, Gabriel, in the company of hunters and trappers, passed the spot on his way to the West

That evening, when the exiles went ashore, the prosperous herdsman who welcomed them proved to be Basil. Evangeline learned that Gabriel had left home that day, too troubled by thoughts of his love to endure the quiet life in his father's house.

For a time Basil helped Evangeline carry on her search. Leaving his peaceful home in the South, the herdsman traveled with the girl to the base of the Ozark Mountains. They were guided by rumors of Gabriel's whereabouts, and sometimes, from the distance, they saw, or thought they saw, his campfire. But when they reached the spot, he had already gone ahead.

One evening a Shawnee Indian woman came into the camp, on her way back to her own people after her husband's murder by Comanches. In the night, after the others were asleep, she and Evangeline exchanged stories. When Evangeline had finished hers, the woman told the tale of Mowis, the bridegroom made of snow, and of the Indian girl who married and followed him, only to see him dissolve and fade with the sunshine. She told of Lilinau, who had followed her phantom lover into the woods until she disappeared forever. Evangeline felt that she, too, was following a phantom.

The next day the party traveled to the Jesuit Mission on the western side of the mountains, where they hoped to hear some word of Gabriel. A priest told them Gabriel had gone to the north to hunt six days before. Because it seemed certain he would pass that way on his journey home in the fall, Evangeline decided to wait at the mission. Basil and his companions returned to their homes.

Autumn and winter passed and spring came, with no news of Gabriel. Finally Evangeline heard that he was camping in the forests of Michigan on the Saginaw River. When she reached his camp, it was deserted and in ruins.

For many years she wandered over the country in search of her lover, but always

1140

she met with disappointment. At last, grown gray, her beauty gone, she became a Sister of Mercy in Philadelphia, where she went because the soft-spoken Quakers reminded her of her own people. When pestilence struck the town, she visited the almshouse to nurse the destitute. One Sunday morning, she saw on the pallet before her a dying old man. It was Gabriel. In his last moments he dreamed of Evangeline and Grand-Pré. Trying to utter her name, he died. Evangeline murmured a prayer of thanks as she pressed her lover to her.

The lovers lie side by side in nameless graves in Philadelphia, far from their old home in the north. But a few peasants who wandered back from exile still keep their story alive.

THE EVE OF ST. AGNES

Type of work: Poem
Author: John Keats (1795-1821)
Type of plot: Chivalric romance
Time of plot: Middle Ages
Locale: A castle
First published: 1820

Principal characters:
MADELINE, a young girl
PORPHYRO, her lover
ANGELA, an old nurse

Critique:

The Eve of St. Agnes is doubtless Keats' most beautiful and compelling composition. Musical in its matchless verse, vivid in colors, sights, and sounds, the poem is generally thought of as a highly idealized picture of the world as imagined by two young, ecstatic lovers. The story itself is built around the ancient superstition that a maiden who retires to her bed after practising a certain ritual on St. Agnes' Eve will be awakened in a dream by her lover. The use of medieval legend and setting add to the romantic effects of the poem.

The Story:

A cold St. Agnes' Eve it was—so cold that the owl with all its feathers shivered, so cold that the old Beadsman's fingers were numb as he told his rosary and said his prayers. Passing by the sculptured figures of the dead, he felt sorry for them in their icy graves. As he walked through the chapel door, he could hear the sound of music coming from the castle hall. He sadly turned again to his prayers.

The great hall of the castle was a scene of feasting and revelry, but one among the merry throng was scarcely aware of her surroundings. The lovely Madeline's thoughts were on the legend of St. Agnes' Eve, which told that a maiden, if she followed the ceremonies carefully and went supperless to bed, might there meet her lover in a dream.

Meanwhile, across the moonlit moors came Porphyro. He entered the castle and hid behind a pillar, aware that his presence meant danger, because his family was an enemy of Madeline's house. Soon the aged crone, Angela, came by and offered to hide him, lest his enemies find him there and kill him.

He followed her along dark arched passageways, out of sight of the revelers. When they stopped, Porphyro begged Angela to let him have one glimpse of Madeline. He promised on oath that if he so much as disturbed a lock of her hair, he would give himself up to the foes who waited below. He seemed in such sorrow that the poor woman gave in to him. She took Porphyro to the maiden's chamber and there hid him in a closet where was stored a variety of sweet meats and confections brought from the feast downstairs. Angela then hobbled away, and soon the breathless Madeline appeared.

She came in with her candle, which blew out, and kneeling before her high arched casement window, she began to pray. Watching her kneel there, her head a halo of moonlight, Porphyro grew faint at the sight of her beauty. Soon she disrobed and crept into bed, where she lay entranced until sleep came over her.

Porphyro stole from the closet and gazed at her in awe as she slept. For an instant a door opened far away, and the noises of another world, boisterous and festive, broke in; but soon the sounds faded away again. In the silence he brought dainty foods from the closet— quinces, plums, jellies, candies, syrups and spices that perfumed the chilly room. Madeline slept on, and Porphyro began to play a soft melody on a lute.

Madeline opened her eyes and thought her lover a vision of St. Agnes' Eve. Porphyro, not daring to speak, sank upon his knees until she spoke, begging him never to leave her or she would die.

St. Agnes' moon went down. Outside the casements, sleet and ice began to dash against the windowpanes. Porphyro told her that they must flee before the house awakened. Madeline, afraid and trembling, followed her lover down the cold, gloomy corridors, through the wide deserted hall, and past the porter, asleep on his watch. So they fled—into the wintry dawn.

EVELINA

Type of work: Novel
Author: Fanny Burney (Madame d'Arblay, 1752-1840)
Type of plot: Sentimental romance
Time of plot: Eighteenth century
Locale: England
First published: 1778

Principal characters:
SIR JOHN BELMONT, an English nobleman
EVELINA, Sir John's unacknowledged daughter
THE REV. MR. VILLARS, Evelina's guardian
MADAME DUVAL, Evelina's grandmother
LORD ORVILLE, whom Evelina married
SIR CLEMENT WILLOUGHBY, a gentleman of fashion
MRS. MIRVAN, Evelina's patroness

Critique:

This novel, written in the epistolary form so popular in the eighteenth century, still attracts attention, chiefly for its portrayal of morals and manners. The author revealed her purpose in her subtitle, *The History of a Young Lady's Entrance into the World*. Even though the reader may be repelled by the sugar-sweetness of a heroine who never draws an unkind breath from the beginning to the end of the story, the reader will be attracted to the descriptions of English social life and the idiosyncrasies of character revealed through the eyes of a seventeen-year-old girl.

The Story:

Evelina, abandoned by her father and her maternal grandmother upon the death of her mother, had been for many years the ward of the Rev. Mr. Arthur Villars, an English clergyman. At last her grandmother, Madame Duval, wrote from France to say that she would take charge of the girl, providing proper proof of the child's relationship were forthcoming. Mr. Villars refused, however, to send Evelina to France. He also objected to the invitation of Mrs. Mirvan, who wanted Evelina to join her family in London. He felt that Evelina, having been brought up carefully at Berry Hill in Dorsetshire, should not be exposed to the unhappiness of London society life, particularly so since her own father, Sir John Belmont,

would not admit his parentage and she was without enough income to permit her to live as the Mirvans did.

After some urging, he finally allowed Evelina to visit Lady Howard, Mrs. Mirvan's mother, at Howard Grove. A short time later Mrs. Mirvan and her daughter, who were delighted with Evelina, secured permission to have her accompany them to London.

Almost at once she was swept into fashionable London life. Having grown up in the provinces, the city was a constant joy to her. She soon met Lord Orville and both were attracted to one another. On several occasions her lack of London manners caused her embarrassment and she expressed a desire to return to Dorsetshire. Sir Clement Willoughby was her chief tormentor.

By chance she met her odious grandmother, the vulgar and presumptuous Madame Duval. On an outing the Frenchwoman became the subject of ridicule when she was pitched into a mudhole. Evelina met other of her relations and found them no better than her grandmother.

Madame Duval, attaching herself to the Mirvans, succeeded in making Evelina most unhappy. Evelina went reluctantly to the opera with her relatives and was made miserable by their crudeness. Hoping to escape them, she joined Sir Clement, but was only further embarrassed when Sir Clement intentionally delayed his coach while escorting her to her lodgings. For that escapade Evelina was severely scolded by her guardian. In a letter to her he indicated that he lived in daily fears for her honor. He was relieved when he heard that the Mirvans were at last returning with her to Howard Grove.

Lady Howard, urged on by Madame Duval, put forth the plan of forcing Sir John Belmont to acknowledge Evelina as his daughter. Mr. Villars did not approve of this action, as he had promised Evelina's mother that the girl would never know her cruel and unnatural father.

At Howard Grove, Evelina unknowingly participated in a cruel joke planned by Captain Mirvan and Sir Clement. Again made a laughing-stock, Madame Duval took to her bed after she had been sent upon a fool's errand and had lost her false curls.

When Sir John Belmont refused to admit that Evelina was his daughter, Madame Duval planned to take Evelina to confront Sir John in person and to demand his recognition. Mr. Villars would not listen to her proposal. He did agree, however, to let Evelina spend a month with her grandmother in London. Evelina was unhappy under Madame Duval's chaperonage because her vulgar relations attempted to use her to ingratiate themselves with her fashionable friends. Sir Clement Willoughby visited Evelina while she was staying with her grandmother, but Madame Duval embarrassed everyone by her uncivil remarks to him. She remembered the joke played on her at Howard Grove.

In her London lodgings Evelina was instrumental in preventing the suicide of Mr. Macartney, an improvised Scottish poet. Out of pity for his plight, she relieved his need with money from her own purse.

At a fireworks display Evelina was again chagrined, having been discovered by Lord Orville while she was in vulgar company.

Madame Duval announced that she hoped to marry Evelina to the boorish young son of Mr. Braughton, a silversmith. Mr. Braughton was Madame Duval's nephew. Evelina was much distressed, the more so when her grandmother's friends attached themselves to Lord Orville in a familiar manner. When Mr. Braughton asked his lordship's custom for any silver the nobleman might want to buy, Evelina felt herself ruined forever in Lord Orville's eyes.

In her distress Evelina wrote to Mr. Villars, who ordered her to return immediately to Berry Hill. From there she wrote to her friend, Miss Mirvan, about her London adventures. A most painful surprise to her was a letter she had received from Lord Orville, to whom she had written to disclaim responsibility for her relatives' crudeness. His reply was so insulting that she became quite ill and had to be sent to a rest home at Bristol Hot Wells, where she went in the company of Mrs. Selwyn, a neighbor.

At the watering place Evelina met many of her fashionable London friends, among them Lord Orville. He was so courteous that she had to forgive him for his impolite letter. As Evelina was beginning to feel at home once more among people of wealth and position, Mr. Macartney appeared and embarrassed her with his importunities.

A new arrival at the baths was Miss Belmont, an heiress reputed to be Sir John Belmont's daughter. Mrs. Selwyn, hearing of the girl's identity, decided to learn more about Miss Belmont. Mrs. Selwyn was convinced that Evelina was the true daughter of Sir John.

Mr. Macartney was trying to return the money Evelina had given him, but she did not want her friends to learn that she had ever known him. She feared that they would suspect her of having had an affair with him. Lord Orville, however, encouraged her to see the unfortunate young poet. From Mr. Macartney, Evelina learned that he believed himself to be an unacknowledged son of Sir John Belmont. Evelina, realizing that she herself must be the sister of Mr. Macartney, did not reveal her knowledge.

When Sir John Belmont returned to England, Mr. Villars was finally stirred to action against him, for by introducing to society the woman who posed as his daughter Sir John was indicating that Evelina was an impostor. Determined that Evelina should have her rights, Mr. Villars prepared to force Sir John to acknowledge Evelina as his daughter.

Through the good offices of Mrs. Selwyn and others the affair was at last untangled. The supposed daughter of Sir John proved to be the daughter of a penniless nurse, who had substituted her own child for Lady Belmont's infant. Evelina, delighted to learn that Sir John's attitude had been the result of error and not neglect, was happily reconciled with her father, who received her warmly. The impostor was treated with great kindness by all concerned as she herself was innocent of the design. She married Mr. Macartney, who was also acknowledged by Sir John. Evelina, as Sir John's daughter, was sought after by Lord Orville, to whom she gladly gave her hand in marriage.

EVERY MAN IN HIS HUMOUR

Type of work: Drama
Author: Ben Jonson (1572?-1637)
Type of plot: Comedy of humors
Time of plot: Late sixteenth century
Locale: London
First presented: 1598

Principal characters:
KNOWELL, an old gentleman
EDWARD KNOWELL, his son
BRAINWORM, Knowell's servant
DOWNRIGHT, a plain man
WELLBRED, his half-brother
KITELY, a merchant
CAPTAIN BOBADILL, a cowardly braggart
DAME KITELY, Kitely's wife
COB, a water carrier
TIB, Cob's wife

Critique:

Every Man in His Humour amused and delighted literary London in 1598. Jonson, a shrewd observer of human foibles, capitalized on these failings to create a new kind of dramatic comedy in accordance with the medieval theory of the four humors—hot, dry, cold, moist. That is to say, each man contains within him these four elements, and when any one of these elements predominates in an individual, that person is given to a peculiar sort of folly and is called "humorous." All comedy, of course, is based on aberration from the normal, but Jonson's conscious design of marking each individual in his play by heightening his principal folly or shortcoming was a new departure in the drama and set the pattern for many subsequent plays by other hands in which the theory of humors was similarly employed. It is believed that Shakespeare acted in this play when it was first produced at The Curtain theater in the summer of 1598. The first published version was the folio edition of 1616.

The Story:

In Hogsden, a conservative suburb north of London's wall, Edward Knowell, a dignified, practical citizen, was some-

what concerned over his son Edward's interest in poetry. Old Knowell was further alarmed at the younger generation's interests when his nephew Stephen, a country simpleton, showed interest in the gentle art of falconry. Old Knowell wished to have his son and his nephew engaged in more practical arts.

One day he was handed a letter obviously meant for his son. The letter, signed by Wellbred, a London gallant, was an invitation to young Knowell to renew his association with a group of young madcaps. Old Knowell, having read the letter, and being convinced that his son was up to no good, had his servant, Brainworm, deliver the letter to the youth in his study, with the directions not to reveal that the letter had been opened. Contrary to orders, Brainworm told his young master that old Knowell had read the letter. The young man, delighted with the prospect of high entertainment in the city, gave little thought to what his father might do.

Meanwhile, in the city, Matthew, an urban fool, called on Captain Bobadill, a spurious cavalier who roomed in the low-class lodgings of Cob, a water carrier. Matthew, his taste having been questioned by Downright, a plain-spoken man,

1147

asked for and received instructions in dueling from the braggart, swaggering city captain.

In his house, nearby, Kitely, a merchant, discussed with Downright the dissolute ways of his brother-in-law, Wellbred, who roomed with the Kitelys. Wellbred had become the leader of a group of scoffers, young men who apparently had no respect for anyone or anything; their greatest sport was to discover fools and make sport of them. Kitely feared that his identity with this sporting crew might endanger his business reputation; besides, he was jealous of his wife. When Matthew and Bobadill called for Wellbred, Bobadill insulted Downright in Matthew's behalf. Kitely, cautious, restrained Downright from avenging his honor on the spot.

Brainworm, young Knowell's ally, appeared in Moorfields disguised as a disabled veteran for the purpose of intercepting old Knowell, who he knew would follow young Knowell into the city to spy on him. Brainworm encountered first, however, young Knowell and his cousin Stephen. To the latter he sold a worthless rapier. Soon afterward he encountered old Knowell. The old gentleman, out of pity, hired Brainworm, who had styled himself Fitz-Sword, as a personal servant.

Inside the city wall, their rendezvous the Windmill Tavern in London's Old Jewry, young Knowell revealed to Wellbred that old Knowell had read Wellbred's letter; the pair agreed that the only recourse was to make a joke of the situation. Stephen, Matthew, and Bobadill provided rare fun for young Knowell and Wellbred. Stephen assumed a ridiculous air of melancholy, which he thought befitted a lovesick poet; Matthew, a poetaster, reflected this melancholy in what he thought was the urban manner. Bobadill provided entertainment with preposterous lies about his military experiences and with oaths which especially impressed rustic Stephen. Brainworm joined the group, revealed his true identity to the satisfaction of the duped Stephen, and reported to young Knowell that old Knowell had come to the city and was stopping at the house of Justice Clement.

Kitely, meanwhile, obsessed with a growing fear that his wife might be unfaithful to him, decided to forego a profitable business transaction in another part of the city. Later he changed his mind, but before he left home he ordered his servant, Thomas Cash, to report immediately the coming to the house of Wellbred and his companions, or of any stranger. The young gallants came to the house shortly afterward. Cash, in desperation, enlisted Cob to carry the message to Kitely. Before Cob left, he was thrashed by Bobadill for making a speech against the use of tobacco.

Having received the message at the house of Justice Clement, where he was doing business, Kitely hurried home, plagued by the imagination of a jealous husband. Cob, meanwhile, asked Justice Clement for a warrant for Bobadill's arrest. When Justice Clement learned about Cob's anti-tobacco speech, he sentenced Cob to jail, but through the good services of old Knowell, who was present, Cob received the warrant instead of a jail sentence.

In Kitely's house, Downright reproached his sister, Mistress Kitely, for permitting their brother, Wellbred, to use her house as meeting place for his mad company. Matthew, to the amusement of young Knowell and Wellbred, read bits of stolen verse to Bridget, Kitely's maiden sister. When Downright asked Wellbred and his followers to leave, rapiers were drawn. After Cash and the other servants had separated the antagonists, Bobadill made brave gestures. As Wellbred and his companions left, Kitely entered excitedly and began a search for young Knowell, whose virtues were being praised by Mistress Kitely and Bridget. He feared the women had hidden the young man in the house.

Armed with a warrant and aroused by Kitely's husbandly apprehensions, Cob went by his house to see that all was well with his wife Tib. He advised her to remain indoors and not to admit anyone.

Meanwhile Brainworm, as the disabled veteran, returned, at the direction of young Knowell, to inform old Knowell that his son could be apprehended at Cob's house, where an assignation was to take place.

Downright arrived in Moorfields while Bobadill entertained young Knowell, Matthew, and Stephen with unbelievable accounts of his prowess as a swordsman. After Downright disarmed Bobadill easily and thrashed him, Matthew, frightened, ran back to the city. Stephen claimed the russet cloak which Downright left at the scene of the fight.

Back in Old Jewry, Kitely continued to be tortured by his jealousy. Brainworm, now disguised as Justice Clement's man, Formal, entered and told Kitely that Justice Clement wished to see him immediately. While Kitely again admonished Cash to guard the house against all interlopers, Wellbred conspired with Brainworm for the marriage of young Knowell and Bridget. Wellbred, ever seeking amusement at the expense of others, suggested to Mistress Kitely that perhaps her husband was a philanderer. At this, Mistress Kitely departed to spy on the activities of her husband. Kitely returned to find his wife absent, and when he was told that she had gone to Cob's house he followed, fearful that he had been cuckolded. Wellbred took the opportunity, while neither of the Kitelys was home, to take Bridget to the church.

After their shameful conduct in Moorfields, Bobadill and Matthew met in the city; Bobadill rationalized their cowardice. They encountered Brainworm, still disguised as Formal, and gave him jewelry and clothing to pawn for the price of a warrant to arrest Downright, who they said wore a russet cloak.

The tricks played by Brainworm, young Knowell, and Wellbred began to rebound on the knavish threesome. Old Knowell went to Cob's house, where he was told by the indignant Tib that she knew no Edward Knowell. At the same time, Mistress Kitely appeared and was suspected by old Knowell of being young Knowell's mistress. Kitely arrived next. He and his wife exchanged bitter words of mistrust, for Kitely suspected old Knowell of being his wife's paramour, Mistress Kitely accused her husband of dalliance with Tib. Cob appeared and thrashed his wife for not obeying him. As a result of misunderstandings all around, Kitely insisted that all concerned present themselves before Justice Clement.

In the meantime, Brainworm, having assumed the disguise of a constable, and accompanied by Matthew and Bobadill, arrested Stephen, who was wearing Downright's russet cloak. Brainworm's mistake was quickly recognized, but when Downright himself approached, Matthew and Bobadill departed in haste. Downright, although Stephen had surrendered the cloak, insisted that the matter be explained to Justice Clement.

Practically all of the principals having gathered in the hall of his house, Justice Clement held an investigation of the misunderstandings which had taken place. Brainworm threw off his disguise and explained his part in the confusion of the day. He was forgiven by his master, old Knowell. Young Knowell and Bridget, now man and wife, entered with Wellbred. Kitely and Mistress Kitely, as well as Cob and Tib, were reconciled after explanations had been made. Justice Clement, having seen peace and trust reëstablished, dedicated the ensuing evening to celebration and conviviality.

EVERY MAN OUT OF HIS HUMOUR

Type of work: Drama
Author: Ben Jonson (1572?-1637)
Type of plot: Comedy of humors
Time of plot: Early seventeenth century
Locale: Not specified, but ostensibly London
First presented: 1599

Principal characters:
  MACILENTE, a malcontent
  CARLO BUFFONE, a scoffer
  SOGLIARDO, a wealthy country fool
  SORDIDO, a rural miser
  FUNGOSO, his son
  PUNTARVOLO, a fantastic knight
  FASTIDIOUS BRISK, a courtier
  SAVIOLINA, a lady of the court

Critique:

Every Man in His Humour having been the tremendous success it was, Jonson, possibly urged on by his fellow investors in the theater, wrote *Every Man out of His Humour* as a companion piece to his earlier success. In this play, produced the following year, Jonson overreached himself: there are too many characters and the plot seems to ramble unconscionably. One explanation for the comparative failure of the play lies in the fact that at the time of its composition Jonson was actively engaged in the so-called War of the Theaters, a controversy in which rival playwrights employed the stage to satirize each other and to ridicule actors of the rival companies. As a play, *Every Man out of His Humour* is a hodgepodge which manages somehow to work out; as personal satire it no longer holds meaning for the modern audience. Its subject and treatment, however, make it a work of particular interest to historians of literature.

The Story:

Macilente, disgusted by the injustices of society, had fled to the country. As he lay idly under a tree he overheard a conversation between the wealthy young farmer, Sogliardo, and Carlo Buffone, a railing cynic whom the rustic bumpkin had chosen as his guide in becoming a gentleman. Macilente winced at Sogliardo's presumption and at Buffone's callous instructions to the foolish Sogliardo to spend his money liberally, to haunt the taverns, to frequent the theater, to have many creditors, and to assume a melancholy air. Buffone, seeing Macilente and knowing him to be a malcontent, hurried away with Sogliardo, but in departing he told Macilente that they were going to Puntarvolo's house.

Still musing under the tree, Macilente next listened while Sordido, a miserly farmer, consulted his almanac and hoped for rainy weather in order that his hoarded grain might soar in value. A farmhand delivered to Sordido a note, an official order for him to bring his grain to market. Sordido scorned the order and swore that he would hide his surplus harvest.

In front of Puntarvolo's house, Buffone and Sogliardo talked with the braggart courtier, Sir Fastidious Brisk. The three watched with amazement Puntarvolo's return from the hunt. Puntarvolo, an old-fashioned, fantastic knight, was given to extravagances in the form of little homecoming plays which he wrote himself. Assuming the role of a strange knight, Puntarvolo approached his house, inquired about the owner, and heard his virtues praised by his indulgent wife and her women. In another part of the play

1150

Puntarvolo wooed his wife in the manner of a knight-errant. Sordido and his son, Fungoso, a law student in the city, appeared. Fungoso was so impressed with the stylish cut of Brisk's clothes that he asked his uncle, Sogliardo, to get him money from Sordido, ostensibly for law books, but actually for a suit of clothes in the latest style. All the while hoping for rain, Sordido reluctantly gave his son money, but not enough.

Reaction varied to Puntarvolo's announcement that he had wagered five thousand pounds at five-to-one odds that he and his wife and their dog could travel to Constantinople and back without a fatal mishap. Buffone saw in this venture material for a colossal joke, while Brisk was interested in investing a hundred pounds in the venture. Fungoso, meanwhile, taken with Brisk's courtly manner and dress, was pleased to learn that his brother-in-law, Deliro, was Brisk's merchant.

The next day Macilente advised his friend Deliro to bridle his doting love for his wife, since this dotage caused the wife, Fallace, to react petulantly to Deliro's affections. Fungoso, wearing a new suit, went to Deliro's house and borrowed money from his sister, Fallace, in order to complete his costume. No sooner had he received the money than Brisk entered in a new suit. Fungoso, frustrated by this new development, wrote his father for more money. Brisk, meanwhile, bragged of his actually non-existent triumphs at court; he also made arrangements with Deliro for mortgaging his land in the country. Fallace, impatient with her work-a-day husband, admired Brisk's courtliness and dreamed of becoming a court lady.

In the aisles of St. Paul's Cathedral, the meeting place of gallants and of small businessmen, Buffone, accompanied by Puntarvolo, tried to find two retainers for his newly-arrived gentleman, Sogliardo. Puntarvolo, who had with him a dog and a cat, explained that his wife had withdrawn from the Constantinople venture and that the cat would go in her place.

Brisk promised to take the hopeful Macilente to court if Macilente would purchase himself a fitting suit of clothes. Actually, it was Macilente's purpose to discover Brisk's true standing at the court. Fungoso and his tailor, ever in pursuit of the latest fashion, studied Brisk's clothes as the knight talked to his companions. And Sogliardo, who desired to have every gentlemanly attainment, retained a braggart down-at-heels rascal, one Shift, as his servant and instructor in the gentle art of smoking tobacco.

The good weather which prevailed in the country became the despair of Sordido. At last, in desperation, he attempted to hang himself, but he was rescued from that folly by the neighboring farmers, who would save him despite his despicable miserliness. The revelation to him of his evil nature caused him to have a change of heart; he vowed to be a kind and generous neighbor henceforward.

Having dressed themselves in new clothes, Brisk and Macilente appeared at the court, Macilente to observe court life and Brisk's deportment. Macilente marveled at the inane discourse between Brisk and Saviolina, a court lady, and he was amused when Saviolina put Brisk out of countenance for his abominable habit of smoking.

Fallace, meanwhile, dreamed of the virtues of courtier Fastidious Brisk and paid no attention to Deliro's efforts to please her. When Macilente told them of Brisk's folly at court, Deliro was determined to foreclose on the knight. Fallace, shocked at Macilente's disloyalty and eager to help Brisk, sent Fungoso, whom she gave money to buy himself a new suit, to warn Brisk of her husband's intentions.

Brisk failed to keep an appointment at the notary's, where he was to contribute a hundred pounds to Puntarvolo's venture. Not finding Brisk immediately, Deliro had time to reconsider his plan. His dotage prevailing, he decided not to

1151

foreclose on Brisk and he renounced Macilente's friendship because Macilente, he felt, had unreasonably urged him to be more realistic in his attitude toward his wife. Sogliardo, meanwhile, was delighted with his man Shift, who pretended to be an ex-highwayman, but who was, in reality, a shiftless, cowardly indigent. Brisk made his belated appearance at the notary's, with the explanation that he had been detained by ladies of the court. Fungoso, having gone to see his tailor, had failed in his mission to intercept Brisk.

Puntarvolo prepared for his journey to Constantinople with his dog and cat. Sogliardo, persuaded by Buffone and Brisk that the time had finally come, decided to become a courtier. All of his acquaintances conspired to make a fool of him. Fungoso, in what he thought was the latest fashion, discovered Brisk to be wearing a new suit and was unhappy.

At the palace foolish old Puntarvolo put his dog in the care of a surly groom. Macilente privately obtained the dog from the groom and poisoned it. Brisk and Puntarvolo told Saviolina that they were presenting to her an incomparable courtier, Sogliardo, and that this courtier enjoyed playing the part of a country boor. Confronted by clownish Sogliardo, Saviolina insisted that she could detect the gentleman in him; she was appalled to discover that Sogliardo, who was not aware of the joke, was a rude peasant.

When Puntarvolo missed his dog, he accused Shift of doing away with the animal and threatened to beat the man. Shift, frightened, confessed, to the disenchantment of Sogliardo, that he had never had the courage to commit even one of the crimes of which he had boasted.

At the Mitre Tavern, Buffone, who could not endure the follies and affectations of court life, greeted his companions. Puntarvolo, dejected by the loss of his dog and the loss of his wager, was chaffed by Buffone. In a rage, Puntarvolo sealed Buffone's lips with sealing wax. When the police arrived, everyone tried to flee. Brisk was seized. Fungoso, hiding under a table, was discovered and held to pay the reckoning for all the company had eaten and drunk.

Macilente, seeing in the situation a chance to rid Deliro and Fallace of their humors, sent Deliro to rescue Fungoso at the tavern and Fallace to the jail to comfort Brisk. Deliro paid the bill at the Mitre Tavern. Fungoso declared that he was through with fashion forever. Macilente then sent Deliro to the jail to obtain Brisk's release, after telling him that by so doing Deliro would be reconciled to his wife. At the jail Deliro, seeing Fallace's interest in Brisk, was suddenly awakened from his dotage. Brisk was doomed to serve a term for his debts. Thus the air was cleared and all who had been taken with a specific folly were cured.

EVERYMAN

Type of work: Drama
Author: Unknown
Type of plot: Moral allegory
Time of plot: Any time
Locale: Any place
Earliest extant version: 1508

Principal characters:
GOD
DEATH
EVERYMAN
GOOD-DEEDS

Critique:

This drama is one of the few morality plays to survive, thanks to four printed versions of the sixteenth century. In addition, *Everyman* is almost the only morality play to appeal at all to modern audiences, and it has been produced several times within our century. Like other dramas of this type, it was written to teach a lesson, its characters being personified abstractions of virtue and vice. With the medieval church services largely conducted in Latin, short plays were adapted to moral teaching for the masses.

The Story:

One day a Messenger appeared to announce a moral play on the summoning of Everyman. In the beginning of his life, he declared, man should look to the ending, for we shall see how all earthly possessions avail little in the final reckoning. At first sin looks sweet, but in the end it causes the soul to weep in pain.

Then God spoke. All living creatures were unkind to Him. They lived with no spiritual thought in their worldly possessions. The crucifixion was a lesson they had forgotten. Man had turned to the seven deadly sins, and every year his state grew worse. Therefore, God had decided to have a reckoning of all men, lest mankind should become more brutish than the beasts.

At an imperative summons Death came to receive his instructions. He was ordered to search out every man and tell him that he had to make a pilgrimage to his final reckoning. Death promised to be cruel in his search for each man who lived outside God's law.

Spying Everyman walking unconcernedly about his business, his mind on fleshly lust and treasure, Death bade him stand still and asked him if he had forgotten his Maker. Then Death announced that God had dispatched him in all haste to warn Everyman. Everyman was to make a long journey, and he was to take with him his full book of accounts. He was to be very careful, for he had done many bad deeds and only a few good ones. In Paradise he would soon be forced to account for his life.

Everyman protested that death was farthest from his thoughts at the time. Death was adamant, setting no store by wordly goods or rank, for when he summoned all men must obey. Everyman cried in vain for respite. Then he asked if he must go on the long journey alone. Death assured him that he could take any companions who would make the journey with him. Reminding him that his life was only his on loan, Death said he would return very shortly; in the meantime Everyman would have an opportunity to find possible companions for his journey.

Weeping for his plight and wishing he had never been born, Everyman thought of Fellowship, with whom he had spent so many agreeable days in sport and play. Fortunately he saw Fellowship close by and spoke to him. Seeing Everyman's sad countenance, Fellowship asked his trouble. Everyman told him he was in deep sorrow because he had to make a journey. Fellowship reminded him of their past friendship and vowed that he would go anywhere with him, even to Hell. Greatly heartened, Everyman told him of Death's appearance and his urgent summons. Fellowship thought of the long trip from which there would be no return and decided against accompanying Everyman. He would go with him in sport and play, he declared, or to seek lusty women, but he definitely refused to go on that pilgrimage.

Cast down by this setback, Everyman thought of Kindred. Surely the ties of blood were strong. His Kindred swore that they would help him in any way they could, but when they heard that Everyman had to account for his every deed, good or bad, they knew at once the last journey he had in mind. They refused in one voice to go with him. Everyman appealed directly to his favorite cousin, who said he would have gone willingly if it had not been for a cramp in his toe.

Still reflecting on his woes, Everyman thought of turning to Goods. All his life he had loved Goods. Goods heard his plea and offered to help him, but when asked to go on that journey to the highest judge of all, Goods promptly refused. Everyman reminded him that money is supposed to right all wrongs. Goods disagreed with him. Anyway, if Everyman took Goods with him he would be the worse off, for worldly goods were not given, only lent.

Everyman became ashamed of having sought unworthy companions. Calling aloud to Good-Deeds, he asked again for help. Good-Deeds answered feebly, for he was lying on the cold ground, bound by sins. Good-Deeds already knew of the projected journey and wanted to go along, but he was too weak to stir. It was revealed that Good-Deeds had a sister, Knowledge, who would stay with Everyman until Good-Deeds could regain strength.

Promptly Knowledge offered to go with him and guide him in his great need. Knowledge led him to Confession, who lived in the house of salvation, to ask for strength for Good-Deeds. Confession in pity gave penance to Everyman to shrive his soul. Accepting penance joyfully, Everyman scourged his flesh and afterward Knowledge bequeathed him to his Savior. Thankfully Good-Deeds rose from the ground, delivered from sickness and woe. Declaring himself fit for the journey, Good-Deeds promised to help Everyman count his good works before the judgment throne. With a smile of sympathy Knowledge told Everyman to be glad and merry, for Good-Deeds would be his true companion. Knowledge gave a garment to Everyman to wear, a garment of sorrow which would deliver him from pain.

Asking Good-Deeds if his account were ready, Everyman prepared to start his pilgrimage. Good-Deeds reminded him that three other companions would go part of the way: Discretion, Strength, and Beauty. Knowledge proposed also the Five Wits, who would be his counselors. After Kindred had called the new companions together, Everyman, now well fortified, set out on his last journey.

Knowledge said that their first stop must be to see the priest, who would give Everyman unction and ointment, for priests perform the seven unctions as intermediaries of God. Surely priests were man's best hope on earth, in spite of the many weak and venal people who somehow were invested with holy orders.

After receiving the last rites from the priest, Everyman prepared to meet Death. Again he was troubled, however, for one by one his companions left him. Even Knowledge refused to go with him into the presence of his Maker. Only Good-Deeds stayed with Everyman until the end. So it is with every man who must die. Knowledge, Strength, Beauty—all the other companions are a help in the journey, but only Good-Deeds can face death.

The Angel greeted Everyman as an elected spouse of Jesus. Taking him on high, he announced that Everyman was thus exalted by reason of his singular virtue. When Everyman's soul was taken from his body, his reckoning was crystal clear. So shall it be with every man, if he will only live well before his doom.

Finally a Doctor appeared to remind all men that on the last journey, Beauty, Strength, Discretion, and the Five Wits forsake every man at the end; only Good-Deeds avail at the final judgment.

EXEMPLARY NOVELS

Type of work: Novellas
Author: Miguel de Cervantes Saavedra (1547-1616)
First published: 1613

> Principal characters:
> RINCONETE, a pícaro
> CORTADILLO, another wandering rogue
> PRECIOSA, a gipsy girl
> CIPIÓN, a dog
> BERGANZA, another dog
> TOMÁS RODAJA, an insane student

Cervantes, the great novelist of Spain's Golden Age (1554-1681), had two ambitions: to compose deathless poetry, and to write excellent drama. As a poet, he finally confessed that he was "more experienced in reverses than in verses." In drama he was no more fortunate. In spite of such confidence that he once signed a contract to supply the finest plays the manager had ever seen or not expect payment, he knew too little about dramatic technique to be successful. Only his short plays continue to be read as "slices of life." One of the most pathetic titles ever given a book was his *Eight Comedies and Eight Interludes Never Performed,* which he could publish only because of the fame acquired through the success of *Don Quixote.*

In his fiction, the story was otherwise. But Cervantes remained a nonconformist. *Don Quixote* was conceived as a parody to laugh out of existence the romances of chivalry, though the last of that lot had appeared nearly half a century earlier. It turned into a deeply human novel that is read today with never a thought of its author's avowed purpose.

He was also the first writer of short stories in Spain, a form quite different from the *ejemplo* or instructive story of the early days of Juan Manuel and the Archpriest of Hita. It was the romantic Italian novella that inspired Cervantes. He added the adjective "exemplary," to indicate that his short fiction contained none of the immorality associated with his Italian models. The modern reader will look in vain, however, for the "useful examples" that he proclaimed them to be.

Of the twelve, some are built on complicated romantic plots that would naturally appeal to a thwarted playwright. Others grew out of his own experiences. Since Spaniards were enjoying tales in which rascally servants satirized the professions of their masters, Cervantes also wrote several picaresque stories, one with dogs as spokesmen. Another deals with a crazy student who believed himself made of glass. In the *Exemplary Novels,* which reveal a care and attention to style not found in *Don Quixote,* Cervantes established himself as a master of this genre.

After a preface, worth preserving for the self-portrait of the author, Cervantes presents, in "Lady Cornelia," a cape-and-sword romance close to the Italian school. Courted and betrayed by an Italian duke, the hapless heroine was finally befriended by two Spanish students to whom a servant had delivered her newborn child, as they passed in the darkness. Eventually they arranged a marriage between her and her betrayer. "The Prevalence of Blood" also deals with a child born of violence, whose beauty, along with the virtue and charm of the wronged mother, won the heart of the libertine father seven years later.

Another of the weaker stories in the volume is "The Spanish-English Lady," about a girl of Cadiz captured by Admiral Howard and carried to England. It, like "The Generous Lover," set in Cyprus and Algiers, reveals how uninterested the author was in authentic local color. He made no attempt to capture the pomp of the Elizabethan court.

"The Two Damsels" is the adventure story of Theodosia, disguised as a man. On a journey in pursuit of the suitor who had promised to marry her, she was recognized by her brother. Later the two came upon another masquerading damsel who was searching for the same vanished lover. After adventures among robbers and a visit to the fleet as it was about to sail for Naples, Theodosia found and married her fleeing sweetheart, while her brother comforted the runner-up in this matrimonial race.

In "The Little Gypsy Girl," a story about idealized Preciosa, Cervantes revealed his ignorance of gipsies. One of Preciosa's suitors, a rich nobleman who spent two years with the tribe in order to woo her, killed a bully. After all the gipsy men had been taken to jail, Preciosa visited the mayor's wife to vouch for their innocence. Then came the explanation of her own charm and discretion. The noble lady recognized Preciosa as her own long-lost daughter.

In "The Illustrious Scullery Maid," one youngster, listing the attractions and adventures offered by various Spanish cities, echoes Cervantes' own nostalgic reminiscences of an ill-spent youth. The youngster and another wealthy sixteen-year-old went disguised on a journey in search of thrills. They stopped at an inn in Burgos because they had heard of a beautiful servant, Costanza, to be found there. So attractive was she that the young men took jobs at the inn to compete with the son of the mayor for her affection. When the mayor himself came to investigate the scullery maid, he was told that she was really the daughter of a wronged widow who had left her at the inn, with half a chain as identification. Shortly afterward, the father of one of the runaways appeared with the other half of the chain. The other runaway married her, his friend was paired off with the daughter of the mayor, and Costanza's original suitor had to be content with the sister of Costanza's husband.

For relief from these romantic cape-and-sword stories, Cervantes attempted a psychological tale dealing with his favorite theme, an April and December marriage. In "The Jealous Estremaduran," a seventy-year-old Spaniard, returning with a fortune from Peru, married a fifteen-year-old girl and shielded her so carefully that the air of mystery surrounding her aroused the curiosity of handsome Loaysa. By dressing as a guitar-playing beggar and drugging the husband with a sleep-producing ointment, he was able to enter the house. Although the girl was too noble to be tempted, the husband discovered them and died of jealousy. Before his death, to punish himself for thinking that at his age he could make a young girl happy, he willed his fortune to her so that she could marry Loaysa.

"A Deceitful Marriage," the most unmoral of these *Exemplary Novels,* serves chiefly as introduction for a better one. A poor soldier married a fallen woman to reform her. She tricked him and got all his money, and he ended up in a Valladolid hospital, through whose window he heard and set down "The Dialog between Cipión and Berganza, Dogs of the Hospital of the Resurrection." In the same way that *pícaros* often satirized their masters' callings, Berganza told of the crookedness he had seen. As a pup, at the Seville slaughter house, he became acquainted with graft. As a sheep dog, he watched shepherds totally unlike the figures in the pastoral novels, men who killed the best sheep and put the blame on wolves. As the pet of a rich merchant, he mocked the ostentation he witnessed. Later, while helping a constable, he was a party to an agreement by which the students of Monipodio's school of crime were to fake a fight, thus enhancing the reputation of the police force. Berganza also served a soldier, a gipsy, a miser, a poet, and the company of actors with whom he had arrived in Valladolid. As he ended his autobiography, the dawn was breaking. The other dog promised to narrate his adventures on the following night.

"Doctor Glass Case" provided Cervantes with other opportunities to criticize social conditions of his time. Some students on their way to the University of Salamanca came upon Tomás Rodaja and took him along as their servant. During his spare time Tomás attended classes and after eight years attained a reputation for brilliance. But an unfortunate love affair drove him insane with the delusion that he was made of fragile glass. His agile mind, however, could still supply answers to any question, and people amused themselves by asking his opinions about professions and customs. Asked if he was a poet, for instance, he replied: "I have never been so foolish as to be a bad poet, nor so bold as to think I could be a good one." Questioned how to avoid envying others, he advised: "Sleep, for while you sleep you are the equal of everybody." Eventually Tomás was restored to sanity, but no one noticed him then. To make a living, he joined the army. He was killed in Flanders.

Best known of all the *Exemplary Novels* is "Rinconete and Cortadillo," an au-thentic story of customs which influenced Charles Dickens. Two fourteen-year-old boys, Pedro de Rincón and Diego Cortado, met on their way to Seville. Since they both boasted of their cleverness and ability as cardsharps, purse snatchers, and general rascals, they joined forces to fleece a mule driver with marked cards. Then they traveled on to the Andalusian capital where, under bad government, crime flourished. To meet competition, the boys enrolled in Monipodio's school for criminals and were nicknamed Rinconete and Cortadillo. They saw flourishing a crime trust where rich people could hire bullies to beat up their enemies and police could pick up protection money. Only a few of the crimes of these rascals are narrated. Cervantes declared the story already overlong, but he promised a sequel later.

In *Exemplary Novels* there are stories whose invention and style would have established Cervantes' reputation among his contemporaries if he had never penned *Don Quixote*. Some are poetic, some realistic. It would be possible to compile a lengthy list of English and French dramatists and novelists who have drawn upon them for inspiration ever since.

EXILES

Type of work: Drama
Author: James Joyce (1882-1941)
Type of plot: Naturalism
Time of plot: 1912
Locale: Merrion and Ranelagh, Dublin suburbs
First published: 1918

Principal characters:
RICHARD ROWAN, an Irish writer
BERTHA, his common law wife
ARCHIE, their son, eight years old
ROBERT HAND, a newspaper editor
BEATRICE JUSTICE, Robert's cousin, a music teacher

Critique:

James Joyce, one of the most influential writers during the first half of the century, was preoccupied, as were many of his contemporaries, with the creation of new and meaningful forms of expression and the effort to speak truly of his age. His constant themes were Irish myths and mores, art, sexuality, and aesthetic integrity. Within this pattern *Exiles* can be considered a part of the continuing development of his genius, since it falls in the period which saw the completion of *A Portrait of the Artist as a Young Man* and the beginning of *Ulysses*. As theater, however, the play lacks the force of Ibsen's work, by which Joyce was greatly influenced; and it lacks also the plasticity and vibrancy of his own fiction. Its importance lies in the fact that this is Joyce's last objective study of the conscience of the artist, his final portrait of the artist as man. The themes are expressed at various levels of conflict; the resolution, where effected, is through integrity and single-heartedness. Both Beatrice and Robert are seen to have compromised with the world or within themselves; thus they are incapable of self-fulfillment. Richard, as the artist, is dependent solely on his own intellectual and emotional values, and the same self-reliance informs his love; he is thus armored against enervating sentimentality and the moral anarchy of the modern world.

The Story:

Richard Rowan and Bertha, unmarried lovers, returned from Italy with their eight-year-old son Archie to Dublin, where, although physically at home, they were in spiritual exile. The two people most involved in their return were Robert and Beatrice, first cousins once engaged to be married. Robert, however, had always been dominated by Richard's ideas and was tenuously in love with Bertha. When he recognized Bertha's love for Richard, he had been gradually drawn to Beatrice, who was in love with him. But she too had always been fascinated by Richard, and had found that without him charming but weak Robert became a mere cipher. Finally, her engagement to Robert had been broken off—a situation from which Beatrice, as she told Richard, was still convalescing.

Richard had thus been the dominant force behind at least three sensitive and intelligent people in their youth. In maturity, his physical passions and his commitment to people still complemented his ideals of freedom and integrity. This fact was demonstrated in a conversation with Robert who, while explaining his eagerness to promote Richard's academic career, had declared that he found in Richard the same faith that a disciple has in his master. Richard answered cryptically that his was a master's faith in the disciple who would eventually betray him. In this fashion he was trying to indicate to Robert, who had uneasily become the editor of a conventional Dublin newspaper, his desire to avoid influencing those he loved while remaining wholly loyal to them.

In somewhat the same fashion Richard desired to be united with Bertha, but not to be bound or to bind, even in love. In Italy, Richard had been absorbed in his writing and Bertha was often sad and lonely. She had remained devoted to him but understood neither his aesthetic standards nor his ethics. In marked contrast was his wholly objective relationship with Beatrice. She had always understood what he wrote and was fascinated by his unique courage. Through his exile they had corresponded about his writing, and on his return Beatrice came to his house to give piano lessons to Archie. Upon renewed contact, Richard found that there was much in Beatrice's character that he could use in his current novel. This was the most vital bond between them.

Through perversity of passion Bertha identified herself with Richard and thus saw his relationship with Beatrice as a love affair. Her concern caused her to crystallize her feeling of loss toward him, and she turned to Robert, whom she had always liked because he too looked up to Richard. She subsequently explored Robert's feelings for her and for a time passively accepted his wooing. Once, when Robert visited the house, he brought Bertha roses, a gesture of courtship which confused and moved her. At that meeting they kissed and Bertha agreed that they must meet somewhere alone and talk together freely. She half promised to meet Robert at his house that evening.

When Richard questioned Bertha about Robert, she answered willingly. At that time he was distressed neither by her involvement nor by Robert's love for her, but he was angered to learn that she was to meet Robert at the same hour as he, at Robert's arrangement, was to meet the vice-chancellor of the university, where Richard was being considered for the chair of romance literature. He felt that this plan was a betrayal of everything that each of them stood for and that Robert was both a fool and a thief. Richard decided to see Robert himself. His intention infuriated Bertha, who felt that he would simply rob her of their friend's love and respect.

Having expected Bertha, Robert was discountenanced by Richard's arrival; but when Richard explained why he had come, Robert was most eager to talk to him. While they talked Richard revealed his own fears and doubts. He felt that by refusing to advise Bertha or to ask anything of her he might have neglected her, as she had accused him. The conflict between personal integrity and love for another person was very real to Richard; he realized that it was an inevitable one, yet he felt that his guilt had destroyed Bertha's innocence. He expressed to Robert his willingness to let her go if Robert felt that she would find fulfillment with him. Faced with this need to accept moral responsibility, Robert faltered. Richard feared that he would ultimately desert Bertha as he had other women in the past.

Richard admitted that he had desired some kind of betrayal that would enable him to redeem, through the rebuilding of his soul, his guilt and shame. In answer Robert wildly suggested a duel, but it would be a duel between the ghost of fidelity on one side, of friendship on the other. Richard declared wearily that such had been the language of his youth, expressing emotions of which he was no longer capable. Completely disoriented by Richard's rejection of his heroic pose, and distracted by his emotions, Robert fled when Bertha arrived.

The talk between Richard and Bertha in Robert's cottage led to a partial resolution of their conflict. Bertha was over-whelmed by Richard's apparent lack of faith in her, while he was angered that she was using Robert's love without herself loving him. For the last time she begged Richard to guide her; he merely repeated his statement of faith in her and left the house. When Robert returned, Bertha was uneasy with him and maintained against all persuasion that she could never betray Richard.

Having survived her period of crisis with Robert, Bertha was repossessed by the problem of Beatrice and Richard.

After a sleepless night she told Richard that she wished she could meet her lover freely. Only later in conversation with Robert, who planned to leave Ireland, did Richard realize what Bertha had meant, that she wished she could freely revive her former relationship with him. Out of this desire she was able to accept Richard's account of his relationship with Beatrice. Thus they arrived at a point where they could stay together while continuing to live as independent individuals, self-exiled from the passions and the romantic notions of their youth.

A FABLE

Type of work: Novel
Author: William Faulkner (1897- 1962)
Type of plot: Religious allegory
Time of plot: 1918
Locale: The Western Front in France
First published: 1954

Principal characters:

THE CORPORAL
THE MARSHAL, Commander-in-Chief of the Allied Armies in France
GENERAL GRAGNON, French Division Commander
THE QUARTERMASTER GENERAL, the Marshal's former fellow student
THE RUNNER, a former officer, in sympathy with the Corporal's aims
THE REVEREND TOBE SUTTERFIELD, an American Negro preacher
THE CORPORAL'S WIFE
MARTHE, the Corporal's younger half-sister
MARYA, the Corporal's feeble-minded half-sister
DAVID LEVINE, a British flight officer
POLCHEK, a soldier in the Corporal's squad
PIERRE BOUC, another soldier in the Corporal's squad
BUCHWALD, an American soldier

Critique:

The end of World War II was only a few months away when Faulkner started this novel about World War I. In search of a more universal background, he left his native surroundings and the fictional world of his Yoknapatawpha County because the battlefields of France seemed more suitable for his religious allegory. Nine years later he completed the novel, probably the most thorough endeavor in the twentieth century to create a mythical work by using elements of the Gospel. Nowhere in the book does the author indicate that this represents a modern version of the Christ story, but it is quite obvious that parts of the story of the Passion and Crucifixion are methodically woven into the novel. It would be useless, however, to indicate comparisons between the New Testament and *A Fable,* as critics are likely to disagree for years to come about the intentions of the author. However, any attempt to describe the novel simply as a partial retelling of the Christ story fails to do justice to a book which, even in its mythical elements, points to the creative power of a strong individualist who defies all efforts of classification for himself and his work.

The Story:

On a Monday in May, 1918, a most unusual event took place on a battlefield in France where French and German troops faced one another after four years of trench warfare. At dawn the regiment under the command of General Gragnon refused to attack. Another unbelievable event occurred when the Germans, who were expected to take advantage of the mutiny, did not move either. At noon the whole sector of the front stopped firing and soon the rest of the front came to a standstill. Division Commander Gragnon requested execution of all three thousand mutineers; he also demanded his own arrest.

On Wednesday the lorries carrying the mutinous regiment arrived at headquarters in Chaulnesmont, where the dishonor brought on the town aroused the people to noisy demonstration. Relatives and friends of the mutineers knew that a Corporal and his squad of twelve, moving in a mysterious way behind the lines, had succeeded in spreading their ideas about peace on earth and good will toward men among the troops. Four of the thirteen men were not Frenchmen by birth; among those only the Corporal spoke French, and he was the object of the crowd's fury.

This situation created uncertainty among the allied generals because a war ended by mutiny was not reconcilable with military principles. To clarify the confusion a conference took place to which a German general was invited, and agreement was reached for continuation of the war.

To young Flight Officer David Levine the unsuspected pause in war meant tragedy. Determined to find glory in battle, but realizing that he might miss his opportunity, he committed suicide. To another soldier, the Runner, the truce at the front was a welcome sign. A former officer, he had rejected submissive principles and abuse of authority by superiors, and he had been returned to the ranks. Having heard about the Corporal from the Reverend Tobe Sutterfield, an American colored preacher who had arrived under unexplainable circumstances in France, the Runner tried to show once again the power of the Corporal's ideas. He forced a sentry, who profiteered by collecting fees for life insurance among the soldiers, to leave the trenches and join a British battalion in a peaceful walk toward the German line. When they showed their empty hands, the Germans also came unarmed to meet the French. A sudden artillery barrage by French and German guns killed the sentry and crippled the Runner.

The man to decide the fate of the mutineers was the Commander-in-Chief of the Allied Armies, an aged French Marshal. The orphaned son of a prominent family, he had attended France's St. Cyr. There his unselfish attitude combined with his devotion to studies had made him an outstanding and beloved student. Especially attracted to him was the man who was now his Quartermaster General. After leaving school, the Marshal had been stationed in the Sahara, where he incurred blood-guilt by sacrificing a brutal legionnaire to tribal justice. Later he spent several years in a Tibetan monastery. In the Middle East he had met a married woman with two daughters. This affair resulted in the birth of a son in a stable at Christmas. The mother died in childbirth, and Marthe, one of the daughters, cared for the boy. When World War I broke out, the Marshal became the Allied commander and the hope of France.

The mutinous troops were kept in a former factory building while awaiting trial. The Marshal, not surprised by the court proceedings, seemed to anticipate all answers. Marthe and Marya, the Corporal's half-sisters, and his wife arrived in Chaulnesmont and in an interview with the Marshal revealed that the Corporal was his son. Marthe had married a French farmer, Dumont, and the boy had grown up on her farm. Soon after the outbreak of war, he had enlisted in the army and received a medal for bravery in action. He had married a former prostitute from Marseilles. Again the old Marshal was not surprised and seemed to know every detail.

On Thursday a meal was served to the squad during which it became known that soldier Polchek had betrayed the Corporal. Another soldier, Pierre Bouc, denied his leader twice. After the meal the Corporal was called away to meet the Marshal. On a hill overlooking the town the Marshal tried to explain the futility of his son's martyrdom. When he promised a secret ocean passage to escape the death penalty, the Corporal refused the offer. Later the Marshal made a last attempt to influence his son with the help of an army priest. Recognizing his own unworthiness before the humble Corporal the priest committed suicide. On the same evening General Gragnon was executed by an American soldier named Buchwald.

On Friday the Corporal was tied to a post between two murderers. Shot, he fell into a coil of barbed wire that lacerated his head. The Corporal's body and his medal were buried on the Dumont farm near St. Mihiel. After the burial a sudden artillery barrage plowed the earth, leaving no trace of the Corporal's grave.

After the war a unit was sent to reclaim a body to be placed in the Unknown Soldier's tomb under the Arc de Triomphe in Paris. As reward they were promised brandy. Near Verdun they obtained a body and drank the brandy. While they were guarding the coffin, an old woman approached. Having lost her mind because her son had not returned from the war, she had sold her farm in order to search for him. Knowing about the mission of the soldiers, she wanted to look at the body. Convinced that the dead soldier was her son, she offered all her money for the corpse; the soldiers accepted and bought more brandy with the money. They secured another body from a field adjoining the Dumont farm. Thus the body of the Corporal reached Paris. Four years later the Runner visited the Dumont farm and picked up the medal.

Six years later the Marshal's body was carried to the Arc de Triomphe, with dignitaries of the Western world following the coffin on foot to pay their respects to the dead leader. As soon as the eulogy started a cripple made his way through the crowd. It was the Runner, who threw the Corporal's medal at the caisson before an angry mob closed in and attacked him. Rescued by the police he was dragged into a side street, where a few curious onlookers gathered around the injured cripple. While he lay in the gutter a man resembling the old Quartermaster General stepped forward to comfort the Runner, who declared that he would never die.

FABLES

Type of work: Didactic poetry
Author: Jean de La Fontaine (1621-1695)
First published: Books I-VI, 1668; Books VII-XI, 1673-1679; Book XII, 1694

Jean de La Fontaine was an easygoing, absent-minded, middle-class Frenchman who became one of the literary ornaments of France's Golden Age. Impervious to discipline—except in his writing—he was a lover of pleasure, a vagabond and dreamer, who had a special talent for attracting the patronage and protection of important people. Thus, he became a hanger-on of Fouquet while that minister of Louis XIV was still wealthy and powerful; and when fate caught up with Fouquet, La Fontaine drifted on to other alliances, chiefly with women, which allowed him to work and live in comfort and security.

The literary career of La Fontaine was somewhat slow in getting started. First, he played with the idea of becoming a churchman or a lawyer. Then he contracted an ill-advised marriage with a romantic adolescent ten years younger than he. Turning his back on these early distractions, he began to write at the age of thirty, encouraged and stimulated by his friendship with Racine and Molière. The first result of his efforts was a fairly successful adaptation of the *Eunuchus* of Terence. This was followed by various short poems and by lively verse tales translated from or inspired by Ariosto and Boccaccio. La Fontaine's career was climaxed by his election to the French Academy, a victory somewhat dimmed by the reaction of Louis XIV, who withheld his confirmation until after the Academy had first installed Boileau.

The celebrated *Fables* of La Fontaine, remarkable for both their range and their poetry, have come to be recognized as their author's greatest achievement. These animal stories in verse, after the style of Aesop and Phaedrus, brought him his greatest contemporary popularity and his surest hold on lasting fame. Public reaction to the *Fables* was immediate and enthusiastic, though some classical critics disapproved of La Fontaine's liberties in versification and his use of colloquial language. His style, however, was perfectly fitted to his subject matter; and Charles Perrault, a contemporary writer of fairy stories and the originator of Mother Goose, declared him greater than the fable writers of antiquity.

The twelve books of the *Fables* were issued at intervals over a period of years which extended from 1668 to 1694. Books I-VI, dedicated to the young Dauphin appeared in 1668; Books VII-XI, bearing a prefatory eulogy to Madame de Montespan, occupied the period between 1673 and 1679; and the final volume, inscribed to the young Duke of Burgundy, was added the year before the author's death.

Born storyteller though he was, La Fontaine was not a particularly original one. It is the pleasure of recognition rather than the joy of discovery which awaits most readers of his early fables. A volume by Phaedrus, published in 1596, has been found to supply most of the stories in his first six volumes, with French folk tales providing the rest. Also, scholars have traced many of the fables in the last six books to translation of some Persian tales in *Le Livre des Lumières* (1644). To compensate for any lack of originality, La Fontaine generally improved on his sources. One critic has summed up the appeal of his fables by commenting on their threefold attraction: children delight in their freshness and vividness; adult readers recognize their subtle reflection of life and character; and critics admire the consummate art of their narration.

Lessons are inherent in the fables, as the first three are quick to show: "The Grasshopper and the Ant" (the rewards of diligence); "The Fox and the Crow" (the dangers of flattery); and "The Frog Who Would Be an Ox" (the error of striving to keep up with those higher placed socially or financially). Yet, since La Fontaine was obviously epicurean by instinct, the "morals" of his fables were far from his chief concern. Always the shrewd, amused observer rather than the preacher, La Fontaine devoted himself to the pictures he could sketch and to the truth he could disclose. Sometimes he omitted the moral entirely; on other occasions he gave it a new twist. For instance, in the second fable of Book II, the author told of the rooster who took a pearl to a jeweler, offering to trade it for a grain of millet. Instead of belaboring the point of the story, La Fontaine reinforced it by adding a parallel (and original) example. In the latter a Blockhead was bequeathed a valuable manuscript which he took to a nearby connoisseur, remarking that he would rather have a halfpenny than the rarity which he had inherited.

After 1668, when La Fontaine brought out the first six books of the *Fables*, several years elapsed before he resumed this type of writing. When he eventually did, the fables were longer and more elaborate than the earlier ones. Often based on Persian originals, they contained subject matter more unfamiliar. They still, however, served the author well in his role as observer and critic, as the introductory fable of Book VII demonstrates: A terrible plague brought the animals together to discover whose sin was being punished by heaven. The lion admitted to serious crimes, including the senseless killing of sheep and shepherds, but no one dared suggest that he be made a sacrifice to placate the gods. Other animals, almost as fierce and strong as the lion, told of their misdeeds but were likewise absolved. Finally the inoffensive ass acknowledged that he had once nibbled grass beside a church. Then the beasts all joined in a clamor for his death; and La Fontaine

concluded with these words, in a biting comparison with human courts of justice:

Thus human courts acquit the strong,
And doom the weak, as therefore wrong.

La Fontaine had apparently abandoned his fables permanently after 1679; however, in 1694, Volume XII appeared in response to a request made by the Duke of Burgundy. This final section showed that the seventy-three-year-old teller of tales had lost none of his former skill. The initial poem, serving as an introduction to the remainder, told of the men of Ulysses' crew and of their transformation into animals. When Ulysses wanted them restored to human form, they protested that they were better off as animals. Using this incident as a springboard, La Fontaine then offered stories, with animals in the leading roles, on which the duke might use his judgment in accepting or rejecting. One of these fulfilled a special desire of the duke, who had asked La Fontaine to write a fable called "The Cat and the Mouse." In it, a young mouse tries to argue a veteran mouser out of eating him, only to be told:

"Youth always hopes its ends to gain,
Believes all spirits like its own:
Old age is not to mercy prone."

Works as widely read as the *Fables* naturally inspired many cross currents of discussion and comment. One interesting speculation, now generally discounted, was Taine's idea that La Fontaine's parables consciously satirized the monarchy of Louis XIV. The more plausible view, however, is that the author was an observer of mankind at large—a gently humorous one, given to a tolerant attitude and dedicated to the glorification of common sense. Fortunately for the effective projection of these qualities, La Fontaine also employed a painstaking art and care which have placed him in the front rank of French literary craftsmen.

THE FAERIE QUEENE

Type of work: Poem
Author: Edmund Spenser (1552?-1599)
Type of plot: Allegorical epic
Time of plot: Middle Ages
Locale: England
First published: Books I-III, 1590; Books IV-VI, 1596

Principal characters:

GLORIANA, the Fairy Queen, representing Queen Elizabeth
THE RED CROSS KNIGHT, representing Holiness
UNA, representing Religion
ARCHIMAGO, a magician *rep, the Devil*
DUESSA, representing Roman Catholicism
BRITOMART, representing Chastity
GUYON, representing Temperance
ARTEGALL, representing Justice
PRINCE ARTHUR, legendary English king *rep. Divine grace*

Critique:

The Faerie Queen was the first sustained poetic creation after Chaucer, and its beauty and poetic power made for it a secure place in our literature as soon as it was given to the world. At present it is generally accorded a high place in the history of English literary art. The Spenserian stanza—nine lines, eight of five feet and one of six, riming ababbcbcc —is a genuine artistic innovation. Combined with his poetic power, Spenser was animated by a high moral purpose. Only six books of the twelve planned by Spenser were completed. The fragmentary seventh book was published in 1609, ten years after his death.

The Story:

Gloriana, the Fairy Queen, was holding her annual twelve-day feast. As was the custom, any one in trouble could appear before the court and ask for a champion. The fair lady Una came riding on a white ass, accompanied by a dwarf. She complained that her father and mother had been shut up in a castle by a dragon. The Red Cross Knight offered to help her, and the party set out to rescue Una's parents.

In a cave the Red Cross Knight encountered a horrible creature, half serpent, half woman. Although the foul stench nearly overpowered him, the knight slew the monster. After the battle, the Red Cross Knight and Una lost their way. A friendly stranger who offered them shelter was really Archimago, the wicked magician. By making the Red Cross Knight dream that Una was a harlot, Archimago separated Una from her champion.

Una went on her way alone. Archimago quickly assumed the form of the Red Cross Knight and followed her to do her harm. Meanwhile the Red Cross Knight fell into the company of Duessa, an evil enchantress. They met the great giant Orgoglio, who overcame the Red Cross Knight and made Duessa his mistress. Prince Arthur, touched by Una's misfortunes, rescued the Red Cross Knight from Orgoglio and led him to Una. Once again Una and her champion rode on their mission.

At last they came to Una's kingdom, and the dragon who had imprisoned her parents came out to do battle. After two days of fighting, the Red Cross Knight overthrew the dragon. After the parents had been freed, the Red Cross Knight and Una were betrothed.

Still hoping to harm the Red Cross Knight, Archimago told Sir Guyon that the Red Cross Knight had despoiled a virgin of her honor. Shocked, Guyon set out to right the wrong. The cunning

Archimago disguised Duessa as a young girl and placed her on the road, where she told a piteous tale of wrong done by the Red Cross Knight and urged Guyon to avenge her. When Guyon and the Red Cross Knight met, they lowered their lances and began to fight. Fortunately the signs of the Virgin Mary on the armor of each recalled them to their senses, and Guyon was ashamed that he had been tricked by the magician.

In his travels Guyon fell in with Prince Arthur, and the two visited the Castle of Alma, the stronghold of Temperance. The most powerful enemy of Temperance was the demon Maleger. In a savage battle Prince Arthur vanquished Maleger. Guyon went on to the Bower of Bliss, where his arch enemy Acrasy was living. With stout heart Guyon overthrew Acrasy and destroyed the last enemy of Temperance.

After sending Acrasy back to the fairy court under guard, Guyon and Prince Arthur went on their way until on an open plain they saw a knight arming for battle. With Prince Arthur's permission, Guyon rode against the strange knight, and in the meeting Guyon was unhorsed by the strong lance of his opponent. Ashamed of his fall, Guyon snatched his sword and would have continued the fight on foot.

The palmer, attending Guyon, saw that the champion could not prevail against the stranger, for the strange knight was enchanted. When he stopped the fight, the truth was revealed; the strange knight was really the lovely Britomart, a chaste and pure damsel, who had seen the image of her lover, Artegall, in Venus' looking-glass and had set out in search of him. With the situation explained, Britomart joined Guyon, Prince Arthur, and Arthurs' squire, Timias; and the four continued their quest.

In a strange wood they traveled for days, seeing no one, but everywhere they met bears, lions, and bulls. Suddenly a beautiful lady on a white palfrey galloped out of the brush. She was Florimell, pursued by a lustful forester who spurred his steed cruelly in an attempt to catch her. The three men joined the chase, but out of modesty Britomart stayed behind. She waited a long time; then, despairing of ever finding her companions again, she went on alone.

As she approached Castle Joyous she saw six knights attacking one. She rode into the fight and demanded to know why they were fighting in such cowardly fashion. She learned that any knight passing had to love the lady of Castle Joyous or fight six knights. Britomart denounced the rule and with her magic lance unhorsed four of the knights. She entered Castle Joyous as a conqueror.

After meeting the Red Cross Knight in the castle, Britomart resolved to go on as a knight errant. She heard from Merlin, whom she visited, that she and Artegall were destined to have illustrious descendants.

Meanwhile Timias had been wounded while pursuing the lustful forester. Belphoebe, the wondrous beauty of the Garden of Adonis, rescued him and healed his wounds. Timias fell in love with Belphoebe.

Amoret, the fair one, was held prisoner by a young knight who attempted to defile her. For months she resisted his advances. Then Britomart, hearing of her sad plight, overcame the two knights who guarded Amoret's prison and freed her. Greatly attracted to her brave rescuer, Amoret set out with Britomart.

At a strange castle a knight claimed Amoret as his love. Britomart jousted with him to save Amoret, and after winning the tourney Britomart was forced to take off her helmet. With her identity revealed, Britomart and Amoret set off together in search of their true loves.

Artegall, in search of adventure, joined Scudamour, knight errant. They met Amoret and Britomart, who was still disguised as a knight. Britomart and Artegall fought an indecisive battle during which Artegall was surprised to discover that his opponent was his lost love,

1168

Britomart. The two lovers were reunited at last, but in the confusion Amoret was abducted by Lust. With the help of Prince Arthur, Scudamour rescued Amoret from her loathsome captor. He wooed Amoret in the Temple of Love, where they found shelter.

Artegall, champion of true justice, was brought up and well-trained by Astraea. When Artegall was of age, Astraea gave him a trusty groom, and the new knight set out on his adventures. Talus, the groom, was an iron man who carried an iron flail to thresh out falsehood. Irene, who asked at the fairy court for a champion against the wicked Grantorto, set out with Artegall and Talus to regain her heritage. With dispatch Artegall and Talus overcame Grantorto and restored Irene to her throne.

Later Artegall entered the lists against a strange knight who was really the disguised Amazon, Radigund. Artegall wounded Radigund, but when he saw that his prostrate foe was a comely woman, he threw away his weapons. The wounded Amazon then rushed on the defenseless Artegall and took him prisoner. Artegall was kept in shameful confinement until at last Talus informed Britomart of his fate. Britomart went to her lover's rescue and slew Radigund.

Continuing his quest, Artegall met two hags, Envy and Detraction, who defamed his character and set the Blatant Beast barking at his heels. But Artegall forbade Talus to beat the hags and returned to the fairy court.

The Blatant Beast, defamer of knightly character and the last remaining enemy of the fairy court, finally met his match. The courteous Calidore, the gentlest of all the knights, conquered the beast and led him, tamed, back to the court of the Fairy Queen.

THE FAIR MAID OF PERTH

Type of work: Novel
Author: Sir Walter Scott (1771-1832) ·
Type of plot: Historical romance
Time of plot: 1396
Locale: Scotland
First published: 1828

Principal characters:

HENRY GOW, smith and armorer of Perth
CATHARINE GLOVER, his sweetheart, the Fair Maid of Perth
SIMON GLOVER, her father
CONACHAR, Simon's apprentice and heir to the chief of Clan Quhele
THE DUKE OF ROTHSAY, heir to Scottish throne
SIR JOHN RAMORNY, his Master of Horse
ROBERT III, King of Scotland
THE DUKE OF ALBANY, his brother
THE EARL OF DOUGLAS, the "Black Douglas"
OLIVER PROUDFUTE, a Perth burgher, a bonnet-maker, and friend of
    Henry Gow
HENBANE DWINING, Ramorny's physician, a Perth apothecary
SIR PATRICK CHARTERIS, provost of Perth

Critique:

Sir Walter Scott in this novel sets his finely-drawn fictional and historical characters against the background of the rise to power of the Earl of Douglas, the Scottish leader who fought against Percy at the famous battle of Chevy Chase. The author is justly praised for his ability to create living beings. The characters of *The Fair Maid of Perth* do not stand out among Scott's greatest creations, but they are believable and interesting; good and bad exist among both the nobility and the citizenry and are present in each individual in varying degrees. It is his picture of human nature that makes Scott's novels worth rereading many times.

The Story:

As Catharine Glover and her father Simon walked to Mass, an unidentified young nobleman, muffled in a cloak, joined them and asked the girl's permission to come to her window the next morning to take part in the traditional Valentine ritual. When she sensibly refused to make any alliance above her social standing, he left her in anger.

A welcome guest, Henry Gow, appeared at the Glovers' that evening; he had just returned from a trip on which he had sold armor throughout Scotland. Although Simon approved heartily of Henry's suit for Catharine's hand, she was disturbed by his propensity for quarreling. His fiery spirit led him to rise up vigorously that evening against Conachar, Simon's Highlander apprentice, who jealously poured a tankard of beer on the armorer and then tried to stab him.

Henry's martial bent was put to better use the next morning when, coming to present himself to Catharine as her Valentine, he discovered a party of men attempting to climb into her room. While fighting them off, he severed the hand of one assailant. Again a mysterious nobleman was involved. When Simon heard his voice he sent Henry into his house and freed the other. In gratitude for Henry's protection, Catharine agreed to be his Valentine; but she would not promise to marry him, even though, as she assured him, she was not in love with Conachar, who had just returned to his Highland home, or any other man.

King Robert was discussing with his confessor the rising power of the Earl of Douglas when that great nobleman arrived at the castle in time to see his son-in-law, the Duke of Rothsay, kiss a traveling glee-maiden. The "Black Douglas," infuriated, threatened to kill both the prince and the innocent girl. The Duke of Albany, King Robert's brother James, and another nobleman calmed the two men, and Rothsay committed the girl to the care of Henry, who had just entered the courtyard engaged in a scuffle with some of Douglas' men. Although he was reluctant to accept such a charge, especially on the day he had become Catharine's Valentine, he took the girl home with him and sent her on to Dundee the next morning.

The council which followed Rothsay's foolish flirtation revealed the tensions surrounding the weak and easily-influenced king. After King Robert had prevented a duel between the arch-rivals, the earls of March and Douglas, March stalked out to join the English. Albany and the prince, too, were obviously struggling for control over king and country.

As these personal conflicts smoldered, the men discussed the enmity between Clans Quhele and Chattan and decided to settle it by setting the bravest men from each group against each other in a combat to be fought before the king. After Douglas had gone, the king and Albany questioned the prince about the early morning disturbance at Simon's house, reported to them by Sir Patrick Charteris, provost of Perth. Confronted with a ring found at Simon's house, Rothsay confessed that he had been present; the ring belonged to Sir John Ramorny, his Master of Horse. Rothsay agreed to dismiss Ramorny, whom both older men regarded as an evil influence over the young prince.

Conachar came back to Perth briefly at Catharine's request that he give refuge to Father Clement, her confessor, who had been accused of heresy. The Highlander told her that he was the son of the chief of Clan Quhele and that his real name was Eachin (Hector) MacIan. As he promised protection for Father Clement, he hinted also at his love for Catharine.

Ramorny, owner of the hand cut off in Perth, planned vengeance on his assailant with Henbane Dwining, an apothecary who was jealous of Henry's power and influence. Having gained only a mild revenge by spreading the tale of Henry's association with the glee-maiden, he was eager to help Ramorny plot Henry's assassination.

That night, as Shrovetide revelers milled about Perth, Oliver Proudfute, a well-meaning but tactless burgher, assured the still angry Simon that Henry was not hiding the glee-maiden; he had seen him send her to Dundee. Then, fearing that he had made matters worse, he escaped from a group of taunting masquers and went to Henry to apologize. Proudfute, who liked to think of himself as a hero but who was really a timid soul, avoided the subject of his visit as long as possible. His belated and sheepish confession served only to deepen Henry's depression over his relationship with Catharine; Henry ordered his friend out, after granting the burgher's request for his helmet and jacket to frighten away assailants. Ironically, these garments caused Proudfute's death, for as he walked down the street imitating Henry's swagger he was struck down from behind and killed.

Rothsay, who had been among the masquers, went to Ramorny's to rouse him to join the gaiety. He was horrified to learn of his missing hand, and he suspected him of attempting revenge when he noticed the surly murderer Bonthron in the room. Ramorny's suggestion that they "allow" Albany to die and force King Robert to abdicate shocked him further. The prince left immediately, vowing to see Ramorny no more and arousing the bitter hatred of his former friend.

When the discovery of Proudfute's body the next morning set off a rumor that Henry was dead, Catharine flew disheveled through the streets to see whether he was safe. Henry's joy at this evidence of her affection was marred by the news of the murder and his realization that he must ignore Catharine's feelings and declare himself the champion of Proudfute's widow.

The provost suspected after a brief investigation that Proudfute's death was the result of the enmity aroused during the Valentine encounter between Henry and Ramorny. The council decided to determine the identity of the murderer by an ancient test, the bier-right, based on the superstition that a body bleeds in the presence of its killer. Ramorny's household was later marched by Proudfute's body but with no result until Bonthron refused the test and chose the alternative, trial by combat. Henry defeated the murderer, who in his confession followed the instructions of Ramorny and Dwining and laid the principal blame on Rothsay. Albany immediately put the prince in the hands of the High Constable to protect him and keep him out of further trouble.

Sir Patrick Charteris came to tell Simon and Catharine that they were to be arrested for heresy. Simon planned to seek asylum with his old friend, Conachar's father, in the Highlands; however, knowing his former apprentice's feelings, he was relieved when the provost offered to take Catharine to Lady Marjory, Duchess of Rothsay.

When he reached his destination, Simon learned that his friend had died, but he was received courteously by the young chief. Conachar confessed to him that he feared the coming combat with Clan Chattan; a coward was not a fit leader for a brave clan. He begged Simon to let him marry Catharine, for he felt that her love would strengthen him. Simon refused, however, to break his word to Henry.

Meanwhile, Ramorny had enticed Rothsay to flee to the former residence of his duchess by telling him that Catharine was coming there. When the girl arrived, thinking Lady Marjory was still there, the prince at first tried to seduce her, but later gave in to her appeal to his honor. He entrusted her to Louise, the glee-maiden, whom he had encountered again by chance.

Ramorny and Dwining starved the prince to death, at the same time spreading a rumor that he was ill. Louise and Catharine discovered what was happening, and the glee-maiden escaped to bring Douglas to the rescue while Catharine tried to get food to Rothsay. Douglas arrived in time to force Ramorny's surrender and save Catharine's life; Dwining poisoned himself to avoid his confederate's fate of death by hanging.

Douglas and Albany decided to keep Rothsay's death secret until after the clan combat on Palm Sunday. That morning Henry volunteered to take the place of a missing Chattan warrior and fought valiantly in order to have a chance to meet Conachar, whom he believed a rival about to wed Catharine. Conachar's foster father sacrificed his eight sons and himself in an endeavor to protect Conachar, but their efforts were useless. When the young leader faced Henry at last, the Highlander fled across the river Tay. Late that day he went to Catharine to tell her of his cowardice before he plunged to his death in the torrent.

Catharine and Henry were married a few months later. Although she was by that time reconciled to her husband's warring impulses, he vowed to take up arms again only in behalf of his country. Their first son had as godparents the Earl of Douglas, Lady Marjory, and Sir Patrick Charteris.

King Robert died soon afterward, broken-hearted by the death of one son and the capture by the English of the other, later James I of Scotland, whom he was sending away to protect him from Albany's power. Albany, acquitted by Parliament of the charge that he was responsible for Rothsay's death, nevertheless did penance for his guilt. His son, who inherited the regency, paid for his father's sins on the scaffold when James I came to the throne, years later.

1172

THE FAITHFUL SHEPHERDESS

Type of work: Drama
Author: John Fletcher (1579-1625)
Type of plot: Pastoral tragi-comedy
Time of plot: Remote antiquity
Locale: Thessaly
First presented: c. 1609

Principal characters:
PERIGOT, a shepherd, in love with Amoret
THENOT, a shepherd, in love with Clorin
DAPHNIS, a modest shepherd, in love with Cloe
ALEXIS, a wanton shepherd, in love with Cloe
THE SULLEN SHEPHERD
AMORET, a shepherdess, in love with Perigot
CLORIN, a hermitess, the faithful shepherdess
AMARILLIS, a shepherdess, in love with Perigot
CLOE, a wanton shepherdess

Critique:

According to John Fletcher's introduction to the play, *The Faithful Shepherdess* was unsuccessful when it was presented on the stage. The reasons are not difficult to find. The characters are highly formalized and completely flat; the plot is very intricate and yet almost entirely predictable, and the verse, although technically of a high order, is hardly robust enough for public performance. Judged by the standards of the masque, however, the play comes off much better. Fletcher is obviously attempting to explore different aspects of love and to extol the virtue of chastity. His characters thus become symbols for certain chaste or unchaste states and the plot a vehicle for juxtaposing, for purposes of comparison or contrast, various carefully balanced sets of characters. The pleasure lies in seeing the theme worked out on these terms, a process which is all the more satisfying because it is made to take place within the narrow and artificial limitations of the pastoral convention.

The Story:

Clorin, who had buried her sweetheart in a woodland arbor, vowed to forsake all of the pleasures of a shepherd's life and devote herself to chaste vigil over his grave, relinquishing it only to cure sick men and beasts through her knowledge of the secret virtues of herbs. So great was the power of her virginity that nothing in the woodland could harm her, and her mere presence had tamed a rough and brutish satyr who became her servant. Among the other shepherds and shepherdesses, however, love affairs of various kinds were progressing. The beautiful Amoret agreed to meet her sweetheart Perigot that night within the wood so that they could plight their troths there beside a sacred well. But Amarillis, a rejected admirer of Perigot, also had plans for the evening. Hoping that Perigot might accept her if he could only be parted from Amoret, she promised the Sullen Shepherd her love if he would break up the meeting. The Sullen Shepherd, who wanted only to satisfy his lust, agreed to carry out any plan she might propose.

Cloe was also seeking a partner for the evening. First she approached Thenot, but he declined her advances because he was in love with the unattainable Clorin. Daphnis, whom she next met, agreed to meet her in the wood, but his modest bearing promised so little that Cloe also made an engagement with Alexis, a youth with a much livelier manner.

After nightfall Amarillis and the Sullen Shepherd prepared to deceive Perigot. Following a magical formula, the Sullen

Shepherd lowered Amarillis into the sacred well, and when he drew her out again she had taken on the form of Amoret. In this shape she met Perigot and attempted to seduce him, but he was so offended by her conduct that he attempted to kill her. Seeing her danger, the Sullen Shepherd used another charm to change her back into her true appearance. Perigot rushed off into the dark wood to find and kill the supposedly lustful Amoret.

Cloe, meanwhile, had met Daphnis and found his intentions to be purer than she had hoped. Making an appointment to meet him later at a certain hollow tree, she went in search of Alexis. This swain's desires were in perfect accord with hers, but their embraces were interrupted by the Sullen Shepherd, who attacked and wounded Alexis. Undoubtedly Alexis would have been killed but for the arrival of Clorin's satyr, who frightened both Cloe and the Sullen Shepherd away and bore Alexis off to his mistress to be healed. Perigot during this time had found the true Amoret, stabbed her, and left her for dead. In this woeful condition she was discovered by the Sullen Shepherd who, wishing to make sure of his bargain with Amarillis, threw her into the sacred well to drown. From this fate she was saved by the river god, who also healed her wounds.

Perigot, thinking Amoret dead, was about to take his own life when Amarillis, seeing that things had gone much too far, attempted to explain the deception that had been worked upon him. In order to convince him, she asked only an hour in which to reappear in Amoret's shape. She had hardly left him, however, when she came upon the true Amoret. Realizing that virtuous love could not be frustrated, she directed the unfortunate shepherdess to the place where Perigot waited; but when Amoret arrived, her sweetheart took her to be Amarillis transformed and, wishing to be revenged, he again stabbed her. Once more the satyr arrived opportunely. As the frightened Perigot fled, the satyr bore Amoret off to Clorin's arbor.

There Clorin had nearly effected Alexis' cure by purging him of lust, but her treatment of Amoret was interrupted because of intemperate influences in the atmosphere. Seeking them out, the satyr found Daphnis and Cloe in the hollow tree. Being innocent of lechery, the young man was dismissed, but Cloe failed the test of chastity to which she was put and was kept for Clorin's ministrations. Perigot, meanwhile, arrived to be cleared of the blood he had shed and to his astonishment found Amoret alive and well. The two were happily reunited. Alexis and Cloe, having been purged of lust, also swore a chaste love to each other.

THE FALL OF THE HOUSE OF USHER

Type of work: Short story
Author: Edgar Allan Poe (1809-1849)
Type of plot: Gothic romance
Time of plot: Nineteenth century
Locale: The House of Usher
First published: 1839

Principal characters:
RODERICK USHER, a madman
MADELINE, his sister
THE NARRATOR, a visitor

Critique:

One of Poe's greatest stories of terror, "The Fall of the House of Usher" combines plot and setting so that they seem one. From the first sentence to the last, the mood of desolation and impending doom never leaves us. There seems to be a series of climaxes, all building to the last horrible one. Poe's choice of words and his figures of speech, always impressive, here seem even more than usual to set a scene of terror and horror. It is little wonder that this short tale should be considered as one of the world's truly great short stories.

The Story:

As the visitor approached the House of Usher, he was forewarned by the appearance of the old mansion. The fall weather was dull and dreary, the countryside shady and gloomy, and the old house seemed to fit perfectly into the desolate surroundings. The windows looked like vacant eyes staring out over the bleak landscape.

The visitor had come to the House of Usher in response to a written plea from his boyhood friend, Roderick Usher. The letter had told of an illness of body and mind suffered by the last heir in the ancient line of Usher, and although the letter had strangely filled him with dread, the visitor had felt that he must go to his former friend. The Usher family, unlike most, had left only a direct line of descent, and perhaps it was for this reason that the family itself and the house had become one—the House of Usher.

As he approached closer, the house appeared even more formidable to the visitor. The stone was discolored and covered with fungi. The building gave the impression of decay, yet the masonry had not fallen. A barely discernible crack extended in a zigzag line from the roof to the foundation, but otherwise there were no visible breaks in the structure.

The visitor entered the house, gave his things to a servant, and proceeded through several dark passages to the study of the master. There he was stunned at the appearance of his old friend. In Usher's cadaverous face his eyes were liquid, his lips pallid. His web-like hair was untrimmed and floated over his brow. All in all, he was a depressing figure. In manner he was even more morbid. He was afflicted with great sensitivity and some strange fear. There were only a few sounds, a few odors, a few foods, and a few textures in clothing that did not fill him with terror. In fact, he was haunted incessantly by unnamed fears.

Even more strangely, he was imbued with the thought that the house itself exerted great influence over his morale, that it had obtained influence over his spirit. Usher's moodiness was heightened by the approaching death of his sister, Lady Madeline. His only living relative, she was wasting away from a strange malady which baffled the doctors. Often the disease revealed its cataleptic nature. The visitor saw her only once, on the

1175

night of his arrival. Then she passed through the room without speaking, and her appearance filled him with awe and foreboding.

For several days the visitor attempted to cheer the sick master of Usher and restore him to health, but it seemed, rather, that the hypochondria suffered by Usher affected his friend. More and more the morbid surroundings and the ramblings of Usher's sick mind preyed upon his visitor. More and more Usher held that the house itself had molded his spirit and that of his ancestors. The visitor was helpless to dispel this morbid fear and was indeed in danger of subscribing to it himself, so powerful was the influence of the gloomy old mansion.

One day Usher informed his friend that Madeline was no more. It was his intention to bury her in one of the vaults under the house for a period of two weeks. The strangeness of her malady, he said, demanded the precaution of not placing her immediately in the exposed family burial plot. The two men took the encoffined body down into the burial vault beneath the house and deposited it upon a trestle. Turning back the lid of the coffin, they took one last look at the lady, and the visitor remarked on the similarity of appearance between her and her brother. Then Usher told him that they were twins and that their natures had been singularly alike. The men then closed the lid, screwed it down securely, and ascended to the upper rooms.

A noticeable change now took possession of Usher. He paced the floors with unusual vigor. He became more pallid, while his eyes glowed with even greater wildness. His voice was little more than a quaver, and his words were utterances of extreme fear. He seemed to have a ghastly secret which he could not share. More and more the visitor felt that Usher's superstitious beliefs about the malignant influence of the house were true. He could not sleep, and his body began to tremble almost as unreasonably as Usher's.

One night, during a severe storm, the visitor heard low and unrecognizable sounds that filled him with terror. Dressing, he had begun to pace the floor of his apartment when he heard a soft knock at his door. Usher entered, carrying a lamp. His manner was hysterical, his eyes those of a madman. When he threw the window open to the storm, they were lifted almost off their feet by the intensity of the wind. Usher seemed to see something horrible in the night, and the visitor picked up the first book that came to hand and tried to calm his friend by reading. The story was that of Ethelred and Sir Launcelot, and as he read the visitor seemed to hear the echo of a cracking and ripping sound described in the story. Later he heard a rasping and grating, of what he knew not. Usher sat facing the door, as if in a trance. His head and his body rocked from side to side in a gentle motion. He murmured some sort of gibberish, as if he were not aware of his friend's presence.

At last his ravings became intelligible. He muttered at first, but spoke louder and louder until he reached a scream. Madeline was alive. He had buried Madeline alive. For days he had heard her feebly trying to lift the coffin lid. Now she had escaped her tomb and was coming in search of him. At that pronouncement, the door of the room swung back and on the threshold stood the shrouded Lady Madeline of Usher. There was blood on her clothing and evidence of superhuman struggle. She ran to her terrified brother, and the two fell to the floor in death.

The visitor fled from the house in terror. He gazed back as he ran and saw the house of horror split asunder in a zigzag manner, down the line of the crack he had seen as he first looked upon the old mansion. There was a loud noise, like the sound of many waters, and the pond at its base received all that was left of the ruined House of Usher.

1176

THE FAMILY AT GILJE

Type of work: Novel
Author: Jonas Lie (1833-1908)
Type of plot: Domestic realism
Time of plot: Nineteenth century
Locale: Norway
First published: 1883

Principal characters:

CAPTAIN JÄGER, an army officer
JÖRGEN, his son
INGER-JOHANNA, his daughter
THINKA, another daughter
MRS. JÄGER, his wife
CAPTAIN RÖNNOW, another officer
ARENT GRIP, a student
GÜLCKE, the sheriff

Critique:

Ranking with Ibsen and Björnson, among nineteenth-century Scandinavian writers, Jonas Lie, unlike the other two, dealt almost exclusively with realistic effects. He was himself in many respects a romanticist, but that part of his personality did not often intrude into his novels. In *The Family at Gilje* the author portrayed the life of his neighbors, not moralizing or preaching but nevertheless changing attitudes and prejudices. His readers seem to experience the problems of characters in his stories, instead of merely witnessing them. It was this ability to project his readers into the plot that made Lie famous in his own time as well as in the present.

The Story:

It was obvious that Inger-Johanna was her father's favorite. He was an army captain, in charge at Gilje. When a fellow officer, Captain Rönnow, stopped at the house, Captain Jäger was delighted because the guest seemed so charmed by Inger-Johanna. Mrs. Jäger was a sister of the governor, and Captain Rönnow told the Jägers that he would petition the governor's wife, with whom he was in favor, to take Inger-Johanna into their home for a year, so that she could learn the ways of society in the city. Gilje was a deserted mountain post and not at all suitable for a young lady of Inger-Johanna's obvious charms.

Captain Jäger wanted his beloved daughter to visit her aunt, but when he learned the cost of the new clothing required, he stormed at his poor wife and could not be quieted. Perhaps his blustering was caused by sorrow at losing his favorite, even though he was happy that she would have such a fine opportunity.

Before Inger-Johanna left, she met a student named Arent Grip, the son of an old friend of her father's. In spite of his radical ideas, the girl found him interesting and was glad that he too would be in the city.

After the departure of his oldest daughter, the captain's house was desolate, for Thinka, another daughter, had gone to work for a judge in Ryfylke. Poor Jörgen, the only son, and a younger daughter were put through hours of lessons to ease their father's loneliness.

Each letter from Inger-Johanna was read again and again. After her first shyness had worn off, she loved her life in the city. Parties and balls delighted her. Both Captain Rönnow and Arent Grip were present at many of the functions, her aunt having secured a place for Grip in her husband's office. The aunt wrote also, confiding that she secretly hoped a match would develop between the girl and Rönnow, who was advancing rapidly and would be a good catch. The aunt was not so fond of Grip. She found him too spirited and unrestrained in expressing his unpopular ideas. But Inger-Johanna had completely won over her aunt, who insisted that the girl return home for a visit and then come back to the city for another season.

During his daughter's visit Captain Jäger was almost gay. Grip called on the family again and arranged to spend much time alone with Inger-Johanna. They took a surveying trip into the mountains with her father and Jörgen, and Grip found Jörgen a bright lad who deserved a better education. In his talks with Inger-Johanna, Grip claimed that fundamentals were all that mattered in life, not the external symbols of success. He wanted people to be themselves, not influenced by worldly values.

Inger-Johanna returned to the city before Thinka came home for a visit. The younger daughter had fallen in love with a young clerk in her uncle's office, but when her relative learned of the affair, he fired the clerk, who was poor and without prospects. Thinka thought often of him after her return home. Her parents urged her to forget him.

Sheriff Gülcke called at Gilje and found Thinka attractive. Because his wife had died only three months before, he could say nothing so soon after his loss; but during his stay he often cast an appreciative eye toward Thinka. She, in the meantime, wrote long letters to her sister, to tell of her love for the poor clerk, for whom she had promised to wait. Inger-Johanna, tiring of balls and city life, wrote that she remained only to please her aunt Grip had changed her way of thinking, making her see the uselessness of such a life.

Jörgen went to the city to school. Grip tutored him, but said that Jörgen should be sent to England or to America to learn a mechanic's trade, because that was the field in which he had great talent. Later Jörgen did sail for England, then to America, a fact which Captain Jäger forever held against Grip.

Thinka was right in her fear that she would never be allowed to marry her clerk. Sheriff Gülcke asked for her hand, and because she was without will to deny her father's wishes, she accepted the older man. After the marriage she was a good and faithful wife, acting almost as a nurse to her husband. He was kind to her and gave her her every desire, but her heart was sad. Inger-Johanna, sorry that her sister had no will of her own, refused to accept the idea that women were to bend to the will of their fathers and husbands.

Inger-Johanna was soon to be tested. Captain Rönnow wrote her father for her hand. It was the proudest moment of Captain Jäger's life. At first Inger-Johanna accepted, for Grip had made no proposal and she knew that Rönnow was the man her father desired for her. Before the wedding, however, she returned suddenly from the city. She admitted to herself and to her family that she could love no one but Grip and could not marry Rönnow. Although her father was bitterly disappointed, he could not force his favorite daughter to marry against her will. Sorrowfully he wrote his old friend his decision.

From that day on Captain Jäger's health rapidly failed. He suffered dizziness and weakness. He was forced to take a leave of absence from his military duties. One day his carriage did not return home. When the servant went to look for him, he found the horse standing at the foot of Gilje hill, the reins loose on the ground. The captain of Gilje was dead.

Twenty years passed. Mrs. Jäger was dead and Jörgen doing well in America. Inger-Johanna, a schoolteacher, taught the children the ideas and ideals she had learned from Grip. He, meanwhile, wandered over the land, a drunkard and an ascetic by turn. He carefully avoided Inger-Johanna, but constantly sought news of her. Finally he went to her school and stood by the window to hear the sound of her voice. He saw her face again as she looked out into the night. He left then, sick with pneumonia. When word of his illness reached Inger-Johanna, she went to him and nursed him until his death. Often he was irrational, at times completely lucid. After his death she knew that he had given her her only reason for living, her spirit for truth and freedom.

THE FAMILY REUNION

Type of work: Drama
Author: T. S. Eliot (1888-   )
Type of plot: Symbolic allegory
Time of plot: Twentieth century
Locale: England
First published: 1939

Principal characters:
AMY, LADY MONCHENSEY, an old lady
HARRY, her son
AGATHA, her sister
DOWNING, Harry's servant
MARY, Amy's ward

Critique:

This play, with references and images borrowed from the Orestes story, has many of the attributes of Greek tragedy. There is a chorus; the Eumenides take a part; and the tone is fatalistic. More than this, however, the treatment is poetical enough to allow complex meanings within a simple dramatic framework. One theme is the decay of an English gentle family, bound by conservatism. Another is the search man makes for a way of life. Probably the whole meaning is to be approached only through allegory. Eliot, in *The Family Reunion*, shows those rare gifts which have made him one of the truly great poets of our time.

The Story:

Amy, Lady Monchensey, was reluctant to have the lights turned on. She had to sit in the house from October until June, for in winter the sun rarely warmed the cold earth of northern England. Since all she could do was measure time, she hardly wanted to make night come too soon.

The whole family, except her three sons, had gathered to celebrate her birthday, and the sons were expected that evening. The conversation while they waited out the time was tasteless. Gerald and Charles, Amy's brothers-in-law, felt that the younger generation did not accept its responsibilities. Ivy and Violet, her younger sisters, agreed that youth was becoming decadent. When they asked Mary her opinion, as a representative of the new generation, Amy's ward was nettled. Nearing thirty, she had always been poor and had remained unmarried; she thought she belonged to no generation.

Amy lived only to keep Wishwood, the family estate, together. Since her husband's death, she had been head of the house. She knew her family, settled in its ways, was getting older; soon death would come as a surprise for them all. Only Agatha, her other sister, seemed to find a meaning in death. Harry, the oldest son, had been gone eight years. Amy hoped he could drop back into the old routine at the family home, but Agatha was doubtful. The past was over; the future could be built only on the present. When Harry came back he could not take up life where he left off, because he would be a new Harry.

The others began speculating. None had liked Harry's wife, a demanding woman who had persuaded him to take her away from Wishwood. On their travels she had been lost at sea, apparently swept overboard in a storm. Amy said they must feel no remorse for her death.

Harry surprised them by being the first of the sons to arrive. When he seemed upset because the blinds were not drawn, the others reminded him that in the country there was no one to look in. But Harry kept staring at the window. He could see the Eumenides, the vengeful spirits. They had been with him a long time, but only at Wishwood could he see them. He greeted the assembled company with an effort.

Harry became impatient when the relatives began talking of all the old things waiting at home for him. Nothing had ever happened to them; they had gone through life half asleep. Harry, however, was doing some soul searching. In mid-Atlantic he had pushed his wife overboard. Now the Furies were always with him.

Only Agatha seemed to understand him. The others thought him overtired and urged him to go lie down for a while. When he left, they decided to invite Dr. Warburton for dinner so that the family doctor could have a look at him.

Charles and Gerald called in Downing, Harry's servant, to question him. Violet and Ivy objected because they feared scandal. Agatha, however, made no objection, because questioning Downing was as irrelevant as calling in Dr. Warburton. Downing seemed to be frank. He hardly thought Harry's wife had had the courage to commit suicide, and while he was a little distrait, Harry had always appeared normal. The only thing amiss that Downing had noticed was that Harry had always been too much with his wife.

Mary appealed to Agatha for help in getting away from Wishwood. She knew that Amy wanted her to stay on and marry Harry; in that way Amy would have a tame daughter-in-law for a companion. But Agatha refused help. Mary should have had the courage to leave earlier; since Harry had returned she could not run away.

When Harry talked with Mary about his fears and doubts, she tried to understand his feeling that change was inevitable. They reminisced of the hollow tree in which they had played as children and of their regret when Amy had it cut

down. Harry saw the Furies again in the window embrasure. Startled by his manner, Mary pulled back the curtains to show that nothing was there.

Dr. Warburton came early for dinner to have a confidential talk with Harry. He tried to attack Harry's disturbance indirectly by warning him that Amy's health was very poor and that Harry must take the burden of Wishwood off her shoulders. Harry recalled the unpleasantness of his boyhood when being good meant pleasing Amy. Abruptly, he demanded to know something of his father. The old doctor assured him that there had been no scandal. His father and mother had just agreed to separate, and his father had gone abroad to die.

A police sergeant came to tell the family that John, having suffered a slight concussion in an auto accident, could not be there for the birthday dinner. Although the family buzzed with the news, Harry shocked them with his statement that it hardly mattered because his brother John was unconscious all the time anyway.

A long-distance call came from Arthur, the other brother. He had been in an accident too, and his license had been suspended for drunken driving.

Still troubled about his father, Harry pressed Agatha for more details. Agatha remembered his father's failings, but his mother had complemented his weaknesses. Then Agatha lost her repressions and told the truth. While Amy was pregnant with Harry, her husband had plotted to kill her. Agatha had talked him out of his scheme; she could not bear to think of destroying the new life Amy was carrying.

At that news Harry felt a great release, for the curse of the house seemed clearer. When the Eumenides appeared again, Harry was no longer frightened. He knew at last that the Furies were not pursuing him; he was following them. Harry decided to leave Wishwood.

Amy, furious at the news that Harry was going away, blamed Agatha, the younger sister who had stolen her husband thirty-five years ago and now was taking her son.

Mary pleaded with Agatha to stop Harry's departure, but to no avail; Harry had crossed the frontier of reality. Then Mary asked her help in getting a situation, perhaps a fellowship, so she could leave too. As the two women became more confidential, they each revealed they had also seen the Eumenides. That knowledge was a bond uniting them outside the stifling confines of Wishwood. When they talked with Downing, he confessed he had seen the Furies but he had paid little attention to them; they were Harry's ghosts.

Just before she died, Amy began to understand what was happening at Wishwood. Agatha and Mary brought in the birthday cake and blew out the candles as they circled around it. The rest of the family began talking about the will.

FAR AWAY AND LONG AGO

Type of work: Autobiography
Author: W. H. Hudson (1841-1922)
Type of plot: Reminiscence and nature notes
Time of plot: Mid-nineteenth century
Locale: Argentina
First published: 1918

Principal characters:
W. H. HUDSON, a sensitive, imaginative boy
MR. HUDSON, his father
MRS. HUDSON, his mother
DOÑA PASCUALA, a neighbor
DON EVARISTO PEÑALVA, another neighbor

Critique:

William Henry Hudson wrote his autobiography while in bed during a six-weeks' illness. On the second day of his illness, beginning to have a clear and vivid vision of his childhood, he decided to write out the picture. The vision stayed with him, and, between bouts of fever and sleep, he continued to record the impressions he had of his early life on the pampas of Argentina. The result was aptly named *Far Away and Long Ago,* for he was an old man writing of his life between the years of three and sixteen. This book, revealing Hudson as a naturalist, a poet, and a mystic, is written in the beautiful and limpid prose of which he was a master.

The Story:

W. H. Hudson's father was a colonist in South America, engaged in raising cattle, running a store, and being so amiable to everyone that he finally lost almost all his possessions. The mother was a stanchly religious New Englander, known in the whole section south of Buenos Aires as a good woman and kind friend. Hudson's parents loved people so well that their house became a regular stopping place for all travelers.

Even in childhood Hudson was interested in people of all sorts and in every kind of bird, animal, and insect. Though there were many children in the family, he himself was almost a solitary wanderer.

At one time his mother, who shared his intense love of nature, was worried because he often stood alone and transfixed. Finally she followed him, only to find he was watching a bird on its nest; she was satisfied that he was not eccentric but that he merely wanted to be by himself.

Hudson believed that in little children the sense of smell was as important to their pleasure as sight and sound. To him, as far back as he could remember, the smells of the pampas grasses and flowers, of the cattle and horses, of the garlic and cumin-seed seasoning, of the Saladero or slaughtering grounds were as vivid as the coloring of the parakeets and flamingos, the feel of bristly thistleweed, or the lovely sounds of flocks of pipits.

The house in which he was born was called "The Twenty-five Ombu Trees" because that many huge, century-old Ombu trees around the house made the place a landmark on the open pampas. There was also one other tree on the place —an unnamed variety—which blossomed so freely and deliciously each November that neighbors, smelling the blossoms on the wind, would come to beg a branch to perfume their own houses.

When the family moved, Hudson found around his second home many other kinds of trees, black acacia, Lombardy poplar, red willow, peach, pear. These he came to love by smell, sight, and touch when he was still too small to wander far from the house.

There were birds—hawks, cowbirds, doves, pigeons, eagles, pipits—and animals, domestic and wild, to entertain him. There were thousands of rats nearby that had to be smoked out periodically. One day, while the men were pouring deadly fumes down the rat holes, Hudson was watching. Suddenly he saw a small armadillo trying to escape by furiously digging a new hole. He caught hold of its scaly tail and tried to pull the animal backwards. The armadillo paid no attention to him but kept on digging, kicking the dirt back into his face. Before long Hudson found himself pulled to the ground as he clung stubbornly to the animal's tail. The contest was small-boy pride against animal desperation, and it was not until his arm had been pulled down into the hole that Hudson let go.

He found snakes fascinating, particularly a colony that lived under the flooring of the house. As he lay in bed, he could hear them moving around, and he often wondered whether they would coil around his legs if he slid to the floor. Until he fell asleep, he could hear their conversations go on, conversations that were a series of sighing sounds, then twenty or thirty ticks, then the sighing sounds again.

When he was six years old, he was given a pony and allowed to roam at will over the pampas. His interests in nature increased, as did his acquaintance with new species.

He also learned to know people better because he learned that his neighbors were invariably kind to a little boy who wanted only to find out what new birds were around.

One place he visited often was Los Alamos, near a stream that was a delight to him because of the running water, the earthly odors, and the numbers of birds. Doña Pascuala lived at Los Alamos; she was old and wrinkled, her hair white, and her face as brown as the cigar she had constantly in her mouth. She was always interested in the Hudsons. One day she came to tell them that rain which had fallen for weeks would surely stop soon. Her saint was St. Anthony, and she had always treated him well with candles, flowers, and devotion. And this was how he treated her! She thought it was time he learned how so much water felt; she had tied a string to his legs and let him down the well with his head in the water, and there he would stay until the rain stopped.

The Hudsons' nearest neighbors were the Royds, the husband a handsome Englishman who wanted to make his fortune from cheese made of sheep's milk, and the wife a huge, indolent woman, a native of good birth. They had colored servants and two daughters. Their younger daughter was, Hudson thought, the most beautiful child he had ever seen. Her constant companion was a child of her own age, a *mulatita*, as dark as the white child was fair, with features so refined that no on supposed her father had been anything but a handsome Englishman. The family and servants lived happily together, but the native servants thought it below them to milk sheep and the cheese project fell through. Then Mr. Royd went to Buenos Aires and slit his throat. His wife considered her meeting with him in her girlhood the great calamity of her life.

As he grew older, Hudson came to know Don Evaristo Peñalva, who was regarded as the grand old man of the plains. At first it was a little difficult for Hudson to reconcile his religious teachings with Don Evaristo's home life, but he realized that all the countryside thought well of the old man who, when called upon, always responded in time of need. The thing that worried young Hudson was that Don Evaristo had six wives all living happily together.

About the time Hudson was fifteen, he caught typhus fever while on a visit to Buenos Aires, an unsanitary town on a plain with no water to be had other than the silted river water bought by the bucketful at the door. While he was ill, he began to realize that he might have to leave all the pleasures of childhood behind him. Before he could reason with himself that he could keep his reactions to nature and make them the basis of his life's work, he was brought down with a case of rheumatic fever so acute that the doctors despaired of his life. The disease left him with a permanently weak heart. He went through a bad time trying to straighten out his religious beliefs until an older brother came back from England and brought him up-to-date on the course of religion vs. science, the battle being fought over Darwin's *Origin of Species*. Then he worked out a philosophy of life which convinced him that he was a mystic. That belief served to make life easier for a man who did not know whether he had one or fifty years left to him.

FAR FROM THE MADDING CROWD

Type of work: Novel
Author: Thomas Hardy (1840-1928)
Type of plot: Psychological realism
Time of plot: 1869-1873
Locale: "Wessex," England
First published: 1874

Principal characters:
GABRIEL OAK, a shepherd
BATHSHEBA EVERDENE, mistress of Weatherbury Farm
SERGEANT TROY, her first husband
FARMER BOLDWOOD, her suitor
FANNY ROBIN, betrayed by Troy

Critique:

This early novel by Thomas Hardy is less marked by the cold fate-ridden philosophy characteristic of his later work. The clarity and realism of the characters hold the reader's interest throughout, and Hardy's poetic style and constant citation of Biblical phrase and incident give the novel a unique quality of language and atmosphere. Although the end of the story has been considered contrived by some, the general structure of the plot leads logically to Hardy's conclusion.

The Story:

Gabriel Oak was a farmer on a small scale, but his honesty, integrity, and ability had won him the respect of all his neighbors. When he heard that a young girl named Bathsheba Everdene had moved into the neighborhood, he went out of his way to see her and fell immediately in love. Gabriel was the kind of man who had to look only once to know that he had found the right woman for him. After seeing her only a few times, he went to her aunt, for whom Bathsheba worked, and asked for the girl's hand in marriage. Although he was refused, he felt that it was the relative, not Bathsheba, who had denied him.

A short time later Gabriel's sheep dog became excited and chased his flock of sheep over a cliff, killing them all. Ruined, Gabriel had to give up his farm and go elsewhere to find work. On his way across the country he happened to pass a burning barn and ran to aid the men fighting the flames. After the fire had been put out, the owner of Weatherbury Farm arrived, and it was suggested that Gabriel be hired as shepherd in return for the fine work he had done. To his surprise, the owner of the farm was Bathsheba Everdene, who had recently inherited the place from her uncle. Gabriel became her shepherd. He was struck by the change in their positions in such a short while. Now Bathsheba was landowner, Gabriel the servant.

On his way to his new quarters Gabriel met a girl standing in the woods. She spoke to him and asked him not to say that he had seen her, and he promised to keep silent. The next morning, while working at his new job, he heard that Fanny Robin, one of Bathsheba's maids, had disappeared, and he rightly guessed that Fanny was the girl he had met. It was suspected that she had gone off to meet a soldier who had been stationed in the area a short time before. This suspicion was correct. Fanny had gone to find Sergeant Troy at his new station, for he had promised to marry her if she came to him. A date was set for the wedding, but Fanny went to the wrong church. When she finally found Troy he refused to make arrangements for a marriage a second time.

Weatherbury Farm prospered, for Bathsheba was a good manager. But, being a woman, she had her caprices. One of these was to send an anonymous valentine to Farmer Boldwood, a conservative, serious man who was her neighbor. Boldwood was upset by the valentine, especially after he learned that Gabriel had recognized Bathsheba's handwriting. The more Boldwood saw of Bathsheba, however, the more deeply he fell in love with her. One day during the sheep-washing he asked her to marry him, but she refused his proposal. Nevertheless, Gabriel and the rest of the workers felt sure that she would eventually marry Boldwood.

About that time Sergeant Troy returned to the neighborhood. Bathsheba was attracted to him at once. Gabriel knew enough of Troy's character to know that he was not the man for Bathsheba and he told her so. Not knowing the story of Fanny Robin, Bathsheba was furious. She and Troy were married soon afterward and the former sergeant became the master of Weatherbury Farm.

With Troy running the farm, things did not go very well. Gabriel was forced to do most of the work of overseeing, and often he was compelled to correct the mistakes Troy made. Troy gambled and drank and caused Bathsheba much unhappiness. Gabriel and Bathsheba were alternately friendly and unfriendly. One day Troy and Bathsheba, riding in a horse cart, passed a young girl walking down the road. Troy stopped the cart and went to talk to her. The woman was Fanny Robin, who was feeble and ill. Troy told her to go on to the next town and there wait for him to come and give her money. As soon as they arrived home, Troy asked Bathsheba for some money. She gave it to him after a quarrel.

Fanny went on to Casterbridge, but she was so weak and ill when she arrived there that she died shortly afterward. When news of her death reached Weatherbury Farm, Bathsheba, not knowing that Troy had been the girl's lover, sent a cart to bring the body to the farm for burial. When the body arrived, Gabriel saw scrawled on the coffin lid a message that both Fanny and a child were in-

side. He erased the last words in his fear that the real relationship of Fanny and Troy might reach Bathsheba's ears. But Bathsheba, suspecting that the coffin concealed some secret, opened the casket late that night. At the same moment Troy entered the room and learned of Fanny's death and the death of his child. Torn with grief, he told Bathsheba that she meant nothing to him, that Fanny had been the only woman he had ever loved. He had married Bathsheba only for her looks and her money. Bathsheba shut herself up in an attic room.

Troy had a beautiful tombstone put up over Fanny's grave, which he covered with roses and lilies. During the night there was a heavy storm and water, pouring from the church roof through the mouth of a gargoyle, splashed on the grave and ruined all his work. Troy disappeared from Casterbridge. News came shortly afterward that he had been caught in a dangerous current while swimming in the ocean and had been drowned.

Bathsheba did not believe that Troy was really dead. But Farmer Boldwood, convinced of Troy's death, did his best to get Bathsheba to promise to marry him if Troy did not reappear within seven years, at the end of which time he would be legally declared dead. One night, at a party Boldwood gave for her, Bathsheba yielded to his protestations of love and said that after the time had passed she would marry him. As she was leaving the party, Troy entered. He had been rescued at sea and had wandered slowly back to Casterbridge in the character of a strolling player.

At his entrance Bathsheba fell to the floor in a faint. Everyone was so concerned for her and surprised by Troy's appearance that they did not see Boldwood when he took down a gun from the wall. Boldwood aimed at Troy and shot him in the chest. Troy died immediately.

Boldwood was tried for the murder, but because his mind had given way he was committed to an institution. Gabriel, who had made every effort to save Boldwood from hanging, had become a leader in the neighborhood. As Bathsheba's bailiff, he managed her farm and that of Boldwood as well. Of her three lovers, he was the only one left.

One day Gabriel went to Bathsheba and told her that he was planning to leave her service. Bathsheba listened quietly and agreed with all he had to say. Later that night, however, she went to his cottage and there told him, by gesture more than by word, that he was the only person left to her now and that she needed both his help and his love. The farmers of the district were all delighted when Bathsheba became Mrs. Oak, and Gabriel became the master of Weather bury Farm.

A FAREWELL TO ARMS

Type of work: Novel
Author: Ernest Hemingway (1898-1961)
Type of plot: Impressionistic realism
Time of plot: World War I
Locale: Northern Italy and Switzerland
First published: 1929

Principal characters:
> FREDERIC HENRY, an American serving with an Italian ambulance unit
> CATHERINE BARKLEY, an English nurse

Critique:

Hemingway combines austere realism and poetic language to present a powerful argument against war and to tell a touching love story at the same time. Possessed of the most remarkable time sense of the period between wars, his disillusioned temperament and technical skill have influenced a whole generation of writers. In spite of its hard-boiled realism of detail and its tragic ending, *A Farewell to Arms* is nevertheless an idealistic book. The novel was dramatized by Laurence Stallings and was made into a motion picture.

The Story:

Lieutenant Frederic Henry was a young American attached to an Italian ambulance unit on the Italian front. An offensive was soon to begin, and when Henry returned to the front from leave he learned from his friend, Lieutenant Rinaldi, that a group of British nurses had arrived in his absence to set up a British hospital unit. Rinaldi introduced him to nurse Catherine Barkley.

Between ambulance trips to evacuation posts at the front, Henry called on Miss Barkley. He liked the frank young English girl in a casual sort of way, but he was not in love with her. Before he left for the front to stand by for an attack, she gave him a St. Anthony medal.

At the front, as Henry and some Italian ambulance drivers were eating in a dugout, an Austrian projectile exploded over them. Henry, badly wounded in the legs, was taken to a field hospital. Later he was moved to a hospital in Milan.

Before the doctor was able to see Henry in Milan, the nurses prohibited his drinking wine, but he bribed a porter to bring him a supply which he kept hidden behind his bed. Catherine Barkley came to the hospital and Henry knew that he was in love with her. The doctors told Henry that he would have to lie in bed six months before they could operate on his knee. Henry insisted on seeing another doctor, who said that the operation could be performed the next day. Meanwhile, Catherine managed to be with Henry constantly.

After his operation, Henry convalesced in Milan with Catherine Barkley as his attendant. Together they dined in out of the way restaurants, and together they rode about the countryside in a carriage. Henry was restless and lonely at nights and Catherine often came to his hospital room.

Summer passed into autumn. Henry's wound had healed and he was due to take convalescent leave in October. He and Catherine planned to spend the leave together, but he came down with jaundice before he could leave the hospital. The head nurse accused him of bringing on the jaundice by drink, in order to avoid being sent back to the front. Before he left for the front, Henry and Catherine stayed together in a hotel room; already she had disclosed to him that she was pregnant.

Henry returned to the front with orders to load his three ambulances with hospital equipment and go south into the Po valley. Morale was at low ebb. Rinaldi admired the job which had been done on the knee and observed that Henry acted like a married man. War weariness was all-pervasive. At the front, the Italians, having learned that German divisions had reinforced the Austrians, began their terrible retreat from Caporetto. Henry drove one of the ambulances loaded with hospital supplies. During the retreat south, the ambulance was held up several times by wagons, guns, and trucks which extended in stalled lines for miles. Henry picked up two straggling Italian sergeants. During the night the retreat was halted in the rain for hours.

At daybreak Henry cut out of the long line and drove across country in an attempt to reach Udine by side roads. The ambulance got stuck in a muddy side road. The sergeants decided to leave, but Henry asked them to help dislodge the car from the mud. They refused and ran. Henry shot and wounded one; the other escaped across the fields. An Italian ambulance corpsman with Henry shot the wounded sergeant through the back of the head. Henry and his three comrades struck out on foot for Udine. On a bridge, Henry saw a German staff car and German bicycle troops crossing another bridge over the same stream. Within sight of Udine, one of Henry's group was killed by an Italian sniper. The others hid in a barn until it seemed safe to circle around Udine and join the main stream of the retreat toward the Tagliamento River.

By that time the Italian army was nothing but a frantic mob. Soldiers were throwing down their arms and officers were cutting insignia of rank from their sleeves. At the end of a long wooden bridge across the Tagliamento military carabiniere were seizing all officers, giving them drumhead trials, and executing them by the river bank. Henry was detained, but in the dark of night he broke free, plunged into the river, and escaped

on a log. He crossed the Venetian plain on foot, then jumped aboard a freight train and rode to Milan, where he went to the hospital in which he had been a patient. There he learned that the English nurses had gone to Stresa.

During the retreat from Caporetto Henry had made his farewell to arms. He borrowed civilian clothes from an American friend in Milan and went by train to Stresa, where he met Catherine, who was on leave. The bartender of the hotel in which Henry was staying warned Henry that authorities were planning to arrest him for desertion the next morning; he offered his boat by means of which Henry and Catherine could escape to Switzerland. Henry rowed all night. By morning his hands were so raw that he could barely stand to touch the oars. Over his protests, Catherine took a turn at the rowing. They reached Switzerland safely and were arrested. Henry told the police that he was a sportsman who enjoyed rowing and that he had come to Switzerland for the winter sports. The valid passports and the ample funds that Henry and Catherine possessed saved them from serious trouble with the authorities.

During the rest of the fall and the winter the couple stayed at an inn outside Montreux. They discussed marriage, but Catherine would not be married while she was with child. They hiked, read, and talked about what they would do together after the war.

When the time for Catherine's confinement approached, she and Henry went to Lausanne to be near a hospital. They planned to return to Montreux in the spring. At the hospital Catherine's pains caused the doctor to use an anaesthetic on her. After hours of suffering she was delivered of a dead baby. The nurse sent Henry out to get something to eat. When he went back to the hospital, he learned that Catherine had had a hemorrhage. He went into the room and stayed with her until she died. There was nothing he could do, no one he could talk to, no place he could go. Catherine walked back to his hotel in the dark. It was dead. He left the hospital and was raining.

THE FATHER

Type of work: Drama
Author: August Strindberg (1849-1912)
Type of plot: Psychological realism
Time of plot: Mid-nineteenth century
Locale: Sweden
First presented: 1887

Principal characters:

A CAPTAIN OF CAVALRY
LAURA, his wife
BERTHA, their daughter
DR. ÖSTERMARK, the village physician
THE PASTOR, Laura's brother
MARGARET, an old nurse
NÖJD, a soldier

Critique:

This play deals with the problem of a man's relationships with his mother and his wife. Rejected by his own mother, the captain had tried to find a mother-wife, who, assuming that role, rejected the lover-husband. Since the wife loathed her role of wife, she tried to undermine the man who had destroyed her maternal relationship to him. The problem here is the battle of the sexes which concerned Strindberg in most of his work. Also a factor in the domestic relationship is the antagonism of science and religion, with the wife showing ignorance and suspicion of the former. The theme of the play is initiated by a relatively trivial problem; that of Nöjd's paternity, which expands first into a study of marital differences and then into an analysis of antagonism between Man and Woman.

The Story:

When a trooper named Nöjd got a servant girl in trouble, the Captain sent an orderly to bring Nöjd to face the Pastor. The culprit, vague about his affair with Emma, hinted that the paternity of her child was uncertain. The Pastor told Nöjd that he would have to support the child, but the soldier claimed that Ludwig should contribute also, since it was possible that Ludwig was the real father. The

Captain declared angrily that the case would go to court. After Nöjd had gone, the Captain berated the Pastor for his gentle treatment of the soldier. The Pastor said he thought it a pity to saddle Nöjd with the support of a child if he were not the real father.

The Captain was married to the Pastor's sister Laura. In his house, complained the Captain, there were too many women: his mother-in-law, a governess, old nurse Margaret, his daughter Bertha. The Captain, worried about his daughter's education, which was being influenced in all different directions by the people around her, deplored the incessant struggle between men and women.

After the Pastor had gone, Laura entered to collect her household money. His affairs near bankruptcy, the Captain asked her to keep an account of the money she spent. Laura asked him his decision about Bertha's education. Laura objected when he announced his intention to send her to town to board with Auditor Säfberg, a freethinker, but the Captain reminded her that a father had the sole control of his children. When Laura brought up the subject of Nöjd's affair, the Captain admitted that the paternity would be difficult to decide. Laura scoffingly claimed that if such were the case even the child of a married woman could be any other man's offspring.

Laura confided to Dr. Östermark, the new village doctor, her suspicion that her husband was mentally ill. He bought books he never read, and he tried to fathom events on other planets by peering through a microscope. He had become a man who could not stand by his decisions, although he was most vehement when he first uttered one.

Speaking privately with his old nurse, the Captain expressed his fear that his family was plotting against him and that something evil was about to happen.

The family quarrel was clearly outlined when Bertha complained to her father that her grandmother was trying to teach her spiritualism and had even told the girl that the Captain, who was a meteorologist by profession, was a charlatan. Bertha agreed with her father that she ought to go away to study, but Laura boasted that she could persuade Bertha to stay home. She hinted again that she could prove the Captain was not Bertha's father.

Dr. Östermark explained to Laura that she had been mistaken about her husband; he had used a spectroscope, not a microscope, to examine the elements on other planets. Still, the doctor said, he would watch the Captain for further signs of insanity. Laura also told the doctor that the Captain feared he was not Bertha's father; quite obviously Laura had planted this idea in the Captain's mind. When he began to worry over his daughter's paternity, old Margaret tried to reassure him.

It became impossible for the Captain to allow his wife to continue her persecution of him. She had intercepted some of his mail, thereby thwarting him in the progress of his scientific ventures. He further accused her of spreading among his friends the idea that he was insane. Afraid that under such provocation he might lose his reason, he appealed to his wife's selfishness. It would be to her best interests for him to remain sane, he said, since insanity might lead to his suicide, which

would invalidate her right to collect his life insurance. She could assure his sanity by confessing that Bertha was not his child, a suspicion which was undermining his sanity.

When she refused to admit a sin of which she was not guilty, he reminded her that in doing so she would gain sole control of Bertha's future. The tables were turned. Now the Captain began to believe that Bertha was not his child and Laura began to insist that she was. The Captain, recalling the circumstances of Bertha's birth, recollected how a solicitor had told Laura that she had no right of inheritance without a child. At that time the Captain had been ill. When he recovered, Bertha had been born.

The Captain understood the power his wife had held over him. He had loved her at first as he would love a mother; she had loathed him after he became her lover. Laura showed him a letter she had forged in which he confessed his insanity and said that she had sent the letter to court. Boasting that she had employed him only as a breadwinner, she declared that she would use his pension for Bertha's education. In anger, the Captain hurled a lamp at her.

Laura succeeded in locking her husband in another room while she examined his private papers. Although the Pastor saw through her scheme, she dared him to accuse her. The doctor arrived with a strait jacket shortly before the Captain, armed with literary evidence of cases in which a child's paternity had been questioned, burst into the room. His talk was so erratic and his raving about conjugal fidelity so wild that when the doctor told him he was insane, the Captain acknowledged his own madness.

Bertha, accusing him of a deliberate attempt to injure her mother, announced that he was not her father if he behaved so badly. The Captain, in reply, told her that her soul was in two parts; one was a reflection of his own, and to preserve it he intended to destroy the part which was not his. He seized a revolver but found it

1193

empty. Bertha ran out screaming.

Old Margaret soothed the raving man by talking softly to him of his childhood, and when he was off guard she slipped the strait jacket on him. Seeing him seated, helpless and dejected, on the sofa, Laura nearly repented the course she had taken as the Captain piteously described his life of torment with mother, wife, and child, all of whom had rejected him. After she had assured him that Bertha was his own child, the Captain, calling to old Margaret for comfort, suffered a stroke. As he lay unconscious Bertha ran to her mother, who caressed her and called the girl her own daughter.

FATHER GORIOT

Type of work: Novel
Author: Honoré de Balzac (1799-1850)
Type of plot: Naturalism
Time of plot: About 1830
Locale: Paris
First published: 1835

Principal characters:
FATHER GORIOT, a boarder at the Maison Vauquer
EUGÈNE DE RASTIGNAC, a young law student
COUNTESS ANASTASIE DE RESTAUD, Goriot's daughter
BARONESS DELPHINE DE NUCINGEN, another daughter
MADAME DE BEAUSÉANT, Rastignac's cousin
MONSIEUR VAUTRIN, Rastignac's fellow boarder
VICTORINE TAILLEFER, another boarder

Critique:

This account of the subtle transformation of Eugène de Rastignac from a naïve provincial to a Parisian gentleman is among the most credible stories in fiction. The story of the ruin of a successful merchant, Goriot, because of his love for two ungrateful daughters is effective but less realistic. These are but a few of the fascinating gallery of characters Balzac assembled at Mme. Vauquer's boarding-house.

The Story:

There were many conjectures at Madame Vauquer's boarding-house about the mysterious Monsieur Goriot. He had taken the choice rooms on the first floor when he first retired from his vermicelli business, and for a time his landlady had eyed him as a prospective husband. When, at the end of his second year at the Maison Vauquer, he had asked to move to a cheap room on the second floor, he was credited with being an unsuccessful speculator, a miser, a money-lender. The mysterious young women who flitted up to his rooms from time to time were said to be his mistresses, although he protested that they were only his two daughters. The other boarders called him Father Goriot.

At the end of the third year, Goriot moved to a still cheaper room on the third floor. By that time he was the common butt of jokes at the boarding-house table, and his daughters visited him only rarely.

One evening the impoverished law student, Eugène de Rastignac, came home late from the ball his wealthy cousin, Madame de Beauséant, had given. Peeking through the mysterious Goriot's keyhole, he saw him molding some silver plate into ingots. The next day he heard his fellow boarder, Monsieur Vautrin, say that early in the morning he had seen Father Goriot selling a piece of silver to an old money-lender. What Vautrin did not know was that the money thus obtained was intended for Goriot's daughter, Countess Anastasie de Restaud, whom Eugène had met at the dance the night before.

That afternoon Eugène paid his respects to the countess. Father Goriot was leaving the drawing-room when he arrived. The countess, her lover, and her husband received Eugène graciously because of his connections with Madame de Beauséant. But when he mentioned they had the acquaintance of Father Goriot in common, he was quickly shown to the door, the count leaving word with his servant that he was not to be at home if Monsieur de Rastignac called again.

After his rebuff, Eugène went to call on Madame de Beauséant, to ask her aid in unraveling the mystery. She quickly understood what had happened, and explained that de Restaud's house would be barred to him because both of Goriot's daughters, having been given sizable dowries, were gradually severing all connection with their father and therefore would not tolerate anyone who had knowledge of Goriot's shabby circumstances. She suggested that Eugène send word through Goriot to his other daughter, Delphine de Nucingen, that Madame de Beauséant would receive her. Delphine, she knew, would welcome the invitation, and would be grateful to Eugène and become his sponsor.

Vautrin had another suggestion for the young man. Under Madame Vauquer's roof lived Victorine Taillefer, who had been disinherited by her wealthy father in favor of her brother. Eugène had already found favor in her eyes, and Vautrin suggested that for a two hundred thousand francs he would have the brother murdered, so that Eugène might marry the heiress. He was to have two weeks in which to consider the offer.

Eugène escorted Madame de Beauséant to the theater next evening. There he was presented to Delphine de Nucingen, who received him graciously. The next day he received an invitation to dine with the de Nucingens and to go to the theater. Before dinner he and Delphine drove to a gambling house where, at her request, he gambled and won six thousand francs. She explained that her husband would give her no money, and she needed it to pay a debt she owed to an old lover.

Before long Eugène learned that it cost money to keep the company of his new friends. Unable to press his own family for funds, he would not stoop to impose on Delphine. Finally, as Vautrin had forseen, he was forced to take his fellow boarder's offer. The tempter had just finished explaining the duel between Victorine's brother and his confederate which was to take place the following morning when Father Goriot came in with the news that he and Delphine had taken an apartment for Eugène.

Eugène wavered once more at the thought of the crime which was about to be committed in his name. He attempted to send a warning to the victim through Father Goriot, but Vautrin, suspicious of his accomplice, thwarted the plan. Vautrin managed to drug their wine at supper so that both slept soundly that night.

At breakfast Eugène's fears were realized. A messenger burst in with the news that Victorine's brother had been fatally wounded in a duel. After the girl hurried off to see him, another singular event occurred. Vautrin, after drinking his coffee, fell to the ground as if he had suffered a stroke. When he was carried to his room and undressed, it was ascertained by marks on his back that he was the famous criminal, Trompe-la-Mort. One of the boarders, an old maid, had been acting as an agent for the police; she had drugged Vautrin's coffee so that his criminal brand could be exposed. Shortly afterward the police appeared to claim their victim.

Eugène and Father Goriot were preparing to move to their new quarters, for Goriot was to have a room over the young man's apartment. Delphine arrived to interrupt Goriot's packing. She was in distress. Father Goriot had arranged with his lawyer to force de Nucingen to make a settlement so that Delphine would have an independent income on which to draw, and she brought the news that her money had been so tied up by investments it would be impossible for her husband to withdraw any of it without bringing about his own ruin.

Hardly had Delphine told her father of her predicament when Anastasie de Restaud drove up. She had sold the de Restaud diamonds to help her lover pay off his debts, and had been discovered by her husband. De Restaud had bought them back, but as punishment he demanded control of her dowry.

Eugène could not help overhearing the conversation through the thin partition between the rooms, and when Anastasie said she still needed twelve thousand francs for her lover he forged one of Vautrin's drafts for that amount and took it to Father Goriot's room. Anastasie's reaction was to berate him for eavesdropping.

The financial difficulties of his daughters and the hatred and jealousy they had shown proved too much for Father Goriot. At the dinner table he looked as if he were about to have a stroke of apoplexy, and when Eugène returned from an afternoon spent with his mistress, Delphine, the old man was in bed, too ill to be moved to his new home. He had gone out that morning to sell his last few possessions, so that Anastasie might pay her dressmaker for an evening gown.

In spite of their father's serious condition, both daughters attended Madame de Beauséant's ball that evening, and Eugène was too much under his mistress' influence to refuse to accompany her. The next day Goriot was worse. Eugène tried to summon his daughters. Delphine was still abed and refused to be hurried over her morning toilet. Anastasie arrived at his bedside only after Father Goriot had lapsed into a coma and no longer knew her.

Father Goriot was buried in a pauper's grave the next day. Eugène tried to borrow burial money at each daughter's house, but they sent word they were in deep grief over their loss and could not be seen. He and a poor medical student from the boarding-house were the only mourners at the funeral. Anastasie and Delphine sent their empty carriages to follow the coffin. It was their final tribute to an indulgent father.

FATHERS AND SONS

Type of work: Novel
Author: Ivan Turgenev (1818-1883)
Type of plot: Social criticism
Time of plot: 1859
Locale: Russia
First published: 1862

Principal characters:
KIRSANOFF, a Russian gentleman
PAVEL, his older brother
ARKADY, his son
FENICHKA, Kirsanoff's mistress
BAZAROFF, Arkady's friend
VASILY, Bazaroff's father
MADAME ODINTZOFF, a widow
KATYA, her younger sister

Critique:

Fathers and Sons is important in the political history of Russia. Turgenev was here the first to use the word nihilist to describe a believer in political anarchy at a time when nihilism was the main current of liberal thought. There are excellent studies of the unsettled Russian peasants just before their emancipation. Beyond this historical importance, *Fathers and Sons* is a novel which dramatizes the conflict and differences between generations. The novel is relatively straightforward in plot and the characters are simply drawn. These characteristics are not common in nineteenth-century Russian novels; the clarity of *Fathers and Sons* is probably a big factor in its popularity.

The Story:

At a provincial posting station Kirsanoff waited impatiently for his son, Arkady, who had completed his education at the university in St. Petersburg. Kirsanoff reflected that Arkady had probably changed, but he hoped his son had not grown away from him entirely. Arkady's mother was dead, and the widower was strongly attached to his son.

At last the coach appeared, rolling along the dusty road. Arkady jumped out. But he was not alone. Lounging superciliously behind was a stranger whom Arkady introduced as Bazaroff, a fellow student. Something in Arkady's manner told Kirsanoff that here was a special attachment. In a low aside Arkady begged his father to be gracious to his guest.

Feeling some qualms about his unexpected guest, Kirsanoff was troubled during the trip home. He was hesitant about his own news, but finally told Arkady that he had taken a mistress, Fenichka, and installed her in his house. To his great relief, Arkady took the news calmly and even congratulated his father on the step. Later Arkady was pleased to learn that he even had a little half-brother.

Very soon Kirsanoff found he had good reason to distrust Bazaroff, who was a doctor and a clever biologist. Arkady seemed too much under his influence. Worse, Bazaroff was a nihilist. At the university the liberal thinkers had consciously decided to defy or ignore all authority—state, church, home, pan-Russianism. Bazaroff was irritating to talk to, Kirsanoff decided, because he knew so much and had such a sarcastic tongue.

Pavel, Kirsanoff's older brother, was especially irritated by Bazaroff. Pavel was a real aristocrat, bound by tradition, who had come to live in retirement with his younger brother after a disappointing career as an army officer and the lover of a famous beauty, the Princess R—. With his background and stiff notions of pro-

1198

priety, Pavel often disagreed with Bazaroff.

Luckily, Bazaroff kept busy most of the time. He collected frogs and infusoria and was always dissecting and peering into a microscope. He would have been an ideal guest, except for his calmly superior air of belonging to a generation far surpassing Pavel's. Kirsanoff, loving his son so much, did his best to keep peace, but all the while he regretted the nihilism which had so affected Arkady.

Kirsanoff was harassed by other troubles. Soon, by law, the serfs would be freed. Kirsanoff strongly approved this change and had anticipated the new order by dividing his farm into smaller plots which the peasants rented on a sharecropping basis. But with their new independence the peasants cheated him more than ever and were slow in paying their rent.

Arkady and Bazaroff, growing bored with quiet farm life, went to visit in the provincial capital, where they had introductions to the governor. In town they ran into Sitnikoff, a kind of polished jackal who felt important because he was one of the nihilist circle. Sitnikoff introduced them into provincial society.

At a ball the two friends met and were greatly taken by a young widow, Madame Odintzoff. Arkady did not dance, but he sat out a mazurka with her. They became friends at once, especially when she found that Arkady's mother had been an intimate friend of her own mother. After the ball Madame Odintzoff invited the two men to visit her estate.

Arkady and Bazaroff accepted the invitation promptly, and in a few days they settled down to the easy routine of favored guests in a wealthy household. Katya, Madame Odintzoff's young sister, was especially attracted to Arkady. Bazaroff, older and more worldly, became the good friend of the widow.

Although Bazaroff, as a good nihilist, despised home and family life, he made a real effort to overcome his scruples. But when he finally began to talk of love and marriage to Madame Odintzoff, he was politely refused. Chagrined at his rejection, he induced Arkady to leave with him at once. The two friends then went on to Bazaroff's home.

Vasily, Bazaroff's father, was glad to see his son, whom he both feared and admired. He and his wife did all they could to make the young men comfortable. At length Arkady and Bazaroff quarreled, chiefly because they were so bored. Abruptly they left, and impulsively called again on Madame Odintzoff. She received them coolly. Feeling that they were unwelcome, they went back to the Kirsanoff estate.

Because Bazaroff was convinced that Arkady was also in love with Madame Odintzoff, his friendship with Arkady became greatly strained. Arkady, thinking all the time of Katya, returned by himself to the Odintzoff estate to press his suit of the younger sister.

At the Kirsanoff home Bazaroff became friendly with Fenichka. He prescribed for her sick baby and even for her. Fenichka, out of friendship, spent much of her time with Bazaroff. One morning, as they sat in a garden, Bazaroff kissed her unexpectedly, to her distress and confusion. Pavel witnessed the scene by accident and became incensed all the more at the strange nihilist.

Although Pavel did not consider Bazaroff a gentleman, he challenged him to a duel with pistols. In the encounter Pavel was wounded in the leg, and Bazaroff left the house in haste, never to return. Pavel recovered from his wound, but he felt a never-ending shame at being wounded by a low nihilist. He urged Kirsanoff to marry Fenichka, and returned to his old life. He spent the rest of his days as an aging dandy in Dresden.

Bazaroff stopped briefly at the Odintzoff home. Still convinced that Arkady was in love with Madame Odintzoff, he attempted to help his friend in his suit.

Madame Odintzoff ridiculed him, however, when Arkady made his request for the hand of Katya. With a sense of futility, Bazaroff took his leave and rejoined his own family.

Vasily was the local doctor, and he eagerly welcomed his son as a colleague. For a time Bazaroff led a successful life, helping to cure the ailments of the peasants and pursuing his research at the same time. When one of his patients came down with typhus, he accidentally scratched himself with a scalpel he had used. Although Vasily cauterized the wound as well as he could, Bazaroff became ill with a fever. Sure that he would die, he summoned Madame Odintzoff to his side. She came gladly and helped to ease him before his death.

Madame Odintzoff eventually made a good marriage with a lawyer. Arkady was happy managing his father's farm and playing with the son born to him and Katya. Kirsanoff became a magistrate and spent most of his life settling disputes brought about by the liberation of the serfs. Fenichka, at last a respected wife and mother, found great happiness in her daughter-in-law, Katya.

FAUST

Type of work: Dramatic poem
Author: Johann Wolfgang von Goethe (1749-1832)
Type of plot: Philosophical allegory
Time of plot: Timeless
Locale: The world
First published: 1790-1831

Principal characters:
FAUST, a student of all knowledge
GRETCHEN, a maiden
MEPHISTOPHELES, the devil
WAGNER, Faust's servant
HELEN OF TROY
HOMUNCULUS, a spirit

Critique:

The philosophical problem of human damnation through desire for knowledge is here presented. Goethe, echoing the eighteenth-century Age of Reason, asserted that man's rationality was the supreme truth in life. This poem contains some of the most beautiful and aspiring passages in all literature. Faust's lofty, anguished cry for one moment in life which would cause him to desire its continuance is echoed throughout the ages in the emotions of all men of all times. The universal problem presented by the play renders it impossible to place the locale of the action or the time of the action, for Faust exists forever and everywhere.

The Story:

While three archangels were singing the praise of God's lofty works, Mephistopheles, the devil, appeared and said that he found conditions on earth to be bad. The Lord tacitly agreed that man had his weaknesses, but He slyly pointed out that His servant Faust could not be swayed from the path of righteousness. Mephistopheles made a wager with the Lord that Faust could be tempted from his faithful service. The Lord knew that He could rely on the righteous integrity of Faust, but that Mephistopheles could lead Faust downward if he were able to lay hold of Faust's soul. Mephistopheles

considered Faust a likely victim, for Faust was trying to obtain the unobtainable.

Faust was not satisfied with all the knowledge he had acquired. He realized man's limits, and he saw his own insignificance in the great macrocosm. In this mood, he went for a walk with his servant, Wagner, among people who were not troubled by thoughts of a philosophical nature. In such a refreshing atmosphere, Faust was able to feel free and to think clearly. Faust told Wagner of his two souls, one which clung to earthly things, and another which strove toward supersensual things that could never be attained as long as his soul resided within his fleshly body. Feeling so limited in his daily life and desiring to learn the meaning of existence, Faust was ready to accept anything which would take him to a new kind of life.

Mephistopheles recognized that Faust was ready for his attack. In the form of a dog, Mephistopheles followed Faust to his home when the scholar returned to his contemplation of the meaning of life. After studying the Bible, he concluded that man's power should be used to produce something useful. Witnessing Faust's struggle with his ideas, the dog stepped forth in his true identity. But Faust remained unmoved by the arguments of Mephistopheles.

The next time Mephistopheles came,

FAUST by Johann Wolfgang von Goethe. Published by Alfred A. Knopf, Inc.

he found Faust much more receptive to his plot. Faust had decided that, although his struggles were divine, he had produced nothing to show for them. Faust was interested in life on this earth. At Mephistopheles' suggestion that he could peacefully enjoy a sensual existence, Faust declared that if ever he could lay himself in sloth and be at peace with himself, or if ever Mephistopheles could so rule him with flattery that he became self-satisfied, then let that be the end of Faust. But Faust had also renounced all things that made life worthwhile to most men. So he further contracted with Mephistopheles that if ever he found experience so profound that he would wish it to endure, then Faust would cease to be. This would be a wager, not the selling of a soul.

After two trials Mephistopheles had failed to tempt Faust with cheap debauchery. The next offering he presented was love for a woman. First Faust was brought to the Witch's Kitchen, where his youth was restored. Then a pure maiden, Gretchen, was presented to Faust, but when he saw her in her own innocent home, he vowed he could not harm her. Mephistopheles wooed the girl with caskets of jewels which she thought came from Faust, and Faust was so tempted that he returned to Gretchen. She surrendered herself to him as a fulfillment of her pure love.

Gretchen's brother convinced her that her act was a shameful one in the eyes of society. Troubled by Gretchen's grief, Faust finally killed her brother. Gretchen at last felt the full burden of her sin. Mephistopheles showed Faust more scenes of debauchery, but Faust's spirit was elevated by the thought of Gretchen and he was able to overcome the evil influence of the devil. Mephistopheles had hoped that Faust would desire the moment of his fulfillment of love to endure. However, Faust knew that enduring human love could not satisfy his craving. He regretted Gretchen's state of misery, and he returned to her; but she

had killed her child and would not let her lover save her from the death to which she had been condemned.

Mephistopheles brought Faust to the emperor, who asked Faust to show him the most beautiful male and female who had ever existed—Paris, and Helen of Troy. Faust produced the images of these mythological characters, and at the sight of Helen, his desire to possess her was so strong that he fainted, and Mephistopheles brought him back in a swoon to his own laboratory. Mephistopheles was unable to comprehend Faust's desire for the ideal beauty that Helen represented.

With the help of Wagner, Mephistopheles created a formless spirit of learning, Homunculus, who could see what was going on in Faust's mind. Homunculus, Mephistopheles, and Faust went to Greece, where Mephistopheles borrowed from the fantastic images of classical mythology one of their grotesque forms. With Mephistopheles' intervention, a living Helen was brought to Faust. It seemed now, with the attainment of this supreme joy of beauty in Helen, that Faust would cry for such a moment to linger forever, but he soon realized that the enjoyment of transitory beauty was no more enduring than his other experiences.

With a new knowledge of himself, Faust returned to his native land. Achievement was now his goal, as he reaffirmed his earlier pledge that his power should be used to produce something useful to man. The mystical and magical powers which Faust had once held were banished so that he could stand before nature alone. He obtained a large strip of swamp land and restored it to productivity.

Many years passed. Now old and blind, Faust realized he had created a vast territory of land occupied by people who would always be active in making something useful for themselves. Having participated in this achievement, Faust beheld himself as a man standing among free and active people as one of them. At the moment when he realized what he had created, he cried out for this moment, so fair to him, to linger on. Faust had emerged from a self-centered egoist into a man who saw his actions as a part of a creative society.

He realized that life could be worth living, but in that moment of perception he lost his wager to Mephistopheles. The devil now claimed Faust's soul, but in reality he too had lost the wager. The Almighty was right. Although Faust had made mistakes in his life, he had always remained aware of goodness and truth.

Seeing his own defeat, Mephistopheles attempted to prevent the ascension of Faust's soul to God. Angels appeared to help Faust, however, and he was carried to a place in Heaven where all was active creation—exactly the kind of after-life that Faust would have chosen.

THE FEDERALIST

Type of work: Political essays
Authors: Alexander Hamilton (1755-1804); James Madison (1751-1836), and John Jay
  (1745-1829)
First published: 1788

Seventy-seven of the eighty-five essays which comprise *The Federalist* were printed serially in New York newspapers between October, 1787, and May, 1788; the remaining eight first appeared in the two-volume edition published in March and May of the latter year. In an attempt to preserve secrecy of authorship, all were signed with the masking signature of "Publius." Although historians are still in dispute over the writers of certain of the papers, the claim has been made that Hamilton wrote sixty; James Madison, fourteen; John Jay, five; and Hamilton and Madison together, sixteen. Lengthy, repetitious, and partisan, they are nevertheless unrivaled as the classic exposition and defense of the principles on which the United States of America was founded.

In the first and concluding essays, Hamilton declared the constitution proposed by the Philadelphia Convention of 1787 to be energetic, perfectly republican, conformable to the state constitutions, and able to guarantee property and liberty. He urged the electorate to shun demagogues who disparaged its proponents as the "wealthy, well-born, and the great," to rise above "obstinate adherence to party," and to fulfill America's destiny as perceived by the framers. Madison joined him in rejecting objections that the new constitution contained no bill of rights or limitation on the reëligibility of presidents. They urged its ratification and subsequent amendment as freer or less crippling compromises than attempts at revision before submitting it to the states. Madison exhorted Americans to fulfill their limitless personal and national personalities, to "improve and perpetuate" the "one, great, and flourishing empire" won by the revolutionary patriots, to compromise a "decent regard for former times" with a rejection of "blind veneration for antiquity," and to be "manly" enough to test innovation and set a "new and noble course." Hamilton admitted that the new constitution was not perfect, but he hailed it as "the best that the present views and circumstances of the country will permit."

Hamilton and Madison cited as authority for the proposed constitution the Continental Congress' summons of the convention to establish *"a firm national government"* on the one hand, "for the sole and express purpose of revising the articles of Confederation" on another, but above all to achieve a constitution *"adequate to the exigencies of government and the preservation of the Union."* Madison insisted that the new document merely expanded on the principles of the articles to invigorate at this "critical" juncture the existing union with "powers commensurate with its objects." He averred that the new method of ratification was more practicable and that the old Congress and the states should not charge with unconstitutionality the convention which they had unconstitutionally summoned. The proposed constitution should be ratified, he said, if only because "it would accomplish the views and happiness of the people," consistent with the assertion in the Declaration of Independence that they could "abolish or alter" governments to effect their safety and happiness. Limiting this right to changing governments by "some solemn and authoritative act," not by transitory whims of the populace or of legislative "cabals," Hamilton denied "that a *party* to a *compact* has a right to revoke that *compact*" by legislative or popular acts. He would, however, exchange the old confederation's shallow foundation of authority delegated by the state legislatures for the constitution's firmer basis of "CONSENT OF THE PEOPLE."

Madison scorned "theoretic" politicians who believed that "reducing mankind to perfect equality in their political rights" would equalize and assimilate their possessions, opinions, and passions. Pronouncing a democracy appropriate to small areas capable of direct government by all citizens, he endorsed a united federal republic, governed through popular representatives, as appropriate to the country and its future growth. He declared this government one of mixed national and federal characteristics because both central and state governments were derived "directly or indirectly from the great body of people" and because the voters' ratification of the new constitution would not be an act by citizens of a consolidated nation, but of independent states. Although the central government would be national in its operation upon citizens as individuals, its extent would be federal in its limitation to "certain enumerated objects." Both Madison and Hamilton envisaged a union more federal than national, in which each state would play a large corporate role in federal elections.

Although Hamilton agreed that the new government would deal with *enumerated* and *legitimate* objects," he emphasized that its laws would be "the SUPREME LAW of the land." As state officials would be bound to its observance by oath, they would become "incorporated" into its operation and "auxiliary to the enforcement of its laws." He discouraged "fettering the government with restrictions that cannot be observed," lest one departure from the "sacred" fundamental law breed precedent for constant infraction. Both he and Madison believed a military establishment necessary to national power and harmless to the states and people because of its dependence on state militia and biennial congressional appropriations. Hamilton frankly urged the use of federal force to suppress insurrections stirred up by demagogues and "desperate debtors" who, like Shays in Massachusetts, might "provoke . . . the people to wild excesses."

Madison foresaw federal improvement of communication by roads and canals, but he denied that the "general welfare" clause added to the government's "few and defined" powers enumerated in the constitution. However, he and Hamilton agreed that the "necessary and proper" clause bred constructive and implied powers useful in achieving the "particular powers" and the overall goal of an efficacious government, saying: "No axiom is more clearly established in law, or in reason, than that whenever the end is required, the means are authorized."

Although agreeing that constitutional laws of the union were the "supreme law of the land," they believed that neither that provision nor complicated and indirect legislative devices could usurp popular liberty, supplant state power, or cloak encroachment on the coördinate departments, because all government action was ultimately limited by popular acceptance and because the new distribution of powers between the executive, judicial, and legislative branches was so well-balanced.

Hamilton and Madison agreed that the new government should be furnished with sure financial sources to accomplish its goal of a more energetic government, whose power to tax was actually less potentially onerous than that of the old one, which had "complete power to REQUIRE of the States indefinite supplies of money for the common defence and general welfare." Hamilton exceeded Madison in advocating an "unqualified" power of taxation, in dismissing distinctions among external, internal, direct, and indirect taxes, and in demanding a power to tax "at least equal" to the union's resources and sufficient to establishing its credit in any contingency; and he candidly disagreed with Madison's contention that federal taxes would fall mainly on foreign trade. He assured those fearful of federal usurpation of taxation that "the prudence and firmness of the people" would safeguard "the constitutional equilibrium between the general and the State governments." Believing that the states' ultimate activity and need for revenue would become *very narrow* after the liquidation of revolutionary debts, he willingly conceded them "independent and uncontrollable authority to raise their own revenues," provided the central government had a monopoly on external taxation and concurrent jurisdiction in internal taxes. He promised that the central government would not attempt to abridge the states' tax resources, but would restrain itself to powers "exclusively delegated" to it or forbidden to the states.

Hamilton's preference for a more centralized government and a limited electorate made him see indirect election of presidents and senators for rather long terms of office, the limited presidential veto, the life tenure of judges subject to good behavior, and the freedom of the states to set voting qualifications as valuable safeguards against egalitarianism. Although admitting that judicial review was not "directly" authorized by the constitution, he praised this process of measuring legislation against that document as consistent with colonial practice, the framers' intent, and common sense. He considered it to be the best means "to secure a steady, upright, and impartial administration of the laws," without which they would be dead letter, and to be an "excellent barrier" against legislative tyranny. He declared such an independent but coördinate judiciary could never endanger liberty or the rights of states because of its interdependence on the executive and legislative branches, which were subject to election by the people and by states. Only such a court, he said, never realized by the Confederation, could secure the constitutional guarantees against *ex post facto* laws and bills of attainder. Life

tenure subject to good behavior for judges was justified, he averred, by the scarcity of men of "sufficient skill" and "requisite integrity."

He considered the federal courts essential to the maintenance of the "majesty of the national authority," brooking neither "NON-COMPLIANCE" nor "DIRECT and ACTIVE RESISTANCE" by individuals or states to the laws of the central government, which operated directly upon the citizens themselves, and from compliance with which states could relieve their citizens, not by "omission or evasion," but only by encroaching upon the union.

Although Madison recognized men's economic motivation, Hamilton made blatant appeal to their materialistic aspirations in which he saw those of farmers and merchants "blended and interwoven." He promised that the new government would multiply the national wealth by providing uniform and sound currency, uniform taxes (mainly on foreign goods, disregarding his own inconsistency), economy in government, and avoidance of excise or sumptuary taxes.

Hamilton and Madison agreed that no one or the "whole mass" of the powers of the new government was unnecessary, improper, or too dangerous to the states. They held that the states would have a constant advantage over the central government through their corporate role in elections, control of militia, and larger bureaucracy. Madison declared that the central government would be "more obsequious than overbearing" toward the states, and that this circumstance accorded with their closer proximity to the people and greater ability to achieve the "supreme object" of securing the "solid happiness" of the people. He and Hamilton agreed that in federal-state controversies the "predilection and probable support" of the people would go to the states.

In such controversies, Madison held that the "ultimate authority" for both union and states was the "great body of citizens." If some "madness" drove the federal government to an "unwarrantable" act, he believed that popular "disquietude" and "refusal to coöperate with the officers of the Union" would be accompanied by "obstructions" thrown up by state officials, neither of which the federal government would long risk. Madison declared the constitutional provision for settling such controversies before the Supreme Court to be the essential alternative to civil war or disunion and to be consistent with the federal nature of the new government.

It was Madison who dubbed opponents of the proposed constitution "Federalists." Unlike Hamilton, he did not fear "faction," which he defined as a number of citizens united to action by common passions or interests "adverse to the rights of other citizens, or to the permanent and aggregate interest of the community." Fearing faction less than its eradication either by loss of liberty or imposition of conformity, he insisted that political diversity would best maintain a government protective of men's diverse and disparate faculties. But he alleged that governmental regulation of conflicting economic and political interests was necessary to achieve approximate justice through the rule of the majority in order to avoid either anarchy or tyranny.

Claiming that essential agreement among the framers had caused them to bury reservations and to sign the proposed constitution, all three authors urged quick ratification of that document as originally submitted, avoiding "delays of new experiments" and disregarding the inconsistent and disunited critics of the federal constitution. Only such a *federal* union, they agreed, would be energetic enough to maintain *any* union; only it could achieve for Americans prosperity at home, respect abroad, security against foreign pressures, settlement of international disputes, regulation of foreign trade, and avoidance of unjust wars.

FELIX HOLT, RADICAL

Type of work: Novel
Author: George Eliot (Mary Ann Evans, 1819-1880)
Type of plot: Political realism
Time of plot: 1832-1833
Locale: Rural England
First published: 1866

Principal characters:
FELIX HOLT, the radical
HAROLD TRANSOME, heir to Transome Court, a radical candidate for Parliament
MRS. TRANSOME, his mother
ESTHER LYON, a refined young woman
RUFUS LYON, her father, a Dissenting minister
MATTHEW JERMYN, a lawyer
MR. JOHNSON, another lawyer hired by Jermyn
PHILIP DEBARRY, a Tory candidate for Parliament
SIR MAXIMUS DEBARRY, his father, owner of Treby Manor
THE REVEREND AUGUSTUS DEBARRY, his brother
THE REVEREND JOHN LINGON, Mrs. Transome's brother
HENRY SCADDON, alias Maurice Christian Bycliffe, a servant in the Debarry household

Critique:

Centered around a political election in a rural area of England at the time of the Reform Bill of 1832, *Felix Holt, Radical* provides a vivid picture of the society of the times. As always in George Eliot's best work, all classes of the society are included in a thorough portrait of rural English life. The novel hinges on character, although it also uses such standard plot devices as an unknown ancestry and a strange will which settles important property in an unexpected way. The characters are skillfully presented: the energetic and unconventional young radical, Felix; the sharp and generous Dissenting minister, Rufus Lyon; the competent, self-satisfied master of Transome Court, Harold Transome. In depth of insight and complexity of character, the novel looks forward to the later *Middlemarch*. Like *Middlemarch*, also, *Felix Holt, Radical* ends in the affirmation of a transcendent love affair, the mating of two people, Felix and Esther, who see beyond the common and trivial experiences of men and share a kind of spiritual force. The romantic hero and heroine transcend the limitations, sympathetically depicted, of the earthbound characters around them.

The Story:

Mrs. Transome, who had long held Transome Court together in spite of financial and legal difficulties and an incompetent husband, eagerly awaited the return of Harold, her younger son. Harold, who had been building up a fortune in Smyrna for the preceding fifteen years, had been called home to take his place as heir to Transome Court after the death of his weak older brother, Durfey. Harold, whose wife was dead, also brought with him a young son.

Mrs. Transome was soon disappointed in Harold. Although he was kind and promised to renovate the somewhat shabby mansion, he did not seem willing to fit into Mrs. Transome's pattern of genteel country life, particularly when he announced that he intended to run for Parliament as a Radical candidate. He seemed, to his mother, to show a surprising knowledge and shrewdness about contemporary English life. In his campaign he received the support of his family's lawyer, Matthew Jermyn, and his uncle, the Reverend John Lingon. Neither had thought of deserting the Tory colors before his arrival.

More understandably committed to the Radical cause was Rufus Lyon, the local Dissenting minister. One day he received a visit from one of his parishioners, a Mrs. Holt, who complained that her son had deliberately stopped the business in patent medicines that she and her late husband had painstakingly established. Her son, Felix, claimed that the business was fraudulent; Mrs. Holt, on the other hand, was convinced that God would not have allowed a fraudulent business to prosper. The minister later sent for young Felix, whom he found highly intelligent, energetic, honest, and independent. Although well educated, Felix was working as a watchmaker in order to feel himself close to the people. The two men soon became close friends. At the Lyons', Felix also met Rufus' daughter Esther, a slight, refined girl educated abroad, who was now teaching the daughters of the rich and reading Byron's poems. The energetic and socially conscious Felix railed at Esther's refinement and aestheticism, but as time passed a strange attraction between the two began to grow. Esther, although she did not know it at this time, was not the daughter of Rufus Lyon. Her mother had been a Frenchwoman, alone and destitute, whom Rufus had found wandering the English streets. Her soldier husband had sent for her, but he had died before she could find him. With her child, she was befriended by Rufus Lyon, who gave up a successful post for her and later married her.

Harold, beginning his election campaign, left the organizing to his lawyer, Matthew Jermyn. Jermyn hired another lawyer, Mr. Johnson, to go to a workers' pub and stir the men into active support of the Radical candidate. Felix Holt was in the pub at the time. Although a Radical, he objected strongly to the rabble-rousing technique used by Johnson and carried his protest directly to Harold. Har-

old, although sympathetic to Felix' point of view, felt himself somewhat indebted to Jermyn, who had helped his mother retain her property through difficult years and an earlier lawsuit. While walking home through the woods, Felix found a purse belonging to Christian, one of the Debarry servants; as a practical joke, the purse had been stolen from his pocket and tossed away while Christian was asleep in the woods. Along with the purse were some papers belonging to Philip Debarry, the Conservative candidate for Parliament.

When Felix took the papers to Rufus Lyon, his friend was amazed to discover evidence that Christian was the first husband of Rufus' French wife and the father of Esther. Through Jermyn, however, Rufus learned that Christian was really a scoundrel named Henry Scaddon who had, in order to save himself, exchanged identities with Maurice Christian Bycliffe, Esther's real father, just before Bycliffe's death. Jermyn also knew that Bycliffe, and therefore Esther, was the real heiress of Transome Court should an old and senile bill-pasting Transome, who had moved to Treby, die. Although Jermyn kept his information for possible use against the Transome family, Rufus Lyon told his daughter of her origins. Meanwhile, Harold Transome kept on campaigning and the friendship between Esther and Felix grew.

On the day of the election, as Felix had feared, the workers rioted. Felix, hoping to quell the riot, led it for a time in a futile effort to lead the workers away from the town. Unsuccessful in his purpose, he was charged with killing a constable. Also trampled in the riot was the old bill-pasting Transome. Esther was now legally the heiress of Transome Court.

Harold Transome, who had lost the election, now turned his attention to Transome Court. Discovering that Jermyn and Johnson, Jermyn's henchman, had been cheating the estate for years, he decided to get rid of Jermyn at once and sue him. Jermyn tried to avoid the suit by telling Harold that the estate really belonged to Esther and that the lawyer would remain silent if Harold dropped proceedings against him. Harold refused to accept the bribe. Later he and his mother invited Esther to live with them at Transome Court. Both were charmed with Esther, and Harold fell in love with her.

Meanwhile, Felix' case was announced for trial. Rufus Lyon, Harold, and Esther testified to Felix' attempts to quell the riot, but he had, though inadvertently, killed a man, and so he was sentenced to four years' imprisonment. Esther's plea was so powerful that it moved even the arch-Tory, Sir Maximus Debarry, who helped petition Parliament to grant Felix a pardon. Felix was soon released.

In the meantime Mrs. Transome had been unhappy that Harold had rejected Jermyn so thoroughly and was attempting to sue him. Harold, claiming that Jermyn was a thief, intended to carry out the suit. In a final burst of fury, Jermyn told Harold the truth: that he was Harold's father and had, during his long affair with Mrs. Transome, saved the estate during several difficult times. Harold was crushed, and only Esther was able to reconcile him to his unhappy mother.

Feeling his illegitimacy keenly, Harold told Esther that he could not, as he had intended, ask for her hand. This declaration saved Esther much embarrassment, for she had already acknowledged her love for Felix. To solve problems for all concerned, Esther signed over all her rights to Transome Court to Harold, returned to her father's house, and soon married Felix.

FÊTES GALANTES and OTHER POEMS

Type of work: Poetry
Author: Paul Verlaine (1844-1896)
Principal published works: Poèmes saturniens, 1866; *Fêtes galantes,* 1869; *La bonne chanson,* 1870; *Romances sans paroles,* 1874; *Sagesse,* 1881; *Jadis et naguère,* 1884; *Amour,* 1888; *Parallèlement,* 1889; *Bonheur,* 1891

The importance of literary groups or "schools" has always been greater in France than in England or America, and much of French literary history can best be understood through the reaction of one school against another. Thus, after the great wave of Romanticism in the 1830's and 1840's, a counterwave was inevitable. This originated in the group known as the "Parnassians," led by Leconte de Lisle (1818-1894) and continued by José-Maria de Heredia (1842-1905), which first made itself known in 1866. The members of the school had two objectives, the first of which was the reformation of the loose metrical methods of the disciples of Hugo and Lamartine and a return to something like the traditional strictness of French prosody. More important, they were reacting against the excessive subjectivity and emotionalism of Romantics like Musset, who in his verse exploited for all it was worth his famous love affair with George Sand. Poetry, according to the Parnassians, should aim at an "abstract beauty" and avoid the cultivation of "private sorrows and their lamentation"; it should be cold and aloof, purely objective. For example, in the famous "Les éléphants," by de Lisle, the great beasts solemnly march across the desert of red sand and as solemnly disappear; "and the desert resumes its immobility." That is all. As James Elroy Flecker, one of the group's few disciples in England, wrote, for a Parnassian "to overlay fine work with gross and irrelevant egoism," as Hugo had done, would be "abhorrent"; and had the movement existed in England, Tennyson "would never have published 'Locksley Hall.'"

It was in the spirit of this school that Verlaine wrote his early poems. But he was never a thoroughgoing Parnassian; occasionally, as in "Un dahlia," he achieved something of the desired objectivity; but even in his first volume there were hints of the much more characteristic manner that was to appear three years later in *Fêtes galantes.* In such a poem as "Nuit du Walpurgis classique" with its description of the garden designed by Le Nôtre, "correct, ridiculous, and charming," there is a distinct foreshadowing of the eighteenth-century fantasies of the subsequent volume. Also included in this first book was one of his most famous poems, "Chanson d'automne," one of those almost wordless little songs that are associated with his later manner.

The publication, between 1857 and 1875, of three books by the brothers Goncourt on various aspects of life and art during the eighteenth century marked another sharp break with the Romantics. As had happened earlier in England, the French Romantics had turned violently against the preceding century, detesting what they considered to be its coldness and artificiality. But as a result of this latest turn of the wheel of taste, this very artificiality became the eighteenth century's greatest charm; and some writers were fascinated by the brilliant, stately society that their grandfathers had overthrown. Verlaine's *Fêtes galantes*—probably his best-known book outside France—was a part of this pattern; in it, as Holbrook Jackson said, "Watteau became literature." It is an evocation of the world of Boucher and Fragonard: the formal gardens, the silks, the fluttering of fans, the tinkling of mandolins in the eternal twilight or moonlight, while abbés, shepherdesses, Pierrot, and Columbine stroll along the paths beside the fountains.

This eighteenth-century bric-a-brac was very charming, but it does not represent Verlaine's most important contribution to French poetry. His chief significance, at least for the literary historian, lies in his connection with the Symbolist movement, which began as an unconscious protest against what has been called the "Spartan creed" of the Parnassians, and which had links with the work of the Impressionist painters. Arthur Symons, who knew many of the writers involved and who translated a few of Verlaine's pieces, called the whole body of late nineteenth-century French literature the "Decadent Movement," which he then divided into "Impressionism" and "Symbolism." It is difficult and perhaps unnecessary to make a distinction between the two. According to Symons, Impressionism gives the truth "of the visible world to the eyes that see it"; Symbolism, "the truth of spiritual things to the spiritual vision." Yet Symons himself cited Verlaine's *Romances sans paroles*, the book which is usually considered the beginning of the poet's Symbolist period, as an example of Impressionism.

It was, then, the effort of the Symbolists to see through outward appearances to inward reality by trying to express "the secret affinities of things with one's soul." It is customary to say that the germ of this point of view is to be found in Baudelaire's poem "Correspondences." The poet saw nature as a "forest of symbols" where "perfumes, colors, and sounds answer one another." This approach resulted in poetry in which the "subject" becomes unimportant or disappears altogether. The "meaning" of the poem is of no more significance than in a musical composition. A remark of Pater's is frequently quoted in this connection: "All art constantly aspires towards the condition of music; and the perfection of poetry seems to depend in part on a certain suppression of mere subject, so that the meaning reaches us through ways not distinctly traceable by the understanding." "Music before everything," Verlaine said in his "Art poétique"; and then, "no color, only the nuance," the finest, most delicate shade, for it is this "nuance" that weds "the dream to the dream." So his later poems became almost literally "romances sans paroles," songs without words, in which the content consists only of half hints and vague suggestions.

In France, this kind of poetry led to the work of Mallarmé, who carried the method much further by composing poems so filled with symbols within symbols, written in a private language in which hardly a word is to be taken in its customary sense, that each poem can mean almost anything—or nothing—and the French claim that his verse is better understood by foreigners. In England, Verlaine was much admired by the minor poets of the 1890's, several of whom—Symons, John Gray, Ernest Dowson—translated some of his poems. And it is certainly possible to see his influence, or that of his school, on some of the early poems of Yeats.

Although Verlaine experienced a religious conversion which found expression in many of the poems in *Sagesse,* his life was a tragic one. He has been called a modern Villon. Almost everyone who has written about him has referred to his childlike qualities. François Coppé said: "Alas, like a child he was without any defense, and life wounded him often and cruelly. But suffering is the ransom paid by genius, and this word can be uttered in speaking of Verlaine, for his name will always awaken the memory of an absolutely new poetry which, in French literature, has acquired the importance of a discovery."

THE FIELDS

Type of work: Novel
Author: Conrad Richter (1890-
Type of plot: Regional romance
Time of plot: Early nineteenth century
Locale: Northwest Territory, later Ohio
First published: 1946

Principal characters:
SAYWARD WHEELER, a woods woman
PORTIUS, her husband
GENNY SCURRAH, her sister
WYITT LUCKETT, her brother
RESOLVE,
GUERDON,
KINZIE,
SULIE,
HULDAH,
SOOTH,
LIBBY,
DEZIA, and
MERCY, her children
JAKE TENCH, a white runner
MISTRESS BARTRAM, a schoolteacher
JUDAH MacWHIRTER, a neighbor

Critique:

The Fields is the second novel in a trilogy, beginning with *The Trees* and ending with *The Town,* which traces the growth of a pioneer settlement in Ohio. In *The Fields* the primeval trees have begun to disappear and farming becomes important. The settlement builds a meeting house and a school, and cabins spring up close to each other along the riverbank. Sayward Wheeler is still the mainstay of her family and of the settlement as well, but Portius, her husband, begins to assume an important position as a schoolteacher and a lawyer. Very little of historical importance happens in the novel, but the reader can feel the gradual lightening of the pioneers' minds as they come out from under the trees and slowly build up their community.

The Story:

Portius Wheeler's family had written from Boston to the trader at the post near Sayward's cabin to inquire about the woodsy girl Portius was living with. Sayward told the trader to write back that she was a woods girl, all right, and she could not read or write, that she had married Portius legally even if the ceremony had taken place while Portius was drunk, but that she was not keeping him from returning to the Bay State because she had not known that his family had written Portius to come home. She said Portius could have gone back if he had had a mind to, but since he wanted to remain she was staying with him.

Genny helped Sayward when the Wheelers' first boy was born. At the time Portius had gone on business to the territory seat. He was away for days. Knowing he was no woods man, Sayward remembered stories of Indian atrocities along the trace. When he finally came home, he would not look at his son, but in his powerful voice told Sayward that the

Chillicothe convention had ratified the constitution. Now they lived in Ohio State. He warmed so to his subject of politics and government in the wilderness that he scared the baby, who yelled until Portius had to look at his son. It was a question of who was the more scared, father or child. Sayward thought Portius should get used to children because she intended to fill the cabin with them.

The handiest meeting place the neighbors had when a circuit rider came around was a sawmill, open to the sky and hemmed in by trees, but Sayward felt that the Lord knew it was His place when folks gathered there. Genny felt His presence too as she sang the hymns, with her beautiful voice reaching out farther than any other. Sayward could not believe it was Genny singing; that was the first time Genny had sung since her husband, Louie Scurrah, went off to the English lakes with her sister Achsa. Portius, a disbeliever, refused to go to the meeting, but Sayward took her son with her and had him christened Resolve.

Sayward had three boys and a girl by the time their township was formed. On Old Christmas Portius asked everybody in the settlement to come to his cabin to make out a taxing list. That was what Sayward liked, a lot of people in the house, particularly in winter when a body was not apt to see neighbors often. They made a party of it. By the time the men worked out the taxing list, everybody realized that their township was a reality.

Sayward named her first girl for her lost sister Sulie. Sayward's Sulie was the liveliest and brightest child she had ever seen, but she never forgot the tokens she had had before Sulie was born. Resolve thought he had seen a strange little black boy, all dressed in white, peeking in the window. The day before Sulie was born, Resolve saw his first colored man, a new hired man in the settlement. He could not stop talking about Caesar's color. When her blonde baby girl came, Say-ward could only sigh with relief. Sulie was burned to death when she was about three years old. Resolve, seeing her charred body in the coffin, pulled at his mother's skirts to show her that it was not their Sulie lying there but the colored boy who had peeked in the window.

The farmers complained so much about night dogs and other wild animals getting their stock that they banded together for one big hunt. Men, closing in from four sides, chased the animals down into a low place called the Sinks. There they fired on the beasts until nothing moved. Wyitt, with a new rifle much like Louie's, joined in the hunt. Later on he realized that there would be no more game left in the woods and he decided to follow his father and head west. He hated not saying goodbye to Sayward, but he was afraid she might keep him on the farm if he did.

The winter Sayward had five children living and one dead followed a cold summer when the crops could not grow. No one had enough meal to last. Portius took Resolve with him into Kentucky when a number of the men from the settlement went there to get meal on credit. The men were gone so long that Sayward had no food left for the children. Weak because she had fed the young ones instead of herself, she went out and shot a turkey, though she could barely hold the gun. Resolve did not come back with Portius. He had broken his leg and had to stay in Kentucky.

The next time the circuit rider came around, the sawmill had been deserted and sprouts had grown up to stand between the meeting-folk and the preacher. Sayward gave a piece of land, over next to the burying ground where Jarv and Sulie lay, for a meeting house. When the men built it she could see it from her doorstep.

The day Resolve came home he went with his father to Judah MacWhirter's. Jude had been wolf-bitten by a slobbering night dog he caught in his cattle pen.

1214

Three weeks later his fits had begun. Between times he was rational and wanted Portius to help him make a will. The night Resolve was there, Jude had to be tied to his bed because his fits were coming faster. Resolve never forgot Jude's dying after begging someone to kill him before he hurt anyone he loved.

Portius and the children wanted Sayward to sell her place and move to the new town upriver, but she could not leave her fields. Instead, she persuaded Portius to start a school, primarily because Resolve wanted so much to learn that he deliberately broke his leg again to have time to read. Portius kept school for a year until his law practice in Tateville grew so large that he spent a good deal of time there. About that time Sayward decided that seven living children were enough and she was not sleeping with Portius.

The children heard that Portius was seeing the new lady schoolteacher who had taken over his school, but they could not tell Sayward. When Mistress Bartram hurriedly married Jake Tench, Sayward insisted upon going to the wedding because she felt sorry for a girl who had to get married and who was obviously not marrying her child's father. Genny told Sayward that folks were saying Portius was the father.

She worked out her feeling of shame without saying anything to Portius. When Sayward's baby Mercy was small, Jake had a celebration for his keelboat, the first built in the township. Sayward, hating to face Jake's wife with the baby that filled the gap between Dezia and Mercy, could not stay home. She had heard that Jake's wife seldom left her cabin, but she was surprised not to find her at Jake's party.

Riding down the river on the keelboat, Sayward realized that a real town was springing up along the river. Now her children no longer deviled her about moving to Tateville. And Portius, after making a fine speech in honor of Jake's industry, was solicitous of her comfort on the boat ride.

Type of work: Novel
Author: Emile Gaboriau (1835-1873)
Type of plot: Mystery romance
Time of plot: 1866
Locale: Paris
First published: 1867

Principal characters:
> M. ANDRÉ FAUVEL, a Parisian banker
> VALENTINE, his wife
> MADELEINE, his niece
> PROSPER BERTOMY, his cashier
> RAOUL DE LAGORS, Valentine's nephew
> LOUIS DE CLAMERAN, an adventurer
> GYPSY, Prosper's mistress
> M. LECOQ, a detective
> FANFERLOT, another detective

Critique:

Gaboriau's mystery stories have always been popular among readers of this type of fiction, and during the latter part of the nineteenth century he had a large following both in France and abroad. Many of our common conceptions of the French Sureté and French detectives come from his work. In Gaboriau's novels the detective is a brilliant individualist who always gets his man by reasoning, theatrics, and agility. M. Lecoq, for instance, is always disguised; not even his fellows at the police department have ever seen his true appearance. Usually he is even disguised from the reader. Gaboriau makes full use of melodrama, extravagant emotions, and improbable motives.

The Story:

Prosper Bertomy, a trusted cashier, came into the bank rather late one morning. Louis de Clameran was impatiently waiting, for the bank had agreed to have his three hundred and fifty thousand francs ready for him that day. Prosper hurried to the safe to get the money, but when he opened the door he discovered that the money was gone.

In great agitation he called for M. Fauvel. When a search failed to reveal the missing money, M. Fauvel called the police. During a preliminary questioning, it was learned that only Prosper and his employer, M. Fauvel, had keys to the safe. Only they knew the word to use on the alphabetical combination. Either M. Fauvel or Prosper had taken the money.

It was unthinkable that dignified, upright M. Fauvel would steal from himself. Prosper, on the other hand, had lost heavily at the gaming tables and he was the intimate of Raoul de Lagors, the dissolute nephew of Mme. Valentine Fauvel. Prosper's richly furnished apartment was presided over by the beautiful but notorious woman known as Gypsy. In the light of these facts, M. Fauvel raised no objection when the police took Prosper off to jail.

As Prosper left the bank, he contrived to throw a folded note to Cavaillon, a young friend. Following the directions, Cavaillon set off to deliver the message. Fanferlot, a detective, followed Cavaillon until the youth turned into an apartment building. There the detective easily cowed Cavaillon and took away the note, which warned Gypsy to flee immediately. Fanferlot, posing as Prosper's friend, delivered the note and induced the frightened girl to move into lodgings at the Archangel, a hotel run by Mme. Alexandre, secretly Fanferlot's wife. Well pleased with himself, Fanferlot went back to headquarters to report.

The examining judge, convinced of Prosper's guilt, pried into the cashier's financial affairs with detailed knowledge of that unhappy man's speculations. He even knew that Gypsy's real name was Chocareille and that she had once been in prison. The judge brought out the fact that Prosper had also been the favored suitor of Madeleine, the niece of the Fauvels, but that the intimacy had been broken off suddenly. Throughout the investigation Prosper stoutly maintained his innocence. Unable to shake his story, the judge sent Prosper back to his cell.

At the Archangel, Fanferlot kept a close watch on Gypsy. One day she received a note asking her to meet an unknown man at a public rendezvous. Fanferlot trailed her to the meeting and saw her talking to a fat man with red whiskers. When they left in a cab, Fanferlot jumped on the springs behind them. As soon as the horses pulled up, he withdrew into an areaway to watch. But no one got out. Gypsy and her escort had given him the slip by getting in one door of the cab and out the other. Dejected at his failure, Fanferlot went to report to Lecoq, his chief.

To his amazement the fat man with red whiskers was in Lecoq's apartment. Lecoq himself, with his great talent for disguise, had been Gypsy's mysterious companion. Then Lecoq showed Fanferlot a photograph of the safe and pointed out a scratch on the door. With sure logic he explained that two people had been involved in the robbery. One held the key and started to open the door; the second tried to draw away the hand of the first. In the struggle the door was scratched.

After Lecoq had convinced the judge that there was no strong case against Prosper, the cashier was released in the company of Lecoq, who had become transformed into the clownish M. Venduret. Prosper put himself completely in the hands of his new friend and the two of them began the work of locating the

guilty parties.

Suspicion pointed to Raoul de Lagors and Louis de Clameran. They had a great deal of influence in the Fauvel household, and Valentine Fauvel seemed greatly taken with her brilliant, handsome nephew. Suspecting a clandestine love affair, Lecoq went to the south of France to ferret out the backgrounds of Raoul and de Clameran. There he learned that in 1841 the de Clameran family had lived on the banks of the Rhone near Tarascon. The family consisted of the old marquis, his older son Gaston, and his younger son Louis. Across the river lived the Countess de la Verberie and her daughter Valentine. Between the two families there had been a feud for generations.

Gaston, the older brother, fell in love with Valentine and often met her secretly. When their affair became known, Gaston defended her honor in a public brawl in which he killed two men. After the fight he fled to South America. The old marquis died from the shock, and Louis left home to lead a life of depravity. Within a few months Valentine gave birth to Gaston's child in England, and her mother sternly took the baby away and placed him with an English family. Later Valentine married M. Fauvel without telling him about her child.

By chance Louis de Clameran discovered Mme. Fauvel's secret. Her son, he claimed, was the man known as Raoul de Lagors. With de Clameran's help the conscience-stricken woman introduced Raoul to her husband as her nephew and made him one of the Fauvel household. Raoul, at the instigation of de Clameran, extorted large sums of money from her.

At last the time came when she had neither money nor jewels left, and de Clameran threatened to expose her. Madeleine, overhearing his threats, loyally stood by her aunt and promised to marry de Clameran to buy his silence. Raoul, playing on his mother's sympathies, persuaded her to give him the key to the bank safe, and she even went with him to rob her husband. At the last moment Valentine regretted her decision, and in her attempts to take away the key she scratched the door. Raoul, ignoring her pleas, took the money from the safe.

When Lecoq told the whole story to Prosper, the cashier was shocked. He had, in an anonymous letter, told M. Fauvel that Raoul was Valentine's lover.

Angry and grief-stricken after reading the letter, M. Fauvel confronted Raoul and his wife. He was threatening to shoot Raoul when Lecoq appeared, unmasked Raoul as an imposter, and returned the stolen money to M. Fauvel. Valentine's real son had died years ago; Raoul had been coached in the part by de Clameran. M. Fauvel forgave his wife's past and was reunited with her.

With his innocence established, Prosper was free to marry Madeleine. De Clameran went mad in prison. Lecoq at last revealed that he had saved Prosper merely to shame Gypsy, who had deserted Lecoq to become Prosper's mistress.

THE FINANCIER

Type of work: Novel
Author: Theodore Dreiser (1871-1945)
Type of plot: Naturalism
Time of plot: About 1850 to 1874
Locale: Philadelphia
First published: 1912

Principal characters:
FRANK A. COWPERWOOD, the financier
LILLIAN SEMPLE COWPERWOOD, his wife
EDWARD BUTLER, contractor and politician
AILEEN BUTLER, his daughter
HENRY COWPERWOOD, Frank's father

Critique:

In this novel characters are more sharply drawn and more dynamic than they are in other of Dreiser's creations. Cowperwood himself, by contrast with Sister Carrie, Jennie Gerhardt, and Clyde Griffiths, is more than a pawn of destiny, a victim of society. He is an aggressive person who fights and plans, who can adapt himself to circumstances and environment. He is both a realist and a fighter. It is plain that Dreiser thought of him as the typical capitalist, the financier.

The Story:

From his very early years Frank Cowperwood was interested in only one thing —making money. When he was still in his teens he made his first successful business transaction. While passing by an auction sale, he successfully bid for a lot of Java coffee, which he sold to a grocer at a profit of one hundred per cent. His family marveled at Frank's ability and his wealthy uncle, Seneca Davis, encouraged him to go into business as soon as possible.

Through several well-paying positions and shrewd speculation Frank acquired enough money to open his own brokerage house. Within a short time he was immensely successful, one of the most enterprising young financiers in Philadelphia.

One day he met Lillian Semple, the wife of a business associate. About a year later her husband died and Frank married the widow. By that time he had accumulated a large fortune, and he was familiar with local and state politicians, among them Edward Butler, who had risen from being a mere collector of garbage to a leading position in local politics. Through Butler Frank met many other influential people as his business and popularity increased.

Frank and Lillian had several children, but the youngsters did not particularly interest him. Rather, his sole interest was his business. His father, Henry Cowperwood, finally became president of the bank in which he was employed. Both Cowperwoods built expensive houses and furnished them luxuriously. Frank bought fine paintings and other rare objects of art.

His home life was not satisfactory. Lillian was older, more passive than he, and her beauty had almost disappeared. By contrast, Edward Butler's daughter Aileen was tremendously appealing. She was young, beautiful, high-spirited. Frank fell in love with her, and in spite of her strong religious training she became his mistress. He rented a house where they met and furnished it with the paintings and statues he had bought.

Though Frank had become one of the financial powers in Philadelphia, he had to plan and scheme continually in order to thwart more powerful monopolists. He managed to acquire large sums from the state treasury through local politicians. The city treasurer, Stener, proved amenable in many ways, and he and Frank became involved in many shady transactions. Frank bought shares in railroads and local streetcar properties.

After the great Chicago fire, some of Frank's investments were in a perilous state. He went to friends and associates and urged them to stand together in order to avoid losses. But so widespread were the effects of the fire that the manipulations of the city politicians were certain to be discovered on the eve of an election. Something had to be done to satisfy indignant reform groups who would demand action when they discovered what had occurred.

In the meantime someone had sent an anonymous note to Edward Butler, telling him that Frank and Aileen were living together. When Frank went to Butler, the contractor refused to help him, and Frank knew that somehow he had discovered his relationship with Aileen. Butler, who had become his enemy, urged the other politicians to make Frank a scapegoat for their dishonest dealings.

As a result Frank and Stener, the city treasurer, were indicted on charges of embezzlement and grand larceny. Ruined financially, Frank pleaded not guilty, but the jury convicted both him and Stener. He appealed, and posted bail to avoid jail. The appeal was denied, although the judges were not united in their decision. As soon as the appeal had been denied, the sheriff was supposed to take Frank to jail until he should be sentenced. But the sheriff was bribed, and Frank had a few more days of freedom. His property was sold to pay his debts. His father resigned his position at the bank.

Frank and Aileen had given up the house where they formerly met. Their meetings now took place at a house in another part of town. Determined to put an end to the affair, Butler and Pinkerton detectives entered the house and confronted the couple. Butler tried various schemes to make Aileen leave Philadelphia, but all failed after Aileen learned that her father had hired detectives to trail her.

Frank was sentenced to four years and nine months in the penitentiary. Aileen remained faithful to him. When Lillian went to visit him, Frank asked her for a divorce. She refused.

After Edward Butler died, Frank's friends managed to get him a parole. At the end of thirteen months in jail, he was freed in March, 1873. Through Wingate, a friend and business associate, he had succeeded in rebuilding his business He had a bachelor apartment where Aileen visited him. Though he was ostensibly still living with his wife, all of the town had long ago known of his relationship with Aileen.

In September, 1873, the panic came. Frank, who had bought stocks cheaply, made a fortune. Several months later he went with Aileen to Chicago, where he planned to reëstablish himself. Lillian got a divorce but remained friendly with the Cowperwood family. She lived luxuriously; Frank, to buy his own freedom, had provided handsomely for her and the children.

THE FINN CYCLE

Type of work: Ballad cycle
Author: Unknown
Type of plot: Historical adventure
Time of plot: Third century
Locale: Ireland
First transcribed: Reputed eleventh-century manuscript

Principal characters:
FINN, leader of the Fianna Erinn
OISIN, Finn's son
OSCAR, Oisin's son
GOLL MAC MORNA,
DERMOT,
KEELTA, and
CONAN THE BALD, Finn's men
NIAM, Oisin's fairy mistress
GRANIA, King Cormac's daughter

Critique:

The Finn Cycle, which is also known as the Fenian Cycle, is a series of ballad tales celebrating the deeds of Finn, a third century Irish hero, and his band of warriors. Their organization, known as the Fianna Erinn, fought and hunted under service to the king of Ireland. The warriors were quite respectable and enjoyed privilege and wealth. The tone of these ballad stories is romantic, and the stories show a delight in sensuous details, with deep feeling for the Irish countryside and glen. Finn himself stands out as a strong, courageous leader who inspired devotion in his men, but he is not without a touch of cunning and treachery. In many respects he is like Robin Hood and King Arthur—a bold hero, a capable leader, a tender lover. Like them, he witnesses the passing of his strength, the dissolution of his band, and the waning of a heroic era.

The Story:

Long ago in Ireland, Cumhal was the leader of the Fianna Erinn, the king's warriors. A rival clan in this group grew envious of Cumhal, took up arms against him, and slew him at the battle of Castleknock. Cumhal's wife Murna gave birth to a boy shortly thereafter. Fearing for his life now that Goll Mac Morna was in power, she gave him to two wise women to rear.

Under these two women the child grew to be a handsome lad. He learned to run faster than the rabbit, to kill deer without hounds, and to bring down birds with his sling. One day, while roaming in the fields, he found a group of boys playing. He joined them and it was soon obvious that he was a match for all of them. In envy the boys tried to kill him, but he overcame seven of them and chased the rest home. From that day he was called Finn, meaning the fair. However, his two nurses felt that since the warriors of the Morna clan would kill him if they found him, he must start off on his own.

Finn gathered a group of youths about him and began to seek adventure. His first exploit was to avenge a woman whose son had been killed by the Lord of Luachar. Finn and his companions stormed the ramparts of the chieftain's castle, recovered jewels Cumhal had lost in battle, and slew the Lord of Luachar and his men. Finn then returned the jewels to the old men who had fought with his dead father in battle.

Finn set out to learn wisdom and the art of poetry from the sage Finegas. While he was with the sage, he caught the salmon of wisdom and accidentally tasted it. Having learned wisdom and the art of poetry, Finn composed a song in praise of May and then set out to become the leader of the Fianna Erinn.

At that time Conn was the ruler of Ireland. He held an annual banquet at which peace was declared among the various clans. When Finn entered the banquet hall unknown, Conn asked him who he was. The king accepted him immediately because he was the son of an old friend. Soon Finn inquired whether he would become captain of the Fianna Erinn if he rid the royal town of the goblin that now haunted it. The king said yes, and Finn set out with a magic spear to slay the goblin. The goblin appeared with his magic harp and enchanted Finn with the music, but with the aid of his spear Finn slew the spirit and returned victorious. Conn kept his word and Finn was made captain of the Fianna Erinn. Faced with the choice of serving his clan enemy or leaving Ireland, Goll Mac Morna chose to serve Finn, and the rest of his men followed him.

Finn was a strong, generous, wise captain who drew the best poets and warriors of Ireland around him. There was his gallant son, Oisin, one of the finest fighters and poets. There was Oisin's son, Oscar, the fiercest fighter of the group. There was Goll Mac Morna, strong and loyal. There was Dermot of the Love Spot, the fair ladies' man of great endurance and agility. There was Keelta, another strong warrior and fine poet. There was Conan the Bald, full of trickery, gluttony, and sloth. There was also Mac Luga, whom Finn instructed in the art of courtesy, and many another brave warrior. Finn was generous to all. But to enter the Fianna Erinn, it was necessary to pass extremely rigorous tests of strength, skill, poise, and poetic ability.

There was the time Finn and his companions gave chase to a doe. The doe far outstripped everyone but Finn and his two hounds. When Finn reached the doe he found his two hounds playing with her and he gave orders for no one to hurt her. That night Finn awakened to find a beautiful woman standing by his bed. She informed him that she had been changed into a deer by the Dark Druid because she would not give him her love and that Finn had restored her to her original form. Finn took her to live with him as his wife. After a few months of happiness Finn was called away to fight the Northmen. Returning victorious, he found his new wife gone; the Dark Druid had come for her in the shape of Finn and unwittingly she had rushed to greet him and he took her away. For three days Finn mourned before returning to his band. Seven years later Finn found a brave young man fighting off a pack of hounds. On calling off the dogs and questioning the boy, Finn learned that this was the son he had had by his wife and that the Dark Druid had come again and taken her away forever. Finn took his son and trained him to be a great warrior-poet.

There was the time Finn and his men were hunting and the giantess Vivionn came seeking Finn's protection from her scorned lover. As she was talking, her lover appeared and thrust his spear into her breast. While Finn and Goll stayed by the dying giantess, the rest of the company set out after the giant. They chased him over hill and plain to the sea, where he escaped after they had gained his sword and shield. Returning, they found the giantess dead. They buried her and mourned her death.

There was the time Finn and his companions were hunting and saw an ugly, clumsy giant coming toward them with an equally ugly old nag. The giant told Finn in an unmannerly way that he wanted to join his band, and Finn reluctantly agreed. Finn's companions turned the giant's horse out to pasture with the other horses, and it immediately began injuring them. Finn told one of his men to ride the nag to death. When the animal refused to move, thirteen men got on its back in jest. Seeing that they were making fun of him, the giant ran off in fury and his nag followed with thirteen of Finn's men on its back. Finn and the rest of his men followed, but they were soon outdistanced when the giant and his nag crossed the ocean.

Then Finn outfitted himself and his men with a ship, food, and gold, and set out across the sea in search of his missing men. At last they came to a huge, slippery cliff. Since Dermot was the ablest, he was sent to investigate the land. Before long Dermot came to a woodland pool where for three days he fought an armed warrior. On the third night he dived into the pool with the warrior and found himself in a land of wonders. He was soon beaten by the men of this land and left for dead. Presently Dermot was awakened by a man who led him into a friendlier kingdom. There he was welcomed by the king, who himself had served in the Fianna Erinn under Finn. In the meanwhile Finn and his men had entered the underground kingdom by another route, and he and his warriors were reunited. They learned that they had been brought there to fight in the service of this underground king against the King of the Well and his allies. In battle Finn and his men proved matchless. After winning the enemy king's daughter, Finn defeated the foe and restored peace to the land. Finn asked for no reward from the king, but when Conan made a jest the king transported the band back to the Irish hills in the space of a second. The whole adventure seemed but a dream.

There was the time the old feud between Finn's clan and Goll's clan reawakened over a dispute about booty. A battle started in the hall and blood was shed until Fergus, the minstrel, awoke and reminded them with his music of the dangers they had shared. So peace was restored.

For many years Finn and his men passed their lives in adventures, in hunts, and in enchantments. But there came a time when the Fianna Erinn began to disintegrate, when Finn's men became unruly and dishonest, and when Finn lost his honor through treachery.

When Finn was an old man, he planned to marry Grania, daughter of the King of Ireland. Grania fell in love with Dermot, the ladies' man, however, and begged him to run away with her. Dermot was extremely reluctant to do so, but Grania bound him by the laws of Fian chivalry and he was forced to abduct her on her wedding night. Finn jealously chased the pair over Ireland. At length Dermot made peace with Finn. One day, while Finn and Dermot were hunting, a boar fatally wounded Dermot. The only way to save Dermot was for Finn to bring him water. Remembering his hurt pride, Finn let the water fall and Dermot died. The King of Ireland then ordered the Fianna Erinn to disband forever. The final blow to the company came at the battle of Gabhra in which Oscar, Finn's grandson, was killed and the Fenians were all but wiped out.

Niam, a fairy princess, then came to take Oisin to an enchanted land where all wishes came true. She sang a magic song to him and he bade farewell to his companions forever. In this land Oisin could love, hunt, and fight without growing old. The time came, however, when he longed to return to Ireland to see his old companions. Niam tearfully let him go, but warned him not to set foot on the soil. On returning to Ireland he found a degenerate race that was both smaller and weaker than the lowliest men of his time. Impetuously, Oisin dismounted from his horse to help the weaklings move a stone and immediately he became an old man. He soon learned that his companions had been dead for three hundred years. Oisin was taken to Saint Patrick. At first there was strong distrust between the two men, but gradually the saint grew to love Oisin's tales of the Fianna Erinn and recorded them. Oisin, on his part, was baptized into the Church.

FINNEGANS WAKE

Type of work: Novel
Author: James Joyce (1882-1941)
Time: A cycle of history
Locale: Dublin
First published: 1939

> *Principal characters:*
> HUMPHREY CHIMPDEN EARWHICKER, also HERE COMES EVERYBODY
> and HAVETH CHILDER EVERYWHERE, a pub keeper
> ANN, also ANNA LIVIA PLURABELLE, his wife
> ISOBEL, their daughter
> KEVIN, also SHAUN THE POSTMAN, CHUFF, JAUN, and YAWN, and
> JERRY, also SHEM THE PENMAN, DOLPH, and GLUGG, their twin sons

From that wonderful passage of revelation and recall as Molly Bloom hovers on the edge of sleep in the closing section of *Ulysses*, there was for James Joyce only one short step to the conception of *Finnegans Wake*. *Ulysses*, centering on the events of a specific day and place, presented an exploration of the thoughts and myriad impressions of the waking mind. *Finnegans Wake*, to which Joyce devoted seventeen years of concentrated effort, attempts to create a total world of nightmare fantasies and half-conscious dream sensations experienced in the sleeping mind during an interval which stretches out to enclose all space and time.

Like *Ulysses*, this novel has called into being an extensive literature of criticism and explications, a process of exegesis needed if the majority of readers are fully to understand Joyce's purpose and accomplishment. In the stream-of-consciousness content of *Ulysses*, however, Joyce had kept the edges of thought and imagery bright and sharp; here everything is blurred and muffled by physical sleep sensuously recorded as well as by the kaleidoscopic nature of Joyce's dream world and the shifting identities of his people as the dreamer pursues erotic fancies or is oppressed by feelings of guilt. Baldly stated, *Finnegans Wake* is the story of a man who in the course of a single night dreams of everything that has ever happened in the world. The dream shapes and memories set free in sleep float up from the subconscious not only in accordance with Freud's principles but also in keeping with Jung's, so that the episodes of the novel and the bewildering array of cross references go beyond the experience of the individual to reflect a state of being which may be vaguely referred to as the collective consciousness of the race.

Some facts about the dreamer are easily ascertainable. He is a man, apparently of Danish descent, named Humphrey Chimpden Earwhicker, and he keeps a pub, the Bristol, somewhere between Phoenix Park and the River Liffey, in Dublin. To Dubliners his name has always been a matter for joking; in addition to its foreign sound it suggests an insect, the earwig, and he is sometimes referred to as H. C. Earwigger. He has a wife, Ann, and three children—Isobel, a daughter now in her teens, and twin sons, Kevin and Jerry. At some time in the past Earwhicker had been involved in a scandal which is never really explained. Apparently he had accosted someone in Phoenix Park, but whether that person was a young girl or a man is never made clear. Although the incident happened a long time ago, Earwhicker still fears investigation by the authorities. Now his old feeling of guilt has been renewed by the fact that on a rowdy Saturday evening in the pub Earwhicker had drunk too much. There had also been some kind of altercation—possibly a drunk had been forcibly ejected—in which insults were exchanged and stones thrown; and this disturbance had reminded Earwhicker of his earlier trouble. When Earwhicker went to bed he was still drunk, and the events of the day disturb his troubled sleep. Since he and his wife no longer feel the passion they once had for each other, his dream does not turn toward her but involves his children. His feeling of guilt is again aroused by the incestuous nature of his dream, but the incest taboo intervenes to transform Isobel into Iseult la Belle and Earwhicker into Tristram, thus severing the father-daughter relationship. By much the same process the other figures in the dream assume different personalities and meanings. Toward morning Jerry, one of the twins, calls out and the mother goes into another room to comfort the child. Earwhicker, only half aware of her going, goes to sleep once more. As the book ends day is breaking and Earwhicker and his wife are about to awake.

But to approach Joyce's novel in this fashion, in terms of narrative and character, is to do violence to his structure and style. *Finnegans Wake* is composed of many elements: an exile's memories of Dublin in his youth, theories of modern psychology, the substratum of myth and legend underlying the history of the race, and Joyce's marvelous command of the resources and texture of language. The book takes its structure from the *Principii d'una scienza nuova* by Giovanni Battista Vico, an early eighteenth-century Italian philosopher. According to Vico's theory, human societies follow a progression of three distinct cycles, the ages of the gods, of great heroes, of ordinary men. Vico also believed that each cycle created its appropriate institutions and forms of government; autocracy gives place to democracy and democracy at last becomes anarchy before the cycle begins again. In the beginning, however, is Godhead, revealed in lightning and the crash of thunder, which leads man to restrain his brutish acts and appetites. In the opening paragraphs of *Finnegans*

Wake such a polysyllabled thunder-clap suggests the Viconian cycle, but it is also associated with the fall of Finnegan the hod carrier. His wake is a noisy affair satisfactorily ended, even though at one stage the corpse, reanimated by the Gaelic word for whiskey, threatens to rise and walk once more. The interment of Finnegan—the Finn MacCool of Irish legend—fades into the landscape of Howth Castle and Environs from which, bearing the same initials, Humphrey Chimpden Earwhicker emerges. Like Finnegan, Earwhicker is a figure of mythopoeic stature, and in the novel he takes on a more universal significance indicated by his successive appearances as Here Comes Everybody and Haveth Childer Everywhere. His transformations on the universal and spiritual level are the essence of the novel. At the same time he functions on a different level indicated by ambiguous family relationships—as Adam fallen from grace because of the incident in Phoenix Park, as Tristram who loved the two Iseults, as Swift, the Irish dean who loved Stella and Vanessa, as the father of Shaun the Postman (Kevin) and Shem the Penman (Jerry).

Ann the wife also undergoes a transformation in the course of the novel. She becomes identified with the River Liffey, personified as Anna Livia Plurabelle, the stream of life eternally flowing toward the sea, the feminine principle into which all the women in the novel finally merge, just as in the end the river merges with the sea. The stream is time to Earwhicker's history, and the Anna Livia Plurabelle sections are not only the finest in the novel but the particular triumph of Joyce's poetic prose.

Joined to these figures are others who function with only slightly less significance in the symbolic texture of the novel: the four old men who act as a kind of chorus but who may be identified at different times as the four apostles, the four points of the compass, the four ancient Irish kingdoms, the Four Masters of Irish legend, the four waves of myth;

Shaun the Postman, who is Kevin and also Chuff, Jaun, and Yawn, the practical man who carries on tradition without knowing the nature of the message he bears any more than the postman knows the contents of the letter he delivers; Shem the Penman, also Jerry, Dolph, and Glugg, who is the writer, the maker of tradition. These figures are at all times surrounded by the history of past and present, shapes of legend and symbol in a dream vision which Joyce attempted to convey by a dream language to which he brought all the resources of his logo-poeic faculty.

The style of *Finnegans Wake* represents a virtual re-creation of language. In this work Joyce exhibits every variety of style in the range of literature and, in order to achieve his multi-leveled effects, a battery of technical devices—the pun, the play on words, telescoped and portmanteau words, parodies, and connotations, to name only a few of the hundreds employed. Because so much of the understanding of the novel depends on linguistic techniques, its effects are auditory rather than visual. It is a book to be heard as well as to be read, for its structural devices within its cyclic outlines are more those of music than of narrative and drama.

Finnegans Wake is a bold experiment in form, meaning, and style. It is repetitious and irritating in its fragmented episodes and its efforts to push language to the limits of expression. Yet it is a tremendous if imperfect fable of the whole of mankind that carries man backward through the history of his moral and social habits to the mystery of his origin, tells the story of his fall, and affirms the promise of his rebirth. From the unfinished final sentence of the novel to its continuation in the first paragraph, with its images of the flowing river, Adam and Eve, and the circle of Howth Castle and its environs, the cycle runs its never-ending course of life, history, and time.

THE FISHER MAIDEN

Type of work: Novel
Author: Björnstjerne Björnson (1832-1910)
Type of plot: Pastoral romance
Time of plot: Early nineteenth century
Locale: Norway
First published: 1868

Principal characters:
PETRA, the fisher maiden
GUNLAUG, her mother
PEDRO, her father
HANS ÖDEGAARD, the pastor's son

Critique:

Björnson's name stands high among Norwegian writers. His ability seems to come not so much from artfully contriving a clever plot or from outlining dramatic scenes, but rather from a deep-bodied spiritual love for mankind which expresses itself in the pastoral and the romantic. In this novel one feels tempestuous simplicity in Petra, the simplicity of the Norwegian peasant who knows the routine of the seasons, the poetry and drama of the church—as reflected in the rites of baptism, confirmation, marriage, and death—and also the passionate simplicity of her devotion to her dramatic art.

The Story:

Pedro Ohlsen, the son of Peter Ohlsen and the grandson of old Per Ohlsen, was not like either his father or his grandfather. They had tended to their businesses like the shrewd, practical men they were. But Pedro was a dreamer. Scolded from morning to night by his father and his schoolfellows, he began to seek out the poor children in the community for companions, among them a sprite-like girl named Gunlaug, whom people called the fisher maiden.

Peter died, leaving enough money for his widow and Pedro to live quietly without working. Pedro devoted his time to flute playing. He and the fisher maiden separated after a quarrel; she thought him a weakling. She left the town.

Nine years later she returned with a child, Petra, a little girl who also became known as the fisher maiden.

One day Petra, audacious as her mother had been, went to steal apples from a tree belonging to Pedro Ohlsen. He caught her and identified her as the child of his lost love. When Petra escaped, she told her mother of the encounter. Gunlaug told her never again to speak to Pedro Ohlsen.

Hans Ödegaard, the pastor's son, asked permission to teach Petra to read, and under his guidance she learned rapidly. Hans was disturbed, for a tragedy had befallen his best friend, and in his grief he could not be persuaded to take up his career. His indifference was a bitter thing for his father, the old pastor. Petra wept when at last Hans left the village. She did not know why.

Young men came to woo Petra. Gunnar, the sailor, was one of her suitors. Another was a stranger who kept his name from her and who mystified her with strange songs and tales. Finally he gave her a gold chain and told her his name was Yngve Vold. Unlike Gunnar, who was poor, Yngve Vold owned his own ship. Both went suddenly to sea. At last Yngve returned and told her that he intended to marry her. He was the richest man in the town. His wealth frightened Petra, for she knew many of the townspeople would not approve of the marriage of the wealthy shipowner and the fisher maiden.

At the same time Gunnar sent her a ring and a love letter. Before she could decide between her two suitors, however, Hans Ödegaard returned, and she realized that he was the man she loved the most.

The next day Hans beat Yngve with his cane for announcing his plan to marry Petra. Hans then told Petra that his life was ruined, for she had betrayed him. Gunnar returned, and he, too, beat Yngve Vold. The whole town buzzed with the gossip that Petra had three men engaged to her, all at the same time.

A mob went to Gunlaug's house and threw stones through Petra's window. Gunlaug aided her daughter to escape from the town by dressing her as a sailor, and Pedro rowed her out to a boat that would take her to Bergen, where she was not known.

In Bergen, Petra was greatly humiliated. The theater attracted her, but because she was awkward and unlettered no theater manager would hire her. At last she left Bergen and made her home among shepherds to the north. A pastor took her in for a time. He was a friend of Hans Ödegaard; and when he learned that Petra also knew Hans, he permitted her to stay in his household. There, for the next three years, she studied the great plays under the pastor and his daughter Signe. At last, however, the pastor became suspicious of Petra and suspected that she was artfully concealing secret admirers. At that difficult time Hans arrived. Signe had brought Hans to the village, for in her letters she had gently explained how much Petra had suffered.

He gradually forgave Petra the harm she had done him and encouraged her desire to go on the stage. Then Pedro Ohlsen died and left Petra enough money to begin her career. Taking her courage from her experience with suffering and her knowledge of life, she followed her greatest desire, happy at the same time in the knowledge that Signe would marry Hans Ödegaard.

FIVE WOMEN WHO LOVED LOVE

Type of work: Novelettes
Author: Ibara Saikaku (c. 1642-1693)
Type of plots: Sentimental romances
Time of plots: Seventeenth century
Locale: Japan
First published: c. 1685

Principal characters:
 SEIJÛRÔ, an apprentice
 ONATSU, his master's younger sister
 OSEN, a young wife
 THE COOPER, her husband
 CHÔZAEMON, a yeast maker
 CHÔZAEMON'S WIFE
 OSAN, a merchant's wife
 RIN, her maid
 MOEMON, the merchant's clerk
 OSHICHI, a young girl
 HER MOTHER
 ONOGAWA KICHISABURÔ, a young samurai
 GENGOBEI, a Buddhist monk, formerly a pederast
 HACHIJÛRÔ, Gengobei's former lover
 OMAN, a young girl

Critique:

The Japanese writer Ibara (sometimes Ihara) Saikaku was both a poet who wrote a prodigious number of seventeen-syllable *haiku* and the leading novelist of the Genroku Period (1600-1868) in Japan. The subjects of his fiction fall chronologically into three distinct types: those dealing with matters of love and the pleasure quarter; those dealing with life among the warrior class; and those dealing with the lives of the merchant class. The *Kô-shoku Gonin Onna,* which has been translated as *Five Women Who Loved Love,* obviously belongs to the first group, and all five of the novelettes of which this work is comprised are based upon actual happenings. The work was first published about 1685. Each story is divided into five chapters. The plots are simple and, with one exception, tragic. The strength of the work lies in its evocation of character and scene. The five heroines are not languishing, leisurely ladies but rather women of character who almost seem to create their tragedies instead of being helplessly fated. Only Oman, the heroine of the last story, is allowed to live happily ever after, and she, in her charming determination to win her love, resembles in some respects Shakespeare's Rosalind.

The Stories:

THE FIRST STORY

Seijûrô, handsome, gallant young man disowned by his wealthy father for his profligacies, apprenticed himself to a shopkeeper and proved hard-working and reliable. When Onatsu, his master's younger sister, fell in love with him, he, after some reluctance, at last fully returned her affection. As an apprentice he was far from an eligible suitor, and so the lovers were forced to elope. Seven hundred gold pieces disappeared at the same time. When the lovers were discovered, Seijûrô, condemned for theft as well as for seduction, was executed. The gold was later found where it had been mislaid. Onatsu went mad for a time. Later she entered a nunnery.

1229

THE SECOND STORY

Osen, a country girl, was married happily to a cooper. When Chôzaemon, the yeast maker, was planning to celebrate the fiftieth anniversary of his father's death, Osen offered to help in the preparations. While she was arranging sweetmeats, Chôzaemon accidentally dropped a bowl on her head, disarranging her hair. Chôzaemon's suspicious, jealous wife accused Osen of adultery. Because she had been unjustly accused, Osen impulsively decided to revenge herself on the wife by truly making love to Chôzaemon, although she cared nothing for him. When her husband, the cooper, discovered the lovers, Osen committed suicide and Chôzaemon was executed.

THE THIRD STORY

Osan's husband had gone to Edo on business. Her maid, Rin, was in love with Moemon, a clerk. Moemon, however, felt coldly toward Rin and only reluctantly agreed to visit her bed. Together, Rin and Osan decided to punish him, and Osan took Rin's place in the bed. The trick had other results, however, when Osan and Moemon found themselves hopelessly in love. After pretending to commit suicide together, they hid in a faraway village for a time. Eventually they were discovered and executed.

THE FOURTH STORY

Oshichi, an innocent young girl, was taken by her mother to find refuge in a temple after their house had burned down. There she met and fell in love with Onogawa Kichisaburô, a young samurai. When Oshichi and her mother returned to their home, the lovers were not able to meet in secret. Oshichi, remembering how she first met her lover, decided to start another fire, but she was discovered, arrested, exposed to shame, and burned at the stake. Kichisaburô, who had been ill, did not know of her death until he accidentally saw her gravestone. At first he planned to commit suicide, but he was persuaded to delay his design until after a talk with his mentor and sworn brother. As the result of his friend's advice Kichisaburô decided to become a monk.

THE FIFTH STORY

Gengobei, a pederast, took priestly vows after the death of Hachijûrô, his lover. Later he fell in love with another boy who returned from the dead to see him again. In his grief Gengobei retired to a mountain hut. Meanwhile, a young girl, Oman, had seen and fallen in love with Gengobei. Determined to win him, she disguised herself as a boy and visited his retreat. There she succeeded in winning Gengobei's love, even after her sex had been revealed. Gengobei left the priesthood and the lovers lived in great poverty together until Oman's parents finally found her. Rejoicing at her recovery, her parents decided to have the two lovers marry and then give their family fortune to Gengobei. Thus Oman's love story came to a happy ending.

FLOWERS OF EVIL

Type of work: Poetry
Author: Charles Baudelaire (1821-1867)
First published: 1857

"Small hands washed, scoured, cared for like the hands of a woman—and with that, the head of a maniac, a voice cutting like a voice of steel"—thus did the observant but uncharitable Goncourt brothers describe Charles Baudelaire, who had already become the subject of innumerable legends in the Paris of the Second Empire. It was said that he had dyed his hair green; that he had been heard to remark in a café: "Have you ever eaten a baby? I find it pleasing to the palate!" But unfortunately for seekers after the sensational, most of the Baudelaire legends have been disproved by later research. Like Poe, he enjoyed creating mystifications about himself.

Flowers of Evil, the volume on which Baudelaire's fame rests, was published in 1857, although some of the poems had appeared in magazines as much as fifteen years earlier, when the author was ruining himself financially by attempting to be a dandy of the boulevards. The book immediately became famous—or notorious —because of a prosecution brought against author and publisher on the grounds of offense against public morals. In the same year a similar charge had been brought against Flaubert for his *Madame Bovary.* Possibly because of the ridiculous position in which the government had found itself in the earlier case, the prosecution of Baudelaire was half-hearted, and the fine of three hundred francs imposed was never paid. Actually, there were only six poems found to be objectionable (the subject of two of them being lesbianism); they were reprinted in a new edition published in Belgium, and are now included in all the standard texts and in some of the English translations.

When Barbey d'Aurevilly wrote of Baudelaire: "His present book is an anonymous drama in which he takes all the parts," he was saying no more than that the poet was a Romantic. No young man of his generation could escape the "Byronic attitude" that had been the Englishman's legacy to Europe. To be grand, gloomy, and peculiar was expected. But in addition to international Byronism, Baudelaire had been exposed to other influences at that time unusual in France. As a boy, he had learned English; hence, he came to know authors such as De Quincey and the Gothic novelists. But most important, he encountered the works of Poe about 1846 and translated much of that work between 1856 and 1865. It was through this translation that Poe began to have an influence upon French literature far greater than any he has ever exerted in America. Baudelaire's admiration of Poe was immense: he called him "the incomparable Poet, the irrefutable philosopher —who must always be quoted in regard to the mysterious maladies of the mind. . . . The Master of the Horrible, the Prince of Mystery." And yet a reading of Baudelaire's poetry does not greatly remind us of that of Poe; the American was not so preoccupied with sex nor do his ethereal, idealized females suggest the tigerish women with smoldering eyes whose nude charms—"ingenuousness united to lubricity"—Baudelaire loved to describe. What Poe gave him was a general interest in the macabre and a feeling for compression, the latter a welcome reaction against the overwhelming verbosity of much Romantic poetry.

Baudelaire's style, at least as it appeared to a contemporary, was described by Gautier as "ingenious, complicated,

FLOWERS OF EVIL by Charles Baudelaire. Translated by George Dillon and Edna St. Vincent Millay. Excerpts reprinted by permission of George Dillon. Published by Harper & Brothers. Copyright, 1936, by Harper & Brothers.

learned, full of shades and of investigations, always pushing back the limits of language, borrowing all technical vocabularies, taking its colors from all palettes. . . . This decadent style is the last word of language called upon to express everything and pushed to the utmost." It is a "gamy" style like that of late Latin, suitable for the "haggard phantoms of insomnia." This, it must be confessed, rather melodramatic description well indicates the peculiar appeal that Baudelaire held for his contemporaries, who felt that "since Louis XIV French poetry has been dying of correctness."

As for his subject matter, the word "morbid" has been applied to it with unfailing regularity. D'Aurevilly called Baudelaire an "atheistic and modern Dante" whose Muse descended into Hell as surely as Dante's had ascended therefrom. The Romantic indulgence in sensation for its own sake he carried to the point at which pleasure becomes revulsion. In what is perhaps his most famous poem, "A Voyage to Cytherea," after the gay opening of the ship setting sail for the island of Venus, we are brought up sharply by

Look at it; after all, it's a poor land,

and are carried remorselessly through the description of the gibbet from which dangles a "ridiculous hanged man" torn by birds, to the final stanza:

In thine isle, O Venus, I found only upthrust
A Calvary symbol whereon mine image hung,
—Give me, Lord God, to look upon that dung,
My body and my heart, without disgust!

Added to all of this was the attitude of world-weariness inherited from Byron. Baudelaire compares himself to a king in whose veins "the green waters of Lethe flow"; to someone who, in a former life, lived among "vast porticoes," tended by slaves whose only task was to discover their master's secret grief. There were also the blasphemies ("Les Litanies de Satan") and the meticulous descriptions of the revolting ("Une Charogne").

Much of Baudelaire's pyrotechnics—even that part which was sincere and not merely intended to shock the bourgeoisie—has lost its effect. A modern reader, accustomed to clinically precise analyses of sex, is not particularly shocked by his lubricities; his blasphemies seem rather juvenile. One wonders what all the fuss was about. But to contemporary poets, English as well as French, he is important as a counter-Romantic in a Romantic age; as the first modern. To quote Peter Quennell: "He had enjoyed a sense of his own age, had recognized its pattern while the pattern was yet incomplete." He enormously extended the frontiers of poetry by showing that it need not be limited to the conventionally "poetic." And there are few readers who will not be forced to admit the truth of the last line of his "Preface":

Hypocrite reader—my likeness—my brother!

FOMA GORDYEEFF

Type of work: Novel
Author: Maxim Gorky (Aleksei Maksimovich Peshkov, 1868-1936)
Type of plot: Psychological realism
Time of plot: Late nineteenth century
Locale: Russia
First published: 1899

Principal characters:
FOMA GORDYEEFF, a gilded youth
IGNAT, his father
MAYAKIN, his godfather
EZHOFF, a brilliant youth
LIUBOFF, Mayakin's daughter

Critique:

Foma Gordyeeff is a study of gilded youth. Foma, the hero, is drawn with profound insight. Ironically, Foma ruins himself not by his worst instincts but by truth and innate nobility. In a similarly keen fashion Gorky describes the rise of the merchant class and the beginnings of the radical intellectuals who gave impetus to the Russian Revolution. Most of the scene centers around the Volga. Although local color enters largely into the work, the moral basis of the novel is universal.

The Story:

Ignat began as a water pumper, but by the time he was forty he was a rich owner of barges and tugs and a determined and ruthless trader on the exchange. At times, however, he was subject to fits of depression when he would carouse with the dregs of the city; sometimes he would exult fiercely when one of his barges burned. He was a huge man with boundless energy. His greatest disappointment was that he had no son; his fat wife had borne only daughters who had died in infancy.

When he was forty-three his wife suddenly died, and within six months he had found a young bride. Natalya was tall and handsome, brought up in a cult of milk drinkers. She was dutiful but

mysterious. Although ordinarily submissive, she had strength of character which made boisterous Ignat afraid to beat her. She died after the birth of Foma, Ignat's long-desired son.

Until he was six, Foma was brought up in his godfather Mayakin's house. Under the watchful, stupid eye of a female relative, he played unimaginatively with Liuboff, Mayakin's daughter. Ignat took back his son then, and Foma's Aunt Anfisa looked after him. Anfisa told him many fanciful tales which whetted the young boy's imagination.

When he was eight Foma discussed the family business with Ignat and was cast down that his father was only a river merchant instead of a pirate. To clear up his misapprehensions, Ignat took the boy on a business trip down the river. Foma got along well with the peasants until he told his father how one worker had been uncomplimentary to the capitalistic class. Ignat knocked the worker down. This incident always seemed brutal to the boy.

At school Foma made two friends: Smolin, a fat, rich boy, and Ezhoff, a quick-thinking poor boy. Foma kept up rather well in his classes because Ezhoff helped him study and prompted him during recitations. In and out of school pranks, Foma was a daring leader. His courage was due in part to his father's wealth, but he was really honest and fearless. As he grew up, Liuboff was the only girl he knew. Mayakin hoped that they would marry and unite the two family fortunes.

When Foma was not yet twenty, Ignat put him in charge of a trading expedition and told the tug captain to keep an eye on the young man. Foma quickly established his superiority over the older captain and took complete command. He did quite well, except that he was often too generous in giving grain to the peasants. He noticed on deck one night a peasant woman with attractive eyes. Although she was older than he, Foma desired to meet her and the captain arranged to have her come to Foma's cabin at night. The woman was thirty, delightfully mature to the naïve Foma. He left her with regret when Mayakin sent a message requiring him to come home as soon as possible.

Mayakin told Foma that his father was in the clutches of a designing woman who had already got large sums of money from him. At first Foma was afraid that Ignat had taken a mistress. To Mayakin the situation seemed even worse; Madame Medynsky had induced Ignat to give liberally to charity. Mayakin had no use for charity. The merchant class, he thought, should use its money to make more money.

For a time Foma helped his father and faithfully attended to business. It was hard work for him, although he was far from stupid. He could see no point in trading, no excuse for amassing a fortune. Liuboff confused him when he talked with her. She read books, to Foma a foolish pastime, for in them he found no answers to his questions. Foma never read much; in polite society he was always ill at ease.

When Ignat died, Foma felt more insecure. Attending a public gathering to dedicate a building to which his father had contributed, he had to leave before the ceremony was over. He did, however, take much interest in Madame Medyn-sky, the moving spirit in his father's philanthropies. Afterward he visited her often and she was very gracious to him, for he was handsome as well as rich. All the while, however, Foma felt troubled, for she seemed to play with his affections. When Foma heard she was an abandoned woman, he refused to believe the tales. In fact, one night he soundly thrashed an official who spoke slightingly of her chastity.

When Mayakin tried to hush up the affair and set Foma back in the path of commercial rectitude, Foma rebelled. He went on a spree with several others and finally wound up on a raft in company with coldly attractive Sasha. Drunk enough to be affected greatly by Sasha's duets with her sister, he cut the mooring lines. As the raft floated away, Sasha swam to shore. She and Foma laughed immoderately as the others in the party floated helplessly down the river.

After some days he and Sasha came upon one of his barges, and Foma forced the captain to let him take command. Promptly he steered the barge into a collision and the craft sank. It was an expensive and scandalous business to raise it. In the midst of their liaison Sasha left Foma. She could not stand his continual questioning as to the purpose of life. When Mayakin heard what had happened to the barge, he took a power of attorney and left Foma to his own devices.

By chance Foma encountered Ezhoff, now a brilliant, satirical journalist. Fascinated by his former schoolmate, he was puzzled because Ezhoff had had so little worldly success. He went with Ezhoff once when the journalist made a revolutionary speech to a gathering of printers, but mostly the two drank together.

At last Foma went home, soberer but scarcely wiser. There he learned Liuboff had become engaged to Smolin, who had turned into an unctuous, polished trader. Mayakin, still hoping to redeem Foma, took him to a ship launching. As he listened to the laudatory speeches and heard the blatant congratulations to the owner, Foma lost control of himself. He compelled the rich businessmen to listen as he probed beneath their smug shells of respectability.

One man had barely escaped trial for seducing a little girl; another had falsely accused his mistress and had her sent to prison; a third had turned out his nephews to starve; still another had kept a bawdy house. As Foma bawled out his terrible accusations, the men fell on him and bound him. His godfather had him confined in an asylum. In after years he could be seen in the streets of the town, shabby, half-witted, and intoxicated. He lived in a little wing off Liuboff's court-yard.

THE FOOL OF QUALITY

Type of work: Novel
Author: Henry Brooke (1703?-1783)
Type of plot: Didactic romance
Time of plot: Eighteenth century
Locale: England
First published: 1766-1770

Principal characters:
HENRY CLINTON, Earl of Moreland
MR. FENTON, his foster father
NED, Henry's friend
FANNY GOODALL, Mr. Fenton's cousin
ABENAIDE, Princess of Morocco

Critique:

In reality, *The Fool of Quality* was an instrument whereby Henry Brooke could expand his views on theology, politics, government, family life, child training, and other philosophical subjects. To these matters he sacrificed plot and character, but not unduly. In spite of the fact that Brooke filled his novel with pathos and the stilted sentiments of the time, the book is still interesting and appealing to any reader who can follow the threads of the plot through a maze of moralizing, anecdote, and illustrative fable. In many ways his sentimentalism is less objectionable than Mackenzie's in *The Man of Feeling.* At the same time the reader can never doubt the complete sincerity of the author.

The Story:

Put out to nurse when he was a baby, Henry Clinton, second son of the Earl of Moreland, saw little of his noble parents and their favorite older son. At the age of five and a half, young Harry, as he was called, made the acquaintance of an old man of the neighborhood, one Mr. Fenton. The old gentleman was so impressed by the innate goodness of Harry's nature that he stole the boy away from his nurse, after leaving a note for the parents telling them that he would one day return their son. It was Mr. Fenton's purpose to train young Harry to become the most accomplished and perfect of men. The parents grieved for a short time but soon forgot the boy in favor of his older brother.

Mr. Fenton removed Harry to a mansion at Hampstead. With them they took Ned, a beggar lad whom Harry had befriended. There Harry's education began. Mr. Fenton, a very wealthy man, gave Harry large sums of money and hundreds of garments to distribute to the deserving poor. It was Harry's task to weed out the deserving from the rascals. At the same time the boys were instructed in academic subjects, body building, and other suitable lessons. Ned had irrepressible spirits and he constantly tormented his teachers. Sometimes Harry joined in the fun, but he was such a good boy that he immediately performed a favor for anyone who might have suffered because of Ned or himself.

Harry was so tender-hearted that he frequently brought whole families to live at the mansion, and gave them money, clothing, and work. Mr. Fenton was highly pleased with the boy, who had purity of heart and a willingness to be instructed in all phases of life. The old gentleman taught him theology, principles of government, moral rules, and many other forms of philosophy.

Harry became the champion of all those who were set upon by bullies, even though the ruffian was often larger and stronger than he. He soundly thrashed many boys and men, then immediately helped them to their feet and became their friend. Once he trounced the son of a nobleman. The mother, not knowing Harry was also an earl's son, would have had him severely punished, but the father saw Harry's good character and defended the lad. Most of the people Harry thrashed became his devoted servants, seeing and loving the nobility of character he possessed.

One day Mr. Fenton called on a lady who had issued several invitations to him. He was delighted to learn that the woman, now Lady Maitland, was his cousin Fanny Goodall. They had in their youth loved each other, but he was many years older than Fanny and there had been nothing but longing on the part of each of them. Now Fanny, recognizing Mr. Fenton, called him Harry Clinton. He was the brother of young Harry's father, the Earl of Moreland; thus he was Harry's uncle. Cast out with a small inheritance, as was the custom with younger sons, he had made his fortune as a merchant, married a wealthy woman, and prospered still more. But his beloved wife, his children, and his dear father-in-law all died, leaving him bereft of any emotion but sorrow. Although he gained a great fortune on the death of his father-in-law, he considered himself the poorest of men. Fanny was also a widow, and the two friends comforted each other as they talked of their sad lives. Mr. Fenton, seeing that Fanny was almost overcome with grief, promised to tell her the rest of his story later, but the good lady was called away before she could hear more.

Harry's education continued. Mr. Fenton, as he was known to all but Fanny, sent him to the prisons to pay the debts of deserving persons, thus securing their release. He continued to take unfortunates home with him, much to the joy of Mr. Fenton. Ned, too, was improving although he still did not have the nobility of character that Harry possessed.

One day Ned's parents were found. Harry had helped some people who had suffered an accident nearby, and these people became friends of the household. By a scar which his old nurse recognized, Ned was known to her and then to his parents. The boy had been stolen in infancy. It was with great joy that the parents greeted their son. Although Ned hated to leave Mr. Fenton and his beloved friend Harry, he went joyfully with his rightful parents.

Countless numbers of people became Harry's friends because of his concern for their well-being. Mr. Fenton sent him and his tutor, one of Harry's charities, to London to learn the ways of the city and the court. Even the king was impressed by the lad. But Harry retained his modesty through all the adulation he received, a fact which added to his popularity. The queen and other noble ladies sought his company, but he eluded them all, making them better, however, for having known him.

When Mr. Fenton learned of the death of Harry's mother and brother, he returned the boy to his father, the Earl of Moreland. Great was that man's joy at finding his lost son. When he learned that the child's abductor had been his own brother, thought dead, the earl was filled with remorse for having treated his brother so badly many years before. The brothers were united publicly and everyone learned that Mr. Fenton was in reality the second son of the house of Moreland. The earl was grateful to his brother for stealing the boy and making a perfect man of him.

Mr. Clinton, as Mr. Fenton was called from then on, told the rest of the story of his life. After the death of his loved ones, he lived in sorrow for many years. Then he married again after almost losing his life in his suit of the girl he loved, Louisa d'Aubigny. They had a lovely daughter called Eloisa. But sorrow again haunted Mr. Clinton, for Louisa died from a fall and Eloisa was washed from a ship and seen no more. The bereaved man had lived in solitude and misery until he had met and abducted Harry.

Not long after learning his brother's story, Harry's father died and the boy became the Earl of Moreland. He now had a huge fortune to spend for charity, and he spent wisely so that those who received would profit from the money in all ways.

Before long, Mr. Clinton learned from his dead wife's brother that he was coming to England, accompanied by Fanny Goodall. For Fanny had married Louisa's brother and thus had become Mr. Clinton's sister-in-law. The old friends rejoiced at their reunion. Fanny was accompanied by a dark Moorish page to whom Harry was instantly attracted. The boy told Harry that he had a sister Abe-naide, as fair as he himself was dark. She would soon accompany their father the emperor, who was coming to England with his wife. The boy had been sent ahead as a page to be trained in genteel conduct. When the girl arrived, Mr. Clinton found her to be the daughter of his own supposedly dead Eloisa, for Eloisa, saved from the sea, had married the Emperor of Morocco. The Moorish princess was, to Harry's extreme surprise, the same page whom he had loved so dearly. She had been in disguise to escape an unwanted royal lover and had continued the deception in order to tease Harry.

The Princess Abenaide and Harry were married, their wedding being blessed with the prayers of the countless hundreds the perfect young man had befriended.

FOR WHOM THE BELL TOLLS

Type of work: Novel
Author: Ernest Hemingway (1899-1961)
Type of plot: Impressionistic realism
Time of plot: 1937
Locale: Spain
First published: 1940

Principal characters:
ROBERT JORDAN, an American fighting with the Spanish Loyalists
PABLO, a guerrilla leader
PILAR, his wife
MARIA, loved by Jordan
ANSELMO, another guerrilla

Critique:

In order to understand Ernest Hemingway's motive in writing *For Whom the Bell Tolls*, it is necessary to know the essence of the quotation from John Donne, from which Hemingway took his theme: ". . . any mans death diminishes me, because I am involved in Mankinde; And therefore never send to know for whom the bell tolls; It tolls for thee." Hemingway wanted his readers to feel that what happened to the Loyalists in Spain in 1937 was a part of that crisis of the modern world in which we all share. The novel tells the story of three days in the life of a young American who had concerned himself with the Loyalist cause in Spain. It is a story of courage, of loyalty, of the human will to endure. *For Whom the Bell Tolls* is a tragic novel, but one of great nobility and compassion. Hemingway is one of the great spokesmen of our time.

The Story:

At first nothing was important but the bridge, neither his life nor the imminent danger of his death—just the bridge. Robert Jordan was a young American teacher who was in Spain fighting with the Loyalist guerrillas. His present and most important mission was to blow up a bridge which would be of great strategic importance during a Loyalist offensive three days hence. Jordan was behind the Fascist lines, with orders to make contact with Pablo, the leader of a guerrilla band, and with his wife Pilar, who was the really strong figure among the partisans. While Pablo was weak and a drunken braggart, Pilar was strong and trustworthy. She was a swarthy, raw-boned woman, vulgar and outspoken, but she was so fiercely devoted to the Loyalist cause that Jordan knew she would carry out her part of the mission regardless of her personal danger.

The plan was for Jordan to study the bridge from all angles and then to make final plans for its destruction at the proper moment. Jordan had blown up many bridges and three trains, but this was the first time that everything must be done on a split-second schedule. Pablo and Pilar were to assist Jordan in any way they could, even to rounding up other bands of guerrillas if Jordan needed them to accomplish his mission.

At the cave hideout of Pablo and Pilar, Jordan met a beautiful young girl named Maria, who had escaped from the Fascists. Maria had been subjected to every possible indignity that a woman could suffer. She had been starved and tortured and raped, and she felt unclean. At the camp Jordan also met Anselmo, a loyal old man who would follow orders regardless of his personal safety. Anselmo hated having to kill but, if he were so ordered, faithful Anselmo would kill.

Jordan loved the brutally shrewd, desperate, loyal guerrillas, for he knew their cruelties against the Fascists stemmed from poverty and ignorance. But the Fascists' cruelty he abhorred, for the Fascists came largely from the wealthy, ambitious people of Spain. Maria's story of her suffering at their hands filled him with such hatred that he could have killed a thousand of them, even though he, like Anselmo, hated to kill.

The first night he spent at the guerrilla camp destroyed his cold approach to the mission before him, for he fell deeply in love with Maria. She came to his sleeping bag that night, and although they talked but little he knew after she left that he was no longer ready to die. He told Maria that one day they would be married, but he was afraid of the future. And fear was dangerous for a man on an important mission.

Jordan made many sketches of the bridge and laid his plans carefully. There his work was almost ruined by Pablo's treachery. On the night before the blowing up of the bridge Pablo deserted after stealing and destroying the explosives and the detonators hidden in Jordan's pack. Pablo returned, repentant, on the morning of the mission, but the damage had been done. The loss of the detonators and the explosives meant that Jordan and his helper would have to blow the bridge with hand grenades, a much more dangerous method. Pablo had tried to redeem himself by bringing with him another small guerrilla band and their horses. Although Jordan despised Pablo by that time, he forgave him, as did Pilar.

At the bridge Jordan worked quickly and carefully. Each person had a specific job to do, and each did his work well. First Jordan and Anselmo had to kill the sentries, a job Anselmo hated. Pablo and his guerrillas attacked the Fascist lines approaching the bridge, to prevent their crossing before the bridge was demolished. Jordan had been ordered to blow up the bridge at the beginning of a Loyalist bombing attack over the Fascist lines. When he heard the thudding explosions of the bombs, he pulled the pins and the bridge shot high into the air. Jordan got to cover safely, but Anselmo was killed by a steel fragment from the bridge. As Jordan looked at the old man and realized that he might be alive if Pablo had not stolen the detonators, he wanted to kill Pablo. But he knew that his duty was otherwise, and he ran to the designated meeting place of the fugitive guerrillas.

There he found Pablo, Pilar, Maria, and the two remaining gipsy partisans. Pablo, herding the extra horses, said that all the other guerrillas had been killed. Jordan knew that Pablo had ruthlessly killed the other men so that he could get their horses. When he confronted Pablo with this knowledge, Pablo admitted the slaughter, but shrugged his great shoulders and said that the men had not been of his band.

The problem now was to cross a road which could be swept by Fascist gunfire, the road that led to safety. Jordan knew that the first two people would have the best chance, since probably they could cross before the Fascists were alerted. Because Pablo knew the road to safety, Jordan put him on the first horse. Maria was second, for Jordan was determined that she should be saved before the others. Pilar was to go next, then the two remaining guerrillas, and last of all Jordan. The first four crossed safely, but Jordan's horse, wounded by Fascist bullets, fell on Jordan's leg. The others dragged him across the road and out of the line of fire, but he knew that he could not go on; he was too badly injured to ride a horse. Pablo and Pilar understood, but Maria begged to stay with him. Jordan told Pilar to take Maria away when he gave the signal, and then he talked to the girl he loved so much. He told her that she must go on, that as long as she lived, he lived also. But when the time came, she had to be put on her horse and led away.

Jordan, settling down to wait for the approaching Fascist troops, propped himself against a tree, with his submachine gun across his knees. As he waited, he thought over the events that had brought him to that place. He knew that what he had done was right, but that his side might not win for many years. But he knew, too, that if the common people kept trying, kept dying, someday they would win. He hoped they would be prepared when that day came, that they would no longer want to kill and torture, but would struggle for peace and for good as they were now struggling for freedom. He felt at the end that his own part in the struggle had not been in vain. As he saw the first Fascist officer approaching, Robert Jordan smiled. He was ready.

THE FORSYTE SAGA

Type of work: Novel
Author: John Galsworthy (1867-1933)
Type of plot: Social chronicle
Time of plot: 1886-1920
Locale: England
First published: 1906, 1920, 1921

Principal characters:
SOAMES FORSYTE, a man of property
IRENE, his wife
OLD JOLYON FORSYTE, his uncle
YOUNG JOLYON, Old Jolyon's son
JUNE, Young Jolyon's daughter
PHILIP BOSINNEY, an architect engaged to June
ANNETTE, Soames' second wife
FLEUR, their daughter
JON, Irene's and Young Jolyon's son
WINIFRED DARTIE, Soames' sister; Monty Dartie's wife

Critique:

Galsworthy's trilogy — *The Man of Property, In Chancery, To Let*—concerns an upper middle-class English family and traces, through the story of a group of related characters, the changing aspects of manners and morals from the Victorian age to the period between wars. In his preface John Galsworthy points to the general theme of the series—the disturbance that Beauty creates in the lives of men, as exemplified by the story of Irene. *The Forsyte Saga* achieves a high point of excellence as social history and art.

The Story:

In 1886 all the Forsytes gathered at Old Jolyon Forsyte's house to celebrate the engagement of his granddaughter, June, to Philip Bosinney, a young architect. Young Jolyon Forsyte, June's father, was estranged from his family because he had run away with a governess, whom he had married after June's mother died.

Old Jolyon complained that he saw little of June. Lonely, he called on Young Jolyon, whom he had not seen in many years. He found his son working as an underwriter for Lloyd's and painting water-colors. By his second wife he had two children, Holly and Jolly.

The family knew that Soames had been having trouble with his lovely wife, Irene. She had a profound aversion for Soames, and had recently reminded him of her premarital stipulation that she should have her freedom if the marriage were not a success. In his efforts to please her, Soames planned to build a large country place. Deciding that June's fiancé would be a good choice for an architect, he bought an estate at Robin Hill and hired Bosinney to build the house.

When Soames made suggestions about the plans, Bosinney appeared offended, and in the end the plans were drawn as Bosinney wished. As the work proceeded, Soames and Bosinney argued over costs that exceeded the original estimate.

One day Swithin Forsyte, Soames' uncle, took Irene to see the house. Bosinney met them, and while Swithin dozed the architect talked to Irene alone. That day Irene and Bosinney fell hopelessly in love with one another. Irene's already unbearable life with Soames became impossible. She asked for a separate room.

There were new troubles over the house. Bosinney had agreed to decorate it, but only if he could have a free hand.

Soames finally agreed. Irene and Bosinney began to meet secretly. As their affair progressed, June became more unhappy and self-centered. Finally Old Jolyon took June away for a holiday. He wrote to Young Jolyon, asking him to see Bosinney and learn his intentions toward June. Young Jolyon talked to Bosinney, but the report he made to his father was vague.

When the house was completed, Soames sued Bosinney for exceeding his highest estimate and Irene refused to move to Robin Hill. When the lawsuit over the house came to trial, Soames won his case without difficulty. That same night Bosinney, after spending the afternoon with Irene and learning that Soames had forced himself on her, was accidentally run over. Irene left her husband on the day of the trial, but that night she returned to his house because there was now no place else for her to go. June persuaded her grandfather to buy Robin Hill for Jolyon's family.

A short time after Bosinney's death Irene left Soames permanently, settled in a small flat, and gave music lessons to support herself. Several years later she visited Robin Hill secretly and there met Old Jolyon. She won him by her gentleness and charm, and during that summer she made his days happy for him. Late in the summer he died quietly while waiting for her.

After his separation from Irene, Soames devoted himself to making money. Then, still hoping to have an heir, he began to court a French girl, Annette Lamotte. At the same time his sister Winifred was in difficulties. Her husband, Monty Dartie, stole her pearls and ran away to South America with a Spanish dancer. When he decided to marry Annette, Soames went to Irene to see if she would provide grounds for his suit. He found that she had lived a model life. While visiting her, Soames realized that he still loved her and he tried to persuade her to come back to him. When she refused, he hired a detective to get the evidence he needed.

Old Jolyon had willed a legacy to Irene, with Young Jolyon, now a widower, as trustee. When Soames annoyed Irene, she appealed to Young Jolyon for protection. Irene went to Paris to avoid Soames and shortly afterward Young Jolyon joined her. His visit was cut short by Jolly, who announced that he had joined the yeomanry to fight in the Boer War. Holly had in the meantime fallen in love with Val Dartie, her cousin. When Val proposed to Holly, he was overheard by Jolly, who dared Val to join the yeomanry with him. Val accepted. June then decided to become a Red Cross nurse, and Holly went with her. Monty Dartie reappeared unexpectedly. To avoid further scandal, Winifred decided to take him back.

Soames went to Paris in a last effort to persuade Irene. Frightened, Irene returned to Young Jolyon. Before they became lovers in deed, they were presented with papers by Soames' lawyer. They decided to go abroad together. Before their departure Young Jolyon received word that Jolly had died of enteric fever during the African campaign. Later Soames secured his divorce and married Annette. Val married Holly, to the discomfiture of both branches of the family.

Irene presented Jolyon with a son, Jon. When Annette was about to give birth to a child, Soames had to choose between saving the mother or the child. Wishing an heir, Soames chose to save the child. Fortunately, both Annette and the baby lived.

Little Jon grew up under the adoring eyes of his parents. Fleur grew up spoiled by her doting father.

Years passed. Monty Dartie was dead. Val and Holly were training race horses. One day in a picture gallery Soames impulsively invited a young man, Michael Mont, to see his collection of pictures. That same afternoon he saw Irene and her son Jon for the first time in twenty years. By chance Fleur and Jon met.

Having decided that he wanted to try farming, Jon went to stay with Val Dartie. Fleur also appeared to spend the week with Holly. Jon and Fleur fell deeply in love.

They had only vague ideas regarding the cause of the feud between their respective branches of the family. Later Fleur learned all the details from Prosper Profond, with whom Annette was having an affair, and from Winifred Dartie. She was still determined to marry Jon. Meanwhile Michael Mont had Soames' permission to court Fleur. When Soames heard of the affair between Annette and Prosper, she did not deny it, but she promised there would be no scandal.

Fleur tried to persuade Jon into a hasty marriage. She failed because Young Jolyon reluctantly gave his son a letter revealing the story of Soames and Irene. Reading it, Jon realized that he could never marry Fleur. His decision became irrevocable when his father died. He left England at once and went to America, where Irene joined him. Fleur, disappointed, married Michael Mont.

When Timothy, the last of the old Forsytes, died, Soames realized that the Forsyte age had passed. Its way of life was like an empty house—to let. He felt lonely and old.

FORTITUDE

Type of work: Novel
Author: Hugh Walpole (1884-1941)
Type of plot: Sentimental romance
Time of plot: Late nineteenth century
Locale: England
First published: 1913

Principal characters:
PETER WESTCOTT, a young writer
STEPHEN BRANT, a friend
CLARE, Peter's wife
BOBBY GALLEON, a student at Dawson's
JERRY CARDILLAC (CARDS), another student
MR. ZANTI, a bookseller
NORA MONOGUE, Peter's friend and adviser

Critique:

Hugh Walpole's novel is likely to attract readers for some time to come because of its sympathetic story. As the title suggests, the author points to the fact that life is not a simple process and that fortitude is the most desirable quality for a young man facing life.

The Story:

Peter Westcott lived with his harsh father and his invalid mother at Scaw House, near the town of Treliss in Cornwall. As he grew up, Peter made friends with Stephen Brant, a farmer who occasionally took the child to the Bending Mule Inn. One Christmas Eve, at the inn, Peter watched Stephen fighting with another man over a girl. That night he arrived home late from the Bending Mule and his father gave him the most severe whipping he had yet received. On another day, Stephen took him to the curiosity shop operated by Zachary Tan. There Peter was introduced to a jovial Mr. Emilio Zanti, from London, who treated the boy with special consideration. At supper that night Peter's father told him that he was to go off to school in Devonshire.

The next phase of Peter's life revolved about Dawson's School, where his best friends were Bobby Galleon and Jerry Cardillac. Bobby was the son of a famous writer. Cardillac, called Cards, was Peter's idol; he was everything which Peter would have liked to have been, and was not. After Cards left at the end of Peter's second year, affairs did not progress so smoothly for Peter. One day he found Jerrard, the best bowler in school, forcing whiskey down the throat of a small boy. Despite the fact that it was the eve of a big game in which Jerrard's services were needed, Peter, in his capacity as a monitor, turned him in to the authorities. Jerrard was expelled, and Dawson's lost the game. On the last day of the term the whole school joined in hissing Peter when he called the roll. Bobby Galleon was the single exception.

He was spared the indignity of returning to Dawson's when the school was closed after the summer holidays because of lack of funds. His father then sent Peter to read law in the office of Mr. Aitchinson in Treliss. Meanwhile Peter became aware of his mother. She had been for many years an invalid who never left her room, and Peter was not encouraged to visit her. One day, when his father was away, Peter went to her room. He found that she was dying as the result of his father's cruel and harsh attitude toward her, and his visit hastened her death. A short time after her funeral Peter again saw Mr. Zanti, who offered the lad a job in his bookshop in London. Peter, finding life at Scaw House intolerable, decided to leave home. On Easter morning he met a little girl who gave her name as Clare Elizabeth Rossiter. According to his plans, Peter left home, but only after fighting with his father.

In London Peter worked in Mr. Zanti's bookshop as an assistant to Gottfried Hanz. Mr. Zanti had found him lodgings with Mrs. Brockett, and there he met Nora Monogue, who encouraged Peter when he began to write. A strange aspect of the bookshop was the great number of people who visited it without buying any books, visitors who passed mysteriously into the back room of the shop. For seven years Peter Westcott worked in Zanti's shop and wrote in his room at Brockett's. In November, 1895, he finished his first novel, *Reuben Hallard,* and began to look for a publisher. One day he again met Clare Rossiter, who had come to call on Nora Monogue. Almost at once Peter found himself falling in love with her. Meanwhile strange things had been happening at the bookstore. When the Prince and Princess of Schloss visited London, one of the visitors to the shop threw a bomb at Queen Victoria as the royal procession passed. Shortly afterward Stephen Brant appeared to take Peter away from the shop. They found lodgings in the slums of Bucket Lane.

Neither of the two was able to find steady employment. When Peter became ill from lack of food, Stephen notified Peter's friend from Dawson's, Bobby Galleon, whom Peter had met in the city. Peter was moved to his friend's house, where Bobby and his wife nursed him back to health. In a short time *Reuben Hallard* was published. It was an immediate success, and Peter Westcott became known in literary circles. Thus he met Mrs. Launce, who was finally instrumental in bringing Peter and Clare together. After they were married, they took a house in Chelsea. There a child was born to Clare, a son named Stephen. But the marriage was not a success. Clare disapproved of Stephen and Mr. Zanti. Peter's second novel brought little money. Back to London came Peter's old school friend, Jerry Cardillac, and Clare became interested in him.

The final blow to Peter's happiness came when little Stephen died. Peter blamed Clare for the child's death. A short time later she left him to join Cardillac in France, after refusing Peter's constant offers to try to make her life as she wanted it. Then Peter's third novel proved a failure. He decided to leave London and return to Scaw House. In Treliss he encountered Nora Monogue; she had been sent to Cornwall because she could live, at the most, only a few weeks. At Scaw House he found his father sodden in drink and sharing the musty house with a slatternly housekeeper. Peter was slipping into the same useless life. But Nora Monogue felt that Peter, now thirty years old, could still be a successful writer, and she used the last of her rapidly failing strength to persuade him to go back to London. As a final resort, Nora admitted that she had always loved him, and her dying request was that he leave his father and return to London to start writing again. So Peter became a man, realizing for the first time that during his whole life his attitude had been childish. He learned fortitude from the dying Nora, and he became the master of his own destiny.

THE FORTRESS

Type of work: Novel
Author: Hugh Walpole (1884-1941)
Type of plot: Historical chronicle
Time of plot: Nineteenth century
Locale: England
First published: 1932

Principal characters:
> JUDITH PARIS, Rogue Herries' daughter
> WALTER HERRIES, Judith's cousin
> JENNIFER HERRIES, another cousin
> ADAM PARIS, Judith's son
> JOHN, Jennifer's son
> ELIZABETH, Walter's daughter
> UHLAND, Walter's son
> MARGARET, Adam's wife

Critique:

The Fortress is part three of the Herries chronicle, which covers more than two hundred years of English social history. The present work portrays the later life of Judith Paris and her quarrel with Walter. The scope of the chronicle is vast, and *The Fortress* alone covers a space of over fifty years and a host of people. Although at times *The Fortress* stalls among the multitude of characters and their gossip, it has considerable narrative power. Walpole must be considered a competent popular novelist.

The Story:

The quarrel between Walter Herries of Westaways and Jennifer Herries, his kinswoman at Fell House, went back a long way. Christabel, Walter's weak mother, had been insulted by Jennifer over the breaking of a fan at a ball, and Walter never forgot the slight to his proud, snobbish family. He resented also the presence of Judith Paris and her illegitimate son, living brazenly, as he thought, at Fell House, so near his own fine house, Westaways. By one method or another he had determined to drive out the whole household. And he might have succeeded had it not been for Judith.

Judith accused her cousin outright of having incited a riot in which Reuben Sunwood, another kinsman, had been killed. Admitting the charge, Walter Herries said he had had no way of foreseeing Reuben's death. He proposed that Jennifer and Judith should sell him Fell House at a fair price and move away. If they did not, Walter would persecute them until they would be glad to leave. When Judith refused, Walter bought Ireby, a high hill overlooking Fell House. There he planned to build a huge mansion to dwarf Jennifer's modest home and he would be there always to spy on the people of Fell House and hurt them. He also reminded Judith of Francis, Jennifer's husband, who had committed suicide. Walter had exposed Jennifer's lover to him, and the coward had shot himself rather than the man who had defiled his home. But Judith defied Walter's angry boasts of his power and cunning.

At Fell House she took complete charge and Jennifer thankfully let her assume management of the household. Since she was firm and headstrong, they did not give in to Walter even when he poisoned their cows.

Uhland and Elizabeth were Walter's children. The girl was beautiful and kind, but Uhland was his father's pride. The son was lame and pampered. At an early age he shared his father's hatred of Judith and her close kin. One day as he walked in the woods he saw his

THE FORTRESS by Hugh Walpole. By permission of the Executors, estate of Sir Hugh Walpole. and of the publishers, Messrs. MacMillan & Co., London. Copyright, 1932, by Doubleday, Doran & Co., Inc.

sister Elizabeth and John, Jennifer's son, together. He ordered his sister to see no more of John. But Elizabeth, who had a mind of her own, refused, knowing that her brother could never bring himself to tell his father. Uhland himself, lame and pale, was much attracted to robust Adam Paris, Judith's son.

As Adam Paris grew up into a strong, rebellious boy, he soon learned that he was illegitimate and that his aunt had taken a lover. The knowledge made him resentful of all restraint and only by the grace of the family name was he allowed to remain at Rugby.

When Walter really began to build on Ireby hill, the countryfolk named his great mansion The Fortress. Walter had carried out his threat to dwarf the house of Judith and to spy on her people. Jennifer was greatly disturbed. Her fear of Walter made her go every day to Ireby and survey the progress made. Finally the strain was too much to bear; Jennifer died quietly from sheer apprehension.

When Walter's family moved into The Fortress they gave a big reception, but even the crowds and the huge fires could not warm the great stone house. Elizabeth, especially, was unhappy in the gloomy, rambling mansion. She and John had agreed not to see each other any more, as marriage seemed an impossibility while their families were enemies. Consequently, when she was invited to visit her Herries cousins in London, she accepted gratefully. But once in fine society, she was troubled. She felt lonely and left out. Mr. Temple, a fat lawyer, pursued her vigorously.

Uhland followed his sister to London. When he saw that Elizabeth could marry the rich and eligible Mr. Temple, he fiercely urged the match. Elizabeth felt more than ever estranged from her family, and when her father wrote and commanded the marriage, Elizabeth promptly and vehemently refused Mr. Temple's awkward proposal. Enlisting the help of a friendly maid, she stole out of the Herries house and took a job as governess with a family named Golightly.

In her new position Elizabeth had little to do. Her employers, however, were common, noisy people and she soon began to detest her place with them. Then her ridiculous employer, old enough to be her father, declared his love for her and his resolution to leave his wife. Terrified, Elizabeth wrote an appeal to John. Forgetting their families' enmity, John and Elizabeth were quietly married.

At the age of twenty-two Adam Paris decided to leave Fell House. He had been threatening to go away for five years, but each time his mother had put him off.

In London Adam found only temporary employment, and in a few weeks he was hungry and penniless. Taken in by chance by the Kraft family, he soon joined the Chartist movement. In that struggle Caesar Kraft became Adam's guide and Kraft's daughter, Margaret, offered Adam sympathy and finally love.

The 1840's were stirring times in England. Widespread unemployment, poverty, and child labor made reform necessary. The Chartists, helped by Adam and many others, planned their big procession to Parliament. Caesar Kraft was a moderate man, and at a Chartist meeting he counseled patience. When the procession was broken up, the hotheads blamed him for their failure, and in the riot that followed Kraft was clubbed to death.

Adam and Margaret were married shortly afterward. Adam's small skill at editing and hack writing kept them going in a tiny apartment. On their visits to Fell House, Margaret was very unhappy. She saw her husband engulfed by his mother's love and herself an outsider. When she broke down one night and wept, Adam began to understand her feelings and desires. From that time on Judith took second place with him, even after they moved to Fell House to stay.

In London John Herries did well, and

as a parliamentary secretary his future seemed bright. But Uhland was madly determined to make John pay for having the impertinence to marry his sister. Everywhere John went he knew Uhland was dogging his path. John was not exactly afraid, but contact with Uhland left him powerless before that great hatred.

In a desperate attempt to shake off his incubus, John met Uhland in a deserted country house. There he suddenly lost his terror of his tormentor and jumped up, daring Uhland to follow him any more. In a mad rage Uhland seized his gun and shot John and then killed himself. So Elizabeth was left with Benjie, her small son. Walter's hate had borne its final, bitter fruit.

In The Fortress Walter lived out his drunken old age with a gaudy housekeeper. Steadfastly he refused to answer Elizabeth's letters or to let her call. Finally, when she was over sixty, Elizabeth heard that her father was seriously ill. She stormed The Fortress, sent the blowzy housekeeper packing, and nursed the old drunkard back to health. So successful was she with the chastened old man that on Judith's hundredth birthday Elizabeth brought her father with her as a guest to Fell House.

FORTUNATA AND JACINTA

Type of work: Novel
Author: Benito Pérez Galdós (1845-1920)
Type of plot: Social chronicle
Time of plot: 1869-1875
Locale: Madrid, Spain
First published: 1886-1887

Principal characters:
FORTUNATA, a woman of the lower class
JUANITO SANTA CRUZ, her lover
MAXIMILIANO RUBÍN, her husband
JACINTA, Juanito's wife
MORENO ISLA, her admirer
COLONEL EVARISTO FEIJÓO, Fortunata's protector

Critique:

Published in four volumes, appearing about five months apart, this realistic study of bourgeois life in Madrid is considered one of the best Spanish novels of the nineteenth century. The longest work of the prolific Benito Pérez Galdós, it re-creates the life of shopkeepers and the professional class during the restoration of the Bourbon regime. The author wrote many sentimental and problem novels, a series of forty-six historical romances, and twenty plays, but his best-proportioned story is this lengthy and thoroughly documented novel of a faithful heart. In addition, the book contains his best-rounded masculine character, Maximiliano Rubín. In every way *Fortunata and Jacinta* illustrates the writer's theory that a novel ought to be an image of life itself.

The Story:

The Santa Cruz dry-goods store in Madrid, established in the eighteenth century, provided an income for Juanito Santa Cruz. Having graduated from the university at twenty-four, he was not yet ready to take his place in the family business. He wanted to enjoy life and Barbara Santa Cruz, his mother, spoiled him. Her chief adviser was a former clerk, Plácido Estupiñá, who smuggled goods into the city in his spare time.

At the home of a fellow student Juanito met the attractive Fortunata and took her as his mistress. Shortly afterward Es-

tupiñá found out about the affair, and Juanito's mother contracted for him a marriage with his beautiful but passive cousin, Jacinta. They were married in May, 1871. When the couple returned from their honeymoon, Fortunata had left Madrid.

The passing years showed Jacinta that she could not have children. Learning some details of her husband's earlier affair with Fortunata, including the fact that his mistress had borne him a son nicknamed Petusin, she wondered whether it was her duty to take care of the child. In the meantime Juanito had been told that Fortunata was back in Madrid. He immediately began to look for her, but his search ended when a lung infection made him an invalid for a long time.

Among Fortunata's admirers was the ill-favored and schizophrenic Maximiliano Rubín, the orphan of a goldsmith, who, like his two brothers, was subject to violent headaches. Thin and weak, he had been brought up by his Aunt Lupe, who allowed him to live in a world of his own imagination. While studying to become a pharmacist, he met Fortunata at a friend's house. Because of her poverty she overlooked his ugliness and took up with him. When she confessed her past, Maximiliano proposed marriage in order to redeem her.

Hearing of his plan, Aunt Lupe sent one of his brothers, a priest, to talk to

Fortunata. The woman said frankly that Maximiliano was the only one of her lovers—except one now married—for whom she had ever cared. The priest proposed that she spend some time in a home for wayward girls; if she benefited by the experience, he would agree to the marriage. After a term in the institution Fortunata married Maximiliano on a day when he was suffering from one of his worst headaches.

Having known beforehand of the proposed marriage, Juanito had taken a room in the boarding-house Fortunata and her husband were to occupy. At first he had intended only to see Fortunata again, but on the night of the wedding her husband was ill and they resumed their old intimacy. Maximiliano, finding out about the affair, quarreled with Juanito, who overpowered the puny pharmacist and sent him to the hospital with an injured larynx. After the fight Fortunata packed her belongings and left her husband.

Juan Pablo, the second of Maximiliano's brothers, spent his afternoons in one café or another with his cronies, among them the elderly Colonel Evaristo Feijóo. While watching the parade marking the restoration of the monarchy in 1874, one of the loiterers saw Juanito and Fortunata sharing a balcony. Through gossip Jacinta learned of her husband's infidelity. When she accused him, he aroused her sympathy for Fortunata by telling how badly she had been treated by her husband. But he did promise to break off relations with the woman. His farewell message, with an enclosure of one thousand pesetas, so angered Fortunata that she went to his house in order to create a scandal. The sight of Jacinta's gentle beauty tempered her anger, however, and while she was trying to decide what to do she saw Colonel Feijóo. He pointed out that, untrained as she was for any career, she had only three choices: go back to her husband, accept the attentions of any man with money to pay her, or take him as her protector.

She chose Feijóo as her lover, at the same time planning to make her future secure after his death and to reinstate herself in the good graces of the Rubín family. On one occasion Fortunata came face to face with Jacinta, who did not know her husband's former mistress. Torn between a realization of Jacinta's beauty and goodness and her hatred for her as Juanito's wife, Fortunata finally blurted out who she really was, much to Jacinta's confusion.

Only one woman present during the encounter knew what to do. Guillermina Pacheco asked Fortunata to come to see her the next day and discuss the situation. The frank conversation between the two women was overheard by Jacinta, who was in the next room. The cruelest blow to Jacinta was Fortunata's insistence that Juanito needed her, since she had given him the son his wife could never bear him. When Fortunata discovered the eavesdropper, her angry words showed that she was still essentially of the lower class.

Later Fortunata had a scene with Maximiliano, who was gradually losing his mind. At last he drove her out of the house. Before long she and Juanito became lovers once more.

Maximiliano, trying to earn a living, worked in a drugstore owned by the Widow Samaniego, but his mental state caused him to make dangerous mistakes in mixing drugs. His employer had two daughters. One was Aurora, the thirty-three-year-old widow of a Frenchman killed while fighting the Prussians in 1870. She wore clothes with a Parisian flair and soon caught the eye of Juanito, as Fortunata learned to her dismay.

In the meantime Moreno Isla had fallen violently in love with Jacinta. Both he and Guillermina Pacheco, bribed by Moreno, tried to convince her that her husband would never be faithful, but Jacinta gave Moreno no encouragement. At the same time Aurora, for her own purposes, tried to convince Juanito that his wife was in love with another man.

Fortunata, pregnant, was afraid to live with Maximiliano any longer. Because he talked constantly of a philosophy of death she hid herself at Aunt Lupe's house. While looking for her, Maximiliano discovered proof that Juanito and Aurora were having an affair. He finally discovered his wife's hiding place after Estupiñá took the news of Fortunata's baby son to the Santa Cruz household. No longer wanting to kill her, Maximiliano forced his way into Fortunata's room, where he told her what he knew about Juanito and Aurora. Although the doctor had ordered her not to leave her bed, Fortunata rushed out to revenge herself on Jacinta's enemy and her own. The exertion caused her death. Before she died she sent a letter by Estupiñá to Jacinta. In it she asked Jacinta to care for Juanito's son.

Being compelled to acknowledge his paternity was a blow to Juanito, for it lost him his wife's remaining esteem. He realized sadly that his philandering had brought him to old age in spirit while he was still young in years, with nothing but an empty and unhappy future before him.

THE FORTUNES OF NIGEL

Type of work: Novel
Author: Sir Walter Scott (1771-1832)
Type of plot: Historical romance
Time of plot: Early seventeenth century
Locale: England
First published: 1822

> *Principal characters:*
> NIGEL OLIFAUNT, Lord of Glenvarloch
> RICHARD MONIPLIES, his servant
> GEORGE HERIOT, a goldsmith, friend of Nigel's father
> MARGARET RAMSAY, Heriot's goddaughter
> THE EARL OF HUNTINGLEN, an old nobleman
> LORD DALGARNO, his son
> LADY HERMIONE, related to Nigel
> DAME SUDDLECHOP, a gossip
> TRAPBOIS, a usurer
> MARTHA TRAPBOIS, his daughter
> JAMES I, King of England

Critique:

In *The Fortunes of Nigel,* Sir Walter Scott surpassed even his former efforts to introduce literally dozens of characters and plots into one novel. Although the multiplicity of people and events and the use of Scottish dialect may make this novel a difficult one for some readers, the reward in the end is worth the effort. For this novel is an exciting tale of intrigue and mystery, one of the great adventure stories in the language. As is also common in stories by Scott, the novel takes much of its romantic atmosphere and dramatic vigor from the author's use of many characters drawn from the lower levels of society. To balance these creatures of his imagination, Scott presents also in the figure of James I, King of England and Scotland, his finest historical portrait.

The Story:

The threatened loss of his family estates in Scotland sent Nigel Olifaunt, Lord of Glenvarloch, and his servant, Richard Moniplies, to London, there to petition King James I for the repayment of large loans made to the crown by Nigel's late father. After Richie Moniplies had made an unsuccessful attempt to deliver his master's petition, he was followed from the court by George Heriot, the royal goldsmith, who went to Nigel and offered to help him gain favor with the king. Heriot gave as his motive friendship with Nigel's late father. He succeeded in presenting Nigel's petition to the king. King James, in royal good humor, ordered Heriot to provide Nigel with money needed to outfit himself properly for an appearance at court, so that he could speak in his own behalf. The king gave Heriot a small crown of jewels, with instructions that the gems were to remain in Heriot's possession until the state repaid him for the money he would lend to Nigel. The state's finances were seriously depleted, and the king was forced to do business by warrant.

While dining at Heriot's house the next day, Nigel met Margaret Ramsay, Heriot's godchild and the daughter of David Ramsay, the royal clockmaker. Margaret promptly lost her heart to Nigel, but because he was a nobleman she was too shy to talk with him. That same night, however, she commissioned Dame Suddlechop, a local gossip, to find out more about Nigel and his business. The dame already knew that Nigel had powerful enemies in court, enemies who were interested in seeing that he was prevented from taking rightful possession of his estates. On the promise of more money in the future, the old gossip agreed to learn all she could about Nigel and his affairs.

Dressed in clothing bought by money advanced by Heriot, Nigel went to the king with his petition. At first he had difficulty in gaining admittance, but at last he managed to see the king. The king confessed that there were no funds available for the debt, but he made a notation on the petition to the Scottish Exchequer and told Nigel that perhaps he could borrow from money-lenders on the strength of the royal warrant. Nigel left the court with Heriot and the Earl of Huntinglen, who had also befriended him because of his father's name.

Anticipating a session with the money-lenders, the three decided to have a paper drawn up, a document which would allow Nigel ample time to redeem his estates by means of the king's warrant. Trusting Heriot and the old earl to handle his business, Nigel devoted himself to becoming acquainted with the earl's young son, Lord Dalgarno. Pretending friendship, Dalgarno in reality began a campaign to undermine Nigel's character and reputation and complete his financial ruin. Dalgarno himself hoped to gain possession of Nigel's estate.

Dalgarno took Nigel to gaming houses and other questionable places until Nigel's reputation began to suffer in the city and at court. At last even faithful Richie asked for permission to leave his service and return to Scotland. Immediately after Richie's departure, Nigel received an anonymous note, telling him of Dalgarno's plot to ruin him. At first Nigel refused to consider such a possibility, but at length he decided to investigate the charges. When he confronted Dalgarno in the Park and accused him of knavery, Dalgarno was so contemptuous of him that Nigel drew his sword and struck Dalgarno. The young courtier was not injured. There was a severe penalty for drawing swords in the Park, however, and Nigel was forced to flee in order to avoid arrest. He was befriended by a young man he had met in a gaming house and hidden

in the house of an old usurer named Trapbois. His refuge was in Whitefriars, known as Alsatia, the haunt of bravos, bankrupts, bully-boys, thieves.

Meanwhile Margaret Ramsay was trying to help the young Scottish lord. In Heriot's house was a mysterious lady who stayed apart in a secluded apartment. She had seen Nigel once, during his first visit at the house. This lady was Lady Hermione, who was in seclusion in Heriot's house following a tragic affair of the heart. Because she was extremely wealthy, Margaret begged her to help Nigel out of his difficulties. Lady Hermione revealed to Margaret that she was of the House of Glenvarloch and thus a distant relative of Nigel's. When Margaret told her of Dalgarno's plot to ruin Nigel, Lady Hermione gave her the money, but warned her not to lose her heart to Nigel, for he was too high-born for a clockmaker's daughter.

Margaret arranged with an apprentice for Nigel's escape. The apprentice was willing to aid her because he was in love with Margaret and had been advised by old Dame Suddlechop that he might win the girl's heart by helping Nigel. In the meantime Nigel killed one of two Russians who had murdered Trapbois. Nigel took Trapbois' daughter Martha with him when he escaped from Alsatia with the help of the apprentice sent by Margaret.

Nigel sent Martha to the house of a ship chandler with whom he had lodged for a time and then set out to find the king and present his own account of the quarrel with Dalgarno. Martha, having had difficulty in gaining admittance to the house where Nigel had sent her, for the ship chandler's wife had disappeared, was discovered and protected by Richie Moniplies, who had returned to London to look for his master and try to help him. Nigel, in the meantime, tried to approach the king. James, believing that Nigel wanted to kill him, called out for help. His attendants seized Nigel and carried him off to the Tower. Dalgarno, one of the royal party, was only too glad to see Nigel imprisoned.

In his cell Nigel was accused by Heriot of adultery with the ship chandler's wife and of duplicity in the disappearance of Martha Trapbois. Nigel denied his guilt in either of these affairs. Heriot, while refusing to believe him, nevertheless said that he would again try to help Nigel for his dead father's sake, and he asked Nigel for the royal warrant. His plan was to collect the money from the state and satisfy the money-lenders who were pressing for the repayment of Nigel's loan. Nigel was in despair when he discovered that the royal warrant had been taken from his baggage.

Through a noble friend, Nigel was cleared of the charge of treason—that is, his supposed attempt on the king's life in the Park. However, he still had to stand trial for drawing his sword against Dalgarno. Richie went to Nigel in his cell and promised to help his master out of his troubles.

In the meantime the king received a letter from the Lady Hermione, in which she charged that Dalgarno was the man who had betrayed her. The king in an attempt to amend the wrong forced Dalgarno to marry Lady Hermione, but after the ceremony Dalgarno informed the king that he now possessed his wife's wealth and through her a claim upon the Glenvarloch estates. If the redemption money were not paid by noon of the following day, he would, he announced, take possession of Nigel's property. Convinced at last that Nigel was the injured party in the affair with Dalgarno, the king informed Richie that his master would be restored to royal favor. Richie, armed with money given to him by Martha Trapbois, paid the mortgage on Nigel's estates. Dalgarno, after trying to show that the redemption papers were gained unlawfully, proceeded on his way to Scotland to claim the property, but on the way he was killed by the same ruffian he had hired to murder Trapbois some time before. His death restored to Lady Hermione the fortune which Dalgarno, as her husband, had claimed. She gave a large portion of her wealth to Margaret and the rest to Nigel, her kinsman. Nigel and Margaret declared their love for each other and were married. During the ceremony Richie appeared with Martha Trapbois, whom he had married. Martha told Nigel that her father had stolen his royal warrant, and by returning the paper to him she made his estates secure. In gratitude to Richie for his part in restoring honor in the court, the king made the faithful servant a knight of the land.

THE FORTUNES OF RICHARD MAHONY

Type of work: Novel
Author: Henry Handel Richardson (Mrs. Henrietta Richardson Robertson, 1870-1946)
Type of plot: Social chronicle
Time of plot: Nineteenth century
Locale: Australia
First published: 1917, 1925, 1929

Principal characters:
RICHARD MAHONY, a doctor
POLLY, his wife
PURDY SMITH, his friend
JOHN TURNHAM, Polly's brother
HENRY OCOCK, Richard's solicitor

Critique:

Written and published separately as three novels, *Australia Felix, The Way Home,* and *Ultima Thule,* this story of Richard Mahony has had wide popularity, and some critics have ranked the trilogy with the great books of this century. The central character is a doctor who starts his practice in humility, reaches dizzying heights, and ends his life a madman. It is also the story of a woman who shared that life completely, spending herself unmercifully in a vain attempt to help her husband find peace of mind. Uncompromisingly realistic, the novel is the most distinguished work of fiction out of Australia.

The Story:

Richard Mahony was ill-suited to life in the Australian gold mines. A moderately successful doctor, he had left his practice in England and gone to the colonies in hopes of a quick fortune. Having found the life of digger completely wrong for him, he had taken what little money and goods he had left and set up a store. But he hated the raw country with bitter passion, and longed for England and his native Ireland.

To that life he brought his bride, Polly Turnham, whom he had met through an old schoolfriend, Purdy Smith. Purdy was as crude as Richard was fastidious. Polly wept at her new home, but she loved her husband, and she set about making the best of matters. The death of her baby matured and quieted her, but it did not kill her spirit.

When her sister-in-law died, Polly gladly cared for her children. Her other brothers and sisters, separated from their home in England, turned to her as they might a mother, and she comforted and encouraged them as she did her husband.

When Richard found his business declining, he decided to sell out and take Polly back to England. But Polly persuaded him instead to stay in Australia and set up a medical practice. With the help of Polly's brother, John Turnham, Richard borrowed enough money to get a decent house and the necessary medical supplies. Henry Ocock, the son of a neighbor and a successful solicitor, arranged a loan and in other ways advised Richard.

Richard had a sudden stroke of luck. On Henry Ocock's advice he had invested a small sum in some mining stock, Australia Felixes. The stock suddenly boomed and Richard found himself overnight a wealthy man. As he prospered, so did his practice, until he had more than he could handle. But Richard began to assume an air that worried Polly. Thinking his old friends uncouth and crude, he wanted Polly to join more fashionable circles. She did so, but she quietly retained the old friendships as well.

After an exhausting illness, brought on by overwork, Richard finally sold out his practice and prepared to return to England. He could return as he had always dreamed he would, rich and honored. They set sail, Richard with pride and Polly with sorrow.

In England, and during their short visit in Ireland, Polly and Richard Mahony were welcomed and entertained. But when Richard settled down to practice medicine again, he was twice scorned as a bushman from Australia, unfit to treat or to meet socially English snobs of the middle class. Worst of all were the snubs to Polly. These Richard could not tolerate, and so they returned to Australia. There Richard learned that his Australia Felix stocks had taken a new turn upward; he was wealthy beyond his wildest dreams. He bought a splendid house and called it Ultima Thule. To Polly's sorrow, he did not return to his practice. Feeling that he could retire and enjoy the quiet he had always longed for, Richard turned to spiritualism and spent long hours in seances with charlatans and quacks, in spite of Polly's remonstrances and those of his friends. In the great house he lived at times like a recluse with his books and fancies. Polly resumed her old ways with her friends and relatives. John, remarried, had been widowed again, and Polly once more had to care for her brother's children and soften his bitterness toward the world. John, successful in business and politics, was still dependent on Polly. Even after he married the third time, he could not find and hold the happiness that came naturally to his sister.

At last Polly and Richard had the family they had hoped for. Polly gave birth to a son and, a year later, twin girls. Although they were getting on in years, Polly and Richard lavished all their love and attention on the children. But Richard was withdrawing more and more from the world, and it was Polly who guided the children through their early days. Their happiness was marred by the death, from cancer, of Polly's brother John. Richard, although he no longer practiced medicine, did everything possible to ease the sick man's pain. Then, because of Polly's grief after John's death, Richard decided to return to England. Ultima Thule was sold before the family left for the land Richard would always call home.

In England, Richard continued his preoccupation with spiritualism. He had for some time, even back in Australia, been bothered by weird dreams which became more frequent and confusing. Richard was convinced that he was actually communicating with the dead, but Polly could see that her husband was deteriorating in body and mind.

The worst blow of all came when he received news that the broker in charge of his financial affairs had absconded from Australia to America. Richard was completely ruined. Leaving Polly and the children to follow later, he left at once for Australia.

On his arrival in Australia, Richard learned that he had left only about three thousand pounds, and he was forced to resume his medical practice. When Polly and the children arrived, she found that in spite of his poverty he had lost none of his grand ideas. As they went from one miserable village to another, Richard's mental deterioration increased rapidly in the squalor in which they lived. His temper was short; he still scorned the old friends as louts to be avoided, and Polly had to meet them in secret. She herself suffered a shock that was almost too much for her to bear when Lallie, one of the twin girls, died a horrible, agonizing death. The tragedy brought Polly and Richard close again, Richard being her only comfort and strength. He insisted that Polly take the two remaining children for a vacation. Alone, Richard could no longer fight his strange dreams and illusions. His dead daughter appeared to him often, and the servant heard him talking to himself like a madman. In his depressed state of mind he lost the pitifully few patients he had.

When Polly and the children returned, she found her husband really ill. After selling the house and her own few trinkets, she moved with Richard to an even more miserable town. There he grew steadily worse and once attempted suicide. Trying to manage, Polly put Richard in a private mental hospital and took a position as postmistress in a hovel far removed from any home they had ever known. When she had no more money to pay the hospital, she placed Richard, now mad, in a public asylum. When she tried to visit him and learned that he was being treated like an animal, she turned to her old friend, Henry Ocock, to help her get Richard out of the institution. At all costs, Richard should not die like a beast.

Richard went home at last. His sanity never returned, but on his deathbed he looked at Polly and called her his dear wife. His words were all the reward Polly needed for her life of sacrifice for the husband buried in a strange land that could never claim his soul.

THE FORTY DAYS OF MUSA DAGH

Type of work: Novel
Author: Franz Werfel (1890-1945)
Type of plot: Historical romance
Time of plot: 1915
Locale: Near Antioch, Syria
First published: 1934

Principal characters:
GABRIEL BAGRADIAN, an Armenian patriot
JULIETTE BAGRADIAN, his wife
STEPHAN BAGRADIAN, their son
TER HAIGASUN, Armenian priest of the village of Yoghonoluk

Critique:

The triumphant defense of the stronghold of Musa Dagh by a small band of Armenians is a moving story in itself. It can only be added that Franz Werfel has, with beautiful restraint, given this narrative of sacrifice and devotion a universal meaning.

The Story:

After twenty-three years spent in Paris, Gabriel Bagradian returned with his wife and child to his ancestral village of Yoghonoluk. He had gone back to Turkey in order to settle the affairs of his dying brother, and after his death Gabriel stayed on in the village to await the end of European hostilities.

One Sunday his son's tutor told him officials had been through the village collecting all passports. To learn what had happened, Bagradian saddled a horse and started for Antioch. There the Kaimakam, or governor, gave only evasive answers about the passport incident. Later, in a Turkish bath, Bagradian heard that the Turkish war minister had ordered all Armenians disarmed and given menial work. From his Mohammedan friend, Agha Rifaat Bereket, Bagradian learned that rich and prominent Armenians would soon be persecuted.

Gabriel was worried. On his return to Yoghonoluk he began to collect data on the number of men of fighting age in the vicinity. Ter Haigasun, the Gregorian priest, told him one day that there

had been a mass arrest in Antioch Bagradian began a survey of Musa Dagh, a mountain which lay between the Armenian villages and the Mediterranean Sea. After having maps drawn of the terrain, Bagradian knew that the plateau with its natural fortifications offered a refuge for his people.

One day a friendly Turkish policeman confided to Bagradian that in three days the village would be ordered to prepare for its trip into exile. Bagradian called a meeting of the people. The Protestant pastor, Nokhudian, and his congregation voted to accept banishment, the rest of the population to defend Musa Dagh. Ter Haigasun was elected leader. The next morning the young men under Bagradian's directions began the construction of trenches and other defenses on Musa Dagh, and at night the people carried provisions up the mountain. Unfortunately there were not enough rifles to go around and very little ammunition, but the men of the village were augmented by army deserters who drifted in from the desert until there were sixty armed men in the community. On the third day the convoy escort arrived. The village pretended to busy itself with preparations for the trip, but that night everyone but Pastor Nokhudian's flock secretly departed for Musa Dagh.

It took five days for the Turks to discover Bagradian's mountain retreat, for

THE FORTY DAYS OF MUSA DAGH by Franz Werfel. Translated by Geoffrey Dunlop. By permission of the publishers, The Viking Press Inc. Copyright, 1934, by The Viking Press Inc.

the woods were so thick and the trenches dug so cleverly that the encampment was not visible from below. During that time the trenches were completed, posts assigned, and patterns for daily living laid down. Everyone was given a task, and the food of the community was held in common so that all might be treated fairly.

The first sortie ended in a victory for the holders of Musa Dagh. The four hundred regulars and gendarmes who boldly attacked, not even seeking cover, were quickly routed and substantial booty of badly needed ammunition, boots, and uniforms was recovered. The second attack came several days later. Turkish howitzers managed to do considerable damage, wounding six non-combatants in the town enclosure and setting the grain depot on fire. Sarkis Kilikian, commander of the south bastion, rigged up a catapult to hurl stones at the attackers. These in turn caused a landslide which killed or maimed half the Turkish force. Young Stephan Bagradian and his friend, Haik, raided the Turkish gun emplacements. Sixteen of the defenders were killed.

Three days later there were again signs of activity in the valley. The Kaimakam had imported families of Arabs to take over the Armenian houses and farms. On Musa Dagh a Greek-American adventurer, Gonzague Maris, who had fled with the Armenians and who had since seduced Juliette Bagradian, tried to persuade her to flee with him under the protection his passport afforded. She was undecided. Bagradian and his wife had grown apart in those troubled times. He was burdened with military duties, and she seemed indifferent to his fate. Bagradian found his only companionship in Iskuhi, a refugee from Zeitun.

The next attack was carried out by two thousand trained Turkish soldiers. In fierce fighting they captured the first line of trenches below the southern bastion. That night Bagradian had his troops counterattack and the trenches were re-taken. The defenders also set a fire which raced down the mountain, driving the Turks into the valley. Musa Dagh was again saved.

Gonzague Maris begged Juliette several times to go away with him, but she did not have the courage to tell her husband she was leaving him. Then Bagradian discovered the lovers together and took his wife off, half-unconscious, to her tent. She was seriously ill with fever. The Greek disappeared of his own accord.

That same night Stephan Bagradian left Musa Dagh, without permission, to accompany his friend Haik, who was being sent to the American consul in Aleppo to ask for intervention on behalf of his people. Haik made his way safely to Aleppo, but Stephan developed a fever and had to start back to the mountain. On the way, the Turks captured and killed him. His body was thrown into the cemetery yard in Yoghonoluk where it was found by some old women who took it to his father. The last of the Bagradians was buried on Musa Dagh.

The next day flocks grazing beyond the fortifications were captured by the Turks. There was now only enough food to last three or four days more.

On the fortieth day on Musa Dagh the people were suffering. It was their third day of famine. Gabriel had planned one last desperate attack for that night, an attempt to reach the valley with his men, capture some high officials as hostages, and return to the mountain. But that afternoon, as Ter Haigasun held a service to petition God for help, Sarkis Kilikian and his deserters broke into the town enclosure to steal ammunition and food. They fled, setting fire to the buildings to cover their escape. The Turks took advantage of their desertion to capture the south bastion. The next day they would capture the plateau.

Kilikian was brought back by deserters who felt it would be better to die with their own people than to be captured by the Turks. He was put to death.

As the Turks prepared to advance at dawn, a French cruiser dropped its first shell into the valley. Its commander had seen the fire in the town enclosure the day before. Approaching to investigate, he had seen the enormous flag the Armenians were using as a distress signal. The Turks retreated into the valley. Bagradian led the weary defenders to the coast and saw them safely aboard a cruiser and a troopship. Then he started back up the mountain for a last view of his son's grave. Exhausted by his ordeal, he fell asleep halfway up the mountainside. When he awoke, the ships were already standing out at sea. He started to signal them but changed his mind. He felt that his life was now complete. Up he climbed until he reached his son's grave. There a bullet from a Turkish scout caught him in the temple. On his son's grave he lay, Stephan's cross on his heart.

FOUR QUARTETS

Type of work: Poetry
Author: T. S. Eliot (1888-   )
First published: 1943

Four Quartets is T. S. Eliot's last book of nondramatic poetry. Written over a period of eight years and published separately, each quartet has the same structure and helps to develop cumulatively the same themes. Eliot has said that transitions in poetry can be similar to those in a symphony or quartet, and these quartets are written in the five-movement sonata form.

The personal and historical significance of the place names which title the poems are the points of departure for the themes developed in the first part of each quartet. The theme of "Burnt Norton"—an old Gloucestershire house—is the nature of time and of personal memories and experience. "East Coker," which is the name of the English village from which Eliot's ancestor left for America in the seventeenth century, is a consideration of the meaning of history and an explanation of the idea of spiritual rebirth. "The Dry Salvages," a group of rocks off the coast of Massachusetts which Eliot knew as a boy, continues the meditations on time and history and includes reflections on human endeavor and further statements on the nature of experience. These themes are all, again, present in "Little Gidding," the name of an Anglican lay community founded by Nicholas Ferrar.

All themes are thus present in each quartet with different emphases, the subsidiary themes are aspects of the major ones and are directly related to them. A difference in these poems from Eliot's earlier verse is that here, although the elements of surprise and rapid transition are still present, the transitional passages are included, whereas in *The Waste Land* they were not. The same symbols also occur in each of the quartets; their

multiple and shifting meanings are resolved in "Little Gidding."

In "Burnt Norton" he writes:

What might have been and what has
been
Point to one end which is always present.

Here there is no placing of experience in time ("do not call it fixity"); it is instead a "stillness." The stillness is the point beyond experience "into the rose-garden." To reach it requires the negation of flesh and spirit. This way of purgation is repeatedly considered and what is required for it is release from desire and compulsion. Meaningful experience is both in and out of time, and life is too full of distraction for this end to be often attained. The description of this distraction is a vivid realization of the contemporary predicament:

Only a flicker
Over the strained, time-ridden faces
Distracted from distraction by distraction.

The passage following these lines on suburban Londoners presents "the way down" towards the dark night of the soul, "desiccation of the world of sense." But there are times in the realm of art when the moment can be prolonged

. . . as a Chinese jar still
Moves perpetually in its stillness.

A further theme in the quartets, the nature and difficulty of poetic creation, follows in contrast to the image of the jar. The struggle with words which "decay with imprecision" introduces the Word which is subject always to temptation. "Burnt Norton" ends with a repetition of the vision of hidden children laughing in the rose-garden, a motif which occurred in the first movement. Such immediacy is contrasted with the usual bleakness of existence.

Time in "East Coker" involves the consideration of the history of man. This, the most despairing of the quartets, comes closest to complete and unredeemed bitterness. The cyclic nature of life and experience is stressed: fields give way to factories which crumble to dust. The life cycle of man and earth is presented as if in a vision after the poet has gone down the dark lane into the somnolent village. The second section begins with a lyric on November, which is followed by a characteristic reversal:

That was a way of putting it . . .
A periphrastic study in a worn-out poetical fashion.

The theme of the bitterness and deception of time mentioned in "Burnt Norton" is expanded here; the wisdom of old men is really folly, and

The only wisdom we can hope to acquire
Is the wisdom of humility.

The concrete description, which in these poems always either immediately follows or precedes the abstract thought, is here that of the descent into subways, which were also used as air-raid shelters during World War II. Thus negation and stillness are combined and the necessity for "waiting" is introduced.

The fourth movement is a lyric on the Christian paradox of life in death and death in life. The symbols are those of a hospital with a "wounded surgeon" and "a dying nurse"

Wherein, if we do well, we shall
Die of the absolute paternal care.

Fire and roses are multiple symbols of destruction and salvation, purgation and resurrection. After the cold fever of death there is purgatory:

Of which the flame is roses, and the smoke is briars.

The fifth section despairs of poetic creation, which, at "every attempt/Is a wholly new start" because the difficulties once conquered are no longer those that face the poet. The resolution of this dilemma is similar to that for the soul: "For us there is only the trying." The final section inverts the opening statement: "In my beginning is my end"; the poet concludes, "In my end is my beginning."

The superb pictures of the Mississippi River and the Atlantic Ocean in "The Dry Salvages" show an increase in the music of the verse which is sustained in "Little Gidding." The river is "a strong brown god" and the sea has "Many gods and many voices." The sea time "is not our time"; "time stops and is never ending." The lyric in Section II speaks of the grief of shipwreck and of those things thought "most reliable" which are "therefore the fittest for renunciation." There is no end to this pain, only the possibility of prayer.

The pattern of the past with its content of meaningful experience is seen here in its historical perspective:

And approach to the meaning restores the experience
In a different form, beyond any meaning
We can assign to happiness.

This passage connects with the reference to Krishna in Section III, one of the many allusions to and quotations of other authors in the quartets. The theory of time is drawn from the philosopher Heraclitus and part of the conclusion of "Little Gidding" from Dame Julian of Norwich. The rose and fire symbolism is reminiscent of Dante, and the conception of the dark night of the soul is that of St. John of the Cross. While awareness of these sources adds considerably to the enjoyment of the quartets, Eliot integrates them so completely and so perfectly controls their place in the poetry, placing them where they have such an exact significance, that the poems can be appreciated and understood without knowledge of source or influence. The poet Krishna is mentioned by name, however, and his words, "fare forward, voyagers" instead of "fare well" are important, as they indicate the essential release from desires and are an exhortation to unselfishness or selflessness.

Section V contains the meaning of the explanation of time's paradoxical aspects:

> But to apprehend
> The point of intersection of the timeless
> With time, is an occupation for the saint.

The images of flowers, sunlight, and music which have recurred throughout these poems symbolize the ordinary man's experiences which, although fragmentary, nevertheless are "hints of grace": "The hint half guessed, the gift half understood, is Incarnation."

The resolution of themes in "Little Gidding" is accomplished by semi-repetitive exposition and some further development. The chapel at Little Gidding is a place "where prayer has been valid." The many allusions to writers and saints and saints who were writers is explained:

> . . . the communication
> Of the dead is tongued with fire beyond the language of the living.

The death of the four elements in Section II opens the way to spiritual resurrection. This lyric is followed by the poet's meeting, after an air raid, with a "familiar compound ghost"—the shade of all his past teachers—who tells him of the grief and failure of old age

> . . . unless restored by that refining fire

> Where you must move in measure like a dancer.

The historical theme is restated in the relationship of the present and the past as a reconciliation of opposites: "History may be servitude,/History may be freedom." And

> Whatever we inherit from the fortunate
> We have taken from the defeated.

The solution of the dilemma of the burden of Divine care for humanity, so bleakly felt in "East Coker," is here seen to be love, which binds us in our desires and alone is able to give the essential release from them.

The end of exploration, of the struggle with words and of all human actions "Will be to arrive where we started/And to know the place for the first time." The moments of personal and historical experience are never lost:

> The moment of the rose and the moment of the yew-tree
> Are of equal duration. A people without history
> Is not redeemed from time, for history is a pattern
> Of timeless moments.

The way of purgation which requires the whole being has led to "complete simplicity" where "the fire and the rose are one."

For all their complexity, *Four Quartets* contains Eliot's most explicit poetry. The poems are specifically Christian, recording the progress of the soul toward salvation. The way in which the themes are at various levels interwoven to augment and illuminate one another, the control of language and rhythm, and the beauty and precision of the images allow some critics to call these quartets Eliot's finest achievement.

FRAMLEY PARSONAGE

Type of work: Novel
Author: Anthony Trollope (1815-1882)
Type of plot: Domestic romance
Time of plot: 1850's
Locale: "Barsetshire" and London
First published: 1861

Principal characters:
MARK ROBARTS, vicar of Framley in Barsetshire
FANNY, his wife
LUCY, his sister
LADY LUFTON, mistress of Framley Court, Mark's benefactress
LORD LUFTON, her son, Mark's close friend
SOWERBY, squire of Chaldicotes, acquaintance of Lord Lufton and Mark
MISS DUNSTABLE, Sowerby's benefactress
DR. THORNE, the man she married

Critique:

This novel is one of the long, leisurely Barchester series. It contains no great moral theme, but it does present some delightful portraits of ecclesiastical characters and other nineteenth-century figures. It is marked by slowly paced development of plot and by conversational interruptions from the author. Without stepping over into sentimentality, but rather maintaining a wise, ironical tone, the novel provides pleasant, heart-warming entertainment.

The Story:

Mark Robarts was the vicar of Framley, an appointment secured through Lady Lufton of Framley, who was very fond of him. He was ambitious, however, and he went to a house party at Chaldicotes, the estate of Mr. Sowerby, of whom Lady Lufton disapproved. Sowerby was notorious for living on other people's money, for he had long since run through his own fortune. While Mark was visiting him, Sowerby played on the vicar's sympathy to such an extent that Mark signed his name to a note for four hundred pounds. From Chaldicotes Mark went to another house party at Gatherum Castle, home of the Duke of Omnium. The Duke of Omnium was also an enemy of Lady Lufton. Mark felt the contacts he would make at these parties would help him in climbing

higher in his career.

When Mark returned home, he told Lord Lufton he had signed a note for Sowerby. Young Lufton could hardly believe a man of Mark's position would do such a thing, for Mark could not afford to pay the note and certainly he would never recover the money from Sowerby. Before Mark told his wife, Fanny, about the debt he had incurred, his father died and his sister Lucy came to live at Framley parsonage. During the next three months Lucy and Lord Lufton became very friendly. Lucy was a small girl without striking beauty, and inclined to be quiet, but when she was with Lord Lufton, she found herself talking with great ease.

When Sowerby's note came due, he asked Mark to sign another for five hundred pounds, a sum which would cover the first note and allow an additional hundred pounds for extras. Mark saw the treachery of Sowerby's scheme, but, unable to pay the note due, he was forced to sign.

Lady Lufton hinted to Fanny that she hoped to find a better match than Lucy for her son, but by this time the two young people had fallen in love with each other. Disturbed also by Mark's attentions to the Chaldicotes set, Lady Lufton sent Mr. Crawley, a strait-laced clergyman from the nearby austere parish of Hogglestock, to remonstrate with Mark. After his visit Mark resolved to act more in accordance with Lady Lufton's wishes.

One day Lord Lufton declared his love for Lucy and asked her to marry him. Lucy, mindful of Lady Lufton's feelings, said she could not love him. Lufton was full of disappointment and grief.

Sowerby informed Mark that the new prime minister had it in his power to appoint the new precentor at Barchester Cathedral. Through Sowerby's influence, Mark received the appointment. He bought a race horse from Sowerby to show his gratitude.

Sowerby, greatly in debt to the Duke of Omnium, was about to lose his estate. Sowerby's sister, Mrs. Harold Smith, was a close friend of Miss Dunstable, a middle-aged spinster whose father had left her a fortune made in patent medicine. Mrs. Smith suggested that Sowerby ask Miss Dunstable to marry him and to say frankly that he wanted her chiefly for her money, since Miss Dunstable herself was a forthright, outspoken woman. Sowerby sent his sister to propose for him. Although Miss Dunstable refused his proposal, she agreed to buy Chaldicotes and let Sowerby live in the house for the remainder of his life. She said she would marry only a man who was not interested in her money.

That man, she thought, was Dr. Thorne, a bachelor physician from Barsetshire. She had informed Dr. Thorne's niece of her admiration for him and the niece had tried to show her uncle how wonderful life would be with Miss Dunstable. He was shocked at the idea of proposing. Though Miss Dunstable talked to him alone at a party she gave in London, Dr. Thorne said nothing at all about marriage. Back home, he decided that Miss Dunstable would, after all, make an admirable wife. He wrote her a letter of proposal and was accepted.

Lord Lufton went to Norway on a fishing trip. While he was away, Mrs. Crawley became ill of typhoid fever at Hogglestock, and Lucy went to nurse her through her sickness. The Crawley children were taken to Framley parsonage against Crawley's will, for he felt they might become accustomed to comforts he could not afford.

Sowerby's second note was coming due. Mark could consider no plan to get him out of his difficulty. If he had to go to jail, he would go. If he had to forfeit the furniture in his house, he would forfeit it. But under no circumstances would he ever put his name to another note.

Lord Lufton returned from Norway and learned from his mother that she thought Lucy insignificant. When he heard Lucy was at Hogglestock, he went there and again asked her to marry him. She replied that she did indeed love him but she would not marry him unless his mother approved. At first Lady Lufton refused to consider the match, but when she saw how determined her son was to have Lucy, she gave in and actually asked Lucy to become her daughter-in-law.

Meanwhile, the bailiffs had come to Framley parsonage to take inventory of the furniture, which was to be sold to pay Mark's obligations. When Lord Lufton discovered what was going on, he dismissed the bailiffs and persuaded Mark to accept a loan for payment of the note.

Sowerby lived at Chaldicotes for only a short time before he disappeared, and Mark was relieved of worry over his foolish debt. Miss Dunstable married Dr. Thorne and, after the departure of Sowerby, moved into the house at Chaldicotes. Lucy married Lord Lufton and became mistress, at least nominally, of Framley Court. Fate seemed to have for each some fair reward.

FRANKENSTEIN

Type of work: Novel
Author: Mary Godwin Shelley (1797-1851)
Type of plot: Gothic romance
Time of plot: Eighteenth century
Locale: Europe
First published: 1817

Principal characters:
ROBERT WALTON, an explorer
VICTOR FRANKENSTEIN, an inventor
ELIZABETH, his foster sister
WILLIAM, his brother
JUSTINE, the Frankensteins' servant
CLERVAL, Victor's friend
THE MONSTER

Critique:

Frankenstein: or, The Modern Prometheus is a weird tale, a wholly incredible story told with little skill. Although not often read now, it is known very widely by name. The endurance of this Gothic romance depends on perhaps two factors. First, Mary Shelley would be remembered if she had written nothing, for she was the wife of Percy Bysshe Shelley under romantic and scandalous circumstances. Indeed, *Frankenstein* was written as a result of a conversation between Byron and the Shelleys. Second, the idea of creating a monster has wide appeal. *Frankenstein* has become part of the popular imagination.

The Story:

Walton was an English explorer whose ship was held fast in polar ice. As the company looked out over the empty ice field, they were astonished to see a sledge drawn by dogs speeding northward. The sledge driver looked huge and misshapen. That night an ice floe carried to the ship another sledge, one dog, and a man in weakened condition. When the newcomer learned that his was the second sledge sighted from the ship, he became much agitated.

Walton was greatly attracted to the man during his convalescence, and as they continued fast in the ice, the men had leisure to get acquainted. At last, after he had recovered somewhat from exposure and hunger, the man told Walton his story:

Victor Frankenstein was born of good family in Geneva. As a playmate for their son, the parents had adopted a lovely little girl of the same age. Victor and Elizabeth grew up as brother and sister. Much later another son, William, was born to the Frankensteins.

Victor early showed promise in the natural sciences. He devoured the works of Paracelsus and Albertus Magnus, and thought in his ignorance that they were the real masters. When he grew older, his father decided to send Victor to the university at Ingolstadt. There he soon learned all that his masters could teach him in the fields of natural science. Engaged in brilliant and terrible research, he stumbled by chance on the secret of creating life. Once he had that knowledge he could not rest until he had employed it to create a living being. By haunting the butcher shops and dissecting rooms, he soon had the necessary raw materials. With great cunning he fashioned an eight-foot monster and endowed him with life.

But as soon as he had created his monster, he was subject to strange misgivings. During the night the monster came to his bed. At the sight of that horrible face, he shrieked and frightened the monster away. The horror of his act prostrated him with a brain fever. His best friend, Henry Clerval, arrived from Geneva and helped to nurse him through his illness. He was unable to tell Clerval what he had done.

Terrible news came from Geneva. William, Victor's young brother, was dead by the hand of a murderer. He had been found strangled in a park, and a faithful family servant, Justine, had been charged with the crime. Victor hurried to Geneva.

At the trial Justine told a convincing story. She had been looking for William in the countryside and, returning after the city gates had been closed, had spent the night in a deserted hut. But she could not explain how a miniature from William's neck came to be in her pocket. Victor and Elizabeth believed the girl's story, but in spite of all their efforts Justine was convicted and condemned.

Depressed by these tragic events, Victor went hiking over the mountainous countryside. Far ahead on the glacier, he saw a strange, agile figure that filled him with horrible suspicions. Unable to overtake the figure, he sat down to rest. Suddenly the monster appeared before him. The creature demanded that Victor listen to his story.

When he left Victor's chambers in Ingolstadt, everyone he met screamed and ran away. Wandering confusedly, the monster finally found shelter in an abandoned hovel adjoining a cottage. By great stealth he remained there during daylight and at night sought berries for food. Through observation he began to learn the ways of man. Feeling an urge to friendship, he brought wood to the cottage every day. But when he attempted to make friends with the cottagers, he was repulsed with such fear and fury that his heart became bitter toward all men. When he saw William playing in the park, he strangled the boy and took the miniature from his neck. Then during the night he came upon Justine in the hut and put the picture in her pocket.

Presently the monster made a horrible demand. He insisted that Victor fashion a mate for him who would give him love and companionship. The monster threatened to ravage and kill at random if Victor refused the request. But if Victor agreed, the monster promised to take his mate to the wilds of South America where they would never again be seen by man. It was a hard choice but Victor felt that he must accept.

Victor left for England with his friend Clerval. After parting from his friend he went to the distant Orkneys and began his task. He was almost ready to animate the gross mass of flesh when his conscience stopped him. He could not let the two monsters mate and spawn a race of monsters. He destroyed his work.

The monster was watching at a window. Angered to see his mate destroyed, he forced his way into the house and warned Victor that a terrible punishment would fall upon the young man on his wedding night. Then the monster escaped by sea. Later, to torment his maker, he fiendishly killed Clerval.

Victor was suspected of the crime. Released for lack of evidence, he went back to Geneva. There he and Elizabeth were married. Although Victor was armed and alert, the monster got into the nuptial chamber and strangled the bride. Victor shot at him, but he escaped again. Victor vowed eternal chase until the monster could be killed.

That was Victor's story. Weakened by exposure, he died there in the frozen North, with Elizabeth, William, Justine, and Clerval unavenged. Then to the dead man's cabin came the monster, and Walton, stifling his fear, addressed the gigantic, hideous creature. Victor's was the greater crime, the monster said. He had created a man, a man without love or friend or soul. He deserved his punishment. So saying, the monster vanished over the ice field.

FRATERNITY

Type of work: Novel
Author: John Galsworthy (1867-1933)
Type of plot: Social criticism
Time of plot: Early twentieth century
Locale: London
First published: 1909

Principal characters:
HILARY DALLISON, a well-to-do writer
BIANCA, his wife, an artist
STEPHEN, his brother
CECILIA, Stephen's wife and Bianca's sister
THYME, daughter of Stephen and Cecilia
MR. STONE, father of Bianca and Cecilia
IVY BARTON, a model
MRS. HUGHS, a seamstress
MR. HUGHS, her husband

Critique:

In both his novels and his plays Galsworthy reflected the social problems of his age. His conscience was bothered by the lack of understanding shown by the members of his own class, the intellectual and moneyed upper middle class. In this novel, as in the others, his social satire is expressed by a delineation of the complacency of the upper classes, rather than by an analysis of the lower classes and their situation. Here also, as in other works, his diagnosis is not profound, nor does he attempt to offer any remedy for the problems he shows. Some readers may feel that this volume shows how Galsworthy's efforts to understand his age and his indignation at what he finds lead to no satisfactory solution in the end. Yet *Fraternity* is generally regarded as one of Galsworthy's best works of fiction, aside from that series of upper middle-class novels upon which his fame rests, *The Forsyte Saga.*

The Story:

Bianca Dallison had begun the chain of events by asking her writer husband to find a model for her painting "The Shadow." Through a friendly artist Hilary had located a girl from the country who suited his wife. The girl, Ivy Barton, was very attractive, and after she had finished posing for Bianca the Dallisons tried to help her find work. They had also found her a place to live with the Dallisons' seamstress, a Mrs. Hughs.

But Ivy Barton, through no fault of her own, began to create trouble in the Hughs household when Mr. Hughs became enamored of her and Mrs. Hughs became extremely jealous. One day Mrs. Hughs told Cecilia Dallison her troubles at home. Cecilia told Mrs. Hughs' story to the rest of the family. The Dallisons, all very much interested in social problems, wished to help the girl and the Hughs family. But the situation was a delicate one. Their interest was heightened by the comment of Mr. Stone that in the lower classes each of them had a counterpart, a shadow, and that everyone was bound together by the bonds of fraternity in the brotherhood of man. Mr. Stone was writing a book on that very subject.

Hilary Dallison found that the girl's work as a model was not regular and that she was finding it necessary to pose in the nude. He found her steady employment as a copyist for his father-in-law,

Mr. Stone, who in his old age had embarked upon his strange philosophical work on the brotherhood of man. Bianca Dallison did not like the idea, for Mr. Stone lived with her and her husband. She began to be extremely jealous of the little model, even though it had been years since she and her husband had lived as man and wife.

In spite of his wife's jealousy, it was Hilary who first investigated the trouble at the Hughs'. He found no one but Mr. Hughs at home. The visit only made the situation worse, for Hughs became convinced that Hilary was having an affair with Ivy. Hughs began to loiter about the Dallison house and to follow the model home when she finished her work with Mr. Stone. When Cecilia also learned that Hughs was beating his wife, the family decided that the situation was dangerous for the model and for Hilary. Cecilia tried to convince Hilary that the girl should be sent away and that he should stop trying to help Mr. and Mrs. Hughs. He only smiled at her suggestions.

Sometime later Hilary followed Hughs when the latter trailed Ivy home. Hilary was somewhat dismayed to discover that Hughs followed only to prevent the girl from meeting anyone else, including Hilary. Nevertheless, Hilary met the girl in a park after she had shaken her follower. Ivy let Hilary notice that her clothing was very shabby, and he, feeling sorry for her, took her into a shop and purchased a complete outfit for her. His deed won her complete devotion; she was in love with Hilary Dallison.

After leaving Ivy at the store where they had purchased her outfit, Hilary went to spend the evening at his club; he knew that his wife would not mind his absence from her. When he got home, however, he found her in his room. They kissed, and for a moment forgot they had agreed not to live as man and wife. Then the moment passed, and Bianca fled to her room. Needing someone to talk to, Hilary went down to Mr. Stone's room and had a cup of cocoa.

The daughter of Stephen and Cecilia Dallison, Thyme, also tried to help the Hughs family. Her interest was the Hughs' tiny baby. She also noted that Ivy had new clothes and guessed that her uncle had bought them for the girl. The word quickly ran through the family, and Stephen, trying to make Hilary see how the others looked at the situation, told him that Bianca was bound to be jealous, even though they did not live as man and wife. Hilary felt that the celibacy she imposed on him had taken away any grounds for jealousy she might have.

That same afternoon Hughs went to the Dallison home and tried to tell Bianca about her husband's affair with Ivy. Although she refused to listen to the man, the incident roused her emotions and suspicions. At least her pride was hurt. That evening Hilary and Bianca tried to talk over the matter, but all they succeeded in doing was hurting each other. Bianca refused to believe that her husband was innocent of any intentions toward the model and had simply bought the girl some clothing because he felt sorry for her.

With his sister-in-law's help, Hilary found another room for Ivy. Hoping to solve the problem of Bianca's jealousy, he also told her not to come to his house to copy for Mr. Stone. When Hughs returned home that night and learned that Ivy had left his house, he beat his wife and wounded her with a bayonet. As a result, he was put into prison for several weeks. During the time he was in prison the Hughs' baby died, for Mrs. Hughs was too upset to nurse him.

Old Mr. Stone became very ill and unhappy at the same time, for he missed the company of the model as well as the copying she had done for him. In an effort to help her father, Bianca sought out Ivy and had her return to be with the old man part of every day. Because of his child's death and the girl's return to work at Hilary's house, it seemed as if the problem would still be unsolved when Hughs returned from prison.

To avoid a repetition of the whole distasteful situation, Hilary resolved to go to Europe. He made up his mind that he would go alone, even though Ivy was in love with him and wished to go along. His wife, because of her conscience, resolved to help the girl in Hilary's absence. When she went to the girl's rooms, however, she found her belongings packed. It dawned on her that in spite of his resolve her husband was taking the model with him. Bianca left the house in a fury just as her husband arrived. Her jealousy and anger were wasted, however, for after she left, when Ivy kissed him, Hilary realized that he could never live for long with a girl from the lower classes. Flinging all the money he had with him on the bed, he left alone. He took rooms for himself in London and then sent a letter to Bianca through his brother Stephen. He told her of his decision to stop seeing Ivy and his further decision not to return to a marriage that was only a mockery.

THE FRENCH REVOLUTION

Type of work: History
Author: Thomas Carlyle (1795-1881)
Time: Last quarter of the eighteenth century
Locale: Paris and elsewhere in France
First published: 1837

Principal personages:
KING LOUIS XV
KING LOUIS XVI
QUEEN MARIE ANTOINETTE
DANTON
MARAT
ROBESPIERRE
TURGOT
NAPOLEON BONAPARTE
COUNT FERSEN, Swedish admirer of Marie Antoinette

The French Revolution is a landmark in the history of nineteenth-century English literature, the work that, after the comparative public failure of *Sartor Resartus* (q.v.), helped to establish Carlyle's star in its ascendancy. In its dramatic picture of the French Revolution it offered the general reader an estimate of an event that had disturbed and shocked the consciences of his grandparents. It offered a measure of revolutionary and socially disruptive movements that was neither optimistic and blindly trustful of progress (here Carlyle differed from Utilitarian friends) nor pessimistic and horrified, as Edmund Burke had been at the time of the Revolution. Finally, and perhaps most important for us, *The French Revolution* was a more successful self-realization for Carlyle than the comparatively nebulous explorations of ideas which we find in *Sartor Resartus*. That earlier work presents us Carlyle's ideas in a kind of cloud formation that conceals whatever terrain of fact and real human experience they float over; *The French Revolution* presents the same ideas brought into relation to and supported by a bewilderingly rich body of facts: the day by day events of the disturbing French years.

Impressive as is Carlyle's method of digesting and arranging the body of facts, still more memorable is the way he commands the facts to do his will. Like an Old Testament prophet, Carlyle rides the hurricane and directs the storm of the fall of absolute monarchy in France. He produces not just another history of a vexed period, full of rationalized information. It is true of Carlyle that his view of one period of history is always on the verge of becoming a vision of *all* human history. The French women who march on Versailles stand for the passionate outbreak of all oppressed human beings, and the sorrows of Marie Antoinette in the Concièrgerie stand for the agonies of all trivial human beings carried to their doom by forces they cannot dominate.

It is possible to indicate some of the means that Carlyle employs to create his apocalyptic vision—a vision, not of last things, but certainly of the forces that combine to drive history onward. The arrangement of the facts is rigorously chronological. The book begins with the death-pangs of King Louis XV; these are at once represented as the death-throes not of one aged monarch but of a regime or way of life that once justified itself but which is now a hollow reality. The book continues with an account of the suicidal follies of the young king, Louis XVI, and his pretty and thoughtless wife, Marie Antoinette. It notices the efforts of some of the king's ministers, Necker, Turgot, and others, to stem the advancing tide: to restore financial soundness and yet provide money for all who thought they

1272

had a right to spend it. Carlyle, often with a somewhat uneven pace which permits him to stop for angry or compassionate meditation when he wishes to point out the "inevitable" chain of disaster and struggle, continues his year by year and month by month account. He tells of the meeting of the Estates General, the Tennis Court Oath, the march on Versailles, the various attempts to frame a constitution, the degeneration of the relation between the royal couple and the Revolutionary Government, the royal family's attempted escape to Varennes, the successive decapitations of king and queen, the succession of leaders who could not lead but had to dictate by harangue and outright terror, and, finally, the end of the revolution at the hands of Napoleon Bonaparte, who brought order with a "whiff of grapeshot" in 1795.

Carlyle, at the end of his work, speaks of a ship that finally is over the bar after much labor and peril from counter winds; and this is certainly the effect of his narrative. Despite its complexity, his story is the single account of a set of events that give a full demonstration of the glories and horrors of revolution, a period of history that was inevitable but not, because of its inevitability, admirable.

In dramatizing a mighty and perilous passage that involved not the French nation alone but all humanity, Thoma Carlyle was able to transform his account of actual events into an apocalyptic statement about man that does not seem to belong to any particular time at all. He did so by means of his style of presentation and by passages of direct, explicit interpretation. Perhaps it is the style that is most decisive. Never before or since has an English-writing historian written a book like this history of Carlyle's. The narrative is couched in the present tense, wearing but hortatory; what occurs happens not in a safely distant past, but here and now. The sentimentality of the French *philosophes* and the ignorant and brutal enthusiasms

of the mob threaten us the readers, as Carlyle drags us through mountains of detail and event. Moreover, Carlyle frequently interrupts the forward movement of the narrative to harangue some of the chief actors in his story—Danton, Mirabeau, Marie Antoinette—and as we read it seems possible that they may listen to him and escape what we well know was their historical fate. Some of the harangues, of course, speak not to the historical personages but to us and suggest that we (even more than a century after the appearance of the book) may escape our historical fate if we will but listen to Thomas Carlyle. Or if we may not escape it, we shall understand it better after reading *The French Revolution*.

Implication becomes explicit in innumerable passages like the following brief one:

Or, apart from all Transcendentalism, is it not a plain truth of sense, which the duller mind can even consider as a truism, that human things wholly are in continual movement, and action and reaction; working continually forward, phasis after phasis, by unalterable laws, towards prescribed issues? How often must we say, and yet not rightly lay to heart: The seed that is sown, it will spring! Given the summer's blossoming, then there is also given the autumnal withering: so is it ordered not with seedfields only, but with transactions, arrangements, philosophies, societies, French Revolutions, whatsoever man works with in this lower world.

A great body of French fact attests to what the drifting clouds of *Sartor Resartus* suggested. It is the "law" of life that social forms become old clothes unless they are worn by the people who have some kind of faith: faith in duty, faith in silent work, faith in, finally, the transcendental, self-realizing movement of some force, some kind of deity which is realizing itself in the total movements of human history and particularly in the great men who rise above themselves and command the attention of the rest of mankind, pointing a finger to show the way all men should "now" go.

Carlyle devoted later books to such demonstration. Cromwell, Frederick the Great, and a whole company of great men in *On Heroes and Hero-Worship* (1841)—all of these so exhort us. The essential tragedy of the French Revolution, as Carlyle saw it, was that here was a congeries of events that cried out for a hero and found only destruction and social chaos. It lacked, among other things, a contemporary like Carlyle to annotate that chaos. But the French people's loss is our gain. Upon their agonies Carlyle rests a view of history as a scroll of events always on the verge of parting and revealing to us—in the heavens or in the depths of our beings—the essential divine plan. *The French Revolution* was actually written and rewritten at 5, Cheyne Row, in London. In spirit, however, it was written on the isle of Patmos in the Aegean where, we were told, a still more famous revelation was composed.

FRIAR BACON AND FRIAR BUNGAY

Type of work: Drama
Author: Robert Greene (1558-1592)
Type of plot: Pseudo-historical chronicle
Time of plot: Thirteenth century
Locale: England
First presented: c. 1589

Principal characters:
HENRY III, King of England
EDWARD, Prince of Wales
LACY, Earl of Lincoln
ROGER BACON, a Franciscan friar
BUNGAY, a Suffolk conjurer
JAQUES VANDERMAST, a German conjurer
ELINOR, Princess of Castile
MARGARET, daughter of the Keeper of Fressingfield Park

Critique:

This chronicle play does not show true dramatic structure; it is simply a series of scenes presenting interesting happenings. Although Greene professed to have used historical material, the action is pure fiction. So far as is known, neither the Emperor of Germany nor the King of Castile ever made a visit to England. For the modern reader the interest of the action lies in the magical powers of Friar Bacon and in the love affair between Lacy and Margaret. *The Honorable History of Friar Bacon and Friar Bungay* is regarded as one of the most notable of pre-Shakespearean dramas.

The Story:

When Prince Edward returned from hunting in a downcast mood, Lacy remarked on his lord's temper. It remained for Ralph, the court fool, to hit on the truth. The hunting party had stopped for refreshments at the keeper's lodge in Fressingfield Park, and Prince Edward had fallen in love with Margaret, the keeper's daughter.

Plans were laid to win Margaret's love for Edward, for the maid was modest and would keep her virtue for her husband. Ralph proposed that Edward should dress in the jester's motley, and Ralph should dress as the prince. They would then go to Oxford and enlist the help of Friar Roger Bacon, since only

magic would win over the girl. Lacy was to go to the fair at Harleston to spy on Margaret there and to press a suit on behalf of the prince.

At Oxford, Friar Bacon and his poor scholar Miles received a deputation of learned doctors. Burden, their spokesman, asked about certain rumors they had heard. It was said that Friar Bacon had fashioned a great head of brass and with it he was going to raise a wall of brass around all of England. Bacon admitted that he planned such a project. Burden doubted whether even Friar Bacon could accomplish such a mighty deed.

To demonstrate his power, Friar Bacon had a devil bring a tavern hostess from Henley, a woman with whom Burden had spent the previous day. Thus the doctors were convinced of Bacon's powers.

At Harleston, Lacy approached Margaret. Although the earl was dressed as a farmer, his manners were so elegant that Margaret was attracted to him. Lacey was minded to press a suit in his own behalf.

At court, meanwhile, King Henry received the King of Castile, his daughter Elinor, and the Emperor of Germany. Negotiations were under way to betroth Elinor to Prince Edward. The princess, having seen a portrait of Edward, was much inclined to love the prince. The emperor had brought with him a German conjurer, Vandermast, to test his powers against the wise men of England. The royal party departed for Oxford to find Friar Bacon.

With the jester disguised as the prince and Edward disguised as a gentleman in waiting, the prince's party met the friar and Miles at Oxford. An argument developed between Miles and the others. To save his scholar, Friar Bacon froze Edward's sword in its scabbard. After rebuking the prince for trying to disguise himself, he invited Edward into his cell. There he let the prince look into a magic glass which showed Margaret and Lacy at Fressingfield.

Friar Bungay was revealing the secret of Lacy's identity to Margaret as Edward watched from afar. Margaret was troubled, for she had fallen in love with Lacy. When Lacy entered, he declared at once his desire to wed Margaret. Friar Bungay was about to perform the ceremony on the spot, but the anguished prince called on Friar Bacon to stop the wedding. The friar obliged by striking Bungay dumb and whisking him away to Oxford.

Edward, posting to Fressingfield in great haste, charged Lacy with treachery and threatened to kill him. Lacy admitted his guilt and prepared to submit, but Margaret pleaded valiantly for the cause of true love and begged Edward to kill her instead. Edward, marveling at his own weakness, changed his mind and gave his permission for Lacy to marry Margaret.

At Oxford, the Emperor of Germany had Vandermast dispute with Friar Bungay. Bungay conjured up the tree that guarded the Garden at Hesperides. In return Vandermast brought in Hercules and commanded him to tear the branches from the tree. Triumphantly the German challenged Friar Bungay to make Hercules stop, but Bungay had to admit that he was vanquished. When Friar Bacon arrived, Hercules, to the emperor's chagrin, ceased his task immediately for fear of Bacon. To demonstrate the eminence of Oxford, Friar Bacon then forced Hercules to transport Vandermast back to Hapsburg.

Two squires came to seek the hand of Margaret. Both were wealthy and insistent, and the keeper asked his daughter to choose between them. Margaret was evasive and put off her answer for ten days, for she was sure Lacy would return by that time. After the squires left, a messenger came with a letter and a sack of gold. In the letter Margaret read that Lacy had chosen to marry a Spanish lady in waiting to Princess Elinor, and he sent the gold as a dowry for her own wedding. In great grief, Margaret gave the gold to the messenger and vowed to enter a convent.

Working in his cell, Friar Bacon was at the climax of his experiments, for he had completed with much labor the brazen head. Tired from wrestling with spirits, he lay down to sleep. Miles was to watch the head and wake his master as soon as it should speak. During the night the head made a great noise and said, "Time is." Thinking those words unimportant, Miles rested on. The head made more noise and said, "Time was." Again Miles did not arouse the friar. A third time the head spoke: "Time has been." Lightning flashed and a great hand appeared and broke the head with a hammer.

Then Miles awoke Friar Bacon, who knew at once that the blundering Miles had ruined his work. No wall of brass would ever surround England. In his wrath the friar sent Miles to wander homeless with a devil to torment him. After he left Oxford, however, Miles made the best of a bad situation. He got on the devil's back and went with him to Hell, where he was engaged as a tapster.

King Henry and the King of Castile were both pleased that Elinor and Edward had made a match. Lacy, thinking still of Margaret, spoke so persuasively of her beauty that the king sanctioned their marriage as well. Elinor was particularly gracious in suggesting a double wedding. The happy Lacy set out for Fressingfield to seek his bride.

Friar Bacon broke the sad news of the brazen head to Friar Bungay. As he finished his tale, two young scholars came in to ask permission to look into Friar Bacon's glass; they wanted to see what their fathers were doing. The fathers, who were the two squires seeking Margaret's hand, were fighting a duel. As the sons watched, the squires were stabbed to death. The sons then fought and each mortally wounded the other. In sorrow, Friar Bacon broke his magic glass.

In spite of her father's remonstrances, Margaret was preparing to enter a nunnery when Lacy rode up to claim his bride. Reproached for his cruel letter, he explained he had written it to test her constancy. Margaret, yielding to his entreaties, accompanied him back to court.

The double wedding was solemnized with royal pomp. Before the wedding feast Friar Bacon made a prophecy of the future of England. He foresaw a period of triumph and peace under a fair ruler who would exalt the glory of England over all other nations. Not understanding that reference to Queen Elizabeth, Henry called the prophecy mystical and led the guests to the dining hall.

FRITHIOF'S SAGA

Type of work: Poem
Author: Esaias Tegnér (1782-1846)
Type of plot: Heroic epic
Time of plot: Eleventh century
Locale: Scandinavia
First published: 1825

Principal characters:
FRITHIOF, a Viking adventurer and fighter
INGEBORG, a noblewoman loved by Frithiof
HELGE, and
HALFDAN, brother-kings in Scandinavia
HRING, a petty king married to Ingeborg

Critique:

Though a tale of ancient Scandinavia, *Frithiof's Saga* was told in a modern spirit by Tegnér when he put the old story into a narrative poem of twenty-four cantos, each canto done in a different meter. Frithiof himself is more akin to a modern hero than he is to the great warriors of other Scandinavian tales, folk heroes like Beowulf. Tegnér's effort is similar to that of Tennyson, in that he attempted to shape the epic material of an ancient Norse story into nineteenth-century poetic form. Although the poem lacks the simplicity and power of true Norse poetry, the imagery is memorable and the lyricism sweet and beautiful.

The Story:

In the ancient days of Scandinavia there was a king named Bele, who had two sons, Helge and Halfdan. King Bele also had a daughter, Ingeborg, a very beautiful girl. As King Bele grew old and near death, he called to him his friend of former days, Thorsten Vikingsson, who had been loyal to the king in peace and battle for many years and who was also near the end of his days. The king told his sons of the help that Thorsten Vikingsson had given him in past days and warned his sons to keep the friendship of Thorsten's son, Frithiof. Frithiof had grown up with the companionship of King Bele's daughter Ingeborg and loved her and her brothers. But after the deaths of King Bele and old Thorsten, who were both laid to rest in burial mounds overlooking a fjord, the sons of Bele forgot the warning that their father had given them, and their friendship toward Frithiof cooled.

When Frithiof, who had long loved Ingeborg sued for her hand from her brothers, they refused his request. Frithiof, angered and humiliated, vowed that he would find his revenge and that he never would carry out his father's request to help the brother-kings.

Not long thereafter, when King Hring made war upon the brothers, they sent for Frithiof to help them. Frithiof, remembering his vows, continued to play at chess and ignored their summons.

King Hring, successful in his campaign against the sons of Bele, made them promise to give him Ingeborg as his wife.

Meanwhile Ingeborg had taken refuge in the temple of Balder. Frithiof, disdainful of the sanctity of the temple, had visited her there, where they exchanged rings. Frithiof thus ran the risk of Balder's wrath.

To punish him for violating the temple, the brother-kings sent Frithiof to collect tribute from the inhabitants of the Faroe islands. Frithiof, with his foster brother, set sail for the Faroes in *Ellida*, the best ship in the North country. It was said of *Ellida* that it could even understand the speech of men.

During the trip a violent storm came up and the ship almost foundered. Frithiof

1278

broke the ring he had received from Ingeborg and gave the shards to his men, so that none of the crew might enter the kingdom of the sea-goddess without gold. When the storm subsided, as it did after the men had conquered a pair of sea-spirits who rode against them on the backs of whales, the ship reached the Faroe islands in safety. Yarl Angantyr, ruler of the islands, let the tribute be collected for friendship's sake, and then Frithiof departed again for his homeland in Scandinavia.

Upon his return Frithiof heard that the brother-kings had burned his hall. Learning that the kings were celebrating the midsummer feast at the grove of Balder, he went there to confront them. Upon his arrival he found few people, but among them were Helge and his queen, who was anointing the image of the god.

Frithiof threw the purse with the tribute money into Helge's face with such force that Helge's teeth were knocked out. As Frithiof turned to leave, he saw on the arm of Helge's queen the great ring of gold he had given to Ingeborg when they had exchanged vows. Frithiof snatched the ring from the queen's arm, and when she fell to the ground because of his violence the god's image overturned into the sacred fire which, blazing up, destroyed the temple.

Helge pursued Frithiof to punish him, but pursuit was impossible because the royal ships had been damaged by Frithiof and his men. In his anger Frithiof pulled with such might upon the oars of his ship that its powerful oars broke like kindling.

Frithiof's violence against Helge and his queen and the double profanation of Balder's temple made the warrior an outcast from his homeland. A true son of the Vikings, he took to the sea and battled with haughty sea-kings, whom he slew. But in spite of his outlawry he permitted traders to travel the seaways unmolested. When he earned great glory as a fighter and much gold through his exploits, Frithiof sought once again to return to his homeland in the North.

Disguising himself as a salt-burner, he visited the land of the brother-kings' enemy, King Hring, who had long since married Ingeborg, Frithiof's beloved. Hring, recognizing Frithiof but keeping his counsel to himself, commanded that the warrior be seated next to him at the head of the table.

Frithiof remained in the hall of King Hring. Ingeborg spoke but little to him, because she was now the wife of another man. But she remembered that she and Frithiof had once exchanged rings, and she was still in love with him.

During his stay with Hring, Frithiof saved the king and Ingeborg from death when their sleigh fell through the ice and went under the water. Frithiof dragged the sleigh, with its occupants and horses, back upon the surface of the ice.

One day, while he and the king were alone in the woods, Frithiof was tempted to kill Hring while he slept, but he conquered his temptation and threw away his sword. Awaking, the king told Frithiof, who was still disguised, that he had known from the first night who his guest was.

Frithiof wished to leave the household of Hring, but the good king would not allow him to depart. Instead, Hring gave up Ingeborg to Frithiof and made the warrior guardian of the kingdom. Soon afterward Hring died and Frithiof was named to follow him upon the throne. When Helge and Halfdan, the brother-kings, went to war against their old enemy, they were defeated. Helge was slain in battle by Frithiof, and Halfdan was made to swear fealty to his conqueror.

THE FROGS

Type of work: Drama
Author: Aristophanes (c. 448-385 B.C.)
Type of plot: Humorous satire
Time of plot: Fifth century B.C.
Locale: Underworld
First presented: 405 B.C.

> *Principal characters:*
> BACCHUS, god of wine and revelry
> XANTHIAS, his slave
> HERCULES, mythological hero
> CHARON, ferryman of Hades
> EURIPIDES, a famous Greek playwright
> AESCHYLUS, another Greek dramatist

Critique:

So vigorous was the mind of Aristophanes that his comedies extant today maintain vitality which is still a sharp and penetrating comment upon human nature. One does not need to be a scholar to understand and love the work of Aristophanes. Satirist for all ages, he wrote to expose the timeless foibles and follies of human nature.

The Story:

Wishing to visit the underworld, Bacchus set out with his slave, Xanthias, to visit Hercules, from whom the god of the vine hoped to get directions for his visit to the lower regions. On the way Xanthias continued to grumble and moan about his many bundles. Xanthias was really riding a donkey, but he complained loudly until Bacchus finally lost patience and suggested that perhaps Xanthias would like to carry the donkey for a while.

Hercules, when consulted, suggested that Bacchus allow himself to be killed and thus arrive in the land of the dead. But Bacchus wanted to go there alive because he was anxious to see and talk to the great playwrights, the critics having told him that all who were good were dead and gone. He was particularly anxious to meet Euripides. Hercules advised him to be content with the playwrights still alive. Bacchus argued that none of them was good enough for him,

and so, after getting directions from Hercules, he started out, Xanthias still complaining about his bundles.

They came to the River Acheron and met Charon, who ferried Bacchus across. The grim ferryman insisted, however, that Bacchus row the boat, and he made Xanthias walk around the margin of the stream since Xanthias had dishonored himself by not volunteering for a naval victory. Xanthias tried to excuse himself on the grounds that he had had sore eyes, but Charon refused to listen.

While Bacchus and Xanthias talked to Charon, a chorus of frogs set up a hoarse croaking, imitating the noisy plebeians at the theater with a senseless kind of hooting. Bacchus sprained his back with his rowing and the frogs thought his groans quite amusing.

Safely on the other side, Bacchus paid his fare and joined his slave. The two met a monster which Bacchus took care to avoid until it turned into a beautiful woman. They found their way with difficulty to the doorway of Pluto's realm. Xanthias still grumbled because he had his heavy bundles.

At the entrance to Hades, Bacchus foolishly pretended to be Hercules—a mistake on his part, for Aeacus, the doorman, raised a clamor over the theft of Cerberus, the watchdog. When Aeacus threatened all sorts of punishment, Bacchus revealed himself as he really was.

1280

Xanthias accused him of cowardice but Bacchus stoutly denied the charge.

Bacchus and Xanthias decided to change characters. Xanthias pretended to be Hercules and Bacchus took up the bundles his slave had carried. But when servants of Proserpine entered and offered Xanthias a fine entertainment, Bacchus demanded his rightful character once more.

Aeacus returned, eager to punish someone, and Xanthias gave him permission to beat Bacchus. Bacchus said that he was a deity; therefore, they should not beat him. Xanthias countered by saying that since Bacchus was an immortal he need not mind the beating. Aeacus decided they both should be beaten soundly.

Aeacus finally decided to take them both to Pluto and Proserpine, to discover who really was the deity. Aeacus said Bacchus was apparently a gentleman and Xanthias agreed wholeheartedly, saying Bacchus did not do anything except dissipate and carouse.

In Pluto's realm they found two dead dramatists, Aeschylus and Euripides, fighting for favor. The rule in Hades was that the most famous man of any art or craft ate at Pluto's table until some more talented man in his field should die and come to Hades. Aeschylus had held the seat Euripides was now claiming.

Aeacus said that the dramatists intended to measure their plays line for line by rules and compasses to determine the superior craftsman. The quarreling dramatists debated, accusing each of the other's faults. Aeschylus said he was at a disadvantage because Euripides' plays died with him and were present to help him, whereas his own plays still lived on earth.

Bacchus offered to be the judge, and each dramatist then began to defend himself. In the midst of their violent quarrel Pluto appeared. Bacchus ordered each to recite from his own works. Euripides seemed to have the worst of this contest, but Bacchus wisely refused to judge so as not to make either playwright angry with him. Pluto wearily insisted that he pick one winner and take his choice back with him to the upper world in order to stop needless rivalry in Hades.

At last Bacchus voted for Aeschylus. Euripides complained at the choice. He was consoled, however, when Pluto said he might be sure of a good meal in the underworld, while Aeschylus would be burdened forever with the task of earning his living by his attempts to reform folly and evil in the world above.

THE FRUIT OF THE TREE

Type of work: Novel
Author: Edith Wharton (1862-1937)
Type of plot: Social criticism
Time of plot: Late nineteenth century
Locale: The United States
First published: 1907

Principal characters:

JOHN AMHERST, an assistant mill manager
BESSY WESTMORE, his first wife, owner of the mills
JUSTINE BRENT, his second wife
MR. LANGHOPE, Bessy's father
DR. WYANT, Justine's former suitor

Critique:

In this novel Edith Wharton is true to form in her investigation of a society of constricted ideas and stillborn inspirations, in which the women are pampered and the men are sheltered from the realities of basic life. More than that, the contrast between the rich, who waste themselves in frivolity, and the workers is brought into painful relief by Edith Wharton's refined but direct prose style. The contrast is embodied in Amherst, who wants to bring his sophisticated intelligence to bear upon the very real problems of the workers, and who is therefore bound to be misunderstood.

The Story:

When Justine Brent, a nurse who was visiting Mrs. Harry Dressel at Hanaford, volunteered to care for Dillon, an operator who had been injured at Westmore Mills, she was approached by John Amherst, the assistant manager of the mills. Amherst deplored the miserable living and working conditions of the mill workers and, since Dillon's accident had been the result of these conditions, wanted to use his case to show the need for improvement to Bessy Westmore, the newly widowed owner of the mills who was due to make an inspection tour the following day.

The next day Amherst conducted Bessy Westmore through the mills.

Bessy, touched by Dillon's case, decided to stay at Hanaford for a while. She recalled that she and Justine had attended school together before Justine's parents had lost their wealth.

Bessy and Amherst made plans to improve the living conditions of the workers, and this association finally led to their marriage. Amherst, hoping to make Westmore Mills a model of humanitarianism, was disillusioned to learn that Bessy was not willing to sacrifice the time or the money to accomplish this end.

Some time later, Justine came to Lynbrook, the Amherst country house, to be a companion to Bessy, who was not feeling well. Amherst, meanwhile, spent most of his time at the mills in Hanaford.

Bessy, to compensate for Amherst's long absences, began to entertain lavishly, at the same time confiding her bitterness and loneliness to Justine. Later, Amherst decided to manage a friend's cotton mill in the South.

Justine wrote to Amherst saying that Bessy needed him. Amherst replied that he would not return and, in a postscript, asked her not to permit Bessy to ride a particularly spirited horse they owned. Bessy, learning of his request, later took the horse out into the frost-covered countryside. There Bessy suffered an accident which seriously injured her spinal cord.

She was taken home and looked after by Dr. Wyant, a local doctor whose proposal Justine had refused some time before. A surgeon and various other consultants were also summoned. Bessy remained paralyzed after an operation; Justine knew that the sick woman would never recover.

By this time Amherst was on a business trip into a remote part of South America, and Bessy's father was in Europe.

One day, while Justine was caring for her alone, Bessy regained enough consciousness from her opiate state to plead with Justine to relieve her pain. Justine, convinced that she was doing the right thing, later gave Bessy an overdose of morphine. When Dr. Wyant came into the room, Justine told him that Bessy was dead. Dr. Wyant seemed to sense what had happened.

A year and a half later, Amherst was back at the Westmore Mills. Bessy had left half her fortune to Cicely, her daughter by her first marriage, and the other half to Amherst. He lived at Hanaford and continued his plans of reconstruction.

In the meantime Justine was taking care of Cicely and an intimate friendship developed between the two. Later, when she went to visit Mrs. Dressel in Hanaford, Justine met Amherst again, a romance developed between them, and they were married. Cicely went to live with her grandfather. Justine took an active part in Amherst's work.

Dr. Wyant, who had left Lynwood and married, now needed money, and he came to Justine and threatened to expose her mercy killing of Bessy unless she arranged to have Amherst write him a letter of recommendation to Mr. Langhope, who could give him a responsible hospital post. Justine, realizing that Dr. Wyant had become a narcotic addict, could not in her conscience arrange a recommendation for him. When she went out of the room, Amherst came in. Learning that Dr. Wyant was in financial straits, Amherst wrote him a letter of recommendation in gratitude for his services to Bessy. On her return Justine told her husband that Dr. Wyant was not qualified for the hospital post. Dr. Wyant, in retaliation, charged Justine with the mercy killing, and left.

Intellectually, Amherst approved of Justine. Emotionally, he was horrified at what she had done. Their relationship became strained.

When Dr. Wyant was appointed to the hospital post, Amherst remembered the letter of recommendation. He knew that if Mr. Langhope were told about Dr. Wyant's addiction to narcotics, the doctor would in turn disclose Justine's crime. Amherst told Justine that if Mr. Langhope thought that she had been in love with Amherst when she killed Bessy, he and Justine would have to give up the mills, go away, and start a new life. Justine secretly went to New York to see Mr. Langhope and told him the truth about Dr. Wyant and herself. She then promised to disappear if Mr. Langhope would continue on his former terms with Amherst. Mr. Langhope agreed.

Justine, returning to Hanaford, told Amherst that Mr. Langhope had taken the news very well. In the course of the following months Amherst's horror of Justine's crime caused their relationship to deteriorate even more. At last Justine went to Michigan to resume her nursing career, thus fulfilling her promise to Mr. Langhope.

A year later Cicely became ill. Mr. Langhope, realizing that she needed Justine's love, asked Justine to come back to Amherst so that she could be close to Cicely. When Amherst learned why Justine had left him, he felt love for her and remorse for his attitude. They continued, however, to feel somewhat estranged.

About a year later Amherst, speaking at the dedication of the mill workers' new recreational center, gave a stirring tribute to Bessy who, he said, had herself drawn up the plans. Justine realized that Amherst was referring to the plans for a gymnasium that Bessy had intended for her own pleasure at Lynbrook, in open defiance of Amherst's wishes. Although angry, Justine kept Bessy's secret.

As they left the dedication, Amherst told Justine how good he felt over improved conditions at the mill. They walked away hand in hand.

THE FUNERAL

Type of work: Drama
Author: Sir Richard Steele (1672-1729)
Type of plot: Comedy of manners
Time of plot: Early eighteenth century
Locale: London
First presented: 1701

Principal characters:
THE EARL OF BRUMPTON, a British nobleman
LADY BRUMPTON, his wife by a second marriage
LORD HARDY, his son by his first marriage
MR. CAMPLEY, Lord Hardy's friend and junior officer
LADY SHARLOT (CHARLOTTE), Lord Brumpton's ward
LADY HARRIOT (HARRIET), Sharlot's sister
TRUSTY, Lord Brumpton's servant

Critique:

The Funeral, Or, Grief à la Mode was Sir Richard Steele's first and best-constructed play, but it is far less serious than his later work. Nevertheless, the drama has moral overtones and some highly sincere social criticism. Through the characterization of the hypocritical widow who gives the play its subtitle, Steele ridiculed manners of the time, as he was to do so often in his later plays and in his familiar essays. Notable in the play are the two young army officers, Lord Hardy and Ensign Campley, who are more reputable and honest than most of their dramatic predecessors, a circumstance probably due to Steele's own career in the military service. Steele boasted, quite rightly, in his preface to the play that his drama was more innocent than the prevalent style of comedy. In many ways his characters and actions show an innocent freshness quite unlike the atmosphere of intrigue found in Restoration drama and the comedies of the early eighteenth century.

The Story:

Young Lady Brumpton was quite happy when her husband, the Earl of Brumpton, died suddenly. A second wife, many years her husband's junior, she could look forward to a lively life as soon as her mourning period was over. Indeed, she intended to begin enjoying life discreetly long before she doffed her widow's weeds.

Meanwhile she had the enjoyment of the earl's entire fortune, for she had persuaded him to disown his only son, Lord Hardy. The task had been easy. The elderly earl, foolishly fond of his pretty young wife, never guessed that she had been plotting against his own best interests and his son's.

The earl's servant, Trusty, remained with his master's corpse when everyone else left it. Much to his surprise and joy, he discovered that the earl had only lapsed into a coma, and before long the nobleman regained consciousness and health. Trusty, seeing an opportunity to prove that his mistress was an intriguer and an adulteress, persuaded the earl to remain hidden and allow everyone to believe he was really dead. The only person taken into the secret was the funeral director, who agreed to keep silent after the earl paid him an amount equal to what the funeral charges would have been.

In addition to planning ways for the enjoyment of her late husband's wealth, Lady Brumpton also gave some thought to the problem of ridding herself of the earl's two teen-age wards, Lady Sharlot and Lady Harriot. The girls were a very real threat to her freedom and to a portion of the earl's estate, since Lady Sharlot was in love with the earl's son and Lady Harriot with his friend Mr. Campley.

Despite the fact that he had been put out of his father's house, Lord Hardy, an officer in the army, refused to believe ill of his father, and with Campley's help he plotted to release the two girls from his stepmother's clutches before some evil should befall them. He was right in his fear; Lady Brumpton planned to have the girls spirited away and seduced by her brother and a friend.

Help for Lord Hardy and Campley came unexpectedly from Trusty, who went to Lord Hardy's apartment and outlined his plan to the earl's son. Lord Hardy, he said, was to send a detachment of troops to the earl's house and the casket containing the earl's body would be turned over to the soldiers. In the meantime, with the help of Lord Hardy's servant and a French seamstress, Campley managed to win Lady Harriot's confidence and persuaded her to escape with him from the Brumpton mansion. They escaped by dressing in the clothes of the French seamstress and a servant girl.

The earl, hidden in the house, eavesdropped on various conversations and learned that his wife had abused him terribly in her conduct with other men and had plotted to bring his son to disfavor. He also learned that the lawyer he had trusted with the drafting of his will had written it in such a way that most of the estate would go, not to the rightful heirs, but to court and legal fees. The earl, seeing his wife as she really was, resolved to reinstate his son as his rightful heir.

When the detachment of soldiers arrived at the house, the casket was delivered to them, but not before a fight between the soldiers and the servants in order to make it seem as if the delivery had not been voluntary. Actually, the casket contained Lady Sharlot. The plot was a ruse to get the girl out of the house before she could be kidnaped and seduced by Lady Brumpton's brother.

As soon as she discovered what had happened and who the commanding officer of the detachment of soldiers was, Lady Brumpton went to confront Lord Hardy. When she arrived, she found Lady Harriot and Campley, who defied her to stop his marriage to the girl. Bitter words were spoken on both sides. At last Lord Hardy entered, to take his turn as the recipient of Lady Brumpton's invective. She railed against him for taking away his father's body and desecrating it. When she had finished, Lord Hardy accused her of poisoning his father, an accusation which made her furious. They went into another room to view the body. When the casket was opened, Lady Sharlot emerged, much to Lord Hardy's joy. His stepmother then told him he had been cut off from his father's fortune, and she handed him the one shilling which had been left to him according to his father's will. She demanded again that he and his soldiers return the body, for she still thought that they had somehow spirited it away. All the while the earl was listening in another room and gaining further evidence that his second wife was entirely dishonorable and evil.

To Lady Brumpton's consternation, the earl showed himself. Although her plans for enjoying a fortune and independence were gone, she felt that the delay was only temporary, for she believed that she could once again put herself in his esteem in spite of the facts he had learned. The earl was not happy to return to a life with an adulteress and a shrew.

Once more Trusty saved the situation. He produced a letter written by a man who had married Lady Brumpton some months before her marriage to the earl. The earlier marriage made the later one void, a fact which took the scheming woman out of the earl's life. The first husband had been induced to write the letter when he saw the earl sitting reading in his study. Like everyone else, he thought that the earl was dead, and he therefore believed the nobleman had returned to haunt him for not telling what he knew about Lady Brumpton's past. Instead of being either a rich widow or a countess, Lady Brumpton found herself the wife of a man who had no money and who was forced to live by his wits. Her plans were utterly undone.

The earl, overjoyed to see his son after many years, promised to reinstate Lord Hardy as the rightful heir to his estates. He also gave his blessing to the approaching marriages between Lord Hardy and Lady Sharlot and Campley and Lady Harriot. He was, indeed, delighted that his two wards were to marry his son and his son's closest friend.

THE GAMBLER

Type of work: Novel
Author: Fyodor Mikhailovich Dostoevski (1821-1881)
Type of plot: Psychological realism
Time of plot: Mid-nineteenth century
Locale: German watering places
First published: 1866

Principal characters:
ALEXEY IVANOVITCH, a young gambler
THE GENERAL, a Russian aristocrat
POLINA, his stepdaughter
MLLE. BLANCHE, a French adventuress
THE MARQUIS DE GRIEUX, a factitious French nobleman
ASTLEY, a young English capitalist
ANTONIDA TARASYEVITCHEV, the General's wealthy old aunt

Critique:

Dostoevski, having done considerable gambling at one time in his life, wrote this short novel with authority. His description of the fatal attraction of gambling to young and old alike is terrifying; for the rest, except for Polina's infatuation for the spurious French marquis, and for Alexey's Slavic penchant for self-torture, *The Gambler* seems a comparative ray of sunlight in the world of Dostoevski's art. Perhaps the background of a fashionable German spa with its international clientele accounts for this effect. Aunt Antonida, if not the most original of Dostoevski's creations, is one of the most delightful, even though she is little more than lightly sketched in.

The Story:

Alexey Ivanovitch returned to Roulettenburg, a German resort, after two weeks in Paris. He was tutor in the family of a Russian general who had come to the resort to repair his dwindling fortune. The General wooed an apparently wealthy young French woman, Mlle. Blanche. Polina, the General's stepdaughter, was attracted to Mlle. Blanche's alleged distant relative, the Marquis de Grieux. Alexey was Polina's creature; he loved her and accepted any humiliation at her hands.

Alexey went to the casino with money Polina gave him. After winning a tidy amount, he felt that his stay in Roulettenburg would affect his life seriously. Believing that he could not lose at the gambling tables, Alexey told Polina that henceforward he would gamble only for himself. But Polina, knowing her power over Alexey, easily persuaded him to share his winnings with her.

An affluent young English capitalist, Astley, came to Roulettenburg and, much to the General's discomfort, diverted the attentions of Mlle. Blanche, who was growing tired of waiting for the General's old aunt to die. The General telegraphed Moscow every day to inquire about the condition of the old lady, who, he was sure, would leave him a fortune.

It was soon evident that Astley was in love with Polina. Alexey, suspecting the French pair to be imposters, wanted to get away from the machinations of Roulettenburg existence, but his love for Polina held him. At the casino he lost a large amount of Polina's money; his possession of the money aroused renewed interest in the General on the part of Mlle. Blanche. The General, it seems, was deeply in debt to de Grieux.

Unable to win with Polina's money, Alexey offered to win with his own and lend her whatever she wanted. Alexey hoped that he could win Polina's love by becoming wealthy through gambling. He confessed his ardent love for her, and when he told her that he could even commit murder for her she impishly ordered him to speak in French to a stuffy German baroness who was passing by with her husband. After Alexey brashly insulted the Germans, he was, in spite of his plea that he was mentally aberrant during the escapade, discharged by the General. Alexey managed to maintain his self-respect when he told the General, who had apologized to the baron for him, that he was capable of making his own apologies, that as the son of a nobleman he objected to the General's patronizing treatment. The General, fearful of the consequences of Alexey's further impetuosities, unsuccessfully tried to mollify the youth.

De Grieux, as mediator, told Alexey that any further indiscretion on his part might spoil the chances of the General's marrying Mlle. Blanche. He also promised that the General would re-employ Alexey soon and would continue, meanwhile, to pay him his salary. Alexey, however, chose Astley to be his second in a duel with the baron. De Grieux then produced a letter from Polina asking Alexey to drop the matter. The young man obeyed, even though he knew for certain that Polina loved de Grieux.

Astley indirectly confirmed Alexey's suspicions that Mlle. Blanche and de Grieux were adventurers. During previous exploits at Roulettenburg, Mlle. Blanche had made advances to the baron and, at the direction of the baroness, had been escorted out of the casino by the police. Alexey suspected the General of being indebted somehow to Mlle. Blanche, and Polina of being involved with the French couple.

The General's old aunt, Antonida Tarasyevitchev, arrived from Moscow with a large retinue. Quite alive, she wickedly chaffed the General on his urgent solicitations and criticized him for squandering his children's inheritance. The General was visibly shocked by her arrival. The old lady, accompanied by the General's party, visited the casino and won fabulously at the gaming tables. In her triumph she gave money to her servants and to beggars.

Polina became more of an enigma to Alexey when she had him deliver a letter to Astley. Despite the General's pleas to the young tutor to prevent Antonida from gambling away her fortune, Alexey and the old lady frequented the casino together. Obsessed with the fever to win, she lost heavily. When she prepared to return to Moscow, she invited Polina to return with her. Polina declined. Antonida, unable to resist one last try at the gambling tables, again lost heavily. She converted bonds into cash and again lost. The old lady now possessed nothing but land and the houses on it; she borrowed money from Astley in order to return to Moscow.

The General's inheritance having been lost at roulette, Mlle. Blanche and de Grieux broke off relations with him and prepared to leave Roulettenburg. The General was a ruined man. Polina was distracted by her impending loss of de Grieux, but she was shaken out of her infatuation when de Grieux offered her consolation money from the proceeds of the General's property, which was mortgaged to de Grieux. In distress, Polina turned to Alexey, who went to the casino and won a fortune for her to hurl in de Grieux's face. She spent the night with Alexey in his hotel room. The next morning she took his money, then threw it in his face. She fled to Astley. Alexey went with Mlle. Blanche to Paris, where he lived with her while she spent his winnings. Tired of the life of an adventuress, Mlle. Blanche, persuaded by Alexey, decided to marry the General.

Alexey, now a confirmed gambler, returned to the gambling tables of the German resort towns. Once he went to jail for debt. In Homburg he saw Astley, who told him that Polina, recuperating from an illness, was in Switzerland with Astley's family. Meanwhile the General had died of a stroke in Paris, and Mlle. Blanche had received his inheritance from

Antonida, who had died in Moscow. Alexey regretfully reminded Astley of Polina's infatuation for de Grieux and was momentarily hopeful when Astley told him that Polina had sent him to Homburg to bring Alexey back to her. Alexey knew that he had no choice, really—he had given his heart and soul to gambling.

THE GARDEN

Type of work: Novel
Author: L. A. G. Strong (1896- 1958)
Type of plot: Impressionistic realism
Time of plot: Early twentieth century
Locale: Ireland
First published: 1931

Principal characters:

DERMOT GRAY, an Anglo-Irish boy who spends his holidays in Ireland
MRS. GRAY, his mother
MR. GRAY, his father
EITHNE, his sister
GRANNY, his mother's mother
GRANDPAPA, his mother's father
BEN McMANUS, Dermot's uncle
AUNT PATRICIA, Ben's wife
CON, their son
EILEEN, their daughter
PADDY KENNEDY, a cripple

Critique:

The qualities which make this novel a book of rare and rich experience are the writer's exquisite, unspoiled perceptions of childhood and his memories of a lost world which delighted a small boy. Behind this tale of nostalgic reminiscence there is a subtle contrast of backgrounds and characters, and this blending of temperamental differences of race and culture gives a more tangible flavor and substance to L. A. G. Strong's biographical novel.

The Story:

The first time Dermot remembered coming into an Irish port he was so young that he had to keep reminding himself to look for his Granny. He, his younger sister Eithne, and his mother came to Dublin each year to spend the summer at Granny's house. Dermot remembered only that there had been a monkey and a cat there the summer before.

After the trip by boat across the Irish Sea, they rode in a carriage, a train, and then a tram before they reached Sandycove, where Grandpapa was leaning over the gate waiting to meet them. To Dermot, as to his mother, the cottage at Sandycove was really home, a place they loved as they could never love their home in England.

Besides such delights as Paddy-monkey and Pucker the cat, Dermot was glad to see once more the comfortable dining-room with its loaded table. He loved the china, the little bone spoon with which he ate his egg, the different foods, and the corner where Grandpapa kept the well-worn books he taught Dermot to read.

Granny's garden was all mixed up in his mind with the Garden of Eden. That summer he spent most of his time there, playing with Paddy-monkey who was chained near the kitchen door, hunting for snails among the plants, investigating the farther reaches of the orchard which he had not known when he was smaller, and helping the gardener chase the half-wild cats that tore down the bushes.

There were two things he did not like about Sandycove. One was the walk far out on the pier in wild weather, while nurse wheeled Eithne. The other was to be surrounded by Granny's gushing friends before and after church. He felt closer to his Grandpapa when the old gentleman stubbornly refused to stand in front of the church with the women but waited instead in a park across the way.

Often on Sunday afternoons Dermot's cousins from Dalkey came to visit, sometimes accompanied by Uncle Ben, a boisterous retired mariner who was also, Dermot discovered, a strict puritan. Of Uncle Ben's four children, two came often: Con, a strapping lad of twenty-one, and Eileen, a lovely girl a few years younger. They were tremendously alive. Dermot, who had always been considered delicate, was exuberant when he was with his cousins.

The McManuses lived at Delgany, on a cliff running down to the sea. Their house was full of all kinds of wonders, such as a telescope, the dried jaws of a whale, a painted wooden pig, a bathroom with no taps. Uncle Ben and his family lived a happy-go-lucky life that left Dermot breathless; it was so unlike the precise life he lived in England. Too, Uncle Ben could answer Dermot's questions in more exact detail than anyone else, excepting perhaps Grandpapa; and even Grandpapa was likely to go on after the interesting part had been answered.

That year Uncle Ben, Con, and Eileen took Dermot in a boat to an island out from their home. There, while they were having their picnic, they looked up to see a ring of goats ranged on the rocks above them. It was a picture Dermot could not forget, and the trip was the first of countless excursions with the McManuses. That fall, as he sailed home to England, he looked back as long as he could see the Dalkey coast. Two years passed before he came back.

In England, before the plumbers laid a pipe in the Grays' yard, Dermot decorated a length of it by printing the plumber's name. Because he had used a chisel for the printing, he pierced the pipe. After it had been laid, the pipe leaked until the yard was a morass. Dermot confessed to his mother his fears that he had ruined the pipe but asked her not to tell his father. She had to tell Mr. Gray, of course, but he spoke kindly to Dermot when he asked the boy to be more careful the next time. A week later Dermot was still amazed at his father's unusual patience. To please Mr. Gray, he decorated the halls with horses' heads in chalk. His father blasted him for defacing the house and Dermot slunk away, cowed by the anger he had inadvertently brought on. He was afraid of his father, but when Mr. Gray became very sick Dermot was afraid for him as well.

After two years the Grays again went to Ireland. They did so each summer until the year of the first World War. As Dermot grew older his Granny hired a crippled lad to teach the boy to fish and to watch over him. It was a grand day when Dermot caught his first conger. Paddy Kennedy and his pals, Long Mike Hogan and Peg-leg O'Shea, taught Dermot a great tolerance for the poor people that he could never have learned elsewhere, but they were careful not to allow any obscenity in his presence. That he learned in his public school.

Mr. Gray always arrived for his holiday just before the time came for the family to return to England. One year he connived with the gardener to rid the place of the worst of the marauding cats that Grandpapa had refused to kill. Mr. Gray, to Dermot's surprise and delight, set the boy to watch for Black Tom and Lord Spenser and let him, without the old gentleman's knowledge, shoot them.

As Eithne grew older she was asked to accompany Dermot to Delgany. The children thrived at the house, adoring their cousins, until it became a ritual for them to spend a full week there each summer. Con, who had never really grown up, always put himself out to make some diversion for Dermot and his sister. If he could think of nothing else, he drove them around the country on his motor bike. Eileen, too, entered into their entertainment. For her Dermot had a fondness verging on adoration.

The last year the Grays went to Ireland Dermot was studying to enter Oxford. That summer Dermot, Con, and Eileen, riding the motor bike to take Eileen to a tennis match, all felt a strange lowering of their spirits at the same time. Soon afterward another bike with two riders passed them and crashed into a post. Con and Eileen took care of the dead man and the injured one. Dermot, finally grown up, realized that he could face such a scene.

Although Eithne was only fourteen, Con asked Dermot if he thought his sister would have him. Dermot recommended that Con wait. He knew, however, that Eithne adored her cousin.

Both Dermot and Con were killed during the war, only a day apart. When Eithne went back to Ireland to visit Eileen and Aunt Patricia, the only ones left in the family, she told them that a letter from Con had arrived just after Dermot died, a letter written the day before Con himself was killed. Eithne had felt torn apart at losing the two who had meant most to her, but she felt better, after reading the letter, to think that Con and Dermot were together and surely happy.

THE GARDENER'S DOG

Type of work: Drama
Author: Lope de Vega (Lope Félix de Vega Carpio, 1562-1635)
Type of plot: Comedy of manners
Time of plot: Late sixteenth century
Locale: Naples
First presented: c. 1615

Principal characters:
DIANA, Countess of Belflor
TEODORO, her secretary
FABIO, a gentleman of Naples
MARCELLA,
DOROTEA, and
ANARDA, ladies in waiting
COUNT FEDERIGO, in love with Diana
THE MARQUIS RICCARDO, also in love with Diana
COUNT LODOVICO, an old nobleman
TRISTAN, Teodoro's lackey

Critique:

The Gardener's Dog has proved to be one of the favorite comedies of Lope de Vega since its first performance, sometime around 1615. It is based on the old tale of the dog who would not eat its food, yet would allow no other dog to have it. Such was Diana. For a time, at least, she herself did not want Teodoro, but she would not let Marcella have him. The play is a comedy of character and manners, reminiscent of some of Shakespeare's work. The technical perfection is amazing when one remembers that this most prolific of all writers turned out more than sixteen hundred plays during his lifetime.

The Story:

The Countess Diana was enraged when she heard that a man had been seen leaving the upper chambers of the palace. He had thrown his cap at the candle, snuffing out the only light so that he could not be identified. Diana sent for her ladies in waiting and questioned them in order to learn who had been visited by a lover during the night. Dorotea and Anarda pleaded innocent, but whispered to Diana that Marcella had a lover in the palace. He was Teodoro, secretary to the Countess Diana herself. Marcella confessed her love but protested that it was a pure love. Teodoro wanted to marry her. Diana gave her consent to the marriage but cautioned Marcella to stay away from Teodoro until the wedding day; otherwise passion might consume honor. After her ladies had left her alone, Diana realized that she too loved Teodoro, but since he was not highborn she could not proclaim her love.

Teodoro, who had indeed been the man involved in the midnight escapade investigated by Diana, feared that he would be found out and banished or executed. But he could not get Marcella out of his heart. Tristan, his lackey, begged him to forget Marcella and never see her again lest Diana punish them both severely, for it had been Tristan who had thrown the cap and snuffed out the candle so that his master would not be recognized while escaping. Soon afterward Diana did learn the truth of the escapade, when she tricked Tristan into revealing his part in the affair. She also sent for Teodoro and subtly hinted at her love for him in a letter she feigned was intended for someone else.

Marcella went to Teodoro and told him that Diana had blessed their betrothal. Confused, Teodoro took Marcella in his arms just as Diana appeared. When he thanked her for giving Marcella to him, their capricious mistress ordered Marcella locked in her room, to await Diana's desires concerning the wedding. Then Diana again hinted that she loved Teodoro, and because of her words he renounced Marcella. To himself he regretted his rejection of Marcella, but he could not put aside the lure of wealth and power that would be his if Diana took him for a husband. Meeting Marcella a short time later, for Dorotea had let her out of the locked room, he spurned her love and disgraced her. Angered, Marcella swore revenge on him and on Anarda, who had, as Marcella learned, betrayed her and Teodoro to Diana because Anardo thought Marcella encouraged Fabio, a gentleman with whom Anardo was in love. Marcella, meeting Fabio, offered him her love and greatly confused that poor man by her words and actions.

Two noblemen, the Marquis Riccardo and Count Federigo, both begged for Diana's hand, and suddenly she sent Teodoro to tell Riccardo that she chose him for her husband. Deserted by the lovely countess before she was really his, Teodoro turned again to Marcella and said that he loved only her. At first she spurned him and declared that she would marry Fabio, but at last love won out over jealousy. Falling into Teodoro's arms, she made him forswear Diana forever. While the lovers called their mistress a devil, an ass, and a bore, they did not know that Diana and Anarda were hidden nearby and listening to their conversation. Suddenly they appeared, frightening the lovers almost to death. Diana dictated a letter to Teodoro, in which she stated that if a noble lady loved a man he dared not love another. When she cautioned him to interpret its meaning correctly, Teodoro again renounced Marcella and told her to marry Fabio in order to please Diana.

Riccardo, appearing in answer to the summons from Diana, was told that Teodoro had misunderstood her words and that she had not intended to marry Riccardo. Teodoro, believing then that his mistress truly loved him, declared his love for her. Instead of listening to his pleas, Diana berated him for daring to speak of love when he was low-born and she a lady. Then he asked her to give Marcella to him, since Diana would not have him. But, like the gardener's dog who would allow no other dog to eat what he himself did not want, she would not let Teodoro have Marcella. Instead, she struck at Teodoro with her knife. He half-believed that she had wounded him because she loved him, and, when she returned and wiped the blood from his wound, he was sure that it was love that made her cruel to him.

Count Federigo and the Marquis Riccardo, hearing that Diana had wounded Teodoro, were convinced that he had threatened her honor, and they decided to have him killed. For their assassin they hired Teodoro's faithful lackey, Tristan, who took their gold and then informed Teodoro of their plot. Tristan had other plans for helping his master.

He had learned of one Count Lodovico, who had lost a son named Teodoro twenty years before. The boy had been captured by the Moors and was never heard of again. Tristan planned to convince the old count that Teodoro was his long-lost son. Then Teodoro would have a family of birth and wealth and would be good enough to wed Diana. Teodoro, too honorable for such knavery, went to Diana and told her that he was going to Spain, to avoid both the death planned for him by her suitors and the torture he endured while in her presence. Diana, not knowing her own mind, alternately told him to leave and to stay. When Marcella went to Diana and asked for permission to accompany Teodoro to Spain, Diana told the girl that she must marry Fabio.

Meanwhile Tristan carried through his plot to make Count Lodovico think Teodoro his lost son, and the old man was delighted at the prospect of having his child returned to him. Before the old count saw Teodoro, Diana, knowing that her true love was to leave her, told him at last that she loved him. Still she refused to marry him because of his humble birth. When Count Lodovico appeared with the announcement that Teodoro was his son, Diana opened her arms to Teodoro and said that they would be married that very night. Marcella, seeing at last that she could never have Teodoro, agreed to marry Fabio.

Teodoro, in one last attempt to save his honor, confessed to Diana that Tristan had tricked the old nobleman into believing Teodoro his own missing son. But by that time Diana had learned that love did not respect position. She declared that they would marry anyway and keep the secret between themselves and Tristan. Federigo and Riccardo confessed their plot to have Teodoro killed, and Diana gave Dorotea to Tristan as his bride. So all ended well, with honor saved and love triumphant. The gardener's dog had made a final choice.

GARGANTUA AND PANTAGRUEL

Type of work: Mock-heroic chronicle
Author: François Rabelais (1490?-1553)
Type of plot: Burlesque romance
Time of plot: Renaissance
Locale: France
First published: Begun 1533; first complete edition, 1567

Principal characters:
GRANGOSIER, a giant king
GARGAMELLE, his wife
GARGANTUA, their son
PANTAGRUEL, son of Gargantua
PANURGE, a clever rascal
FRIAR JOHN OF THE FUNNELS, a lusty monk

Critique:

The book Rabelais titled *The Lives, Heroic Deeds and Sayings of Gargantua and His Son Pantagruel* is a vast panorama of an amiable dynasty of giants. The characters are prodigious eaters and drinkers, gay and earthy. The five books which contain the adventures of a galaxy of types are loosely held together by the main actors. Discursive and monumental, *Gargantua and Pantagruel* is an astounding achievement. *Rabelaisian* and *gargantuan* as adjectives indicate the opinion of many readers. But Rabelais had a serious purpose. He demonstrated heroically his theme that the real meaning of life is to expand the soul by knowing all the sources of experience.

The Story:

Grangosier and Gargamelle were expecting a child. During the eleventh month of her pregnancy, Gargamelle ate too many tripes and then played tag on the green. That afternoon in a green meadow Gargantua was born from his mother's left ear.

Gargantua was a prodigy, and with his first breath he began to clamor for drink. Seventeen thousand nine hundred and thirteen cows were needed to supply him with milk. For his clothing the tailors used nine hundred ells of linen to make his shirt and eleven hundred and five ells of white broadcloth to make his breeches. Eleven hundred cowhides were used for the soles of his shoes.

At first Gargantua's education was in the hands of two masters of the old school, Holofernes and Joberlin Bridé. Seeing that his son was making no progress, however, Grangosier sent him to Paris to study with Ponocrates. Aside from some mishaps, as when he took the bells from the tower of Notre Dame to tie around his horse's neck, Gargantua did much better with his studies in Paris.

Back home a dispute arose. The bakers of Lerné refused to sell cakes to the shepherds of Grangosier. In the quarrel a shepherd felled a baker, and King Picrochole of Lerné invaded the country Grangosier baked cartloads of cakes to appease Picrochole, but to no avail, for no one dared oppose Picrochole except doughty Friar John of the Funnels. Finally Grangosier asked Gargantua to come to his aid.

Gargantua fought valiantly. Cannon balls seemed to him as grape seeds, and when he combed his hair cannon balls dropped out. After he had conquered the army of Lerné, he generously let all the prisoners go free.

All his helpers were rewarded well, but for Friar John, Gargantua built the famous Abbey of Thélème, where men and women were together, all could leave when they wished, and marriage and the accumulation of wealth were encouraged.

When he was more than four hundred years old, Gargantua had a son, Pantagruel. Pantagruel was a remarkable baby, hairy as a bear at birth and of such great size that he cost the life of his mother. Gargantua was sorely vexed between weeping for his wife and rejoicing for his son.

Pantagruel required the services of four thousand six hundred cows to nurse him. Once he got an arm out of his swaddling clothes and, grasping the cow nursing him, he ate the cow. Afterwards Pantagruel's arms were bound with anchor ropes. One day the women forgot to clean his face after nursing, and a bear came and licked the drops of milk from the baby's face. By a great effort Pantagruel broke the ropes and ate the bear. In despair, Gargantua bound his son with four great chains, one of which was later used to bind Lucifer when he had the colic. But Pantagruel broke the five-foot beam which constituted the footboard of his cradle and ran around with the cradle on his back.

Pantagruel showed great promise as a scholar. After a period of wandering he settled down in Paris. There he was frequently called on to settle disputes between learned lawyers. One day he met a ragged young beggar. On speaking to him, Pantagruel received answers in twelve known and unknown tongues. Greatly taken by this fluent beggar, Pantagruel and Panurge became great friends. Panurge was a merry fellow who knew sixty-three ways to make money and two hundred fourteen ways to spend it.

Pantagruel learned that the Dipsodes had invaded the land of the Amaurots. Stirred by this danger to Utopia, he set out by ship to do battle. By trickery and courage, Pantagruel overcame the wicked giants. Their king, Anarchus, he married to an old lantern-carrying hag and made the king a crier of green sauce. Now that the land of Dipsody had been conquered, Pantagruel transported there a colony of Utopians numbering 9,876,543,210 men, besides many women and children. All these people were very fertile. Every nine months each married woman bore seven children. In a short time Dipsody was populated by virtuous Utopians.

For his services and friendship Panurge was made Laird of Salmigondin. The revenue from this lairdship amounted to 6,789,106,789 gold royals a year, but Panurge managed to spend his income well in advance. Then, thinking to settle down, Panurge began to reflect seriously on marriage, and he consulted his lord Pantagruel. They came to no conclusion in the matter because they got into an argument about the virtues of borrowing and lending money. But the flea in his ear kept reminding Panurge of his contemplated marriage, and he set off to seek other counsel.

Panurge consulted the Sibyl of Panzoult, the poet Raminagrobis, Herr Tripa, and Friar John. When all the advice he received proved contradictory, Panurge prevailed on Pantagruel and Friar John to set out with him to consult the Oracle of the Holy Bottle. From Saint Malo the party sailed in twelve ships for the Holy Bottle, located in Upper India. The Portuguese sometimes took three years for that voyage, but Pantagruel and Panurge cut that time to one month by sailing across the Frozen Sea north of Canada.

The valiant company had many adventures on the way. On the Island of the Ennasins, they found a race of people with noses shaped like the ace of clubs. The people who lived on the Island of Ruach ate and drank nothing but wind. At the Ringing Islands they found a strange race of Siticines who had long ago turned to birds. On Condemnation Island they fell into the power of Gripe-men-all, Archduke of the Furred Law-cats, and Panurge was forced to solve a riddle before the travelers were given their freedom.

At last they came to the island of the Sacred Bottle. Guided by a Lantern from Lanternland, they came to a large vineyard planted by Bacchus himself. Then they went underground through a plastered vault and came to marble steps. Down they went, a hundred steps or more. Panurge was greatly afraid, but

Friar John took him by the collar and heartened him. At the bottom they came to a great mosaic floor on which was shown the history of Bacchus. Finally they were met by the priestess Bacbuc, who was to conduct them to the Bottle. Panurge knelt to kiss the rim of the fountain. Bacbuc threw something into the well and the water began to boil. When Panurge sang the prescribed ritual, the Sacred Bottle pronounced the one word, "trinc." Bacbuc looked up the word in a huge silver book. It meant drink, a word declared to be the most gracious and intelligible she had ever heard from the Sacred Bottle. Panurge took the word as a sanction for his marriage.

THE GAUCHO: MARTÍN FIERRO

Type of work: Poem
Author: José Hernández (1834-1886)
Type of plot: Adventure romance
Time of plot: Nineteenth century
Locale: Argentina
First published: Part the First, 1872
                   Part the Second, 1879

        Principal characters:
           MARTÍN FIERRO, the gaucho
           CRUZ, his friend
           PICARDIA, Cruz' son
           TWO SONS OF MARTÍN FIERRO

Critique:

Although it is not well known in the English-speaking world, the tale of Martín Fierro has had great popularity in the South American countries, particularly in Argentina. Fierro gave hope to a people long oppressed by the government and cheated by corrupt officials. He became a legend and his tale was repeated over and over again. Hernández himself was identified with his hero, and everywhere he went he was idolized as the spokesman for the gaucho. It is said that much of the romantic appeal of the poem is lost in translation; nevertheless, the English version is musical, vigorous, and exciting.

The Story:

Martín Fierro was a gaucho, born and raised on the rolling plains of Argentina. A gaucho was a mixture of the Spaniard and the Moor, transplanted to South America and mixed again with aboriginal Indians. He was God-fearing, brutal, superstitious, ignorant, lazy, and kind. His type was but a passing one, but while he roamed the plains he became a legend. Martín Fierro played his guitar and sang his songs, songs that told of his unhappiness and the sorrows of the gaucho all over the land.

There was a time when Martín had a home and a wife and children to comfort him. He had owned land and cattle and a snug house. He rode the plains and lived in peace with his neighbors. Then officers appeared to take Martín and his neighbors away from their homes and families to serve the government in wars with the Indians. Martín was among those chosen because he had not voted when the judge was up for election, and the judge said that those who did not vote helped the opposition. The government promised that the gauchos would serve only six months and then be replaced. Martín took his horse and clothes and left his wife and children.

The men lived in filth and poverty. Complaints brought a staking out and lashes with leather thongs. There were no arms; the colonel kept the guns and ammunition locked up except when the Indians attacked. The Indians came and went as they pleased, killing, plundering, and taking hostages. They pulled babies from mothers' arms and killed them for sport. But the Indians were not much worse than the officers. The men had no pay, no decent food. They wore rags, and rats crawled over them while they slept.

At last Martín escaped and returned to his home. There he found his wife and sons gone, the house destroyed, the cattle and sheep sold by the government. Martín swore revenge and set out to find his sons.

He was soon in more trouble. He killed a Negro in a fight. Another swaggering gaucho picked a quarrel and Martín killed him. These killings brought the police after him. They had tracked him down and were about to kill him when one of their number joined him in fighting the others. Cruz, his new friend, fought so bravely that the two of them drove off or killed their attackers.

Cruz, telling Martín his story, sang it like a true gaucho. He had lost his woman to the commandante of the army and so had left his home. He, too, had killed a man and been hunted by the law before an influential friend got him a pardon and a job with the police. But Cruz had no heart for the police. Seeing Martín prepared to fight against great odds, he had decided to join him. The two decided to leave the frontier and go to live among the Indians.

Martín and Cruz traveled across the desert to the land of the savages. But before they could make friends and join a tribe, they were captured by a raiding party. For two years they suffered tortures inflicted by the Indians; then they were allowed to pitch a tent and live together, still under guard. They had to ride with the savages on raids against the Christians. When smallpox ravaged the tribe, Cruz gave his life by nursing a chief who had been kind to them.

Martín was alone once more. At last he escaped from the Indians. He rescued a white woman who had been beaten with the bowels of her own baby son. After weeks of weary travel they returned to the plains, where Martín left the woman with a rancher and went on his way. He knew by then that even the evils of the government were better than life with savage Indians.

Martín, returning to his homeland, learned that he was no longer wanted by the government. The judge who had put him into the army was dead and no one any longer cared about the Negro and the gaucho he had killed in fair fights. In his new freedom he went to a racing meet and there was reunited with two of his sons. From them he learned that his wife was dead and that they had also been tortured and cheated by the government.

The older son sang his song first. He had been arrested and convicted for a killing which he did not do. Beaten, starved, abused, he spent a long time in the penitentiary. In his loneliness he had had no friend to share his woes. He cautioned all who heard his tale to keep away from the law, for the law was not for the gaucho.

The second son sang his song. An aunt died and left him some property. The judge appointed a tutor who robbed the boy of his inheritance and beat him and starved him. Penniless, Martín's son had roamed the land like a tramp until he was sent to the frontier with the army.

Father and sons sat singing and talking when a stranger called Picardía appeared and sang his song. Like the others, he had been sent to serve in the army and endure the tortures of the wicked officials. At the end of his song Picardía told Martín that he was the son of Cruz, Martín's old friend. The friends celebrated the meeting with wine and song, and while they sang a Negro joined them. He and Martín held a singing match, a common thing among the gauchos. The Negro sang that he was the brother of the Negro Martín had killed long years before and that he would avenge the death. Before they could fight, other gauchos stepped between them and sent Martín, his sons, and Picardía on their way.

They rode only a short distance together, then separated to seek new lives, each man alone. Before they departed, Martín Fierro gave the young men some advice out of his own experience. He told them to be true to their friends, to give every man his due, to obey the law, and never to cheat. If ever a woman should win their hearts, they must treat her well and be true. The four scattered, each one taking a new name from that day on. Martín, ending his song, commended his words to gauchos everywhere, for they came from the wisdom of an old man. Then he laid down his guitar, never to sing again.

THE "GENIUS"

Type of work: Novel
Author: Theodore Dreiser (1871-1945)
Type of plot: Naturalism
Time of plot: 1889-1914
Locale: Alexandria, Illinois, Chicago, and New York
First published: 1915

Principal characters:
EUGENE WITLA, an artist, the "genius"
THOMAS WITLA, his father, a sewing machine agent
SYLVIA, and
MYRTLE WITLA, his sisters
STELLA APPLETON, Eugene's first love
ANGELA BLUE, a schoolteacher, later Eugene's wife
MARGARET DUFF, a laundry worker, Eugene's first mistress
RUBY KENNY, an artist's model
MIRIAM FINCH, a sculptress in New York
CHRISTINA CHANNING, a singer in New York
M. ANATOLE CHARLES, an art dealer
FRIEDA ROTH, a young girl in Alexandria
CARLOTTA WILSON, a gambler's wife, Eugene's mistress
DANIEL SUMMERFIELD, head of an advertising agency
OBADIAH KALVIN, head of a publishing company
MARSHALL P. COLFAX, a publisher
FLORENCE J. WHITE, Eugene's associate and enemy
MRS. EMILY DALE, a wealthy socialite friend of Eugene
SUZANNE, her daughter
MRS. JOHNS, a Christian Science practitioner

Critique:

The "Genius" traces the career of Eugene Witla, an artist haunted by a search for beauty which leads him to fall in love with many women during his lifetime. Yet the search for beauty brings no more enduring peace or value than do the searches for material security or social success that mark other Dreiser novels. Beauty, in Dreiser's terms, is transitory and relationships shift back and forth so that the artist, like the ordinary human being, is unable to alter any of the significant circumstances of his experience or control his own destiny. The novel contains a great deal of social detail in its pictures of the worlds of art and publishing and of New York life in the early years of this century. Another theme is the tendency of money and commerce to corrupt art.

The Story:

Eugene Witla, a sensitive seventeen-year-old boy, lived with his parents and his two sisters in Alexandria, Illinois. Eugene had little idea of what he wanted to do, although his aspirations were vaguely artistic. His father, a sewing machine agent and a respectable member of the middle class, got him a job setting type for the local newspaper. His first enthusiasm was for a local girl named Stella Appleton, but even this affair did not keep Eugene, unhappy in his restlessness, from leaving the small town and going to Chicago to seek his fortune.

When he first went to Chicago, Eugene supported himself by moving stoves, driving a laundry wagon, and collecting for a furniture company. While at the laundry, he met the passionate young Margaret Duff and began his first real love affair. About this time he also met, through mutual friends, a schoolteacher named Angela Blue, a fair-haired beauty who represented everything fine and elegant to impressionable young Eugene.

Eugene began attending art classes at night at the Chicago Art Institute. There he demonstrated some talent, particularly in his class in life drawing, for he seemed to have a special sensitivity in conveying the beauty of the human form. While at the Art Institute, he met a model, Ruby Kenny, and she soon became his mistress. But Ruby, like Margaret, was from the lower classes and made her charms easily available to men. Eugene finally left them both, preferring the finer and more fragile beauty of Angela. Engaged to the young teacher, he left Chicago to seek his artistic fortune in the wider world of New York.

In New York, Eugene painted powerful and realistic pictures of what he saw in the city, and began, from time to time, to sell a few of his paintings. After several years he became moderately successful. Some of the women he met, like Miriam Finch and Christina Channing, began to educate him in the well-read and knowledgeable polish of the New York artistic world. Christina became his mistress for a short time; that sophisticated affair somewhat baffled Eugene. But in spite of his new polish and elegance, he still remembered Angela. Returning to the Middle West to visit her, he seduced her and then, feeling his responsibility, married her and took her back to New York. Angela felt that all her dreams of happiness had been fulfilled.

Eugene's work impressed M. Anatole Charles, manager of a distinguished firm of art dealers in New York. M. Charles held an exhibit which, a great success, marked Eugene as a powerful and rising young artist. Full of enthusiasm, he and Angela went to Paris. The show held when he returned was less successful; people felt that his work in Paris had not been fresh or unusual. While in Paris,

Eugene had also begun to suffer a vague malaise, a lack of energy and purpose. He did not, at that time, realize that his marriage was causing his uneasy and restless feeling.

Eugene and Angela returned to Alexandria for an inexpensive rest. While there, Eugene met eighteen-year-old Frieda Roth and found her attractive. Since he was twenty-nine by this time, Frieda represented for him a renewed interest in youth and beauty. Angela was able to stop this relationship before it advanced further than a few kisses stolen under the trees. Afterward Eugene and Angela left Alexandria and stayed at several resorts until their money ran out. Angela then returned to her parents, while Eugene returned to New York to reëstablish his reputation as an artist.

Eugene, still restless, found himself unable to paint, and he took a job doing manual labor for the railroad in a town near New York. While there, he met and had a passionate affair with his landlady's married daughter, Carlotta Wilson. Again Angela heard of the affair and came to reclaim Eugene. They decided to try to start again in New York.

Eugene worked for a newspaper and then as art director for an advertising agency. His boss there, Daniel Summerfield, was a tyrant who broke his promises and failed to pay Eugene adequately. Eugene left for another job with the advertising department of the *North American Weekly*, under the directorship of Obadiah Kalvin. Successful there, he moved to Philadelphia to accept a $25,000 job as head of the advertising for all books and publications directed by Marshall P. Colfax. When Eugene was made a vice president, the other vice president, Florence J. White, felt that Eugene's job and salary were unnecessary. White was jealous of Eugene and the two became enemies.

Eugene became greatly successful, both financially and socially. His marriage was hollow, but both he and Angela seemed to accept the situation and to cope with it fairly well. Although Eugene had money enough to retire, his financial success had bred in him a desire for greater financial success, and he had lost the will to paint. His artistic lassitude was matched by the emotional emptiness of his marriage.

About this time Eugene met Mrs. Emily Dale, a rich socialite. They exchanged visits and became friendly. One day, Mrs. Dale brought Suzanne, her eighteen-year-old daughter, to tea. Eugene fell in love with Suzanne at first sight, and all the yearning of his search for beauty returned. Soon Eugene and Suzanne were meeting and they confessed their love for each other. Brought up a cultured and sophisticated young woman, Suzanne was willing to become Eugene's mistress. Filled with romantic ideas about becoming an artist's mistress, she insisted, however, on telling her mother of her plans, for she thought that her mother would surely approve. But Mrs. Dale did not approve. Angela, when she discovered the affair, decided that the only way to hold Eugene was to have a baby, despite the fact that doctors had warned her against having children. Angela, who had become a Christian Scientist, believed that her firm faith and will would permit her to have the child. Mrs. Dale took her daughter to Canada to get her away from Eugene. When he tried to follow Suzanne to Canada, Mrs. Dale, through Florence J. White and the threat of scandal to the firm, was able to have him fired from his job. Eugene, having lost both his job and Suzanne, returned to comfort Angela during her ordeal.

After Angela died giving birth to a daughter, also named Angela, Eugene had his sister Myrtle come East to help him make a home for the child. For a time, in his desolation, Eugene began to read Christian Science, but he failed to find comfort or salvation in its message.

When Eugene and Suzanne met by accident on the street two years later, they were each too self-conscious to acknowledge the existence of the other. Living sanely with his daughter and Myrtle and her husband, Eugene began to paint again. He had several shows, was sponsored again by M. Charles, and became a popular and fairly successful artist. He began to weave romantic dreams around his daughter Angela, thinking of the time when she would grow up and they could search for beauty together. In spite of his new awareness of man's inability to control his fate, of the delusions that belief in beauty or belief in Christian Science represented, Eugene's emotional impulse toward beauty was still strong enough to keep him fashioning impossible dreams for himself and his daughter.

THE GENTLEMAN DANCING MASTER

Type of work: Drama
Author: William Wycherley (1640-1716)
Type of plot: Satiric comedy
Time of plot: Seventeenth century
Locale: London
First presented: 1672

Principal characters:
MR. GERRARD, a young gentleman of the town
MR. MARTIN, his friend and ally
MR. PARIS (MONSIEUR DE PARIS), an affected Gallophile
MR. JAMES FORMAL (DON DIEGO), a merchant
HIPPOLITA, his daughter, enamored of Mr. Gerrard but engaged to her cousin, Mr. Paris
MRS. CAUTION, Mr. Formal's widowed sister
PRUE, Hippolita's disingenuous maid
MISTRESS FLIRT, a woman of the streets

Critique:

This play, the second produced by Wycherley and the most derivative of the four, takes its title and its general theme from a play by Calderón. The style of the play, too, is somewhat in the manner of Molière and through him goes back to the *commedia dell' arte,* with its brisk criticism of affectation and its elaboration of the gulled father, the saucy maid, the languorous lover, and other farcical types. Wycherley possessed sufficient talent, however, to convert his borrowed materials into a play much copied in later years, particularly by Sheridan, and one still appealing to a modern audience or reader.

The Story:

Mr. James Formal, who made his living in trade with the Spanish and who admired their pride and gallantry to the point of affecting their manners, had confined his fourteen-year-old daughter Hippolita, recently returned from boarding school, to the house for a period of a year. During his absence his sister, the widow Caution, acted the part of a duenna to see that Hippolita's virtue was protected in the Spanish manner. In spite of the soured old woman's puritanical wishes—she was adept at sensing sin since it was always on her mind—from her balcony the young girl carried on a flirtation with a young gentleman who frequented a neighboring inn.

Several days before Mr. Formal was due to return, Mr. Paris, his nephew and a suitor for the hand of Hippolita, arrived in London after a brief stay in France which had made of him a slavish imitator of French dress, manners, and idiom without in the least understanding his own ridiculousness. Since only he had access to the young lady's presence, she made of him a willing dupe in order to make the acquaintance of the tall, handsome Gerrard. As a jest, M. de Paris— as the silly coxcomb called himself—challenged Gerrard to contrive a meeting with the young lady whom he had seen only from a distance but of whom he was enamored.

Accepting the challenge, Gerrard broke into Hippolita's chamber, proposed a hasty elopement, and was caught in a near-embrace by her returning father. Hippolita, her actions always covered by her resourceful maid, cleverly pretended that Gerrard, who was unable to dance a step, was the dancing instructor hired at the behest of her husband-to-be, who would not have a wife without such French refinement as the ability to dance. The deception was further extended by M. de Paris who, blinded as he was by his own ego and splendor in dress and speech, helped the lovers at every turn. Mrs. Caution, immediately suspicious of the true situation, repeatedly warned the affected Spanish grandee of a father, who proudly protested that he would never permit such an affair to occur under his roof. Mr. Formal, in fact, took a liking to the supposed dancing master and urged him to come three times a day in order that his daughter could learn as rapidly as possible before her imminent marriage. At the same time he took a dislike to his ridiculous nephew and forced that embarrassed but docile young man to change to a Spanish costume and English speech, a calamity in the eyes of the young Gallophile. Meanwhile, Hippolita carried off her flirtation to the point of elopement, a conspiring innocent who allowed herself to be pursued only to become the pursuer. Paris, in turn, had become embroiled in an affair with Mistress Flirt, begun in the inn where he went to scheme against Gerrard.

The dancing lessons were never taken, thanks to the modesty of the young woman who at first would not dance before witnesses and who later plotted to pit her father against her aunt and her betrothed in order to get them all out of the way. The insistence of the suspicious aunt only aroused Mr. Formal's ire; he was sure that he could protect the honor of his daughter as well as manage family affairs. His dislike for Paris, who ridiculed his Spanish ways, dress, and attitudes, and his admiration for the punctual dancing master further misled the proud father, who postponed the wedding for another day in order that skills might grow apace.

Plans for the elopement were hastened by Gerrard's interest in Hippolita's twelve hundred pounds and the hiring of a coach and six, the romantic young girl's dream of the perfect rig in which to flee with her lover. The young gallant, in spite of his attempts to learn dancing between lessons, felt also that he would soon be discovered as an impostor and

would then find himself the victim of Spanish revenge. Confiding in Paris, Hippolita begged him to maintain the deception lest the whole compromising situation be disclosed. Paris, ironically, played the part of the jilted lover without knowing it. Spanish care, prudence, and circumspection were his allies.

Only the slight diversion of family strife protected the lovers on the night of the planned elopement. Mr. Formal, not satisfied with his prospective son-in-law's loss of French affectations, made him learn Spanish ways as well, to the tune of dance instructions from a blackamoor. The ridiculous young man was so disconsolate that he repulsed even the advances of Hippolita's maid, the designing Prue, who, being better acquainted with the comforts of love, suffered more than the others did from the household restrictions. Sibling rivalry now reached a climax when Mr. Formal convinced himself that what Mrs. Caution had said all along was true. Furthermore, Hippolita took Gerrard's haste to elope as an indication he was marrying her only for her money, and she refused to leave with him as they had planned. When Gerrard, believing that the game was lost, revealed to all that his plans had gone awry, his remarks were interpreted to mean only that his pupil would not learn. He then escaped the threat of exposure by breaking the strings of a fiddle which would have proved him unmusical. Reinstated in Mr. Formal's good graces, he was asked to bring the musicians for the wedding celebration.

When he appeared for the last lesson, Gerrard and Hippolita were reconciled. Convinced that he loved her for herself alone, she assured him that she did, after all, have twelve hundred pounds—a fact she had denied earlier to test his devotion. Gerrard, no longer needing obsequious, dandified Paris as an ally, cuffed him soundly, treatment which the craven fellow did not take amiss, so sure was he that this was his wedding day. In fact, he blunderingly helped the lovers by protecting Hippolita, the parson, and Gerrard from the wrath of the rightfully indignant father and held Mr. Formal off long enough for the marriage ceremony to be performed.

Mr. Formal, unwilling to admit that he had been duped, acted the part of willing collaborator and told his spiteful sister and the effeminate Paris that he planned the wedding especially for their discomfiture.

Paris was outdone a second time when Mistress Flirt bound him to so many illicit promises as to make matrimony seem much less binding by comparison.

THE GENTLEMAN USHER

Type of work: Drama
Author: George Chapman (c. 1559-1634)
Type of plot: Romantic comedy
Time of plot: Seventeenth century
Locale: Italy
First presented: c. 1602

Principal characters:
DUKE ALPHONSO
PRINCE VINCENTIO, his son and rival
MARGARET, a beautiful young noblewoman
COUNT LASSO, her father
BASSIOLO, usher to Lasso
COUNT STROZZA, Vincentio's friend
MEDICE, the duke's favorite
CORTEZZA, Lasso's sister

Critique:

Though not the equal of Shakespeare's great comedies, *The Gentleman Usher* approaches them in richness and variety. Delightful comic scenes are interwoven with the serious story of a father and son's rivalry for a young girl. The play contains a wide range of successful characterizations; among them, the figure of Bassiolo, the self-satisfied and gullible usher, is especially memorable. The action, slow in starting, moves rapidly from the middle of the play to the conclusion.

The Story:

Prince Vincentio was deeply in love with Margaret, a gentlewoman of the court, but his courtship was inhibited by the fact that his father, Duke Alphonso, was also in love with the girl. Since the duke was not a man to tolerate opposition, it was unthinkable for Vincentio to become his father's open rival. When he disclosed his feelings to his close friend, Count Strozza, his friend encouraged him to carry on his suit in secret.

Meanwhile, the duke was planning a boar hunt near the home of Count Lasso, Margaret's father. It was not the hunt that interested the duke, but the festivities at Lasso's house that would follow, for he hoped that he would be able to advance his cause with Margaret during the feast. The duke's chief ally in this cause and his favorite courtier at the moment was Medice, a base lord noted for his poor apparel and his illiteracy. Contemptuous and suspicious of this upstart, Strozza and Vincentio grasped every opportunity to ridicule him.

When the duke arrived at Lasso's castle, where elaborate preparations had been made for his entertainment, he was bound as a captive. His men, dressed in costumes, explained to Margaret that he was a captive to her charms. She unbound him and, though she fully understood the duke's intentions, treated the matter as a compliment and jest.

Acting for his master, Medice sought information about Margaret. Aware of her coolness toward the duke, he believed that she must have another lover. To discover the name of this person, he plied Margaret's aunt, Cortezza, with sack. For his troubles he got some shameless flirting from the old hag and also a hint that Vincentio might be the guilty person.

During the festivities Vincentio himself was seeking the services of a go-between. Finally, acting on Margaret's suggestion, he approached her father's usher, Bassiolo, a pompous fool quite susceptible to Vincentio's flattery. Vincentio, treating Bassiolo as an equal, embraced him and asked that he be called Vince. He gave the usher a jewel and hinted that Bassiolo could expect a high position when Vincentio became duke. Bassiolo, because of his self-conceit, had no idea that Vincentio was secretly laughing at him. When the prince brought up the subject of exchanging letters with Margaret, the usher immediately volunteered his services.

As arranged, Bassiolo brought Margaret a letter from Vincentio, but she, wishing to implicate the usher, refused it on the grounds of her attachment to the duke. After an argument against her marriage to an old man, Bassiolo forced Vincentio's letter upon her. When she had read the letter, she told Bassiolo to answer it. His missive, indited in a turgid style, she declined to send, telling him that it sounded too good for a woman's writing. Her own letter to Vincentio, she dictated to the usher.

Medice, angered by Strozza's mockery, also felt that Strozza stood in the way of his advancement. He decided, therefore, to get rid of him by having one of his men kill the young count during a hunt. The man succeeded in hitting Strozza with an arrow, but failed to kill him. The doctor who treated him said that he would have to cut the flesh around the wound in order to remove the arrow, but Strozza, in a highly agitated state, refused this operation. Cynanche, his wife, counseled Christian patience, but with no immediate effect.

When Bassiolo brought Margaret's letter to Vincentio, the prince pretended to believe that it did not really come from her. The usher, responding exactly as Vincentio hoped he would, offered to bring Margaret to prove her authorship. Vincentio, meanwhile, had decided that the only way to forestall his father's plans was to marry Margaret immediately. When she came, they performed their own marriage ceremony by knitting a scarf around each other's arms and making their vows. As they were completing their simple rite, news came of the wounding of Strozza.

As a result of his wife's ministrations,

Strozza's spirits had improved. Freely submitting himself to the will of heaven, he had been relieved of pain. His humility had also brought him new powers of understanding. He predicted that the arrowhead would fall out of his side on the seventh day.

Medice, pursuing his investigations in the meantime, had Cortezza rob Margaret's jewel box. There the letter from Vincentio was discovered. When the affair was revealed to Duke Alphonso, he thundered enraged threats against his son. Cortezza, believing that she knew the secret trysting place of the two lovers, offered to reveal it, and Medice and the duke made plans to discover Vincentio and Margaret at their next meeting.

Lasso, in the meantime, had also begun to suspect his daughter, and a conversation in which he threatened her and her supposed lover was overheard by Bassiolo. The usher, terrified at the prospects of punishment for his complicity, began to suspect that the prince had been making a fool of him. When he notified Margaret that he intended to reveal the truth to her father, she reminded him that he had railed against the duke, forced Vincentio's letter upon her, and written a letter for her to Vincentio, a letter still in her possession. Realizing that he was trapped, Bassiolo claimed he had spoken of betrayal only in jest. When Margaret ordered him to arrange a meeting for her with Vincentio, he immediately complied.

Hidden in the room where the two lovers met were Duke Alphonso, Medice, Lasso and Cortezza. Bassiolo, again proud of his part in the intrigue, freely insulted the unseen duke and Medice. At last the eavesdroppers revealed themselves. Vincentio, warned by the usher, made his escape. The duke, saying that his son would suffer death or banishment, ordered Medice to capture him. After Medice had left and the duke had taken time for reflection, he sent a man after Medice to see that Vincentio was not harmed.

Margaret, determined that she would not be forced into marriage with the duke, borrowed from Cortezza an ointment that would cause horrible blisters on the skin. After covering her face with this ointment, she visited Alphonso, revealed her disfigurement, and denounced him for his actions. This blow to the duke was followed quickly by a second one: news was brought that Medice, against his orders, had wounded Vincentio. With Vincentio, when he was brought in, was Strozza, who had recovered, the arrow having fallen from his side as he had predicted. Strozza charged the duke with being a tyrant; and Duke Alphonso, seeing before him the consequences of his deeds, humbly accepted the rebuke and expressed his fervent wish that he could undo his actions. So possible tragedy was averted. Vincentio, although seriously wounded, would recover, and he desired to marry Margaret in spite of her terrible disfigurement. She at first refused his offer because she felt he could only pity her, not love her. But this obstacle was removed when a doctor revealed that he could remove the blisters from her face. Bassiolo, expecting punishment, received instead the commendation of the duke. Medice, after admitting that he had misrepresented himself as a nobleman, was exiled. Duke Alphonso, happy at the turn of events, gave his blessing to the marriage of Vincentio and Margaret.

GEORGIA SCENES

Type of work: Short stories and sketches
Author: Augustus Baldwin Longstreet (1790-1870)
Time: 1780-1830
Locale: Georgia
First published: 1835

It was an auspicious moment for American literature when the presses of the *Augusta State Rights Sentinel* issued a collection of pieces that had appeared in that newspaper, for this book, born in obscurity, was *Georgia Scenes, Characters, Incidents, &c., in the First Half Century of the Republic* by "A Native Georgian." The author was not a professional man of letters, but rather one of those wonderfully versatile gentlemen who flourished in nineteenth-century America. Lawyer, judge, politician, Methodist minister, newspaper publisher, and educator (at various times president of Emory College, Centenary College, the University of Mississippi, and the University of South Carolina), Augustus Baldwin Longstreet was ideally suited to the task of writing an informal social history of the southwestern frontier. An educated man (Yale), but no scholar, his activities brought him into personal contact with the whole range of men and manners in the growing country. Although *Georgia Scenes* now enjoys a position as a minor classic, it appealed to its own times as a new and exciting vein of writing. Edgar Allan Poe heralded it as an "omen of better days for the literature of the South," and the reading public called for twelve editions by 1894.

Georgia Scenes is significant on several counts. It is a pioneer work of realism and one of the milestones in the local color movement. Longstreet's careful use of dialect foreshadows a whole school of writing that reached a culmination of sorts with Joel Chandler Harris' Uncle Remus tales. As a humorist, Longstreet is intimately connected with the great tradition of rough-and-tumble frontier humorists. In this category he is a real precursor of Mark Twain, and there is much in *Georgia Scenes* that would not be out of place in *Huckleberry Finn*. Finally, Longstreet wrote with satirical intent, and an argument can be made for his claim to a position among the forerunners of the revolt from the village movement.

Although he was not a literary theorist, Longstreet seems to have worked out a rough theory of realism. It would be folly to consider *Georgia Scenes* an accidental combination of lucky hits. The preface to the first edition shows that the author's aim was to record accurately the details of the life he had observed: "They [the sketches] consist of nothing more than fanciful *combinations* of *real* incidents or characters. . . . Some of the sketches are as literally true as the frailties of memory would allow them to be. . . . The reader will find in the object of the sketches an apology for the minuteness of detail into which some of them run, and for the introduction of some things into them which would have been excluded were they merely the creations of fancy." However, Longstreet was a reporter with a purpose; he applied realism as the handmaiden of social criticism. Like *The Spectator*, which he appears to have admired, Longstreet exposes the follies and vulgarities of his times for the purpose of reforming men and manners. A number of the sketches close with didactic tags. But the author was too much of "A Native Georgian" to advocate replacing good American social norms with foreign modes. He wishes to see a standard of natural, unaffected American manners prevail. Rarely, if ever, does Longstreet miss an opportunity to ridicule or scorn European manners or even imported culture. On the subject of greetings between women he remarks: "The custom of kissing, as practised in these days by the *amiables,* is borrowed from the French, and by them from *Judas.*" The whole of a rather thin sketch, "The Song," is devoted to the horrors of Continental music and the absurdity of American girls who study it.

The nineteen sketches of *Georgia Scenes* are roughly divided into two groups—those dealing chiefly with men and those which deal with women. In their original periodical publication, the sketches appeared as two series signed with two pseudonyms. These general categories do not circumscribe the material. A whole world of rural and urban life is packed into the fairly slim volume: brawls, shooting matches, horse races, balls, inns, old wives, young bloods, country schools, high society, and Negroes. As Longstreet noted in his preface, there is an abundance of detail. But it is not intrusive, for these are not tightly plotted stories. The term *sketches* describes them perfectly: generally brief descriptive pieces which excel at catching atmosphere, very much like the form of Washington Irving's *Sketch Book* pieces.

The two best-known and most frequently anthologized sketches in *Georgia Scenes* are concerned with the cruder aspects of rural life. In "The Horse-Swap," a professional trader called the "Yellow Blossom" is outduped while trying to pass off a horse with a terrible sore under the saddle. In this sketch Longstreet shows a sympathy for animals that is completely characteristic of the volume. Not only does he pity the suffering of dumb beasts, but he also sees that savage treatment of animals brutalizes the human beings who inflict it. There is probably nothing else in American literature, before Jack London, quite like "The Fight." In the story two bully-boys who have always avoided an encounter are pushed into a brawl by a disagreement between their wives. During the course of the knock down and drag out fight an ear, a finger, part of a nose, and part of a cheek are bitten off. A minor character

in "The Fight" is of considerable interest. Ransy Sniffle is a diseased runt whose greatest delight is starting fights between other people. The brutality of fights is also scored in "Georgia Theatrics," which shows a man rehearsing all the parts in a bloody fight.

Although Longstreet never uses a Negro as a leading character, he takes great pains to transcribe the speech of Negroes, and in this respect he was ahead of his time. The practical joker of "The Character of a Native Georgian" asks a colored woman to sell him half a live chicken, and she protests: "Name o' God! what sort o' chance got to clean chicken in de market-house! Whay de water for scall um and wash um? . . . Ech-ech! Fedder fly all ober de buckera-man meat, he come bang me fo' true. No, massa, I mighty sorry for your wife, but I no cutty chicken open." Longstreet is equally careful to reproduce the dialect of backwoods whites. In "A Sage Conversation" he records the talk of three old women sitting by the fire: "Indeed, I have a great leanin' to sweats of yerbs, in all ailments sich as colds, and rheumaty pains, and pleurisies, and sich; they're wonderful good." This interest in colloquial speech is closely associated with the author's interest in folk customs, as can be seen in "The Turn Out," which describes the custom of giving pupils a holiday if they can turn out (barricade out) the teacher.

Longstreet's crusade against the barbarity of rural sports is most evident in "The Gander Pulling" and "The Turf." In the latter a Negro jockey is killed, and the comment Longstreet puts into the mouth of a woman spectator is worthy of Mark Twain at his bitterest: "I declare, had it not been for that little accident, the sport would have been delightful."

One sketch in *Georgia Scenes* is not by Longstreet. "The Militia Company Drill," by Oliver Hillhouse Prince, gives an account of a wildly undisciplined muster. It is as good as the other pieces and merits inclusion in the volume.

After Augustus B. Longstreet mounted the ladder of respectability he came to feel that *Georgia Scenes* was an undignified work. Though he continued to write, he wrote nothing else that has survived; only one book gives him a literary eminence he probably never expected.

GERMINAL

Type of work: Novel
Author: Émile Zola (1840-1902)
Type of plot: Naturalism
Time of plot: Nineteenth century
Locale: France
First published: 1885

Principal characters:
ÉTIENNE LANTIER, a socialist laborer
MAHEU, a miner
MAHEUDE, his wife
CATHERINE,
ZACHARIE,
JEANLIN, and
ALZIRE, Maheu children
CHAVAL, another workman

Critique:

One of the first books written about the conflict between capital and labor, *Germinal* was based on an actual strike that took place in France in 1884. Completely realistic, the book manages to exaggerate the truth without blaspheming it. Its most commendable quality is its lack of preaching. In a literary sense Zola triumphs here by portraying mob scenes with a painter's success. The emotions and movements of masses of people are so completely depicted that the characters in the story become mere results of the pressure of events around them. The idea of socialism and the nature of the men who uphold it is a principal theme here, yet the book is no manifesto in spite of its social intent.

The Story:

Étienne Lantier set out to walk from Marchiennes to Montsou looking for work. On the way he met Vincent Maheu, another workman, called Bonnemort because of successive escapes from death in the mines. Nearing sixty, Bonnemort suffered a bad cough because of particles of dust from the mine pits.

Bonnemort had a son whose family consisted of seven children. Zacharie, the eldest son, twenty-one years old; Catherine, sixteen years old, and Jeanlin, eleven, worked in the mines. In the morning, as they were dressing, they listened to the sounds of Levaque leaving the next door apartment. Soon afterward Bouteloup joined the Levaque woman. Philomène Levaque, the eldest daughter and Zacharie's mistress, coughed from her lung ailment. Such was the life of those who worked in the mine pits.

Étienne was given a job in the mine. He descended the mine shaft along with Maheu, Zacharie, Chaval, Levaque, and Catherine. At first he mistook the latter for a boy. Chaval, during lunch time, roughly forced the girl to kiss him. This act angered Étienne, although the girl insisted that the brute was not her lover.

The head captain, Dansaert, came with M. Négrel, M. Hennebeau's nephew, to inspect Étienne, the new worker.

There was bitterness among the workers, danger lurking in the shafts, and so little pay that it was hardly worth working. Étienne, however, decided to stay in the mine.

M. Grégoire had inherited from his grandfather a share in the Montsou mines. He lived in peace and luxury with his wife and only daughter, Cécile. A marriage had been arranged between Cécile and Négrel.

One morning Maheude, Maheu's wife, and her small children went to the Grégoires to seek help. They were given warm clothing but no money, since the

Grégoires believed working people would only spend money in drinking and nonsense. Maheude had to beg some groceries and money from Maigrat, who kept a shop and who would lend money if he received a woman's caresses in return. He had Catherine in mind. But Catherine, escaping him, met Chaval that night and allowed him to seduce her. Etienne happened to witness the seduction and was disillusioned by the young girl.

Étienne quickly adapted himself to the mine, so expertly that he earned the profound respect of Maheu. He made friends with the other workers. Only toward Chaval was he hostile, for Catherine now openly showed herself the man's mistress. At the place where Etienne lived he would chat with Souvarine, a friendly man who despised the company of women. Étienne discussed a new movement he had heard about from his friend Pluchart, a Lille mechanic. It was a Marxist movement to free the workers. Étienne who had come to loathe the working conditions and the lives of the miners and their families, hoped to collect a fund to sustain the forthcoming strike. He talked about his plan to Rasseneur, with whom he boarded.

After Zacharie married his mistress Philomène, the mother of his two children, Étienne came to the Maheu household as a boarder. Night after night he urged them to accept his socialistic point of view. As the summer wore on he gained prestige among the neighbors. His fund grew. As the secretary he drew a small fee and was able to put aside money for himself. He began to take on airs.

The threat of strike was provoked when the company lowered the wages of the workers. As a final blow to the Maheus, a cave-in struck Jeanlin, leaving him a cripple. Catherine went to live with Chaval, who had been accusing her of sleeping with Étienne. In December the miners struck.

While the Grégoires and the Hennebeaus were at dinner arranging the plans for the marriage between Cécile and Négrel, the miners' delegation came to see M. Hennebeau, but he refused to give any concessions. The strike wore on through the weeks while the workers slowly starved. Étienne preached socialism and the strikers listened; as their misery increased they became more adamant in their resistance to M. Hennebeau. The endless weeks of strike at the Montsou mines ended in a riot when the people advanced to other pits to force the workers to quit their labors and join the strike. All day the mob destroyed property and raged against their starvation.

Catherine had remained faithful to Chaval, but when, during the riot, he turned renegade and ran to get the gendarmes, she deserted him to warn her comrades, especially Étienne.

Étienne went into hiding, assisted by Jeanlin, who had become a street urchin and a thief. The Maheu family fared poorly. Crippled Alzire, one of the younger children, was dying of starvation. Everywhere neighbors quarreled fretfully over trifles. Étienne frequently slipped into Maheu's house for a visit. For the most part he wandered alone at night. After the strike had been going for two months, there was a rumor that the company was bringing strikebreakers to the pits, Borain workers. Étienne began to despair. He suggested to the Maheus that the strikers bargain with M. Hennebeau, but Maheude, who once had been so sensible and had resisted violence, shouted that they should not give in to the pressure of their want.

One night at Rasseneur's, while Étienne was discussing matters with Souvarine, Chaval and Catherine entered. The animosity between Étienne and Chaval flared up, and they fought. Chaval, overpowered, ordered Catherine not to follow him but to stay with Étienne. Left alone, Catherine and Étienne were embarrassed and confused. Étienne had no place to take the girl. It was not possible for her to go home, since Maheude could not forgive her for having deserted the family and for working during the strike. Resignedly, Catherine went back to her lover.

After Catherine had gone, Étienne walked by the pits, where he was a witness to the murder of a guard by little Jeanlin. Étienne dragged the body away and hid it.

When the strikebreakers began to work, the strikers stormed the entrance to the pit and threatened the soldiers who were on guard. After a while the soldiers fired into the mob. Maheu was among those killed. Twenty-five workers had been wounded and fourteen were dead.

Company officials came to Montsou to settle the strike. The Borains were sent away. Étienne's popularity ended. He brought Catherine home and began to stay at Maheu's house again. The bleak house of mourning filled Étienne with remorse.

Souvarine resolved to leave Montsou. Before he went, he sneaked into the pit and committed enough damage to cause a breakdown in the shafts. That same morning Étienne and Catherine decided that they must go back to work. Chaval managed to be placed on the same work crew with Étienne and Catherine. Repeatedly the two men clashed; Chaval still wanted Catherine.

Water began rushing into the shaft. Below, Chaval, Étienne, and the rest were trapped when the cage made its last trip up and did not come down again. The people above waited and watched the mine slowly become flooded by subterranean torrents of water.

Négrel set about to rescue the entombed workers, for as long as they were below they must be assumed to be still alive. At last he and a rescue party heard faint thumpings from the trapped workers. The men began to dig. An explosion injured several of them and killed Zacharie.

Meanwhile the trapped workers had scattered, trying to find a place of safety. Etienne and Catherine came upon Chaval in the gallery to which he had climbed. There the animosity between the two men led to a fight which ended when Étienne killed Chavel. Alone, the two lovers heard the rescuers' tapping. For days they continued to answer the tapping. Catherine died before the men outside reached them. Étienne was still alive when help came.

After six weeks in a hospital Étienne prepared to go to Paris, where more revolutionary work awaited him.

GERMINIE LACERTEUX

Type of work: Novel
Authors: Edmond (1822-1896) and Jules (1830-1870) de Goncourt
Type of plot: Naturalism
Time of plot: Nineteenth century
Locale: Paris
First published: 1865

Principal characters:
GERMINIE LACERTEUX, a maidservant
MADEMOISELLE DE VARANDEUIL, Germinie's employer
MADAME JUPILLON, Germinie's friend
MONSIEUR JUPILLON, Madame Jupillon's son and Germinie's lover
MONSIEUR GAUTRUCHE, another lover of Germinie

Critique:

The story of Germinie Lacerteux is not a pretty one, nor did its authors mean it to be a pretty tale. They consciously set out to show how the life of a very minor figure in the city of Paris could contain the real essence of tragedy, despite the heroine's low station. According to Zola, a great admirer of the Goncourt brothers, the study of the lower classes in fiction began with this novel. The story of Germinie, a servant, is presented with the clinical detachment of the dissecting room. No details are spared the reader, and the emotions, pains, and joys of such a life are carefully analyzed in realistic fashion. The authors, who neither condemned nor praised, but simply presented what they saw, are the literary forerunners of such American novelists as Stephen Crane, Frank Norris, and Theodore Dreiser.

The Story:

Germinie Lacerteux, left an orphan at the age of four years, was taken care of by her sisters. At the age of fourteen she was sent to Paris to live with an older sister who had settled with her husband in the city. Not wishing to pay for all the expenses of the child from their own meager income, the sister and her husband found Germinie a job as a waitress in a café. After she had worked in the café for several months, she was seduced by one of the waiters. Becoming pregnant, she suffered many indignities from her relatives because she would not say to them that she had literally been raped; they thought she had invited seduction. Her child was born dead, and her sickness almost killed Germinie. Finally a retired actor took pity upon her and hired her as a maid and companion. For Germinie this was a step upward in the world; unfortunately for her, the old actor died within a few months. Germinie then filled a host of positions as maid to kept women and boarding-school mistresses.

One day the maid of Mlle. de Varandeuil died suddenly, and through the influence of her sister Germinie was given the position. Mlle. de Varandeuil was an old maid. Her father had prevented her from being anything but a servant to him until his death, so that Mlle. de Varandeuil had few friends and acquaintances. Other members of her family had died, and she herself was an old woman. She had a sufficient income to live more or less comfortably, but it could not tolerate many extravagances. In her old age she needed someone to look after her, as much a companion as a maidservant.

For a time after her entry into the service of Mlle. de Varandeuil, Germinie was a devoted Christian. She spent a great deal of time at church and went to confession regularly. Through her devotions she fell in love with a young priest, but he, sensing her state of mind, sent her to another confessor and refused to speak to her. When he took that course of action, Germinie's devotions ceased.

Germinie's next devotion was to her

sister's niece, who was left to Germinie's care when the mother died. But Germinie's happiness was short-lived, for the child was taken to Africa by another sister. When word came by letter that the child was ill and the sister's husband out of work, Germinie sent everything she could to aid the stricken child and the family that was taking care of her. After depriving herself of necessities for two years, Germinie learned that the child had died shortly after leaving Paris and that the letters from the aunt and uncle were only a ruse to get Germinie's hard-earned money.

About that time a dairy store was opened very close to the house in which Germinie lived with Mlle. de Varandeuil. In her dealings with the store Germinie found a friend in Madame Jupillon, the proprietress. Madame Jupillon had a son, who was at a trade school learning to become a glove maker. Germinie, quite taken with the youngster, often went with his mother to see him on visiting days. One day, when Madame Jupillon was ill, Germinie went by herself to the school. Upon her arrival she learned that the young man was in trouble because some questionable books had been found in his possession. Germinie helped him out of his difficulty, but when she tried to lecture him found herself unable to do so.

Soon Germinie realized that she had a great deal of affection for the young man, who was ten years her junior. In order to be near him and to have company, she spent a great deal of time with the Jupillons, who took advantage of her willingness to help in the store. She was exceedingly jealous when Jupillon was attracted to a woman of notoriety and did everything she could to keep the two apart. By her actions she left herself open to the advances of young Jupillon, who was not above taking advantage of her unselfish devotion.

Germinie was extremely happy as the lover of young Jupillon; she had a need, both physically and psychologically, for someone to love. But she soon discovered that Jupillon spent much time in the company of other women. To help keep him for herself, Germinie spent all her money to buy him a place in which to open his own business, meanwhile providing him with an apartment of his own. But shortly after she had done so much for him Germinie was turned away from Jupillon's door by another woman who had become his mistress. In the meantime Germinie had become pregnant; a baby daughter was born. Since it was impossible to keep the child at home while acting as Mlle. de Varandeuil's maidservant, Germinie farmed out the child. The death of the baby a few months later brought Germinie great sorrow.

Some time after she had been turned out by Jupillon, the young man was unfortunate enough to be called for military service. He had no money to secure his release, but he knew that he could get the money from Germinie, who still loved him. Germinie, after some trepidation, went into debt to keep her false lover near her. She was compelled to borrow so much money that the bare interest on it took everything she could spare from her small income.

As the years passed Jupillon took less and less interest in Germinie, so that she finally gave him up and turned to liquor for comfort. Drunkenness became her one joy, although she managed to keep the secret of her vice to herself; old Mlle. de Varandeuil never even guessed the truth. Everyone noticed, however, that she had become slovenly in her person and in her work. Mlle. de Varandeuil kept her on only because the old woman could not stand the thought of a new servant in the house. Germinie had two grave problems: she had no one to love, and she was miserably in debt because of a man who cared nothing for her.

At last Germinie found herself approaching forty years of age. About that time she met a man in his fifties, a painter, and took him as a lover. She did not love Gautruche except as an object upon which her pent-up affections could be lavished. Before long she felt much better, behaved much better, and was a better servant to her mistress. But Gautruche saw in her only a servant for himself, and he believed that she would be only too happy to leave her job and marry him. Much to his surprise, she refused his offer of marriage, and the two parted forever. Once again Germinie was left with no one who cared for her or upon whom she could lavish her affections. She turned in her desperation to picking up any man she could find on the streets. One night, as she roamed Paris looking for a lover, she saw Jupillon. She followed him to a house and spent the night outside in the rain, while waiting for a chance to see him again. The next morning she was desperately ill with pleurisy. She kept on working in spite of her illness, until her condition became much worse. At last Mlle. de Varandeuil sent her to a hospital and there Germinie died. After her death all her secrets were revealed, for everyone to whom she owed money attempted to collect from her employer. At first Mlle. de Varandeuil was outraged; then she came to realize the agony and frustration of Germinie's life, and felt only pity for the wretched girl.

GETTYSBURG

Type of work: Short stories
Author: Elsie Singmaster (Mrs. E. S. Lewars, 1879-1958)
Types of plots: Historical chronicle and regional realism
Times of plots: 1863-1913
Locale: Gettysburg, Pennsylvania
First published: 1913

> *Principal characters:*
> MARY BOWMAN, widowed during the battle
> YOUNG PARSONS, a recruit from Gettysburg
> COLONEL FRANK HASKELL, of the Thirty-sixth Wisconsin Infantry
> GUNNER ADAM CRISWELL, a blind veteran
> FREDERICK DAGGETT, a military substitute
> GRANDFATHER MYERS, an aged veteran

Critique:

Gettysburg gave Elsie Singmaster's writing its center and its roots, and this collection of her short stories is one of the best books ever written about the battle fought there and its aftermath. Living on the site of that great conflict, the writer heard at first hand the stories of many men and women who remembered vividly the events of those three decisive days of July first, second, and third, 1863. The people of that time are dead and buried now, but Elsie Singmaster has preserved their recollections in this book, to which she gave the simple yet evocative title, *Gettysburg*. Her treatment is both realistic and legendary. The book opens with a picture of the town when news came that a battle was to be fought there, continues with an account of the battle and the Confederate retreat, and ends with a group of stories dealing with characters whose experiences are presented in retrospect—blind Gunner Criswell, whose name was missing from the roll of honor; old Daggett, the substitute who had been cheated of honor and pay; Grandfather Myers, who saw the marching ranks once more before he died; Mary Bowman, widowed during the fighting, who saw General Early on his white horse, the ghostly leader of that grim retreat through wind and rain. *Gettysburg* may be read as a work of fiction. The stories, however, are based on actual people and events.

The Stories:

Mary Bowman, scraping lint for wound-dressings, found it difficult to keep her mind on her work. Close by, her three small children played that they were General Early and his ragged Confederate troops, who had passed through Gettysburg several days before. Yesterday Union soldiers had marched into town and headed toward Chambersburg. Mary Bowman was glad that the village was not to see fighting, thankful that her husband was with Hooker's unengaged forces. But she had dreamed of marching men in the night. Suddenly uneasy, she went to her front door. Hannah Casey, a neighbor, came from her garden across the street. While they stood talking a soldier rode by and warned them to take shelter. The Army of Northern Virginia was advancing from the north, the Army of the Potomac from the south. The women looked at each other in dismay as cannon roared threateningly from the ridge west of town.

For months young Parsons had dreamed of fields filled with dead men. Sometimes he wanted to run away.

Marching along the dusty road from Taneytown, he suddenly realized that the army was moving toward Gettysburg, where he had been born. Firing sounded in the distance. As his company marched that night past the cemetery where his father was buried, he could stand the thought of death and battle no longer. Turning, he ran blindly through the darkness to his mother's farmhouse. Finding the door locked, he entered through a window and crept upstairs to his own bed. He awoke in late afternoon, to find the house empty, his mother nowhere about. Looking from a window, he saw men in blue and other men in gray skirmishing outside. His fears forgotten, he began to fire on the Confederates. All that afternoon he and the Union soldiers held the strategic ground around the Parsons house, where, toward evening, his friends carried him with a bullet wound in his throat. Lying on the kitchen floor, he saw his mother as she came from the cellar where she had hidden herself when the firing began. On Parsons' face was a look of peace; he had come home.

Near a clump of trees, on the third day of the battle, Colonel Frank Haskell waited in a stone-fenced field. Around him were long lines of infantry, re-formed since yesterday's fighting. A mile away, on the opposite ridge, Lee's men also waited. The cannonading began. Smoke drifted across the field. Men fell, but still the Union lines waited. The bombardment ended with heavy, ominous silence. Then through the smoke the Confederate ranks appeared, eighteen thousand men, a rolling sea of gray. Shells, shrapnel, canister failed to stop them. When the Union lines began to waver, the young officer drew his sword and urged his men back. The troops were fighting hand to hand as the smoke closed down. Then the Confederate charge broke. By a clump of trees behind a stone wall Pickett's charge ended in defeat.

Although she had been forewarned, Mary Bowman was startled by the sound of reveille on the morning of November 19, 1863. The night before a train from Washington had brought President Lincoln to Gettysburg for the dedication of a cemetery for the dead soldiers. Out there on the battlefield, among the unknown dead, lay Mary Bowman's husband, for whom she had looked in vain. Sad and embittered by her loss, she went to the ceremony only because the judge, a kindly man concerned for her welfare, insisted that she take her children. She heard little that the orator of the day said, for her mind was on the wounded she had nursed, on the grim debris of the battle she had uncovered in her search. As she turned to leave, someone said that the President was about to speak. Abraham Lincoln, lank and sad-faced, spoke only a few words, but, hearing them, Mary Bowman took heart. It was as if he were telling her to be of good comfort, that her duty was to the living as well as the dead.

The explosion which cost Gunner Adam Criswell his eyesight on the second day of the battle had not disabled him. A vigorous old man, he returned to Gettysburg with his friend, Carolus Depew, in September, 1910, for the dedication of the great monument containing the names of all Pennsylvania soldiers who had fought in the battle. While Carolus looked for his own name, a boy read to the blind man the names of those in Criswell's battery. The townspeople had opened their homes to the old soldiers; Criswell and Depew stayed with Professor James and his wife. Another guest was a pompous general who took credit for the plan to inscribe the veterans' names on the monument. The next day Criswell went to the exercises with Mrs. James. Afterward the general offered to find the blind man's name on the memorial tablets. Then Criswell told them what he himself already knew. His name had been overlooked.

Frederick Daggett had fought as a substitute. The other man had promised him a thousand dollars, but the money had never been paid. All Gettysburg, knowing Daggett as a drunkard and braggart, laughed at his foolish story. Congressman Ellison Brant, arriving in Gettysburg on the eve of Memorial Day, was unable to find accommodations or a guide until Daggett offered his services. Brant, impatient and demanding, was dissatisfied with the old man's efforts and tried to pay him off contemptuously in the crowded lobby of the Keystone Hotel. Before all the people there, Daggett demanded his thousand dollars, for he had recognized Brant as the man who had cheated him years before. The politician reached for his checkbook before he realized that his gesture was an admission of guilt. Hurriedly he wrote the check. Daggett took it and deliberately tore the slip of paper in two. Ragged and disreputable, he could always boast that he had thrown away a thousand dollars.

Grandfather Myers, invalided home after Chancellorsville, had watched the Confederates retreating through rain and mud from Gettysburg. Ever since, he had regretted the illness which had kept him from offering food or comfort to the tired, defeated men. He himself was an old man when the state militia held a summer encampment on the battlefield. His son, daughter-in-law, and grandchildren went to see the review, but Grandfather Myers stayed at home because there was no room for him in the buggy. That afternoon he dressed himself in his blue uniform. He was sitting on the front porch when a detachment of the National Guard came marching by on maneuvers. To the old man they were Lee's soldiers in retreat, their uniforms yellow with dust instead of tattered and rain-soaked. When they asked for water he could only nod smilingly. At last he had given Lee's men something. He could die content.

Although Mary Bowman lived to see the fiftieth anniversary of the battle, she never talked of those days. But she remembered all her life her husband, lost on that battlefield, the voice of Abraham Lincoln, and most vividly of all the figure of General Early, as she had seen him riding by on his white horse, the spectral leader of a stumbling, ghostly host on that rain-muffled retreat toward Hagerstown.

1323

GHOSTS

Type of work: Drama
Author: Henrik Ibsen (1828-1906)
Type of plot: Social criticism
Time of plot: Nineteenth century
Locale: Rosenvold, Norway
First presented: 1881

Principal characters:
MRS. HELEN ALVING, a widow
OSWALD ALVING, her son, an artist
MANDERS, pastor of the parish
JACOB ENGSTRAND, a carpenter
REGINA ENGSTRAND, his daughter, in Mrs. Alving's service

Critique:

Ghosts is Ibsen's effort to substitute the modern scientific concept of heredity for the Greek idea of Fate. But there is more to the play than merely a study in degenerative heredity; it is a mordant attack upon society and the standards by which it lives. Ibsen explicitly says that these standards were responsible for the tragedy of Mrs. Alving, and in so doing he tossed a bombshell into the conventional and even the liberal thought of his day. The play can still be read as a study in what has come to be known as the science of semantics—the disruptive effect caused when words or concepts are, in society, divorced from the realities for which they are supposed to stand.

The Story:

Pastor Manders called on Mrs. Helen Alving on the eve of the tenth anniversary of her husband's death, to discuss certain details concerning the opening of an orphanage in memory of her late husband. The pastor found Mrs. Alving in the best of spirits, for her son Oswald, an artist, had returned from Paris to attend the dedication of the memorial to his father. Although he was now twenty-six, Oswald had lived away from his parents since he was seven, and Mrs. Alving was delighted at the prospect of having her son spend the entire winter with her.

Oswald had idealized his father, for in her letters his mother had always pictured Captain Alving as a sort of hero. The boy's own memories of his father were confined to one incident in his childhood when his father had taken him on his knee and encouraged him to smoke a large meerschaum pipe. Oswald remembered this episode, and upon his return home he took a certain pride in lighting up his father's old pipe and parading in front of his mother and Pastor Manders.

Pastor Manders did not approve of smoking; in fact, he did not approve of anything which could even loosely be interpreted as sin. He did not approve of Oswald's bohemian way of life in Paris and blamed Mrs. Alving's neglect for her son's ideas. He reminded Mrs. Alving that hardly a year after her marriage she had come to him willing to leave her husband, and that he had sent her back to her duty. This was an act Manders considered the greatest moral victory of his life.

Mrs. Alving thought it high time that Manders be informed of the truth about her late husband. Years before, when he advised her return to Captain Alving, the minister had been quite aware of her husband's profligacy. What he did not know was that the profligacy continued after his wife's dutiful return. Her entire relationship with her husband consisted largely of helping him into bed after

GHOSTS by Henrik Ibsen. Published by Charles Scribner's Sons.

one of his drinking bouts, and on one occasion she had surprised him making love to her own maidservant. But the most abominable aspect of the situation was the fact that she had discovered, soon after her marriage, that her husband was diseased and her son would have to go through life with his father's curse upon his head. Manders' religious influence and Mrs. Alving's cowardice had conspired to keep silence.

Now it began to look as if the moral consequences would play themselves out. While Mrs. Alving and the minister talked, Oswald was attempting familiarities in the adjoining dining-room with the maid, Regina, his own stepsister. To Mrs. Alving it seemed as if this act were the ghost of her unhappy marriage, for Regina, ostensibly the daughter of a drunken carpenter named Jacob Engstrand, was actually the result of Captain Alving's escapade with the maidservant, the discovery of which had sent Mrs. Alving flying to Pastor Manders for solace and help. Engstrand had been willing to turn Regina over to Mrs. Alving for her education and care. Now, however, he had other ideas for the girl's future. He planned to enlist her aid in the establishment of a seamen's home. But Regina had other plans for herself, and saw no reason why she should throw herself away on worthless and irresponsible sailors when she might have the heir of a wealthy family.

Oswald himself, unaware of any blood relationship, wanted to marry Regina. He confided to his mother that before he left Paris he had gone to a doctor regarding a feeling of malaise which robbed him of his ambition to paint. The doctor had commented on the sins of fathers. Oswald, knowing only the picture of his father that his mother's letters had given him, was furious, and he thought he had brought about his own downfall. He told his mother that he wanted to marry Regina and make what was left of his life happy. Mrs. Alving realized that at last she must tell the two young people the truth. But before she had a chance to do so, news came that the orphanage which was to have been Captain Alving's memorial was afire.

When the orphanage caught fire, Manders and Engstrand were in the carpenter shop nearby. After the fire, Engstrand accused the pastor of dropping a lighted candle wick into some shavings. Though not guilty, Manders was frightened because of his position in the community. When Engstrand offered to take the blame for the fire in return for enough money from the remainder of Captain Alving's fortune to build his sailor's home, the self-righteous Manders agreed to this blackmail and promised to help Engstrand in the transaction.

Mrs. Alving told Oswald and Regina the story of their late father. She tried to explain why Alving had been doomed from the beginning. When it was revealed that she was really Alving's daughter, Regina was angry, feeling that she should have been reared and educated as a lady. She preferred to cast her lot with Engstrand. Alone with his mother, Oswald revealed the final horror; an affliction had already attacked his brain and would result in complete regression to childhood. Mrs. Alving assured her son that she would always be by his side to take care of him. Oswald urged his mother to kill him if the need should arise. Shocked, Mrs. Alving refused when he showed her the morphia tablets he had brought with him. They were still talking at daybreak. Mrs. Alving blew out the light. But while she stood and looked in horror, Oswald sat crying childishly for the sun.

GIANTS IN THE EARTH

Type of work: Novel
Author: O. E. Rölvaag (1876-1931)
Type of plot: Regional romance
Time of plot: Late nineteenth century
Locale: The Dakotas
First published: 1924-1925

Principal characters:
PER HANSA, a Norwegian settler
BERET, his wife
OLE,
ANNA MARIE,
HANS KRISTIAN, and
PEDER VICTORIOUS, their children

Critique:

Giants in the Earth is a tremendous contribution to our understanding of pioneer life. Perhaps some day it will be condensed into a saga, its story sharpened down into the short, keen points of myth and its Per Hansa viewed as an American folk hero. It is important to realize that Rölvaag, writing in the tradition of Western Europe, and writing for a European audience, was able to blend old and new and to create a story which an American audience would accept. The theme of the novel is a great one: man's struggle with the stubborn earth. This theme is of principal importance to Americans. It is the story of man bearing his memory of other lands into a new country, and out of that experience building a new homeplace and a new people.

The Story:

Per Hansa moved all his family and his possessions from Minnesota into the Dakota territory. His family consisted of his wife, Beret, and three children, Ole, Anna Marie, and Hans Kristian. Beret was fearful and sad, for she had been uprooted too often and the prairie country through which they traveled seemed bleak, lonely, savage.

Per Hansa staked out his claim near the family of Hans Olsa at Spring Creek. Then Beret announced that she was carrying another child. Money was scarce. Per Hansa faced overwhelming odds and thoughts of the great risks he was taking kept him awake long after Beret and the children slept. Being something of a poet, Per Hansa thought at times that the land spoke to him, and often he watched and listened and forgot to keep to his work as he cleared his land and built his house. He labored from before dawn until after dark during those long, northern summer days.

When Indians came and drove away the settlers' cows, only Per Hansa had the courage to follow after them. Only he had the sense to doctor a sick Indian. Beret mistrusted his wisdom for foolishness and there were harsh words between them. The grateful Indian gave Per Hansa a pony. Then Per Hansa went on a buying expedition and returned with many needed supplies and, what was more, news of coming settlers.

The next summer Per Hansa discovered claim stakes which bore Irish names. The stakes were on his neighbor's land; the homesteaders had settled where others had already filed claim. Secretly he removed the stakes and burned them, but not before Beret realized what he was doing. She began to worry over her husband's deed. Per Hansa sold some potatoes to people traveling through and awoke the slumbering jealousy of his neighbors.

In midsummer more people arrived, the settlers who had set out the stakes that Per Hansa had burned. They called the Norwegians claim jumpers, but after a fight they took up other land nearby. Per Hansa managed to sell some of his goods to them. That fall more Norwegians came. The little community was thriving. But Beret, depressed by the open spaces and her fear that her husband had done a bad thing, brewed a dark remorse within herself. Day by day she brooded over her lonely life, and she covered her window at night because of her nameless fears. At least Per Hansa on his infrequent trips around to different settlements met other people.

When winter came Per Hansa rested. He could sleep long hours while the winds blew outside, but his wife worried and fretted. He began to quarrel with her. Soon, however, he noticed that his neighbors were suffering hardship and privation. The unmarried young men who had settled near the Hansas were planning to desert the settlement. It required all his ability to convince them to stay and to face the desolate, bitter winter to its end.

The settlers began to talk of a school which would move from house to house so that the parents might learn English along with the children.

During the winter Per Hansa became lost in a blizzard and only his tremendous strength and courage saw him and his oxen safely through the storm to the Trönders' settlement. The following day, forgetting how Beret must be worrying about him, he stayed on and cut a load of wood to take back home with him.

His next expedition was to bargain with the Indians for furs. He suffered greatly from exposure and lost two toes through frostbite.

When spring came, Per Hansa could not wait to get into his fields to plant his wheat. His friends thought he was planting too early. And so it seemed, for snow fell the next day and freezing weather set in. Determined not to lose heart, Per Hansa decided to plant potatoes in place of the wheat. Beret took to her Bible, convinced that evil was working its way into their lives. Then, unexpectedly, their wheat came up.

Another couple arrived. They were exhausted with travel, the wife saddened by the death of her son on the prairie. Per Hansa and Beret took them in. When they moved on, greater despondency seized Beret. She felt some doom was working its way closer and closer to her life.

That summer grasshoppers destroyed much of the grain. Most of Per Hansa's crop was saved, but Beret took his good fortune only as a sign that the underground trolls, or evil spirits, were planning greater ruin for her and her husband.

In the following years the scourge of the grasshoppers returned. Many of the settlers were ruined. Some starved. Some went mad. One summer a traveling Norwegian minister took up residence with them to plan a religious service for the whole community. His coming worked a change in Per Hansa's household. Per Hansa took courage from it and consolation, but deeper and stranger grew the reveries in Beret's mind. Because it was the largest house in the district the minister held a communion service in Per Hansa's cabin. Disconnected parts of the service floated all that week in Beret's head. Her mind was filled with strange fancies. She began to think of Peder Victorious, her youngest child, who was born on the prairie, as a savior who would work their salvation.

As the autumn came on, the great plains seemed hungry for the blood and strength of those who had come to conquer it.

That winter Hans Olsa froze his legs and one hand. In spite of all that Per Hansa and the others did for their neighbor, Hans Olsa grew weaker. Beret stood beside him, predicting that he had not long to live. She put into the sick man's mind the idea to send for the minister. Per Hansa thought that Hans Olsa was weak in calling for a minister and that the way to throw off illness was to get out of bed and go to work. He had never spared himself, nor had he spared his sons. He was the man to go for the minister, but this time he was unwilling to set out on a long winter journey. Hans Olsa was a good man; he did not need a minister to help him die. The weather itself was threatening. However,

Per Hansa reconsidered. His sons were digging a tunnel through snow to the pigsty. Inside, his wife was preparing a meal for him. They watched as he took down his skis and prepared to make the journey for the sake of his dying friend. He did not look back at his house or speak farewell to Beret as he started out.

So Per Hansa, on his errand of mercy, walked into the snowstorm. There death overtook him.

GIL BLAS OF SANTILLANE

Type of work: Novel
Author: Alain René Le Sage (1668-1747)
Type of plot: Picaresque romance
Time of plot: Seventeenth century
Locale: Spain
First published: 1715, 1724, 1735

Principal characters:
GIL BLAS, a rogue
SCIPIO, his secretary
DON ALPHONSO, his patron

Critique:

The Adventures of Gil Blas of Santillane is a long novel made up of many disconnected episodes. One of the first works to introduce thieves, vagabonds, and vulgar peasantry into fiction, it is a precursor of the realism of Flaubert and Balzac. The setting is supposedly Spain, but the characters and settings are in reality French, and particularly Breton. The appeal of this book comes from the skilled narration of exciting tales, and from its author's shrewd insight into the minds of his picturesque characters.

The Story:

Blas of Santillane retired from the wars and married a chambermaid no longer young. After the birth of Gil, the parents settled in Oviedo, where the father became a minor squire and the mother went into service.

Happily, Gil Perez, Gil Blas' uncle, was a canon in the town. He was three and a half feet high and enormously fat. Without his aid, Gil Blas would never have received an education. He provided a tutor for his nephew and at the age of seventeen Gil Blas had studied the classics and some logic.

When the time came for him to seek his fortune, the family sent Gil Blas to Salamanca to study. The uncle provided him with forty pistoles and a mule. Shortly after setting out, Gil Blas was foolish enough to join the train of a muleteer who concocted a story that he had been robbed of a hundred pistoles and threatened all his passengers with arrest and torture. His purpose was to frighten

the men away so that he could seduce the wife of one of the travelers. Gil Blas had some thought of helping the woman, but he fled upon the arrival of a police patrol.

Gil Blas was found in the woods by a band of ruffians who had an underground hideout nearby. Under Captain Rolando, they made Gil their serving-boy. After an unsuccessful attempt to escape, he set out to ingratiate himself with the captain. At the end of six months he became a member of the gang and embarked on a career of robbery and murder. One day the robbers attacked a coach, killed all the men, and captured a beautiful woman. Since she was well-born and modest, Gil Blas resolved to rescue her. Waiting until the robbers were asleep, he tied up the cook and escaped with the woman, whose name, he learned, was Donna Mencia. She was very grateful for her rescue, and, dressing Gil Blas in fine clothes, she presented him with a bag of money. So he went on his way, comparatively rich and comfortable.

On his travels he met Fabricio, a former schoolmate who had become a barber. Scornful of Gil's intention to study, Fabricio soon prevailed upon him to go into service as a lackey. As it turned out, Gil was well adapted to flattery and intrigue, and he soon became proficient by serving a variety of masters, among them Doctor Sangrado, a physician. The doctor's one remedy for all maladies was forced drinking of water and frequent bleeding. Gil Blas won the doctor's esteem and was permitted to at-

1329

tend poor patients in his master's place. During an epidemic, he made a record as good as that of Sangrado; all of their patients died.

Another master was Don Matthias, a fashionable man about town. By means of a little judicious thievery and daring, Gil Blas found his new life highly satisfying. Each day was spent in eating and polite conversation, every night in carousing. During this service Gil dressed in his master's clothes and tried to get a mistress among the titled ladies of the town. An old lady who arranged these affairs introduced him to a grand lady who was pining for a lover. Gil was disillusioned when he went with Don Matthias to the house of Arsenia, an actress, and found that his grand lady was really a serving-maid.

After Don Matthias was killed in a duel, Gil attended Arsenia for a time. Later he went into service in the household of Aurora, a virtuous young woman who grieved because a student named Lewis paid no attention to her charms. At Gil's suggestion, Aurora disguised herself as a man and took an apartment in the same house with Lewis. Striking up a friendship with him, Aurora skillfully led him on. Then she received him in her own house in her proper person, and soon Lewis and Aurora were married. Gil Blas left their service content with his part in the romance.

On the road again, Gil was able to frustrate a band of robbers who had planned to kill Don Alphonso. Thus Gil and the don began a lasting friendship.

After losing a situation because he learned that the duenna had an ulcer on her back, Gil next took service with an archbishop. His work was to write out the homilies composed by the archbishop. After he had won his master's confidence, the churchman made Gil promise to tell him when his homilies showed signs of degenerating in quality. After a stroke, the archbishop failed mentally, and Gil told him his homilies were not up to the usual standard. In his rage, the archbishop dismissed Gil, who learned in this manner the folly of being too truthful.

Engaged as secretary by the Duke of Lerma, prime minister of Spain, Gil soon became the duke's confidential agent. Now Gil was in a position to sell favors, and his avarice grew apace with his success in court intrigue. During this successful period, he engaged Scipio as his servant. Gil's high position enabled him to secure the governorship of Valencia for Don Alphonso.

Gil became involved in high court scandal. At the request of the prime minister, he acted as pander for the prince of Spain, the heir apparent. About the same time Scipio arranged a wealthy marriage for Gil with the daughter of a rich goldsmith. But one night the king's spies caught Gil conducting the prince to a house of pleasure and Gil was confined to prison. Faithful Scipio shared his imprisonment. After months of sickness, Gil was released and exiled from Madrid. Fortunately Don Alphonso gave Gil a country estate at Lirias, and there he and Scipio settled to lead the simple lives of country gentlemen. Attracted by Antonia, the daughter of one of his farmers, Gil married, but his happiness was brief. After Antonia and his baby daughter died, Gil became restless for new fields. The prince was now king, and Gil resolved to try court life again. He became an intimate of the new prime minister, Count Olivarez. Once again he was employed to arrange a liaison for the king, a mission that turned out badly. Forced to resign, Gil returned for good to Lirias.

There he made a second marriage with a girl named Dorothea. Now content, Gil Blas hoped for children whose education would provide amusement for his old age.

THE GILDED AGE

Type of work: Novel
Authors: Mark Twain (Samuel L. Clemens, 1835-1910) and Charles Dudley Warner (1829-1900)
Type of plot: Social satire
Time of plot: Nineteenth century
Locale: United States
First published: 1873

Principal characters:
> WASHINGTON HAWKINS, a young Westerner
> LAURA HAWKINS, his adopted sister
> COLONEL BERIAH SELLERS, an improvident optimist
> PHILIP STERLING, a young engineer
> HARRY BRIERLY, his friend
> SENATOR DILWORTHY, a member of Congress
> RUTH BOLTON, a Quaker

Critique:

Satire was Mark Twain's forte, and in this novel his wit finds a wide range. In fact, he and his co-author planned to attack almost every aspect of contemporary society. The weakness in the story lies in its co-authorship; it hangs in uncertain balance between sober reality and sheer hilarity, with no clear demarcation between the two attitudes. Mark Twain's contribution can easily be recognized by readers familiar with the humorist's style. The book was apparently intended to do for the novel what *The Knight of the Burning Pestle* did for the drama. Diffused in its effects, the novel does contain one memorable element, the unforgettable character of Beriah Sellers.

The Story:

Squire Hawkins of Obedstown, Tennessee, received a letter from Colonel Beriah Sellers asking Hawkins to come to Missouri with his wife Nancy and two Hawkins children, Emily and George Washington. Moved by the colonel's eloquent account of opportunities to be found in the new territory, the family traveled West. On the journey they stopped at a house where a young child was mourning the death of his mother. Taking compassion on the orphan, Hawkins offered to adopt him. His name was Henry Clay.

The travelers boarded the *Boreas,* a steamboat headed up the Mississippi. In a race with a rival the two boats collided, causing a fire on the other steamboat and killing or injuring scores of passengers. In the confusion Hawkins found a stray child, Laura, whose parents apparently had died in the fire. The Hawkinses, although now burdened with four children to care for, took hope in the promise of Tennessee lands which they still owned.

After a tiresome journey they reached their new home, a log cabin surrounded by a dozen or so other ramshackle dwellings. There Colonel Sellers helped the Hawkinses start their new life. But Squire Hawkins did not prosper as he had hoped and before long his affairs became hopelessly involved.

Ten years later found Colonel Sellers living in Hawkeye, a town some distance away. Squire Hawkins, by that time, was impoverished. Clay had gone off to find work and Laura, now a beautiful young girl, volunteered to do so. Washington and Emily could not decide what to do. Clay brought money to the destitute family and paid Washington's stagecoach fare to Hawkeye, where he found Colonel Sellers as poorly off as the Hawkins family. But Colonel Sellers was a magnificent talker. His fireless stove became a secret invention, his meager dinner a feast, his barren house a mansion, and under the spell of his words Washington's dismal prospects were changed to prospects of a glowing future. Colonel Sellers spoke confidentially of private deals with New York bankers and the Rothschilds. He confided that he was working on a patent medicine which would bring him a fortune.

Colonel Sellers took Washington to the real estate office of General Boswell. It was arranged that the young man should live with the Boswells while working for the general. Before long he fell in love with Boswell's daughter Louise.

Squire Hawkins died, leaving his family only the lands in Tennessee. Among his papers Laura found some letters from a Major Lackland, who apparently had come across a man believed to be Laura's father. Before Hawkins could get in touch with the man, he had disappeared. Laura's doubtful parentage made her an object of scorn in the region.

Two young New Yorkers, Philip Sterling and Harry Brierly, set out for Missouri to work as construction engineers for a railroad company. In St. Louis they met Colonel Sellers, who entertained them with boasts about his investments and treated them to drinks and cigars. When he showed embarrassment at having lost his money, Philip relieved him by paying the bill.

In Philadelphia, Ruth Bolton, the daughter of Eli and Margaret Bolton, both Quakers, received a letter from Philip. Rebelling against the rules of the Friends, she told her parents that she wanted to do something different, perhaps study medicine.

Colonel Sellers continued to befriend the two young men in St. Louis. He went so far as to suggest that the railroad should be built through Stone's Landing, a small village not along the route planned for the road. Like the colonel, Harry was a man of imagination. When their money ran out, Harry and Philip went to an engineers' camp near Hawkeye, and the colonel joined them to plan the city to be built there.

Philip and Harry arrived in Hawkeye eight years after the death of Squire Haw-

kins. The Civil War had been fought; the Hawkinses were still supported by Clay, and Laura had become a beauty. During the war she had married a Colonel Selby, who, already married, had deserted her when his regiment was transferred. After that calamity she turned her eye upon Harry Brierly, who fell in love with her.

When Senator Dilworthy went to Hawkeye to investigate Colonel Sellers' petition for funds to improve the area, the senator met Washington Hawkins. Thinking Washington a fine young man, the senator hired him as a secretary. Laura charmed Senator Dilworthy to such an extent that he invited her to visit his family in Washington.

Ruth Bolton was in school at Fallkill, where she stayed with a family named Montague. On their way to New York, Philip and Harry stopped to see her. Philip was disappointed in the manner in which Ruth accepted him. Alice Montague was kinder to him; Ruth seemed too attentive to Harry. In Washington, Harry saw the appropriation for Stone's Landing passed by Congress. When the New York office sent no money with which to pay the workers at Stone's Landing, Harry went to New York to investigate. Speculation was everywhere; even Mr. Bolton decided to buy some land near the railroad in Pennsylvania. Unfortunately, Harry learned that the cost of obtaining the Congressional appropriation had been so high that there was no money left to pay for the work at Stone's Landing.

Hired by Mr. Bolton, Philip went to develop the natural resources of a tract of land in Ilium, Pennsylvania. He became a frequent visitor at the Boltons'.

Senator Dilworthy invited Laura to come to Washington, where she immediately became a belle—much to Harry Brierly's consternation. Many people believed her an heiress. The senator attempted to use her influence in getting congressmen to vote in favor of a bill in which he was interested. At a party Laura saw Colonel Selby, who had come to

Washington to claim reimbursement for some cotton destroyed during the war. When the former lovers met, Laura knew she still loved Selby and the two began to be seen about town together. When he left Washington, Laura followed him to a New York hotel, where she shot him.

The opening of the Ilium coal mine found Philip and Harry hard at work. Before they had located the main vein, however, Mr. Bolton went bankrupt and surrendered all his property to his creditors, and Philip was able to buy the Ilium tract. Ruth, graduated from medical school, had gone to work in a Philadelphia hospital. Harry was in New York, a witness at Laura's murder trial. Philip, hoping to read law in the squire's office, visited the Montagues in Fallkill. Mr. Montague, seeing value in Philip's mine, offered to finance a further excavation.

Laura's trial attracted much attention. Claiming that she was insane, her lawyer tried to show that her mind had been deranged from the time she lost her parents in the river boat fire.

Senator Dilworthy's bill, a measure to establish a university for Negroes on the Hawkins land in Tennessee, had been for some time in committee. Washington Hawkins and Colonel Sellers expected to make a fortune when the bill passed. Then Dilworthy, up for reëlection, attempted to buy votes and was exposed, and his bill was defeated on the floor of the Senate. Washington and Sellers were crestfallen.

Laura was acquitted of the murder charge. Penniless, she tried to begin a lecture tour, but on her first appearance she found only an empty auditorium. On the streets she was attacked by angry citizens and driven home to a cold room, where she died of grief.

Philip finally found coal in his shaft, but his elation subsided when a telegram from the Boltons told him that Ruth was gravely ill. He hurried to her bedside, where his presence helped to hasten her recovery.

THE GLASS KEY

Type of work: Novel
Author: Dashiell Hammett (1894-1961)
Type of plot: Mystery romance
Time of plot: 1930's
Locale: New York area
First published: 1931

Principal characters:
NED BEAUMONT, gambler and amateur detective
PAUL MADVIG, his friend and the city's political boss
SENATOR HENRY, Madvig's candidate for reëlection
JANET HENRY, his daughter
SHAD O'RORY, Madvig's rival
OPAL MADVIG, Madvig's daughter
BERNIE DESPAIN, a gambler owing Ned money

Critique:

In this detective novel Hammett has followed the customary pattern but has varied the circumstances so as to give the story an interesting twist. In addition to tracking down the murderer, the hero also breaks up a bootlegging gang and gives the city officials something about which to worry. The novel has stylistic qualities above the ordinary. It is an excellent example of the modern school of hard-boiled realism.

The Story:

Ned Beaumont reported to his friend, Paul Madvig, the political boss of the city, that he had found the dead body of Taylor Henry in the street. Taylor was the son of Senator Henry, Madvig's candidate for reëlection. When Madvig failed to show much interest, Ned told his story to the police. Next day he went to collect from Bernie Despain the thirty-two hundred and fifty dollars that he had won on a horse race and found that Bernie had vanished, leaving behind twelve hundred dollars worth of Taylor's I.O.U.'s. Ned had himself appointed special investigator in the district attorney's office so that he could work on Taylor Henry's case. What he really wanted to do was to find Bernie and get his money.

His first step was to get the help of Madvig's daughter Opal, who had been meeting Taylor secretly. Ned had found no hat on Taylor the night of the murder. Opal got one for him from the room she and Taylor had rented. Then Ned went to New York to a speakeasy that Bernie frequented. Bernie came in accompanied by a burly bodyguard who, when Ned asked for his money, struck Ned a terrific blow. With the help of Jack Rumsen, a private detective, Ned trailed Bernie from the hotel where he was staying to a brownstone house on Forty-ninth Street. There he told Bernie that he had planted Taylor's hat behind a sofa cushion in Bernie's hotel room and would leave it there for the police to find if Bernie did not pay him the money. Bernie paid off.

Back from New York, Ned went to see Farr, the district attorney. Farr showed Ned an envelope enclosing paper on which were typed three questions implicating Madvig in Taylor's murder. Meanwhile Madvig had decided to have the police close down several speak-easies belonging to Shad O'Rory, gangster and ward boss. O'Rory reopened the Dog House, where Ned went to get information. O'Rory had him tortured for several days. Finally he escaped. He was taken to a hospital.

There he had many callers, including Madvig and Janet Henry, Taylor's sister. Opal Madvig went to tell Ned she was sure her father had killed Taylor. Ned assured her he did not believe Madvig had committed the murder. Partly recovered, he left the hospital against orders.

Shortly afterward Ned and Madvig dined with Senator Henry and his daughter Janet. Ned made Janet admit that she secretly hated Madvig, who was in love with her.

Ned went to see Madvig and told him that even his henchmen were beginning to betray him because they thought he had committed the murder. Madvig admitted Taylor had followed him out of the Henry house that night, that they had quarreled, and that he killed Taylor with a brown, knobby cane which Taylor had been carrying. Madvig claimed that he had then carried the cane away under his coat and burned it. Ned later asked Janet to look for the cane. She said it was with some others in the hall of their home. She also told him of a dream in which she and Ned had found a house with a banquet spread inside; they had to unlock the door and let out a great many snakes before they could go in to enjoy the food.

Ned went next to Farr's office and signed an affidavit telling of Madvig's confession. Then he went to a bar where he found Jeff, O'Rory's bodyguard. In a private room upstairs he accused Jeff of a gangster killing planned by O'Rory. O'Rory walked in on them and in the ensuing quarrel Jeff strangled O'Rory. Ned had a waiter call the police to the scene.

Ned went to the Madvig home, where Madvig's mother said that Madvig was nowhere to be found and that Opal had unsuccessfully attempted to commit suicide. Next morning Ned went to Senator Henry's house and told the senator that Madvig had confessed. It was all Janet and Ned could do to keep the senator from rushing out to kill Madvig. The senator asked Janet to leave him alone with Ned. Ned told him that Janet hated Madvig. The senator insisted he was not going to permit the murderer of his son to go unpunished. Then Ned accused the senator of killing Taylor, of wanting to kill Madvig so that he would not testify against him, of caring more for his own reëlection than for the life of his son. The senator confessed that he had interfered in a street quarrel between Taylor and Madvig and had asked the political boss to leave him with his son. Madvig had done so after giving him the cane Madvig had taken away from Taylor. The senator, angry with his son because of the quarrel he had forced upon Madvig, had angrily struck Taylor with the cane and killed him. He had then carried home the cane. After hearing the old man's confession, Ned refused to leave him alone because he feared the senator would kill himself before the police arrived.

Next day Janet begged Ned to let her go with him to New York. She said the key to the house in her dream had been of glass and had shattered just as they opened the door because they had had to force the lock. When Madvig came in, he learned that he had lost Janet, that she was going away with Ned Beaumont.

THE GLASS MENAGERIE

Type of work: Drama
Author: Tennessee Williams (1914-   )
Time: 1930's
Locale: St. Louis, Missouri
First presented: 1945

Principal characters:
AMANDA WINGFIELD, a woman who lives in illusion
TOM, her son
LAURA, her crippled daughter
JIM O'CONNOR, the gentleman caller

This drama of illusion has been much praised for its tenderness, gentleness, and fragile charm. The first of Williams' plays to achieve commercial success, it launched him upon a spectacular career in the American theater. Some have claimed that he never again succeeded in regaining the height that he here attained, and that his subsequent work, popular though it may have been, is anticlimactic.

The action of the drama, involving only four characters, is built around Amanda and her effect upon her son and daughter. Infuriating and pathetic by turns, Amanda, an incurable romantic, lives by and for the illusions of her youth, when she was—or thinks she was—the belle of a small Southern town in the Delta region. It is the ghost of this lost past that she constantly conjures up in a pitiful and futile effort to obliterate the grim reality of lower middle-class life in St. Louis. She has been deserted by her husband; she now lives only for her children, for whom she sincerely wants happiness and security. It is the irony of the story, however, that, by her insistent nagging, her endless repetition of anecdotes from her romanticized version of her girlhood, and her inability to face the actualities of her situation, she has crushed her daughter and alienated her son. At one moment she can envelop herself in exaggerated "Southern charm"; at the next, she can be an unbearable shrew.

Laura, the daughter, is the most pitiable of the three members of the family. A cripple and so abnormally shy that she cannot have even the most ordinary re- lationships with people, she takes refuge in her "glass menagerie," a collection of small glass animal figurines that symbolizes the fragility of her life and her retreat from reality. She is hopelessly inadequate to play the role of "Southern belle" that her mother wishes her to assume or even to make a marriage that will give her security. She has cared for only one boy during her life—a pompous high school hero. Jim O'Connor is the type, to be found in every school or college, who never in later life measures up to his youthful promise. He is now working in a warehouse, trying hard to "improve himself," but still only a clerk. When Tom, who does not know that his sister had ever known Jim, brings him home to dinner, Laura has her one moment of happiness and her one escape from the world into which she has retreated.

After the dinner that Amanda has produced in a desperate effort to impress him, Jim, in his awkward fashion, does give Laura a flash of self-confidence, enough to enable us to see what she might become if she could ever break out of her shell. Too unworldly to handle the situation, she is dazed with happiness when Jim kisses her. But Jim, crude as he may be, is fundamentally honest enough to confess that Laura can expect nothing of him, for he is engaged and will be married soon. And so the momentary illusion of happiness collapses around Laura just as the illusion of success collapses around Amanda. It is the final irony of the play that Amanda, who blames the entire catastrophe on her son,

1336

drives him from her in their final quarrel with the accusation that he is a dreamer who lives in a world of illusion.

Tom, the frustrated son, is the least successful of the characters, for he is the familiar type of the young man with literary ambitions imprisoned in the deadly monotony of a job in a warehouse. Indeed, with his anguished revolt against his family, his furious outcries against his fate, and his final escape, he seems to have stepped out of a novel by Thomas Wolfe. We can feel desperately sorry for him because he is burdened with the care of a nagging mother and a crippled sister; however, since his inner life and his literary gifts are described rather than seen, he remains unconvincing and shadowy, even though the whole story of the play is seen through his memory.

From the point of view of theatrical technique, the play holds much of interest. Williams uses the long and involved stage directions first made popular by Shaw, plus a very elaborate and complicated set of stage devices. The question of the validity of such technical tricks remains an open one. Shaw's use of elaborate stage directions, which all too frequently turned into lengthy and tiresome preachments, succeeded in splitting a play into two aspects: the play as produced, in which these little essays naturally could not appear, and the play as published, in which these comments were extremely important. In the printed version of *The Glass Menagerie*, Williams makes a modified use of this device. His elaborate stage directions comment on the situation as well as give the reader some of the advantages of the spectator.

He also employs the device of using Tom as both the narrator of and commentator on the action, somewhat as in the role of a Greek chorus, and as a character in the play. Further, Williams has devised a complicated set of stage effects—rather like the tricks used in a Dos Passos novel —to point up the mood of his play. The question might well be raised of how legitimate this theatrical sleight of hand may be. Should not a dramatist be able to rely on the significance of his fable without calling on so much mechanical ingenuity to get it presented?

Although, in a pantomime scene at the end of the play, Amanda achieves something like dignity as she comforts Laura, it cannot be said that the play reaches the heights of genuine tragedy. The characters, pathetic though they may be, are too shallow, too trivial, to have in them the qualities of tragic greatness. The point has been made that this is a story of "lives of quiet desperation" and that the choice of the 1930's for the setting deliberately contrasts these lives with an increasingly violent world in which illusion can have no place. Perhaps this is part of the human condition of our times and therefore the only possible subject for a serious dramatist. Yet it remains true that the mood of the play is pathetic, not tragic, and that Williams has created a drama of gentle pathos rather than one of high tragedy.

GOAT SONG

Type of work: Drama
Author: Franz Werfel (1890-1945)
Type of plot: Symbolic allegory
Time of plot: Late eighteenth century
Locale: A Slavic countryside
First presented: 1921

Principal characters:

GOSPODAR STEVAN MILIC, a farmer
MIRKO MILIC, his son
MIRKO'S MOTHER
STANJA VESILIC, Mirko's betrothed
JUVAN, a student
THE PHYSICIAN

Critique:

The damage that can be done by the fear and superstition of an ignorant people is amply demonstrated in *Goat Song*, in which the rebirth of brutishness in man is symbolized by the birth of a human monster. In their zeal to find a sacrifice for their sins, the peasants and gipsies elevate the human monster to sainthood and then sacrifice a young girl to him. This is a dynamic plot, the horror touched with mysticism and poetic symbolism.

The Story:

Stanja Vesilic was the betrothed of Mirko Milic. The parents had arranged the marriage, as was the custom. It was a marriage of convenience, the exchange of money for position in the community. It was the custom also for the bride-to-be to stay in the groom's home for a month, in order that she might learn the ways of her prospective mother-in-law. Neither Stanja nor Mirko took much interest in the arrangements. It was to be and that was all.

Unknown except to a very few was the existence of another son born to Stevan Milic and his wife. This boy, now grown, was a human monster, hidden from the world and his brother in a little cottage. He crawled on all fours like a goat and at times let out terrible screams which had to be explained away to passers-by. The mother had never seen the child since his birth, he having been suckled by a servant girl, but her heart yearned for him even while she knew she could never see him lest the secret of his existence be revealed.

A physician called and urged them to place the monster in a home for such beings, but when Stevan learned that his name must be registered, he would not allow the plan to be carried through. No one must learn the secret. At last Stevan decided to kill his son so that the creature would be free of his troubles and Stevan and his wife free of worry about him. But when Stevan took his gun and went to the hut, he found that the physician, who had visited the monster in the name of science, had left the door open and the monster had escaped. Now he was really free.

The farmers of the area had been plagued by vagabonds and gipsies seeking to settle near the village. Most of these wanderers had once lived on land nearby and wanted a little of it again. When their leaders went to the council with their petition, the wealthy farmers would not listen to their pleas. Stevan presided at the council on the night the monster disappeared, his mind so filled with his own fear that he did not really hear the pleas of the gipsies. He ordered them away, telling them that they were the lucky ones, smiled on by fortune. His actions and words convinced everyone present, even the other elders of the council, that he was a madman.

The intellectual leader of the vagabonds was Juvan, a student. He stirred up his followers to kill and plunder the farmers who would not give them land. Stanja and Mirko talked with him. Each hated Juvan, but Stanja was drawn to him in spite of her hate. Feeling compassion for Juvan's homeless people, she wanted Mirko to join him in getting land. But Juvan insulted Stanja, and so the two men prepared to fight. Before they drew blood, the gipsies found the monster and ran to Juvan with the news. The ignorant gipsies thought the monster had been sent to punish them for their greed. Juvan, who knew the monster was the secret hidden by Stevan Milic, planned to use his knowledge to enforce his will on the landowners.

The monster was taken in bonds to the church and installed behind the altar, hidden from view. The gipsies secured arms, thought by the villagers to be provided by the monster, and attacked the peasants. As they murdered and plundered, thinking always that they were appeasing the monster, Juvan used the creature to work the mobs into a frenzy. At last they demanded to see the monster. Their lust for blood lessening, they wished to see the strange god who would avenge all their wrongs and return their homelands.

When they gathered at the church, Stevan, his wife, their son Mirko, Stanja, and the elders appeared. The mob would have killed them if Juvan had not silenced the rioters. Stevan tried to bargain with Juvan: if Juvan and his mob would lay down their arms and release the monster, the gipsies would be forgiven and allowed to take some land.

After forcing Stevan to claim the monster as his son in the presence of all the people, Juvan said that the monster would be released only to Stanja, who was to go in and cut the creature's bonds. Mirko and his father and mother tried to get the girl to flee, but by that time Juvan ruled her completely. Scorning the words of everyone, she took the knife to cut the bonds. Mirko attacked Juvan and was instantly killed by a guard. Mirko's mother was happy, without understanding why she wanted her good son dead.

Stanja went into the sanctuary to free the monster, while the mob sang in ecstasy. When Juvan tried to go to Stanja, to save her, the mob held him back and demanded a sacrifice to the unknown god. Suddenly the doors to the altar opened of their own accord, and the monster stood in the shadows before them.

Soldiers came to the farms and villages and drove off the gipsies. The monster had fled into the woods and there burned, or so they said. Juvan, taken prisoner, was to be hanged. The farmers were now poor, but Stevan was strangely happy. He felt young, now that his sons were dead. He and his wife had found each other again after their guilty secret had been disclosed.

Now that her betrothed was dead, Stanja's parents came to take her home. But Stanja, refusing to go, begged to stay with Stevan Milic and his wife. Because she told them that she was still true to their son they kept the girl and loved her as their own. When Juvan was brought to Stanja under guard, the privilege of the condemned, he told her that he loved her, that she had changed him, by her sacrifice to the monster, from an animal knowing only lust to a man wanting a woman's love. Stanja loved Juvan too and wished to die with him, but he insisted that she live so that he would leave a part of himself on earth when he went off to his death on the gallows.

Later the hangman went to Stanja and

the mother told them that he had found the monster lying dead in the charred forest but with not a hair singed. The mother wept that there would never be a trace of the son she had carried in sorrow and in secret. Stanja told her she was wrong. Before long the girl would be delivered of the monster's child.

THE GODS ARE ATHIRST

Type of work: Novel
Author: Anatole France (Jacques Anatole Thibault, 1844-1924)
Type of plot: Historical satire
Time of plot: 1793-1794
Locale: Paris
First published: 1912

Principal characters:
ÉVARISTE GAMELIN, a young painter
MAURICE BROTTEAUX, Évariste's friend, a maker of dancing dolls
MME. GAMELIN, Évariste's mother
MME. DE ROCHEMAURE, wife of the king's former procurer
JEAN BLAISE, a printseller
ÉLODIE, his daughter
PÈRE LONGUEMARE, a Barnabite monk
JACQUES MAUBEL, a young gallant
JULIE GAMELIN, Évariste's sister
ATHENAÏS, a prostitute
MARAT, and
ROBESPIERRE, French revolutionaries
HENRY, a dragoon
PHILIPPE DESMAHIS, an engraver

Critique:

The Gods are Athirst is a satire deal-ing with the Reign of Terror which fol-lowed the French Revolution. Although the excesses of the period are satirized, the satire also delves more deeply, dem-onstrating the folly and the inhuman brutality of a mind committed to a po-litical cause or party. The romantic artist, Évariste Gamelin, begins by feeling a genuine desire to commit himself to the cause of the revolutionary Jacobins and ends by ordering the execution of his closest friend. From a rational and hu-mane point of view, Anatole France de-plores the idiotic barbarism of causes and the self-righteous cruelty of those con-vinced that they were reforming society. The characters are primarily abstractions, each designed to represent an idea cur-rent at the time: Évariste is the foolish romantic swayed into inhumanity by his allegiance to the cause; his friend Brotteaux is the atheist and intellectual, executed because he will not join and will not abandon his integrity; Élodie, a kind of symbol of France itself, is purely physical, without ideals or convictions or fidelity to anything, and she, alone of the three principal characters, survives. In brilliantly satiric fashion, Anatole France probed the excesses of devotion to the cause of the state, but in probing them he made it clear that their origin was the brutal, self-deceiving, self-glorifying, irra-tional nature of man himself.

The Story:

Évariste Gamelin, a young man who lived with his mother, was a not very tal-ented pupil of Jacques David, the painter. The only one of Évariste's paintings that gained any recognition was a canvas de-picting the story of Orestes and Electra. People claimed that Évariste's painting of Orestes was really a self-portrait.

An older artist, Maurice Brotteaux, lived in the garret of the Gamelin house in 1793. A former nobleman, he made his living creating Punch and Judy dolls.

Évariste became an active member of the Jacobins, genuinely believing that their success and complete control would bring about a new and better era for all the people in France. He even had a plan to change playing cards from pictures of kings, queens, and jacks to symbols of liberty, equality, and fraternity, but his fellow revolutionaries would not finance his designs. Brotteaux, on the other hand, was an atheist, an intellectual, a skeptic without faith in the goodness of the masses.

Évariste tried, unsuccessfully, to sell his new designs for playing cards to Jean Blaise, a printseller. Évariste was in love with Blaise's daughter Élodie, who finally got Évariste, far more naïve than she, to propose to her. When Élodie confessed that she had had a lover, Évariste was certain that it must have been a cynical aristocrat who had used her cruelly. On political grounds he forgave her.

One day, while Brotteaux and Évariste were waiting in a breadline, a woman screamed that her purse was gone and pointed to a cleric, Père Longuemare, as the thief. People, all excited, ran about accusing Longuemare of being a Capuchin, a member of an order opposed to the Jacobins, even though, by his speech, he was clearly a Barnabite. Brotteaux defended the cleric, but to no avail until the woman found that she had had her purse all along. The idealistic Évariste believed the incident demonstrated that, in the new society, people were so eager for justice they would leave their places in the breadline to find a thief. The wiser Brotteaux realized that they simply wanted to accuse others. He later gave Père Longuemare a place of refuge in his garret.

Mme. de Rochemaure, whose late husband had been a procurer for the king, was an intriguer who pretended revolutionary ardor. She, trailed by Henry, a young dragoon, was interested in using her new revolutionary connections to make more money. She wanted to meet Marat, who she had heard was easily swayed by flattery, to interest him in some Swiss financial speculations, but Marat was killed by Charlotte Corday before Mme. de Rochemaure had her chance. She did, however, manage to use her connections to get Évariste a post as a juror on the Grand Tribunal, the group of Jacobins responsible for trying political crimes. On his first day on the Grand Tribunal, Évariste made an impassioned plea for justice and the tribunal then voted not to execute an innocent man. Évariste was so excited that, later, he allowed the experienced Élodie to seduce him; the corruption of the innocent had begun.

Tiring of Henry, Mme. de Rochemaure wrote a letter to an old friend who had left France. In it she quoted a few of Brotteaux's witty remarks about the new state. Henry, jealously believing that Mme. de Rochemaure had become Brotteaux's mistress again, stole the letter and turned it over to the authorities. Both Mme. de Rochemaure and Brotteaux became politically suspect. In addition, the loyal "citoyens" began to say that Brotteaux's dolls were really meant to be caricatures of Jacobins. When Brotteaux was arrested, a prostitute named Athenaïs, whom he had once befriended, protested and cried out, "Long live the king!" as the soldiers took Brotteaux away. Athenaïs was also arrested.

The Grand Tribunal became far less just and bloodier. Trials were no longer held; prisoners were brought up in lots of fifty, convicted, and sent away to be executed. Évariste applauded the efficiency of the new arrangement.

Évariste's sister Julie had, a few years earlier, run away to England with her lover. When they returned to France, they were captured and the lover was condemned to death. Even old Mme. Gamelin tried to intercede for Julie's lover with Évariste. But Évariste was an adamant supporter of the new justice, confirming the symbolic fact that his portrait of Orestes was really a self-portrait. Besides his cruelty to his sister, Évariste was obsessed with the desire to discover and punish Élodie's first lover. He thought that the man must be Jacques

Maubel, a quiet but aristocratic young gallant. There was no evidence to support this claim, but Évariste, irritated by Maubel's lack of faith in the people, had Maubel arrested and executed. In reality, Élodie's first lover had been Henry, now a dragoon but in those days a clerk. Élodie, the symbol of France itself, was so impressed by Évariste's cruel power in having Maubel killed that she loved her tribune more than ever.

Brotteaux, Père Longuemare, Mme. de Rochemaure, and Athenaïs were all brought up before the Grand Tribunal, convicted without trial, and executed in the same lot of fifty. Évariste did not say a word. A short time later Robespierre, feeling that enough blood had been shed, tried to reform the Grand Tribunal, but the people turned on him and killed him. Soon the mob switched again and killed the members of the Grand Tribunal, including Évariste. For a time, Paris was bathed in anarchy and chaos.

The mob, as irresponsible as the tribunes had been, killed many, both aristocrats and peasants, political supporters and opponents. After Paris had become quiet and orderly again, Élodie became the mistress of a calm, nonpolitical, young engraver named Philippe Desmahis. Two people entirely unconcerned with politics or causes, governments or liberty, they managed to survive the grim Reign of Terror.

THE GOLD BUG

Type of work: Short story
Author: Edgar Allan Poe (1809-1849)
Type of plot: Mystery romance
Time of plot: Early nineteenth century
Locale: South Carolina
First published: 1843

Principal characters:
THE NARRATOR
WILLIAM LEGRAND, who found the gold bug
JUPITER, his colored servant

Critique:

One of the best known of all American short stories, "The Gold Bug" grips its readers with the eternal fascination of the detective story. Poe, regarded by some critics as the greatest genius of American literature, has here combined romance and adventure in a tale of buried treasure. There are inaccuracies in geography and measurements, defects in character portrayal, but these are quickly forgotten in the fascinating web Poe weaves of a mystery and its solution.

The Story:

William Legrand had been reduced to poverty by a series of misfortunes. In order to avoid the embarrassment of meeting friends of his more prosperous days, he left New Orleans and went to live on Sullivan's Island, near Charleston, South Carolina. It was a small island, usually uninhabited except for Legrand and his colored servant, Jupiter. Jupiter would not leave his master, even though he was a free man and could have found work to support himself in comfort.

Winters on the island were mild and fires were usually unnecessary, but on a night in October when a friend from Charleston visited Legrand, he found Legrand and Jupiter away from the house and a fire blazing in the fireplace. The two returned soon after from a quest for entomological specimens. Legrand was in rare good humor. He had stumbled upon an entirely new specimen, a bug of gold. On his way home he had met a Lieutenant G——, who took the bug to ex-amine it. Because the friend could not examine it before morning, Legrand took from his pocket an old piece of parchment and drew a picture of the specimen.

As the friend took the drawing, Legrand's dog entered, jumped upon the guest, and licked his face in joy. When the friend finally looked at the paper, he found that the drawing resembled a human skull. Legrand, somewhat disgruntled at this slur on his drawing, took the paper back and prepared to throw it into the fire. After one last glance, however, he paled visibly, rose and seated himself at the table. Then he carefully placed the paper in his wallet. As Legrand appeared distracted and a little sulky, the friend canceled his plans for spending the night and returned to Charleston.

About a month later the friend received a visit from old Jupiter. The servant reported that his master was not well. Going around as if in a daze, Legrand worked constantly at a cipher. Once he had eluded Jupiter and stayed away the whole day. Jupiter knew that the gold bug was to blame, for it had bitten Legrand on the day he captured it. Jupiter knew that the bug was the reason for Legrand's talk about gold in his sleep. He produced a letter from his master begging the friend to return to the island with Jupiter.

At the island the friend found Legrand in a state of great excitement. Filled with plans for an expedition to the mainland, he asked the friend to accompany him. After getting Legrand's promise that he would consult a doctor before long, for the man was obviously deranged, the friend joined Legrand and Jupiter in their adventure. Taking the dog with them, they left that evening. Jupiter carried picks and shovels for the three. Legrand took with him the gold bug, attached to a long cord.

After traveling about two hours, they stopped at the foot of a huge tulip tree situated near an almost inaccessible hill. There Legrand commanded Jupiter to take the bug and climb the tree to the seventh limb. Jupiter obeyed, climbing out to the very tip of the limb. On the outer edge he found a human skull, nailed to the wood. Then Legrand told him to drop the bug through the left eye of the skull. After this strange act, Jupiter climbed down. Legrand, working in feverish anxiety, then began a series of measurements. By the light of lanterns, the men, following Legrand's lead, dug out a hole four feet in diameter and seven feet deep. When they failed to unearth the treasure Legrand obviously thought he would find, he questioned Jupiter again about the eye through which he had dropped the gold bug. The old man, they learned, had mistakenly dropped the bug through the right eye. Again Legrand measured and drew circles. By that time the friend shared Legrand's excitement. Again they dug, and at last they came upon an old chest, too heavy to move. Prying open the lid, their eyes fell upon gold and jewels of unbelievable value. They later computed that the total worth was over a million and a half dollars. Leaving Jupiter and the dog to guard what they could not carry, Legrand and his friend took one load home. Then they returned and with Jupiter carried the rest of the treasure back to the island.

Legrand told his friend in detail how he had solved the riddle of the treasure. The piece of parchment upon which he had drawn the picture of the gold bug had been found near the bug, on the beach. Although the paper had been blank on both sides when he drew the picture, the friend had seen the shape of a skull. He remembered then that the dog had leaped on the friend, causing the paper to come near the fire. Heat from the fire had brought out the outline of a skull. Legrand, seeing the skull when he took the parchment, had begun a feverish attempt to solve its meaning. By dipping the paper in warm water, he had found a numerical code. Deciphering had long been a hobby of his, and thus after a month he had found the secret of the parchment. It was his belief that the treasure was a fabulous one believed to have been buried by Captain Kidd. Even after he had deciphered the numbering, transposing the figures into words, he had had trouble finding the location of the landmarks revealed in the writing. But on the day he had slipped away from Jupiter he had discovered the hill and the tree. On the day of their search Jupiter's mistake about the left eye had caused an error, but the rectifying of that error had brought the treasure to light. The deciphered code had instructed that a bullet was to be dropped through the left eye of the death's head. Legrand, using the gold bug, wished only to punish his friend for suspecting his sanity.

THE GOLDEN ASS OF LUCIUS APULEIUS

Type of work: Tale
Author: Lucius Apuleius (125?-?)
Type of plot: Picaresque romance
Time of plot: Early second century
Locale: Greece
First transcribed: Second century manuscript

Principal characters:
LUCIUS, a traveler
CHARITES, a Greek lady
LEPOLEMUS, her husband
THRASILLUS, in love with Charites
MILO, a usurer
PAMPHILE, his wife
FOTIS, her maid

Critique:

The Golden Ass is a rich repository of gusty, fantastic anecdotes. In tone it is bawdy and realistic; in approach it is a mixture of fancy and shrewd observation. An allegory runs through the story, the maturing of man, but the symbolism is dim and inconclusive. Two notable themes distinguish Apuleius' work—the metamorphosis of the hero into an ass, which is a reworking of an earlier Greek tale, and a lengthy retelling of the story of Cupid and Psyche.

The Story:

When Lucius set out on his travels in Thessaly, he happened to fall in with two strangers who were telling unusual stories of the mysterious life of the region. At the urging of Lucius, one of the strangers, a merchant named Aristomenes, told of his strange adventure in Hippata, the chief city of Thessaly.

Aristomenes had gone to the market to buy honey and cheese, but he found that a rival merchant had been there before him and had bought up the supply. As he turned sadly away, he spied his friend Socrates, clad in rags, sitting on the ground. Socrates had fallen among thieves, who beat him and robbed him even of his clothes. Touched by his friend's plight, Aristomenes led him to an inn, bathed and clothed him, and took him to his own chamber to sleep.

Socrates warned of the woman who kept the inn, a carnal woman possessed of magical powers. When she saw a comely man, she wanted him for a lover; if he refused, he was changed into a beast or bird. Aristomenes was a little frightened; he barred the door securely and moved his bed against it for safety. Socrates was already sleeping soundly.

About midnight two hags came to the door, which fell away at their approach. One bore a torch and the other a sponge and sword. While the landlady stood over Socrates and accused him of trying to get away from her, the two hags seized his head, thrust the sword into his throat, and reached in and took out his heart. They caught all his blood in a bladder. Then they put the sponge in the gaping throat wound.

In the morning Socrates looked like a whole man. The two friends crept away quietly, without arousing the landlady. A few miles out of town, they stopped to eat. Socrates, after eating a whole cheese, leaned over to drink from the stream. As he did so, the wound in his throat opened, the sponge fell out, and Socrates fell dead.

Warned by this story of what he might expect in Thessaly, Lucius presented his letter of introduction to Milo, a rich

---

THE GOLDEN ASS OF LUCIUS APULEIUS by Lucius Apuleius. Published by Liveright Publishing Corp.

usurer. He was well received in Milo's house. Attracted by Fotis, a buxom maid, Lucius hung around the kitchen admiring her hair and hips. She agreed quickly to come to his room that night as soon as she had put her mistress, Pamphile, to bed. Fotis was as good as her word, and several nights were passed agreeably enough.

In the city Lucius met a cousin, Byrrhaena, a rich gentlewoman. She invited him to dine and at dinner warned him of the witch Pamphile. Full of wine, Lucius on his way home saw three thugs trying to get into Milo's house. He rushed on them and slew them with his sword. The next day was the Feast of Laughter. As an elaborate hoax, Lucius was arrested and tried for murder in the public place. At the last minute the three "corpses" were revealed to be three bladders, blown up and given temporary life by Pamphile.

One night Fotis let Lucius look through the keyhole of Pamphile's bedroom. To his amazement, Lucius saw the witch smear herself with ointment and turn into an eagle that flew away in majestic flight. Filled with envy, Lucius demanded of Fotis that she smear him with ointment and turn him into an eagle. Fotis consented but with reluctance.

At a propitious time Fotis stole a box of ointment and smeared Lucius, but to his horror he found himself turned into an ass instead of an eagle. He looked around at the mocking Fotis, who professed to have made a mistake and promised to get him some roses in the morning. If he would only eat roses, he would turn into a man again. So Lucius resigned himself to being an ass for the night.

But during the darkness thieves broke into Milo's house, loaded much of Milo's gold on Lucius' back, and drove him out on the road. That morning Lucius saw some roses along the way, but as he was about to eat them he suddenly thought that if he turned into a man in the company of thieves they would surely kill him. He trotted on until they came to the thieves' lair, which was governed by an old woman.

On another night the thieves took captive the gentle Charites, whom they had abducted from her wedding with Lepolemus. Charites wept bitterly. To console her, the old hag told the story of Cupid and Psyche.

There was a merchant who had three daughters. The two older girls, well-favored, were soon married off. The youngest, a true beauty, was admired by all who saw her. No man came to woo her, however, for Venus had become jealous of her beauty and had put a spell upon the girl.

In despair, the parents consulted an oracle, who told them to expose the girl on a rocky cliff, where she would become the bride of a loathsome beast. The sorrowing couple obeyed, and the lovely virgin was exposed one night on a cliff. After she had been left alone, a gentle wind whisked her down into a rich castle.

That night a man with a caressing voice, but whose face she never saw, made her his wife. For a while she was content not to see her husband, but at last her jealous sisters persuaded her to light a lamp in order to see his face. When she did, she learned her husband was Cupid, who had succumbed to her charms when Venus had sent him to make her fall in love with a monster.

Although the girl was pregnant, Venus refused to recognize her son's marriage with a mortal. Then Jupiter took pity on her and brought her to heaven. There he conferred immortality on her and named her Psyche. So Cupid and Psyche became the epitome of faithful love.

Lepolemus, the resourceful bridegroom, rescued Charites by ingratiating himself with the robbers and becoming one of their band. Watching his chance, he made them all drunk and chained them. Setting Charites on the back of Lucius, Lepolemus took his bride home and returned with a band of aroused citizens, who killed all the thieves of the den.

Lucius was given over to a herdsman of Charites, and for a time he lived a hard life as a mill ass. One day news came of the death of Lepolemus, who was killed on a hunting trip with his friend, Thrasillus. In a dream, Lepolemus told Charites that Thrasillus had killed him. When Thrasillus came wooing Charites soon afterward, she pretended to listen to his proposals. He came to her chamber late one night, and there the old nurse of Charites gave him wine. When he was drunk, Charites took a pin and pricked out both his eyes.

These irregularities of their owners made the shepherds uneasy. In a body they left Charites' estate and struck out on their own. Lucius passed through several hands, some good owners, some bad. He bore his lot as best he could, but he could never be a proper ass because he still longed to eat bread and meat. One of his owners discovered this peculiarity and exhibited Lucius as a performing ass.

As a performer Lucius led an easier life. Now that spring was approaching, he hoped to find some roses. In the meantime he enjoyed himself; he even had a rich matron as his mistress for a few nights. But when his master proposed to exhibit him in a cage, making love to a harlot, Lucius decided to rebel.

He escaped and sought the aid of Queen Isis. Taking pity on Lucius, she caused a priest to carry a garland of roses in a parade. The priest offered the flowers to Lucius, who ate them eagerly. Once again Lucius became a man.

THE GOLDEN BOWL

Type of work: Novel
Author: Henry James (1843-1916)
Type of plot: Psychological realism
Time of plot: c. 1900
Locale: England and the Continent
First published: 1904

> *Principal characters:*
> MR. VERVER, a wealthy American living in England
> MAGGIE VERVER, his daughter
> PRINCE AMERIGO, an Italian nobleman married to Maggie Verver
> CHARLOTTE STANT, a school friend of Maggie Verver
> MRS. ASSINGHAM, a friend of the Ververs and the Prince

Critique:

This novel is full of the subtleties of the minds of cultured people. It is a collection of psychological shades and discriminations which are, at times, overwhelming to the reader, and it is also a forerunner of modern expressionism in literature. The novel is completely aloof from the homely realities of life. The characters are shut off in a world of their own, a world which will not tolerate crudities.

The Story:

Maggie Verver was the daughter of a wealthy American widower who had devoted all his life to his daughter. The Ververs lived a lazy life. Their time was spent in collecting items to decorate their own existence and to fill a museum which Mr. Verver was giving to his native city back in the United States. They had few friends. Maggie's only confidante was Mrs. Assingham, the American-born wife of a retired British army officer.

It was Mrs. Assingham who introduced the Ververs to Prince Amerigo, a handsome, quiet young Italian nobleman who struck Maggie's fancy. When she informed her father that she would like to marry the Prince, Mr. Verver provided a handsome dowry so that the wedding might take place.

A few days before the wedding a painful scene occurred in Mrs. Assingham's home, where the Prince and Charlotte Stant, deeply in love with each other, met to say goodbye. Each was penniless and a marriage had been out of the question. Since both were friends of Maggie, the present situation was painful for them. As a farewell lark they spent the last afternoon in searching for a wedding present for Charlotte to present to Maggie. In a tiny shop they discovered a golden bowl which Charlotte wished to purchase as a remembrance for the Prince from her. He refused it because of superstitious fears that a crack in the golden bowl might bring bad luck.

After the wedding of the Prince and Maggie, the lives of the pair coincided with the life that the Ververs had been living for years. Maggie and her father spent much of their time together. The Prince, although he did not complain, was really only a convenience that they had purchased because Maggie had reached the age when she needed to have a husband.

After a year and a half a baby was born to the Prince and Maggie, but the child made no apparent difference in the relationships between the girl and her father or the girl and her husband. Maggie decided that her father also needed a wife. She went to Mrs. Assingham and told her friend that she planned to have Charlotte Stant marry her father. Charlotte was a quiet person aware of the love between the girl and her father, and she was the sort of person who would be so thankful to marry a wealthy man that she would cause little trouble. Neither Maggie nor Mrs. Assingham put this aspect into words, but it was tacitly understood.

Mr. Verver, anxious to please his daughter in this as in everything else, married Charlotte a short time later. This second marriage created a strange situation. Maggie and her father both took houses in London where they could be together a great deal of the time. The association of father and daughter left the Prince and Charlotte much together. Maggie encouraged them to go out, to represent her and her father at balls and dinners. But Maggie did not know that her husband and her stepmother had been intimate before her own marriage to the Prince.

Several years went by in this manner, but slowly the fact that there was something strange in the relationships dawned upon Maggie's sensitive feelings. She eventually went to Mrs. Assingham and poured out her suspicions to her. Mrs. Assingham, in full knowledge of the circumstances, decided to keep silence.

Maggie resolved to say nothing of her suspicions to anyone else. But her attitude of indifference, her insistence in throwing the Prince and Charlotte together, aroused their suspicions that she knew they had been sweethearts, that she suspected them of being lovers after marriage.

Each one of the four speculated at length as to what the other three knew or suspected. Yet their mutual confidence and love prevented each one of them from ever asking anything of the others.

One day Maggie went shopping for some unusual art object to present to her father on his birthday. She accidentally happened into the same shop where the Prince and Charlotte had gone several years before, and she purchased the golden bowl which they had passed over because of its flaw. The following day the shopkeeper visited her. The name and address had told him that she was the wife of the Prince who had passed up the bowl years before. He knew that the existence of the crack would quickly come to the attention of the Prince, and so he had hastened to inform Maggie of the flaw and to return part of the purchase price. He also told her of the Prince's first visit to the shop and of the young woman who had been with him. Maggie then knew that the Prince and Charlotte had known each other before her marriage and that they had spent an afternoon together the day before she was married. She was upset. Again she confided in Mrs. Assingham.

Having learned that there was no serious relationship between the Prince and Charlotte, Mrs. Assingham informed Maggie that she was making a great ado over nothing at all. To point up her remark, she raised the bowl above her head and smashed it to the floor, where it broke into several pieces. As she did so, the Prince entered the room and saw the fragments of the bowl. After Mrs. Assingham's departure he tried to learn how much Maggie knew. Maggie and her husband agreed to say nothing to either Maggie's father or to Charlotte.

Charlotte, too, began to sense that something had disturbed Maggie, and she shrewdly guessed what it was. Then Maggie tried to realign the relationships of the four by proposing that she and Charlotte stay together for awhile and that the Prince and her father go to the Continent to buy art objects. This proposal was gently put forward and as gently rebuffed by the other three.

Maggie and her father began to realize that their selfishness in trying to keep up the father-daughter relationship which they had had before her marriage was wrong. Shortly after that selfishness had been brought into the open and discussed by Maggie and Mr. Verver, Charlotte told Maggie that she wished to return to

America and to take her husband with her. She bluntly informed Maggie she was afraid that if Mr. Verver continued to live so close to his daughter he would lose interest in his wife. Mr. Verver agreed to accompany Charlotte back to the United States. It was a difficult decision for him to make. He realized that once he was away, Charlotte would never agree to his coming back to Europe to live.

On an autumn afternoon Mr. Verver and Charlotte went to have tea with Maggie and the Prince before leaving England. It was almost heartbreaking to Maggie to see her father's carriage take him out of sight and to know that her old way of life was really ended. The only thing which kept her from breaking down completely was the look on the Prince's face as he turned her face away from the direction her father's carriage had taken. At that moment, seeing his eyes, Maggie knew she had won her husband for herself and not for her money.

GOLDEN BOY

Type of work: Drama
Author: Clifford Odets (1906-1963)
Type of plot: Social allegory
Time of plot: 1930's
Locale: New York
First presented: 1937

Principal characters:
    JOE BONAPARTE, a prize fighter
    TOM MOODY, a fight manager
    LORNA MOON, his mistress
    MR. BONAPARTE, Joe's father
    EDDIE FUSELI, a gunman

Critique:

Clifford Odets began his theatrical career as an actor with the Theatre Guild and was later one of the founders of the Group Theatre, which presented some of his plays. His early work was received with enthusiasm by the critics, but his later efforts have proved disappointing. *Golden Boy*, written in 1937, was described by Odets as an allegory, and some of the individual scenes and much of the dialogue represent him at his best. Dealing with a young Italian violinist who becomes a prize fighter in order to gain money and fame, the fable reflects the fight of every individual for a place in the world. The play has been praised as good entertainment, but it has also been denounced for its episodic, movie-like construction.

The Story:

Tom Moody, a fight manager, and Lorna · Moon, his mistress who wanted to marry him, were having an argument about Tom's wife, who would not give him a divorce. Tom, wanting money for the divorce, needed to find a winning fighter. While they were talking, Joe Bonaparte arrived to tell them that Moody's fighter had broken his hand and could not fight that night. Joe, whom nobody knew, persuaded them to let him substitute, and he won.

Joe, a musician, had always wanted a good violin, and his father had bought him one for his twenty-first birthday. When Joe returned home, his father, who had not been told of the fight, had read of it in the papers and was very much distressed. He tried to persuade Joe to give up fighting and continue his study of music, but Joe wanted to fight. His father, hurt, did not give him the violin.

Joe fought well after that, but there was a serious conflict between the sensitive musician that he truly was and the brutal fighter he had to be. He held back in the ring, fearing that he would ruin his hands for the violin. When Moody tried to persuade him that fame and money would be more important than music, he succeeded only in antagonizing Joe, who threatened to quit. Lorna agreed to try to persuade Joe to reconsider. Joe was basically a musician, but he had been laughed at and hurt by people. Fighting was not a part of his nature, but he wanted to fight back and music could not do that for him. While he was explaining all this to Lorna, he had already decided to remain in the ring.

When Joe was preparing for a fight tour, Mr. Bonaparte asked Lorna to help the young man find himself. When he tried to give Joe the violin, the boy refused it. Then he asked for a blessing which his father refused to give.

Joe's tour was a great success except for

one fight. He had not fought well on that occasion because he had seen a man with a violin and was reminded of his music and his own past. Moody realized that Joe had to be prevented from having any contact with his family and his past.

The fight world changed Joe's personality. He liked the money and the notoriety. He bought a Duesenberg, which he drove recklessly, and he became difficult to manage. Eddie Fuseli, a gambler and a gunman, wanted to buy a piece of Joe, and Joe agreed, to Moody's dislike. He told Lorna to take care of Joe in her own way.

Joe fell in love with Lorna and asked her to give up Moody. She denied loving Joe and said that she could not leave Moody because she felt sorry for him. Joe knew that she was not telling the truth when she began to cry. They talked about their love and Joe demanded that she tell Moody at once. She said that she would, but when she went to tell him she learned that his wife had agreed to a divorce and that they could be married in a few months. With this knowledge she was unable to tell him about her love for Joe. Later Joe had an argument with Moody and demanded that Lorna tell Moody about their love. Although Lorna denied that there was anything between them, she confessed the truth to Moody when they were alone again.

One night Mr. Bonaparte came to see Joe fight. Fuseli was disturbed because he did not want Joe to see his father, but Joe saw him anyway. He also saw Moody and Lorna together. Mr. Bonaparte, seeing that Joe had completely changed, finally gave his blessing to Joe's career. Joe cried after his father left. During the fight Mr. Bonaparte went back into the dressing room rather than see the fighters hurt each other. Joe returned after he had won the fight, but when his trainer attempted to remove the gloves, Joe told him that he would have to cut one of them off. His hand was broken.

Now that he could never be a musician, Joe was all fighter. Moody and Lorna announced that they were getting married in a few days. Because Joe was still in love with Lorna, it was obvious that his unhappiness was hurting his career. While Joe was fighting badly in his most important match, Fuseli blamed Lorna and threatened to kill her. But Joe returned to the dressing room a victor. A few moments later they were all told that the other fighter had died after being floored by Joe's knockout punch. Everyone left the dressing room except Lorna and Joe. She told him that she loved him and asked him to go back to his music. He showed her his mutilated hands. However, he decided to give up fighting, and he and Lorna went for a wild ride in order to celebrate.

Fuseli, Moody, and the others, not knowing where Joe and Lorna had gone, went to Joe's home and drank and talked while they waited for his return. The telephone rang in the middle of an argument to decide who would own Joe in the future. Joe and Lorna had been killed in an automobile accident. Mr. Bonaparte left to claim Joe's body and bring him home where he belonged.

THE GONDOLIERS

Type of work: Comic opera
Author: W. S. Gilbert (1836-1911)
Type of plot: Humorous romance
Time of plot: 1750
Locale: Venice and Barataria
First presented: 1889

Principal characters:
THE DUKE OF PLAZA-TORO, a Grandee of Spain
THE DUCHESS OF PLAZA-TORO, his wife
CASILDA, their daughter
LUIZ, the duke's attendant
INEZ, an old nurse
DON ALHAMBRA DEL BOLERO, the Grand Inquisitor
MARCO PALMIERI, and
GIUSEPPE PALMIERI, gondoliers
GIANETTA, and
TESSA, flower girls

Critique:

Another of the favorite comic operettas of Gilbert and Sullivan is *The Gondoliers, Or, The King of Barataria.* Unlike most of their works, which were set in England and which poked gentle fun at Victorian customs and institutions, *The Gondoliers* has an Italian background. But the tone is the same, light and humorous throughout. It was the last truly successful operetta on which Gilbert and Sullivan collaborated before the famous break in their personal and business relationship.

The Story:

Twenty-four lovely maidens were in love with two gondoliers of Venice. In order to be fair, the two young gondoliers, Marco and Giuseppe Palmieri, had themselves blindfolded and then each caught a girl. The lucky ones were Gianetta and Tessa, and the two couples went off to be married.

A short time later the Duke of Plaza-Toro, a Grandee of Spain, arrived with his duchess and his daughter Casilda. They were accompanied by the duke's attendant, Luiz. The duke had come to Venice penniless, to pay his respects to the Grand Inquisitor and to learn the whereabouts of Casilda's husband. For much to that young lady's surprise, her father told her now that she had been married when a baby to the son of the King of Barataria. The king had become a bigoted Wesleyan Methodist and the Grand Inquisitor, to punish the turncoat king, had spirited his baby son away to Venice. Now the king was dead, killed in an uprising of his people, and the son, Casilda's husband, was entitled to the throne.

Casilda heard the news with mixed emotions. She would like to be queen but, unknown to the duke and duchess, she and the attendant Luiz were lovers. Luiz knew something of the story which had so surprised Casilda, for his mother, Inez, had been the baby prince's nurse. But Luiz could not persuade Casilda to renounce the marriage; the prospect of being a queen was stronger than love. But when the Grand Inquisitor received the duke and his wife and daughter, he had confusing news. He had given the baby to a worthy gondolier, to be reared with that man's own son. The gondolier had died from drink and gout, and the children, also gondoliers, could not be told one from another. However, the nurse to whom the young prince had been entrusted still lived. She would be sent for in the hope that she could identify the rightful king. Should she have difficulty making a decision, she would be tortured until she chose the right one.

The Grand Inquisitor thought the problem was almost solved. Coming upon Marco and Giuseppe and their new brides, he announced that one of them was the King of Barataria. Since he was not sure of the rightful king, a matter which could not be determined before the nurse arrived and settled the point, they must both go to Barataria and rule as one.

Marco and Giuseppe hated a monarchy and loved a republic, but when they found that they, as one, were kings, they suddenly loved a monarchy as well. Under their rule everyone would be equal, and their fellow gondoliers would be given important positions so that no one would serve another. The only drawback was that they must leave their new wives for three months, until the nurse could arrive and make her decision. The Grand Inquisitor did not disclose the fact that one of them already had another wife, the bride of his infancy. Gianetta and Tessa sadly bade their husbands goodbye, each one seeing herself a queen in three short months. The two kings sailed away for Barataria.

Three months went by. The government of the new rulers was indeed strange. The kings lived in the attic and did all the work while the gondoliers, now officers of state, reaped all the advantages reserved formerly for the monarch. Since the two men were one king, they were given only enough food for one man until their subjects relented and gave them a double portion. But the new rulers were pleased with their republican monarchy and thought it only right that they should serve their subjects for the privilege of being king.

Missing female company, the kings thought often of their wives. They were happily surprised, therefore, when Gianetta and Tessa and the other girls arrived in Barataria before they had been sent for. The two wives wanted to know instantly who was queen, but since the nurse had not yet appeared no decision could be made.

When the Grand Inquisitor found the two wives established in Barataria, he was forced to tell Marco and Giuseppe that one of them was a bigamist. He explained about the infant marriage and told them that the duke, the duchess, and Casilda, the real queen, were even then in Barataria. Inez, the nurse, had also arrived and was in the torture chamber, about to make her decision and name the rightful king.

When Casilda saw the two gondoliers, really one king, she told them that she would be a dutiful wife to whomever she married. She could never love either of them, however, for she loved another. The duke, disturbed by the lack of discipline and formality around the castle, tried to train the kings to be more courtly. They tried, but they were after all just simple gondoliers and could do nothing in a regal way.

At last the Grand Inquisitor brought forth Inez, the nurse who would identify the rightful king. When asked who he was, Marco or Giuseppe, she confessed that he was neither. When the lads were small, traitors had come to steal the prince away and she had substituted her own son. The real king was Luiz, the attendant loved by Casilda. So everyone was happy. Casilda was both a queen and the wife of the man she loved. The gondoliers were restored to their profession, one they much preferred to the responsibilities of royalty. Singing lustily, they departed, leaving the republican monarchy in the capable hands of King Luiz and Queen Casilda.

GONE WITH THE WIND

Type of work: Novel
Author: Margaret Mitchell (1900-1949)
Time: 1861-1873
Locale: Atlanta and Tara Plantation, Georgia
First published: 1936

Principal characters:

SCARLETT O'HARA, a Georgia belle
RHETT BUTLER, an unscrupulous profiteer, her third husband
ASHLEY WILKES, a sensitive neighbor, loved by Scarlett
MELANIE WILKES, Ashley's wife
GERALD O'HARA, the master of Tara Plantation, Scarlett's father
ELLEN O'HARA, Scarlett's mother
CHARLES HAMILTON, Melanie's brother, Scarlett's first husband
FRANK KENNEDY, Scarlett's second husband
MISS PITTYPAT, Melanie's maiden aunt
INDIA, Ashley's sister
MAMMY, Scarlett's nurse
BONNIE BLUE, child of Scarlett and Rhett

Gone with the Wind, one of the best-selling novels of all time, is the story of the subjugation of a proud people by war and the harsh "reconstruction" that followed. Swept along with these events is the beautiful, headstrong daughter of a wealthy plantation owner who, when reduced to poverty and hardship in the wake of Sherman's cruel and vicious destruction of the countryside, used her feminine wiles to regain her lost wealth. Having at last attained this goal, she was unable to hold the one man she really loved.

A historical romance of prodigious proportions, this first novel by an unknown author went through twelve printings within two months of publication. Its 1,037 pages enthralled millions, the sales in a single year exceeding two million copies. The novel has been translated into two dozen languages and even after more than twenty years, sales continue at a pace brisk enough to please any publisher. The motion picture lived up to Hollywood's most studied superlatives and no other photoplay has even approached its world-wide popularity.

The unprecedented success of Margaret Mitchell's only novel may be attributed to a combination of the author's style—a sustained narrative power combined with remarkable character delineation—and the universality of her subject, the struggle for survival when the accustomed security of civilized life is abruptly swept away and the human spirit suddenly stands alone. In spite of the fast-moving narrative, one is aware of this underlying thread of universality, this familiarity with human tragedy that all men can understand.

Perhaps the most lasting impression one gets from the novel, however, is the skill with which Miss Mitchell handles her characterizations. Scarlett O'Hara is, without question, one of the memorable characters in fiction. So lifelike did she become in the public mind that the producers of the motion picture preferred not to risk an established actress in the role and be accused of miscasting; they sent to England for a relatively unknown young actress to portray the fire and passion flashing from the tempestuous Scarlett.

The story of Scarlett O'Hara alone would be reason enough for a best seller; many books have achieved such eminence on far less. This daughter of Irish temper and French sensibilities displays stark and bold emotions that grip the reader. He follows her intense, futile love for Ashley Wilkes, her spiteful marriage to Charles

Hamilton, her opportunistic stealing of her sister's fiancé Frank Kennedy, her grasping arrangement of convenience with Rhett Butler. He is sometimes appalled at her callous use of her sex to gain her ends; he looks in vain for some sign of lofty ideals in this woman; and yet, in spite of all this, he finds laudable her will to survive and her contempt for her conquerors.

Three other characters stand out, admirably drawn but not quite inspiring the amount of interest created by Scarlett. Rhett Butler, dissolute son of Charleston blue bloods, is a cynical, materialistic blockade runner who consorts openly with the enemy and scoffs at patriotic ideals. Forceful, masculine, he is accustomed to taking what he wants. His one unfulfilled desire is the love of Scarlett and this frustration finally breaks his spirit. When at last, after several years of unhappy marriage, he gains her love as Ashley defaults, Rhett, now a bitter, fleshy toper, has already reached his decision to leave her.

Ashley Wilkes, the weak-willed object of Scarlett's misguided passion, depicts the impractical idealist dependent on a stronger will to solve life's problems for him. When Scarlett observes his unstable reaction to his wife's death she is finally able to see him as he really is. Shorn of his cavalier manners and the aura of courtly romance she had bestowed upon him, he becomes in her eyes an ineffectual weakling and the sterility of her forbidden love is at last apparent.

Melanie, in a way the winner despite her death at the end of the novel, found happiness and tranquility in her devotion to her insecure husband. Reticent, ladylike, saccharine, but intellectually attuned to Ashley, there is never any question that she, not Scarlett, should be Ashley's wife.

High-spirited Scarlett was sixteen when the Civil War began. She fancied herself in love with Ashley Wilkes, the sensitive, sophisticated son at a neighboring plantation, but he did not acknowledge her love. Upon the announcement of his engagement to his soft-spoken cousin Melanie Hamilton, Scarlett impetuously married Melanie's brother Charles, to that surprised young man's pride and delight. Less than a year later Scarlett was a war widow and an unwilling mother.

Here the novel loses the tempo of leisurely plantation life and takes on the urgency of a region at war. Leaving her father's plantation, Tara, Scarlett traveled twenty-five miles to Atlanta to stay with her dead husband's relatives. Later, as Atlanta was besieged by Sherman's troops, Scarlett returned home to Tara through the battle lines at night in a wagon provided by Rhett. With her were Melanie and Ashley's day-old son whom Scarlett had delivered as guns sounded in the distance.

Approaching Tara through the battle-scarred countryside she saw that most of the plantation mansions had been looted and burned by the enemy. Tara had been spared as a headquarters, though the outbuildings and baled cotton had been burned and the hogs, cows, and chickens killed. Scarlett's mother, too ill with fever to be moved as the soldiers approached, died with her beloved Tara filled with Yankee conquerors. Her father's mind, unable to stand these shocks, was gone. Now the sheltered Southern belle was faced with the formidable prospect of feeding, from a plantation stripped bare by the ruthless invaders, her father, her child, two sisters, Melanie, and the few servants who remained faithfully behind when the others ran off.

These are the events that helped to shape the character of Scarlett O'Hara and they explain the hardness, the avarice, that prompted many of her actions. For example, she was determined to hold on to Tara and when the carpetbaggers arbitrarily levied an extra three-hundred-dollar tax with the expectation of taking over the property for unpaid taxes, Scarlett unhesitatingly married storeowner Frank Kennedy, who was engaged to her sister Suellen, and he dutifuly paid the three-hundred-dollar tax.

The art of Margaret Mitchell makes such reprehensible acts seem normal under the circumstances, for the author has skillfully brought us along the same harsh road Scarlett has traveled and we, being thus exposed to the same experiences, understand, even condone, her responses.

Once Scarlett had learned the law of the jungle her native abilities came into their own. Borrowing money from Rhett, she bought and operated successfully a sawmill and soon was financially secure. When Frank was killed by occupation troops she married Rhett, who had amassed half a million dollars during the war as a blockade runner. But even the birth of a child, Bonnie Blue, did not bring happiness to this union because of the love for Ashley to which Scarlett absurdly clung. Rhett, always jealous of this will-of-the-wisp emotion, was unable to cope with what he could not understand. Ironically, Rhett overcame his love for Scarlett just as she was discovering that it was he, not Ashlev, whom she loved. When she tried to tell him this, Rhett announced brusquely that she was too late, that he was leaving her forever. There was no mistaking the finality of his words but, characteristically, Scarlett, the self-confident schemer, would not accept them as such.

Gone with the Wind is not a happy book. There are flicks of humor, but for the most part a deadly seriousness pervades the novel and in the end the callous, grasping cynicism of the leading characters mocks them and, properly, only an empty loneliness remains.

A natural question concerns the position of Gone with the Wind and its author in world literature. On the strength of her one novel Margaret Mitchell certainly cannot be called a great author. Whether her outstanding book will rank as a great novel will not be decided by those who consider the question at this early date. If the work eventually achieves first rank, it will be because Scarlett O'Hara continues to convey to future readers the same essence of human behavior that we ourselves see in her now.

THE GOOD COMPANIONS

Type of work: Novel
Author: J. B. Priestley (1894-   )
Type of plot: Picaresque romance
Time of plot: The 1920's
Locale: England
First published: 1929

Principal characters:
MISS TRANT, a well-to-do British woman
INIGO JOLLIFANT, a teacher at a boys' school
JESS OAKROYD, a workman
SUSIE DEAN, a comedienne
JERRY JERNINGHAM, a dancer

Critique:

J. B. Priestley's novel is a very human portrayal of a group of his contemporary Britishers in the 1920's. In many ways the novel is reminiscent of the work of Charles Dickens, both in characterization and in atmosphere. The descriptions of the English countryside and towns are particularly good. With such descriptions the author effectively sets the locale of the various parts of the novel. The best character of the novel is the Yorkshire workman, Jess Oakroyd. His northern dialect is a source of amusement both to the characters in the novel and to the reader, and he is the English parallel to the almost mythical American Yankee who says little, thinks much, and ends up by proving more astute than the sophisticated people about him.

The Story:

Jess Oakroyd was a stolid, proper sort of Yorkshireman, but his wife's nagging, coupled with the sarcastic remarks of his son, finally forced him to pack a small basket of clothes and set off to travel about England. His adventures began immediately, for he got a ride in a large van loaded with stolen goods. The driver of the van and the driver's helper left Jess at an inn in a small hamlet after having robbed him while he was asleep. Rudely awakened by the innkeeper, Jess had no money to buy his breakfast. Setting off afoot, he came upon another van, in which a man was attempting to repair a battered peddler's stall. In return for Jess' help, the owner gave him breakfast and a ride. Jess stayed for three days with the peddler, who sold fancy balloons.

After leaving the balloon trade, the Yorkshireman set out to walk the roads of England once again. Within the hour he came upon a stalled car and helped the woman driver to start the motor. The woman was Miss Trant, who had inherited several hundred pounds from her father. Since all her previous adventures had been in the realm of historical novels, Miss Trant had also decided to travel over England. At the age of thirty-five she was already an old maid.

While they were getting the car started, rain began to fall, and Jess and Miss Trant headed for a little tearoom nearby. There they met Inigo Jollifant and an odd-looking companion who was carrying a banjo. Inigo had begun his adventures on the previous Monday evening, as had Jess and Miss Trant.

An instructor at a boys' school, Inigo had been unhappy there because of the petty tyranny of the headmaster and his termagant wife. On Monday evening he had been dismissed because he became drunk and played the piano in celebration of his twenty-sixth birthday. Inigo, too drunk to do the prudent thing, had packed a knapsack and set out on his travels immediately. In the railroad station of a small town he had met his banjo-carrying companion, Morton Mitcham, a professional entertainer.

In the tearoom the shrewish woman proprietress was berating a group of customers who were unable to pay their bill. The banjo player recognized them as members of a theatrical troupe stranded, as they explained, when their manager ran away with a young woman and their funds.

On impulse, Miss Trant decided to take over the stranded company. That night they made plans for taking the show on the road once more. The new troupe took the name of The Good Companions. It was made up of an elderly comedian, a young and pretty comedienne named Susie Dean, Morton Mitcham, a dancer named Jerry Jerningham, a girl singer, and an older couple who sang duets. Miss Trant was the manager, Inigo the accompanist, and Jess, at Miss Trant's insistence, the handyman.

Their first appearance was in the little town where Miss Trant had found them. The show was not successful, but their second engagement, at a seaside hotel, met with obvious favor. The most appreciated actors were Jerry Jerningham and Susie Dean, who were aided by the gay songs which were written for their acts by Inigo Jollifant. For several weeks the routine of the company was one of rehearsals and performances, with train rides between two or three-night engagements in each town.

As the weeks passed, Inigo Jollifant fell in love with Susie Dean, who laughed at him, saying she could not fall in love and marry until she had become a musical comedy star and had played in London. Miss Trant was having a delightful experience. All her life had been spent in the sleepy village of Hitherton in southern England, where ner father had settled upon his retirement from the army. Her theatrical associates were far more interesting than the small sedate group of her father's village friends.

Next The Good Companions played in an almost deserted mill town in the Midlands. The mills had been shut down for some months and the townspeople had little money or interest in a traveling vaudeville troupe. Since the audiences were small and not sympathetic, the troupe became dispirited and almost broke up. But Jess Oakroyd persuaded the troupe to stick with Miss Trant, since she would lose her money if they did not carry on with their engagements.

At last the fortunes of the troupe had a turn for the better. Inigo Jollifant composed new tunes for the acts which met with great success. His love affair, however, did not fare as well. Susie Dean could not understand why he did not take his music as seriously as he did his writing for literary periodicals. She felt sure that he was making a mistake in trying to be a second-rate essayist when he could be a first-rate song writer.

The Good Companions finally had a long engagement in a series of prosperous manufacturing towns. The large audiences they drew began to recoup the money Miss Trant had invested. They became bold enough to engage a large hall for a stand of several nights. In the meantime Inigo went to London, where a famous producer listened to his new songs. Inigo, determined to help Susie become a top-ranking musical comedy star, refused to let the producer use his songs unless the man went with him to hear Susie Dean.

The first night in the large auditorium was disastrous. The operator of the local motion picture houses hired toughs to start a riot and set fire to the hall during the performance. The producer from London was punched on the nose in the melee and so refused to hear any more about either Inigo's music or Susie Dean. Miss Trant was injured during the riot.

Finally, when the future looked darkest, an elderly woman took a fancy to Jerry Jerningham. She married him and put her money and influence at his disposal. The result was that an even greater producer gave Susie Dean her chance at musical comedy in London and bought Inigo's music.

The troupe disbanded; but at Jerningham's request the other performers found excellent places with the same producer. In the hospital Miss Trant met a doctor with whom she had been in love for many years, and she prepared to marry him as soon as she was well. Jess Oakroyd did a little detective work in connection with the riot. With the help of the balloon peddler, he discovered who had hired the men to start the rioting and set fire to the theater. Held responsible for the disturbance, these men had to take over Miss Trant's debts for the damages.

After solving the mystery of the riot, Jess went back to his home in Yorkshire, for he had had a telegram from his son telling him that Mrs. Oakroyd was seriously ill. She died shortly thereafter and Jess made preparations to continue his traveling. He decided to visit his married daughter in Canada, for he had discovered that even a man as old and settled as he could become addicted to the pleasures of adventuring away from home.

THE GOOD EARTH

Type of work: Novel
Author: Pearl S. Buck (1892-   )
Type of plot: Social chronicle
Time of plot: Early twentieth century
Locale: Northern China
First published: 1931

Principal Characters:
WANG LUNG, a Chinese farmer
O-LAN, his wife
LOTUS BLOSSOM, his concubine
PEAR BLOSSOM, his slave
NUNG EN, Wang Lung's oldest son
NUNG WEN, Wang Lung's second son
THE FOOL, Wang Lung's first daughter

Critique:

In an almost pastoral style, *The Good Earth* describes the cycle of birth, marriage, and death in a Chinese peasant family. The book is written realistically, without any overt attempts to awaken sympathy for any of the characters. It is the absorbing story of Wang Lung's life on the farm, his trip to the city when starvation threatens, and of his life until it is time for him to be claimed by the good earth.

The Story:

His father had chosen a slave girl to be the bride of Wang Lung, a slave from the house of Hwang, a girl who would keep the house clean, prepare the food, and not waste her time thinking about clothes. On the morning he led her out through the gate of the big house, they stopped at a temple and burned incense. That was their marriage.

O-lan was a good wife. She thriftily gathered twigs and wood, so that they would not have to buy fuel. She mended Wang Lung's and his father's winter clothes and scoured the house. She worked in the fields beside her husband, even on the day she bore their first son.

The harvest was a good one that year. Wang Lung had a handful of silver dollars from the sale of his wheat and rice. He and O-lan bought new coats for themselves and new clothes for the baby. Together they went to pay their respects, with their child, at the home in which O-lan had once been a slave. With some of the silver dollars Wang Lung bought a small field of rich land from the Hwangs.

The second child was born a year later. It was again a year of good harvest.

Wang Lung's third baby was a girl. On the day of her birth crows flew about the house, mocking Wang Lung with their cries. The farmer did not rejoice when his little daughter was born, for poor farmers raised their daughters only to serve the rich. The crows had been an evil omen. The child was born feeble-minded.

That summer was dry, and for months no rain fell. The harvest was poor. After the little rice and wheat had been eaten and the ox killed for food, there was nothing for the poor peasants to do but die or go south to find work and food in a province of plenty. Wang Lung sold their furniture for a few pieces of silver, and after O-lan had borne their fourth child, dead with bruises on its neck when he saw it for the first time, the family began their journey. Falling in with a crowd of refugees, they were lucky. The refugees led them to a railroad, and with the money Wang Lung had received for his furniture they traveled on a train to their new home.

In the city they constructed a hut of mats against a wall, and, while O-lan and the two older children begged, Wang Lung pulled a ricksha. In that way they spent the winter, each day earning enough to buy rice for the next.

One day an exciting thing happened. There was to be a battle between soldiers in the town and an approaching enemy. When the wealthy people in the town fled, the poor who lived so miserably broke into the houses of the rich. By threatening one fat fellow who had been left behind, Wang Lung obtained enough money to take his family home.

O-lan soon repaired the damage which the weather had done to their house during their absence; then, with jewels which his wife had managed to plunder during the looting in the city, Wang Lung bought more land from the house of Hwang. He allowed O-lan to keep two small pearls which she fancied. Now Wang Lung had more land than one man could handle, and he hired one of his neighbors, Ching, as overseer. Several years later he had six men working for him. O-lan, who had borne him twins, a boy and a girl, after their return from the south, no longer went out into the fields to work, but kept the new house he had built. Wang Lung's two oldest sons were sent to school in the town.

When his land was flooded and work impossible until the water receded, Wang Lung began to go regularly to a tea shop in the town. There he fell in love with Lotus and brought her home to his farm to be his concubine. O-lan would have nothing to do with the girl, and Wang Lung was forced to set up a separate establishment for Lotus in order to keep the peace.

When he found that his oldest son visited Lotus often while he was away, Wang Lung arranged to have the boy

marry the daughter of a grain merchant in the town. The wedding took place shortly before O-lan, still in the prime of life, died of a chronic stomach illness. To cement the bond between the farmer and the grain merchant, Wang Lung's second son was apprenticed to Liu, the merchant, and his youngest daughter was betrothed to Liu's young son. Soon after O-lan's death Wang Lung's father followed her. They were buried near one another on a hill on his land.

When he grew wealthy, an uncle, his wife, and his shiftless son came to live with Wang Lung. One year there was a great flood, and although his neighbors' houses were pillaged by robbers during the confusion, Wang Lung was not bothered. Then he learned that his uncle was second to the chief of the robbers. From that time on he had to give way to his uncle's family, for they were his insurance against robbery and perhaps murder.

At last Wang Lung coaxed his uncle and aunt to smoke opium, and so they became too involved in their dreams to bother him. But there was no way he could curb their son. When the boy began to annoy the wife of Wang Lung's oldest son, the farmer rented the deserted house of Hwang and he, with his own family, moved into town. The cousin left to join the soldiers. The uncle and aunt were left in the country with their pipes to console them.

After Wang Lung's overseer died, he did no more farming himself. From that time on he rented his land, hoping that his youngest son would work it after his death. But he was disappointed. When Wang Lung took a slave young enough to be his granddaughter, the boy, who was in love with her, ran away from home and became a soldier.

When he felt that his death was near, Wang Lung went back to live on his land, taking with him only his slave, young Pear Blossom, his foolish-witted first daughter, and some servants. One day as he accompanied his sons across the fields, he overheard them planning what they would do with their inheritance, with the money they would get from selling their father's property. Wang Lung cried out, protesting that they must never sell the land because only from it could they be sure of earning a living. He did not know that they looked at each other over his head and smiled.

GOODBYE, MR. CHIPS

Type of work: Novelette
Author: James Hilton (1900-1954)
Type of plot: Sentimental romance.
Time of plot: 1870-1933
Locale: An English boys' school
First published: 1933

Principal characters:
MR. CHIPS, an old schoolmaster
MRS. WICKETT, his landlady
BROOKFIELD BOYS

Critique:

This charming story of an old school-master was written when the young journalist, James Hilton, was given an assignment to produce a Christmas story for an English newspaper. The almost instantaneous success of the book determined to a large degree the wide public reputation of its author. The novel consists largely of a series of happy and sad reminiscences of a beloved and almost legendary teacher who, sitting in his little room one gray November day, thinks of the many years he has spent in a boys' school.

The Story:

Chips was old — eighty-five — but of course, he thought, far from ill. Dr. Merivale had told him he should not venture out on this cold November day, but he also added that Chips was fitter than the doctor himself. What Chips did not know was that the doctor had told the landlady, Mrs. Wickett, to look after him; Chips' chest clouded in bad weather.

Chips sank into his armchair by the fire, happy in the peace and warmth. The first thing about his remembered career set him laughing. He had come to teach at Brookfield in 1870, and in a kindly talk old Wetherby, the acting head, advised him to watch his disciplinary measures. Mr. Wetherby had heard that discipline was not one of Chips' strong points. On the first day of class, when one of the boys dropped his desk top rather too loudly, Chips assigned him a

hundred lines and had no trouble after that. The boy's name was Colley—Chips seldom forgot a name or a face—and years later, he remembered, he taught Colley's son, and then his grandson, who, he said pleasantly, was the biggest young nitwit of them all. Chips was fond of making little jokes about the boys, who took his jibes well and grew to love him for his honesty and friendliness. Indeed, Chips' jokes were regarded as the funniest anywhere, and the boys had great sport telling of his latest.

Remembering these things, Chips thought growing old was a great joke, though a little sad. And when Mrs. Wickett came in with his tea, she could not tell whether Chips was laughing or crying. Tears were spilling down his withered cheeks.

Brookfield had known periods of grandeur and decay. When Chips arrived there, the school was already a century old and regarded as a place for boys whose lineage was respectable but seldom distinguished. Chips' own background was not distinguished, either, but it had been hard for him to realize that his mind was not the type to assume leadership. He had longed to work his way into the position of headmaster, but after many failures he knew that his role was one of teaching, and he gave up his administrative ambitions. But he grew to love his students. They would often come to chat with him over tea and crumpets. Sometimes they remarked, as they left, what a typical bachelor old Chips was.

It was painful to Chips that no one at Brookfield remembered his wife. He had married Kathy Bridges at forty-eight, and even now he wondered how the miracle had taken place. He had seen a girl waving from the top of a rocky ledge one day when he was out walking, and thinking her in trouble he set out to rescue her. On the way he sprained his ankle, and Kathy had assisted him. It was a remarkable love, for she was years younger than he. But Kathy left an enduring mark upon Chips. He grew more lenient with the boys, more understanding of their problems, and more courageous in his teaching. Ironically, Kathy died on April first, in childbirth, and that day, not realizing the tragedy that had befallen Chips, the boys played April Fool jokes on the stricken teacher.

Chips began to remember the war years. Names of boys whose faces he could still vizualize were read out in chapel from the casualty lists. When the headmaster died and no one could be found to fill his place, Chips was asked to head Brookfield. Standing in his tattered gown, which was often considered disgraceful by newcomers, he read out the names as tears filled his eyes. Even now, sitting in front of the fire, he could recall that roll, and he read it over to himself, remembering the faces that had looked so hopefully at him in the classroom.

One day he was meeting a Latin class while German bombs were crashing nearby. The boys squirmed in their seats as the explosions sounded nearer and nearer, but Chips quietly told them that they should never judge the importance of anything by the noise it made. Then, asking one of the more courageous lads to translate, Chips chose from Caesar a passage which was particularly apt because it dealt with German methods of

fighting. Later the boys told how Chips stood steady and calm, and they remarked that even though they might consider Latin a dead language, it was nevertheless valuable at times.

After the war Chips gave up his headmastership and returned to his room at Mrs. Wickett's. Now, fifteen years later, he was always asked to greet visiting dignitaries who came to Brookfield. He was amused to find that many of the barons, Parliament members, and war heroes had been his former pupils, and he remembered their faces, though now, to his chagrin, he often forgot their names. He would make amusing, appropriate remarks, not always complimentary, and the visitors would shake with laughter. Sometimes during those postwar years, he was asked to make little speeches at school banquets, and because of his reputation for funny sayings his audience would laugh uproariously, often before Chips reached the point of his jokes. Chips was privileged now; his eccentricities only made him more loved at Brookfield. Indeed, Chips was Brookfield.

Chips thought of the rich life he had led. There were so many things for laughter and sorrow. Now, as he sat by the fire, he heard a timid knock at the door, and a youngster, much abashed, came in. He had been told that Chips had sent for him. The old man laughed, knowing that this was a prank the old boys often played on a newcomer, and he saved the boy from embarrassment by saying that he had sent for him. After conversation and tea, Chips dismissed the boy in his abrupt but kindly fashion. The boy waved as he went down the walk.

Later that youth thought of Chips sadly and told his comrades that he had been the last to tell him goodbye. For Mr. Chips died quietly in his sleep that cold November night.

GORBODUC

Type of work: Drama
Authors: Thomas Norton (1532-1584) and Thomas Sackville (1536-1608)
Type of plot: Romantic tragedy
Time of plot: Before the Saxon invasion of England
Locale: England
First presented: 1562

Principal characters:
GORBODUC, aged King of England
VIDENA, his queen
FERREX, and
PORREX, their sons
AROSTUS,
PHILANDER, and
EUBULUS, Gorboduc's counselors
DORDAN, counselor to Ferrex
HERMON, parasite and confidant of Ferrex

Critique:

Written and put on the stage during Elizabeth's reign, this play had direct political implications for the time. It pretended to show how England in the past had been thrown into turmoil when the land was left without a proper heir. Certainly the authors and many of the people who saw and read the play realized that its hints to the heirless queen were broad indeed. The play was first presented at the Christmas revels of the Inner Temple, in London, and the lawyers and magistrates and courtiers who witnessed it must undoubtedly have been wondering what course the throne would take if Elizabeth died without providing for a successor. In the history of English drama this play is important as the first play written in blank verse in English and because it was among the first English tragedies to employ a domestic political theme. In structure it followed the classical drama of Seneca.

The Story:

Gorboduc, King of Britain and last of the line beginning with the legendary Brute, decided that he would not wait until his death before handing over the rule of his kingdom. In addition, he decided that he would set aside the rule of primogeniture and divide Britain between his two sons, Ferrex and Porrex. To Ferrex, the older, he planned to give all lands south of the Humber River; to Porrex, the younger, he intended to give those lands north of the Humber.

Calling in his chief advisers, Gorboduc told them what was in his mind. Arostus was in complete agreement with the king's wishes, but Philander and Eubulus warned of the dangers of the plan. Although they admitted that the king would be able to aid his sons in the early years of their reigns, they felt that the sons might not be willing to take advice from their father after he had placed great power in their hands. The advisers also warned that when the authority of the kingdom was divided the allegiance of the people might be divided, and they pointed out that Ferrex might very well resent having to share the kingdom with a younger brother, since custom made it the rule that the firstborn son inherited the entire kingdom. Last of all, they warned Gorboduc that history had proved a kingdom divided was easier prey to foreign conquest.

Gorboduc listened to his counselors. When they had finished speaking, however, he told them his mind was made up, that he felt the advantages to be gained by dividing the kingdom during his lifetime outweighed the disadvantages. Accordingly, he set his plan in operation, not knowing that his queen, Videna, was extremely jealous of her older son's prerogatives and hated the younger son for receiving a part of the kingdom which she felt rightfully belonged in its entirety to Ferrex.

Gorboduc sent trusted advisers of his own with each of the princes when they took over their separate domains, but before long both sons began to disregard their father's counselors. Instead, they listened to young men who preyed upon their vanities. Ferrex began to seek the advice of a parasite named Hermon, a man who flattered the young ruler's ego. Hermon told Ferrex that as the older son he should not have been given such a meager part of Britain and that, according to custom and his own ability, Ferrex should have been made ruler of the entire domain.

More than flattering Ferrex, Hermon told him that the younger king beyond the Humber was jealous of the older brother and was plotting to invade the kingdom of Ferrex. Dordan, the elderly counselor sent to Ferrex by Gorboduc, prevailed enough on the young man so that Ferrex made only secret preparations against a possible attack by his brother.

Meanwhile, north of the Humber, the same situation had developed. Porrex, the younger son, scorned the wise advice of his father's counselor and turned to a flattering parasite, who told Porrex about the secret plans being made for war by Ferrex. Porrex, who distrusted his brother, decided that a preventive war was the best solution to the problem, and he set out to invade the kingdom south of the Humber.

Dordan sent a letter to Gorboduc advising him of the state of affairs between the two brothers. The aged father-king called his trusted men about him to ask their advice. While the council met to seek a solution, word came that Porrex had invaded the older brother's kingdom and had murdered Ferrex with his own hand.

Queen Videna, when she heard what had happened to her beloved older son, swore she would be avenged on Porrex.

She vowed that he was no longer a son of hers but a criminal to be punished for his evil deeds.

Porrex, sent for by his father, appeared at Gorboduc's court and readily admitted invading his brother's kingdom and murdering his brother-king. Porrex said that he was genuinely sorry that the deed had been committed, but that he still felt the murder justified. He swore that Ferrex had tried to have him poisoned and that he had killed Ferrex in order to save his own life. Gorboduc, not knowing what to do until he had investigated the situation further, sent Porrex from his sight until he should send word that he wanted the young man's presence.

Scarcely had the young man left his father when he was killed by his mother, who thereby avenged the murder of Ferrex. The Britons, outraged at such conduct on the part of their rulers, then rose up in arms and murdered both Gorboduc and Queen Videna.

The nobles of Britain, left without a leader, tried to put down the uprising of the common people. They feared that if they did not quell the revolt at once the country would be weakened and left prey to some invading power. The nobles saw themselves, their families, their lands, and the whole country threatened by the tragedy that had destroyed the royal house. But even the nobles could not agree on a course of action.

When a number of them met in a solemn conclave to organize against the uprisen rabble, they learned that the Duke of Albany, filled with ambition to become ruler, had raised an army and set out on a campaign to make himself master of Britain. King Gorboduc's counselors advised the other nobles to join together to put down the duke, since he wished to usurp the throne. Faced by a common danger, they at last chose a new king for Britain, the old line having become extinct with the deaths of Gorboduc and his two sons.

GRAND HOTEL

Type of work: Novel
Author: Vicki Baum (1888-1960)
Type of plot: Social chronicle
Time of plot: 1920's
Locale: Berlin
First published: 1930

> *Principal characters:*
> BARON GAIGERN, a gambler and thief
> ELISAVETA ALEXANDROVNA GRUSINSKAYA, a ballerina
> OTTO KRINGELEIN, a junior clerk of the Saxonia Cotton Company
> HERR GENERALDIREKTOR PREYSING, manager of the Saxonia Cotton Company
> DR. OTTERNSCHLAG, a retired physician
> MISS FLAMM (FLAEMMCHEN), a public stenographer and model

Critique:

In this novel Vicki Baum uses a time-honored device of fiction by bringing together a group of characters in a particular time and place, and showing how they react upon and influence each other. The parallel, concurrent actions of her characters are well synthesized into a picture of European society in the period between wars.

The Story:

Through the revolving doors of the Grand Hotel in Berlin came people from various walks of life. The meetings of these people and their effects upon one another thereafter were as varied as the people themselves. Each one had his own life, his own worries, and his own problems, and each pursued his own selfish ends.

Baron Gaigern was living in luxury at the hotel. He never seemed to lack money and he possessed well-tailored clothes. The baron, however, was a gambler and a thief staying at the hotel for the purpose of stealing Elisaveta Alexandrovna Grusinskaya's famous pearls, which had been given to the ballerina by the Grand Duke Sergei. Gaigern's plan to steal the pearls was based on a timing of Grusinskaya's actions. One night he crawled along the outside of the building to the dancer's room, where she kept her jewels in an unlocked case. That night Grusin-

skaya returned earlier than usual and found him in her room.

Grusinskaya, the aging ballerina, knew that her youth was slipping away from her. On that particular night, feeble applause after one of her best numbers made her leave the theater before the performance was over and return to her room at the hotel. When she discovered Gaigern in her room, he convinced her that because he loved her he had come to sit there while she was away at the theater. Willing to believe him, she let him stay with her the rest of the night. The next morning, before she awoke, he replaced the pearls in their case. Grusinskaya left Berlin that morning and Gaigern promised to meet her in Vienna three days later.

Still in need of money, Gaigern decided to get it from the wealthy and apparently ailing provincial in room 70. Gaigern did not suspect that the rich provincial, Otto Kringelein by name, was in reality only a junior clerk of the Saxonia Cotton Company of Fredersdorf. Kringelein at forty-six, had learned that he was dying, and he decided that before his death he would see something of life after years of being bullied at the office by his superiors and at home by his wife Anna. With a small legacy left him by his father, his savings in the bank, and a loan on his

---

life insurance policy, he planned to live the life of a rich man for a few weeks before he died. On the morning Grusinskaya left Berlin, Gaigern met Kringelein and took him to be outfitted by his own tailor. In the evening they went to the boxing matches and then to a gambling casino. Kringelein paid for the evening's entertainment, for Gaigern admitted that he was without funds. Gaigern had hoped to win enough money to pay his way to Vienna, but he lost steadily. Kringelein won thirty-four hundred marks. They ended the evening at the Alhambra, a shabby night club, where Kringelein became ill. On the way back to the hotel Gaigern stole Kringelein's pocketbook. Later in Kringelein's room, he returned it at Dr. Otternschlag's insistence.

Dr. Otternschlag, a middle-aged physician badly disfigured in the war, spent one or two months every year at the Grand Hotel. He did nothing, went practically nowhere, and seemed to have no interests whatsoever. He had begun to show a slight interest in Kringelein when Gaigern intruded. It was Otternschlag who gave Kringelein a hypodermic to lessen his pains, but after a polite word of thanks to the doctor Kringelein turned to Gaigern, whom he begged to remain with him. Otternschlag was forgotten.

In the morning Kringelein received a letter from his wife, complaining about the inconveniences of the house in which they lived, a house owned by the Saxonia Cotton Company. Kringelein angrily stamped down to Generaldirektor Preysing's room to air his grievance. Herr Preysing had married the daughter of the owner of the Saxonia Cotton Company years before and had gradually worked himself up to the position of manager. He was in Berlin to bring about an amalgamation between his company and the Chemnitz Manufacturing Company, a merger necessary to forestall huge losses for the Saxonia Company. When Preysing saw that the representatives of the Chemnitz Company were about to re-

ject his offer, he told a lie which he knew would win him their consent. He assured them that a trade agreement existed between the company and Burleigh & Sons, importers, of Manchester, England. The merger was then signed. During his stay in Berlin, Preysing had hired a stenographer, Miss Flamm, a beautiful girl who worked part time as a photographer's model. Preysing became quite enamored of her. When she hinted that she would be willing to travel with him as his secretary, Preysing decided to go to Manchester and confer with the English company. He asked Flaemmchen, as he called her, to accompany him and she agreed, after setting her price at one thousand marks. Preysing immediately engaged an adjoining room for her at the Grand Hotel.

That night Preysing was in Flaemmchen's room when he heard a noise in his own room and went to see what it was. There stood Gaigern in his pajamas. Preysing saw that his billfold was missing from the table where he had placed it, and he demanded its return. Gaigern threatened to shoot. Preysing seized a bronze inkstand and hit Gaigern over the head with it, killing him. Flaemmchen ran to call for help. Kringelein heard her and opened his door, to have her fall unconscious into his arms. He took her in and when she regained consciousness he learned the whole story from her. He then went down to Preysing's room, gathered up Flaemmchen's clothes, and told Preysing to call the police. When they arrived, Preysing was arrested and his plea of self-defense after robbery seemed weak, for Gaigern had had no gun on him. Preysing stayed in jail for three months. During that time his affair with Flaemmchen was exposed, his wife divorced him, and his father-in-law discharged him. Meanwhile Kringelein and Flaemmchen, having become friends, decided to go to England together.

Lives had been changed by chance meetings. Gaigern, the strong, vital man, was now dead. Preysing, the respectable citizen, was in jail accused of murder. Otternschlag, who claimed to have no interest in life, found when he tried to commit suicide that he wanted very much to live. Meek, downtrodden Kringelein began to assume the authority that came with responsibility, responsibility in the form of Flaemmchen. The tired and aging ballerina, Grusinskaya, had left the hotel feeling young and loved once more. And as their rooms were vacated one by one, new visitors entered the hotel where life, mysterious or stupid or cruel, went on.

THE GRANDISSIMES

Type of work: Novel
Author: George W. Cable (1844-1925)
Type of plot: Regional romance
Time of plot: 1804
Locale: New Orleans
First published: 1880

Principal characters:

HONORÉ GRANDISSIME, head of the Grandissimes
THE DARKER HONORÉ GRANDISSIME, his quadroon half-brother
AGRICOLA FUSILIER, Honoré's uncle
AURORA NANCANOU, a young widow
CLOTILDE NANCANOU, her daughter
JOSEPH FROWENFELD, a young American
DR. KEENE, Joseph's physician and friend
PALMYRE, a freed slave

Critique:

George W. Cable knew intimately the Creole society of New Orleans, and this novel re-creates for the reader a segment of American life which has vanished forever. Through the author's attempt at reproducing Creole dialect, the book acquires a unique flavor. The plot presents the tragedy of the Negro in a more effective and more truthful manner than do many modern books on the subject.

The Story:

Honoré Grandissime and Aurora Nancanou, both members of the Creole aristocracy, met at a masked ball and fell in love at first sight. Each was unaware of the other's identity. Honoré was a young merchant, the head of the Grandissime family. Aurora, a young widow, was the daughter of a De Grapion. Honoré's uncle, Agricola Fusilier, had killed Aurora's husband in a duel, after he had accused Agricola of cheating at cards. Agricola won the duel, cleared his honor, and collected the gambling debt, the entire estate of Aurora's husband. Aurora and her daughter Clotilde, were left penniless. Agricola gave Aurora's estate to Honoré and made him a wealthy man.

Shortly afterward Joseph Frowenfeld, a young American immigrant, arrived in New Orleans with his parents and sisters. All were stricken with fever; only Joseph

survived. The lonely young man formed a friendship with his physician, Dr. Keene. Joseph and Honoré met by chance one day and found a common interest in their concern over the injustice of slavery and the caste system of New Orleans society. Honoré's life however depended upon these institutions. Joseph wished to have them wiped out at once.

Deciding to earn his living as a druggist, Joseph opened a small shop and soon became friendly with his aristocratic landlord. The landlord was actually Honoré's half-brother and he bore the same name, but he was not acknowledged as a member of the family because he was a quadroon. He was called the darker Honoré.

Joseph found another new friend in old Agricola. He was also struck by the charm of Aurora and Clotilde when they called to make purchases. He learned more about Aurora from Dr. Keene. The physician told him about Palmyre, a freed slave who had once been Aurora's maid. The girl hated Agricola. One night Joseph was awakened by pistol shots nearby. A few minutes later Dr. Keene and several others entered the shop with the wounded Agricola; he had been stabbed, and his companions had fired upon his assailant.

Several days later Aurora called upon her landlord in order to make some ar-

1372

rangements about the rent she could not pay. She knew her landlord's name was Honoré Grandissime, but she did not connect this name with the man she loved. Upon learning that they were half-brothers, Aurora was upset and her family pride caused her to be harsh with Honoré.

When Dr. Keene fell sick, he asked Joseph to attend one of his patients. The patient was Palmyre, who had been wounded as she ran away after stabbing Agricola. Joseph promised Dr. Keene to keep her trouble a secret and went to dress the wound.

Joseph paid his last visit to the wounded Palmyre, now almost recovered. Palmyre begged him to help her make the white Honoré love her. But Palmyre's maid, misunderstanding the conversation, thought that Joseph had wronged her mistress. She struck him over the head, and Joseph reeled groggily into the street. Some passing pedestrians, seeing him emerge bleeding from Palmyre's house, drew a natural inference, and soon everyone knew about Joseph's misfortune. Only Clotilde and Honoré believed him innocent.

Public feeling was running high against the Americans, and Joseph found himself despised by most of the Creoles. Both his liberal views and his trouble at Palmyre's house were against him.

Honoré's conscience bothered him. He felt that he unjustly held Aurora's property, but he also knew he could not return it to her without ruining the finances of her family. But he made his choice. He called upon Aurora and Clotilde and presented them with their property and the income from it. Now he could not declare his love for Aurora; if he did so, his family would think he had returned the property because of love instead of a sense of justice.

On his way home from Aurora's house, Honoré met the darker Honoré with Dr. Keene. The physician had risen from his sickbed because he had heard of Honoré's call at Aurora's house. Dr. Keene, also in love with Aurora, was jealous. His exertion caused a hemorrhage of the lungs, and the two Honorés carried him home and watched over him.

While they attended the sick man, the darker Honoré proposed to his brother that they go into partnership, so that the darker Honoré's money could save the family from ruin. His brother accepted the offer. But this action turned Honoré's family against him. Agricola led an unsuccessful lynching party to find the darker Honoré. Not finding him, the mob broke the windows of Joseph's shop as a gesture against liberal views in general.

Aurora set Joseph up in business again on the ground floor of her house and made Clotilde a partner in the store. Brought together in this manner, the two young people fell in love. At the same time, the darker Honoré lay wasting away for love of Palmyre, who was trying to revenge herself upon Agricola by voodoo spells. When Agricola could no longer sleep at night, his family determined to catch Palmyre in her acts of witchcraft. They caught her accomplice, but Palmyre escaped.

Meanwhile the darker Honoré went to Joseph's store to get some medicine for himself. Meeting Agricola, who insulted him, the darker Honoré stabbed Agricola and escaped. The wounded man was carried upstairs to Aurora's house to die; there the two families were united again at his deathbed. Agricola revealed that he had once promised to Aurora's father a marriage between Aurora and Honoré.

The darker Honoré and Palmyre escaped together to France. There he committed suicide because she still would not accept his love.

Joseph finally declared his love for Clotilde. But Aurora would not accept Honoré's offer of marriage because she thought he had made it out of obligation to Agricola. Then Honoré made his offer again as a man in love. As a last gesture of family pride Aurora refused him, but at the same time she threw herself into her lover's arms.

THE GRANDMOTHERS

Type of work: Novel
Author: Glenway Wescott (1901-   )
Type of plot: Regional chronicle
Time of plot: 1830-1925
Locale: Wisconsin
First published: 1927

Principal characters:
ALWYN TOWER, a young boy
HENRY TOWER, his grandfather
ROSE TOWER, his grandmother
JIM TOWER, his uncle
EVAN TOWER, another uncle
FLORA TOWER, his aunt
RALPH TOWER, his father
MARIANNE TOWER, his mother

Critique:

The heritage which Alwyn Tower studied as he pored over the family albums is the heritage of most Americans. The struggles of the pioneers of the Tower family were the struggles of all pioneers. Glenway Wescott has told a story of the loves and hates, the madness, the strength, and the weakness found in the histories of all families. The characters are vivid and authentic, the events realistic and moving. The writer must have loved the people about whom he wrote; he portrays them so sympathetically. *The Grandmothers* is a truly American story.

The Story:

During his childhood, Alwyn Tower spent many hours poring over the family albums, for everything any of his ancestors or relatives had done was interesting to the boy. He begged his Grandmother Tower to tell him stories of her childhood and stories about her children and other relatives. Often the old lady could not remember what he wanted to know, and sometimes she seemed reluctant to talk about the past. But piece by piece, from his Grandmother Tower, his parents, his aunts and uncles, and from the albums, Alwyn learned something of what he wanted to know.

Alwyn's Grandfather Tower died when the boy was twelve years old, and so his memories of that old man were rather vague. Grandfather Tower's chief interest during his old age was his garden, where he never allowed his grandchildren to go without his permission. He had failed at farming, but he was the best gardener in that part of Wisconsin.

Grandfather Tower had come to Wisconsin from New York. Like so many others, he had planned to get rich in the new West; like so many others, he had failed. He had been a young boy full of dreams when he first cleared the wilderness for his farm. He fell in love with and married Serena Cannon, and shortly afterward went off to the Civil War. When he returned, Serena was ill with a fever and died soon after, leaving a baby boy. Grandfather Tower could never love another as he had loved Serena. Because the boy needed a mother, however, he married Rose Hamilton, who had been jilted by his brother Leander. Serena's boy died, a week before Rose bore his first child. After that life seemed unimportant to Henry Tower. There were more children, some a small pleasure to him, some a disgrace. But they seemed to be Rose's children, not his. Part of Grandfather Tower had died with

Serena, and although he lived to be eighty-two years old, he had never seemed to be completely alive as far as Alwyn was concerned.

Grandmother Tower, too, had come to Wisconsin when she was a child. Growing up in the wilderness, she suffered all the hardships of the pioneers —hunger and cold and fear of Indians. When she was in her early teens she met and fell in love with Leander Tower. When the Civil War came, Leander enlisted, and the girl went to stay with Serena Tower. While Serena lay ill with fever, the young girl cared for her and the baby. Leander returned, but he had changed. Although he could not explain himself clearly, Rose knew that he no longer wanted to marry her. After Serena's husband came home and Serena had died, Leander went to California. Rose married Serena's widower and bore his children, but like him she was only partly alive. She never ceased to love Leander, but she was faithful to Grandfather Tower, even after Leander returned to Wisconsin. To Alwyn, she was a quiet, serene woman, resigned to life, but not unhappy with her lot.

Alwyn learned about many of his more distant relatives as he studied the albums and listened to the stories of his elders. There was his Great-Aunt Nancy Tower, who had been insane for part of her life. There was his Great-Aunt Mary Harris, who had been married three times and had traveled all over the world. Grandmother Tower said that Great-Aunt Mary was a real pioneer. She had seen her first husband killed by Southerners because he sympathized with the Union. Her second husband was a drunken sot who beat her, and often she had to beg for food to stay alive. After her second husband divorced her, she married one of the Tower men, and for the first time she knew happiness and prosperity.

Old Leander Tower seemed to be happy only when he was helping a young boy. His younger brother Hilary had dis-appeared in the war, and it seemed almost as if Leander were trying to find a substitute for his brother.

Alwyn knew his father's brothers and sisters quite well. His Uncle Jim was a minister who had married a rich woman, and they took Alwyn to live with them in Chicago, giving the boy his only chance for a good education. Uncle Jim's wife persuaded her husband to give up preaching. After her death he continued to live with her mother and sisters and to humor their whims. Alwyn liked his Uncle Jim, but he could not admire him.

Uncle Evan, a deserter in the Spanish-American War, had gone west to live after taking a new name. Once or twice he came home to visit his father, but both men seemed embarrassed during those meetings. Grandfather Tower had always been ashamed of Evan, and during the last visit Evan made the old man refused to enter the house while his son was there.

Aunt Flora was an old maid, although she still thought of herself as a young girl. She had had many chances to marry, but she was afraid of the force of love, afraid that something hidden in her would be roused and not satisfied. It was a mysterious thing she could not understand. She turned to Alwyn, giving him her love and accepting his, for she could love the young boy whole-heartedly, having nothing to fear from him. When she was twenty-nine years old, she fell ill and died. Alwyn thought she looked happy as she took her last breath.

Alwyn's father, Ralph Tower, had always wanted to be a veterinarian, for he had a way with animals. But Uncle Jim had been the one chosen for an education, and after Uncle Evan deserted and went west, Ralph had to take over the farm for his father. He was never bitter; merely resigned. Perhaps he would have envied Jim if it had not been for Alwyn's mother.

His parents had one of the few really happy marriages in the family, Alwyn realized as he watched them together.

Alwyn knew something of the girlhood of his mother. Her parents had hated each other fiercely, and had taken pleasure in showing that hatred. Alwyn's mother was a lonely child until she met Ralph Tower. Sometimes it embarrassed Alwyn to see his parents together because they revealed so much of their feeling for each other.

Alwyn realized that the Towers were one of the last pioneer families in America. He knew that in his heritage there was a deep religious feeling, a willingness to accept poverty and hardship as the will of God. His heritage was a disordered one; a deserter, an insane woman, a man and a wife who hated each other, an uncle who lived on the wealth of his wife's mother. But these people were just as much a part of him as were the others. Alwyn knew that his life would be a rearrangement of the characters of the others. He knew that he could understand himself if once he understood his people.

THE GRAPES OF WRATH

Type of work: Novel
Author: John Steinbeck (1902-   )
Type of plot: Social criticism
Time of plot: 1930's
Locale: Southwest United States and California
First published: 1939

Principal characters:
TOM JOAD, an ex-convict
PA JOAD, an Okie
MA JOAD, his wife
ROSE OF SHARON, Tom's sister
JIM CASY, a labor agitator

Critique:

In *The Grapes of Wrath* Steinbeck has achieved an interesting contrapuntal effect by breaking the narrative at intervals with short, impressionistic passages recorded as though by a motion picture camera moving quickly from one scene to another and from one focus to another. The novel is a powerful indictment of our capitalistic economy and a sharp criticism of the southwestern farmer for his imprudence in the care of his land. The outstanding feature of *The Grapes of Wrath* is its photographically detailed, if occasionally sentimentalized, description of the American farmers of the Dust Bowl in the mid-thirties of the twentieth century.

The Story:

Tom Joad was released from the Oklahoma state penitentiary where he had served a sentence for killing a man in self-defense. He traveled homeward through a region made barren by drought and dust storms. On the way he met Jim Casy, an ex-preacher; the pair went together to the home of Tom's people. They found the Joad place deserted. While Tom and Casy were wondering what had happened, Muley Graves, a die-hard tenant farmer, came by and disclosed that all of the families in the neighborhood had gone to California or were going. Tom's folks, Muley said, had gone to a relative's place preparatory to going west. Muley was the only sharecropper to stay behind.

All over the southern Midwest states, farmers, no longer able to make a living because of land banks, weather, and machine farming, had sold or were forced out of the farms they had tenanted. Junk dealers and used-car salesmen profiteered on them. Thousands of families took to the roads leading to the promised land, California.

Tom and Casy found the Joads at Uncle John's place, all busy with preparations to leave for California. Assembled for the trip were Pa and Ma Joad; Noah, their mentally backward son; Al, the adolescent younger brother of Tom and Noah; Rose of Sharon, Tom's sister, and her husband, Connie; the Joad children, Ruthie and Winfield; and Granma and Grampa Joad. Al had bought an ancient truck to take them west. The family asked Jim Casy to go with them. The night before they started, they killed the pigs they had left and salted down the meat so that they would have food on the way.

Spurred by handbills which stated that agricultural workers were badly needed in California, the Joads, along with thousands of others, made their torturous way, in a worn-out vehicle, across the plains toward the mountains. Grampa died of a stroke during their first overnight stop. Later there was a long delay when the truck broke down. Small business people along the way treated the migrants as enemies. And, to add to the general misery, returning migrants told the Joads that there was no work to be had in California, that conditions were even worse than they were in Oklahoma. But the dream of a bountiful West Coast urged the Joads onward.

Close to the California line, where the group stopped to bathe in a river, Noah, feeling he was a hindrance to the others, wandered away. It was there that the Joads first heard themselves addressed as *Okies*, another word for tramps.

Granma died during the night trip across the desert. After burying her, the group went into a Hooverville, as the migrants' camps were called. There they learned that work was all but impossible to find. A contractor came to the camp to sign up men to pick fruit in another county. When the Okies asked to see his license, the contractor turned the leaders over to a police deputy who had accompanied him to camp. Tom was involved in the fight which followed. He escaped, and Casy gave himself up in Tom's place. Connie, husband of the pregnant Rose of Sharon, suddenly disappeared from the group. The family was breaking up in the face of its hardships. Ma Joad did everything in her power to keep the group together.

Fearing recrimination after the fight, the Joads left Hooverville and went to a government camp maintained for transient agricultural workers. The camp had sanitary facilities, a local government made up of the transients themselves, and simple organized entertainment. During the Joads' stay at the camp the Okies successfully defeated an attempt of the local citizens to give the camp a bad name and thus to have it closed to the migrants. For the first time since they had arrived in California, the Joads found themselves treated as human beings.

Circumstances eventually forced them to leave the camp, however, for there was no work in the district. They drove to a large farm where work was being offered. There they found agitators attempting to keep the migrants from taking the work because of unfair wages offered. But the Joads, thinking only of food, were escorted by motorcycle police in to the farm. The entire family picked peaches for five cents a box and earned in a day just enough money to buy food for one meal. Tom, remembering the pickets outside the camp, went out at night to investigate. He found Casy, who was the leader of the agitators. While Tom and Casy were talking, deputies, who had been searching for Casy, closed in on them. The pair fled, but were caught. Casy was killed. Tom received a cut on his head, but not before he had felled a deputy with an ax handle. The family concealed Tom in their shack. The rate for a box of peaches dropped, meanwhile, to two-and-a-half cents. Tom's danger and the futility of picking peaches drove the Joads on their way. They hid the injured Tom under the mattresses in the back of the truck and told the suspicious guard at the entrance to the farm that the extra man they had had with them when they came was a hitchhiker who had stayed on to pick.

The family found at last a migrant crowd encamped in abandoned boxcars along a stream. They joined the camp and soon found temporary jobs picking cotton. Tom, meanwhile, hid in a culvert near the camp. Ruthie innocently disclosed Tom's presence to another little girl. Ma, realizing that Tom was no longer safe, sent him away. Tom promised to carry on Casy's work in trying to improve the lot of the downtrodden everywhere.

The autumn rains began. Soon the stream which ran beside the camp overflowed and water entered the boxcars. Under these all but impossible conditions, Rose of Sharon gave birth to a dead baby.

1378

When the rising water made their position no longer bearable, the family moved from the camp on foot. The rains had made their old car useless. They came to a barn, which they shared with a boy and his starving father. Rose of Sharon, bereft of her baby, nourished the famished man with the milk from her breasts. So the poor kept each other alive in the depression years.

GREAT EXPECTATIONS

Type of work: Novel
Author: Charles Dickens (1812-1870)
Type of plot: Mystery romance
Time of plot: Nineteenth century
Locale: England
First published: 1860-1861

Principal characters:
PIP, an orphan
JOE GARGERY, Pip's brother-in-law
MISS HAVISHAM, an eccentric recluse
ESTELLA, Miss Havisham's ward
HERBERT POCKET, Pip's roommate
MR. JAGGERS, a solicitor
ABEL MAGWITCH (MR. PROVIS), a convict
COMPEYSON, a villain

Critique:

Miss Havisham was deserted on her wedding day. Pip gave help to an escaped prisoner hiding in a marsh. From these two events Dickens weaves an amazing story of vindictiveness on one hand and gratitude on the other; and both of these motives affected Pip's life, for Miss Havisham had marked him as one of her victims, and the prisoner had sworn to reward the small boy who had helped him in the marsh. Although an absorbing tale, this is also a gloomy one, not lightened by Dickens' usual capricious characterizations. There are few moments to relieve the reader from the pressure of Pip's problems in life.

The Story:

Little Pip had been left an orphan when he was a small boy, and his sister, much older than he, had grudgingly reared him in her cottage. Pip's brother-in-law, Joe Gargery, on the other hand, was kind and loving to the boy. In the marsh country where he lived with his sister and Joe, Pip wandered alone. One day he was accosted by a wild-looking stranger who demanded that Pip secretly bring him some food, a request which Pip feared to deny. The stranger, an escaped prisoner, asked Pip to bring him a file to cut the iron chain that bound his leg. When Pip returned to the man with a pork pie and file, he saw another mysterious figure in the marsh. After a

desperate struggle with the escaped prisoner, the stranger escaped into the fog. The man Pip had aided was later apprehended. He promised Pip he would somehow repay the boy for helping him.

Mrs. Joe sent Pip to the large mansion of the strange Miss Havisham upon that lady's request. Miss Havisham lived in a gloomy, locked house where all clocks had been stopped on the day her bridegroom failed to appear for the wedding ceremony. She often dressed in her bridal robes; a wedding breakfast moldered on the table in an unused room. There Pip went every day to entertain the old lady and a beautiful young girl, named Estella, who delighted in tormenting the shy boy. Miss Havisham enjoyed watching the two children together, and she encouraged Estella in her haughty teasing of Pip.

Living in the grim atmosphere of Joe's blacksmith shop and the uneducated poverty of his sister's home, Pip was eager to learn. One day a London solicitor named Jaggers presented him with the opportunity to go to London and become a gentleman. Both Pip and Joe accepted the proposal. Pip imagined that his kind backer was Miss Havisham herself. Perhaps she wanted to make a gentleman out of him so he would be fit some day to marry Estella.

In London Pip found a small apartment set up for him, and for a living companion he had a young relative of Miss Havisham, Herbert Pocket. When Pip needed money, he was instructed to go to Mr. Jaggers. Although Pip pleaded with the lawyer to disclose the name of his benefactor, Jaggers advised the eager young man not to make inquiries, for when the proper time arrived Pip's benefactor would make himself known.

Soon Pip became one of a small group of London dandies, among them a disagreeable chap named Bentley Drummle. Joe Gargery came to visit Pip, much to Pip's disturbance, for by now he had outgrown his rural background and he was ashamed of Joe's manners. But Herbert Pocket cheerfully helped Pip to entertain the uncomfortable Joe in their apartment. Plainly Joe loved Pip very much, and after he had gone Pip felt ashamed of himself. Joe had brought word that Miss Havisham wanted to see the young man, and Pip returned with his brother-in-law. Miss Havisham and Estella marked the changes in Pip, and when Estella had left Pip alone with the old lady, she told him he must fall in love with the beautiful girl. She also said it was time for Estella to come to London, and she wished Pip to meet her adopted daughter when she arrived. This request made Pip feel more certain he had been sent to London by Miss Havisham to be groomed to marry Estella.

Estella had not been in London long before she had many suitors. Of all the men who courted her, she seemed to favor Bentley Drummle. Pip saw Estella frequently. Although she treated him kindly and with friendship, he knew she did not return his love.

On his twenty-first birthday Pip received a caller, the man whom Pip had helped in the marsh many years before. Ugly and coarse, he told Pip it was he who had been financing Pip ever since he had come to London. At first the boy was horrified to discover he owed so much to this crude ex-criminal, Abel Magwitch. He told Pip that he had been sent to the colonies where he had grown

rich. Now he had wanted Pip to enjoy all the privileges he had been denied in life, and he had returned to England to see the boy to whom he had tried to be a second father. He warned Pip that he was in danger should his presence be discovered, for it was death for a prisoner to return to England once he had been sent to a convict colony. Pip detested his plight. Now he realized Miss Havisham had had nothing to do with his great expectations in life, but he was too conscious of his debt to consider abandoning the man whose person he disliked. He determined to do all in his power to please his benefactor. Magwitch was using the name Provis to hide his identity. Provis told Pip furthermore that the man with whom Pip had seen him struggling long ago in the marsh was his enemy, Compeyson, who had vowed to destroy him. Herbert Pocket, who was a distant cousin of Miss Havisham, told Pip that the lover who had betrayed her on the day of her wedding was named Arthur Compeyson.

Pip went to see Miss Havisham to denounce her for having allowed him to believe she was helping him. On his arrival he was informed that Estella was to marry Bentley Drummle. Since Miss Havisham had suffered at the hands of one faithless man, she had reared Estella to inflict as much hurt as possible upon the many men who loved her. Estella reminded Pip that she had warned him not to fall in love with her, for she had no compassion for any human being. Pip returned once more to visit Miss Havisham after Estella had married. An accident started a fire in the old, dust-filled mansion, and although Pip tried to save the old woman she died in the blaze that also badly damaged her gloomy house.

From Provis' story of his association with Compeyson and from other evidence, Pip had learned that Provis was Estella's father; but he did not reveal his discovery to anyone but Jaggers, whose housekeeper, evidently, was

Estella's mother. Pip had learned also that Compeyson was in London and plotting to kill Provis. In order to protect the man who had become a foster father to him, Pip with the help of Herbert Pocket arranged to smuggle Provis across the channel to France. There Pip intended to join the old man. Elaborate and secretive as their plans were, Compeyson managed to overtake them as they were putting Provis on the boat. The two enemies fought one last battle in the water, and Provis killed his enemy. He was then taken to jail, where he died before he could be brought to trial.

When Pip fell ill shortly afterward, it was Joe Gargery who came to nurse him. Older and wiser from his many experiences, Pip realized that he need no longer be ashamed of the kind man who had given so much love to him when he was a boy. His sister, Mrs. Joe, had died and Joe had married again, this time very happily. Pip returned to the blacksmith's home to stay awhile, still desolate and unhappy because of his lost Estella. Later Herbert Pocket and Pip set up business together in London.

Eleven years passed before Pip went to see Joe Gargery again. Curiosity led Pip to the site of Miss Havisham's former mansion. There he found Estella, now a widow, wandering over the grounds. During the years she had lost her cool aloofness and had softened a great deal. She told Pip she had thought of him often. Pip was able to foresee that perhaps he and Estella would never have to part again. The childhood friends walked hand in hand from the place which had once played such an enormous part in both their lives.

THE GREAT GALEOTO

Type of work: Drama
Author: José Echegaray y Eizaguirre (1832-1916)
Type of plot: Social satire
Time of plot: Nineteenth century
Locale: Madrid, Spain
First presented: 1881

Principal characters:
DON JULIAN, a rich Spanish businessman
TEODORA, his young and beautiful wife
ERNESTO, a young dramatist befriended by Don Julian
SEVERO, Don Julian's brother
MERCEDES, Severo's wife

Critique:

A long prologue to *The Great Galeoto*, spoken by Ernesto and Don Julian, clearly expresses the purpose of the play. Echegaray, a rebel against the limitations of the dramatic form, wished to place the whole of society on the stage and to use as motivations not the personal impulses of members of the cast of characters, but the nebulous motivations that arise out of the interactions of groups of people within the social framework. Thus it is that in this drama Echegaray shows the results of slander on the part of many people against the characters placed on the stage. The motivation for the action is not given by the characters we see; the whole of Madrid acts upon them behind the scenes. The problem of dramatic limitations upon reality, which is the basis of *The Great Galeoto*, makes it immediately comparable to another modern play dealing with similar problems, Pirandello's *Six Characters in Search of an Author*.

The Story:

Ernesto, a young playwright, was taken into the home of Don Julian, a rich businessman who had been a close friend of Ernesto's father. Ernesto was working on a great play, but he had difficulty in putting down on paper what was in his mind. As he told Don Julian, his play was to include everyone and to reflect the whole world, not simply a part of it, but the laws of the drama made it impossible for him to put down what he wished to say within

the space and symbols of a play. Don Julian, a practical man, told Ernesto to go get some sleep and be ready to go partridge shooting the next day. After Don Julian left, Ernesto's eye fell on a work by Dante. From it he took the title for his play, *The Great Galeoto*, after a character in the love story of Paolo and Francesca.

The following evening Don Julian and his wife Teodora sat watching the sunset. Don Julian told Teodora that he was afraid Ernesto was unhappy because they had done so much for him, that Ernesto felt he owed them much which could never be repaid. Ernesto joined them and in the ensuing conversation readily admitted his belief that he was living on charity and that people were talking about him. Don Julian said the situation could be remedied and suggested that Ernesto become his secretary, thus repaying, in the eyes of the world, what Julian gave him. Ernesto was pleased by the proposal and accepted.

Don Julian left the room. As the sun went down and Teodora and Ernesto continued to talk, Severo, Don Julian's brother, entered with Mercedes, his wife. Severo and Mercedes voiced their suspicions of the other two to one another and said that the whole city of Madrid was speaking of the affair going on in Don Julian's house between his young wife and the young man he had befriended. After the men left the room Mercedes even told Teodora about the slander that was being voiced in the city. Severo went to pass on the same information to Don Julian.

When Don Julian rejoined his wife, he expressed his anger that Severo should dare to insult his honor and Teodora's by bringing such slander into his home. Don Julian insisted that Ernesto remain in his house as he had before.

Ernesto, told of the slander by Severo's son, left Don Julian's fine home to live in a garret. At first Don Julian was glad, thinking that there might have been some truth in the town's gossip. Later he arrived at a different conclusion and went to invite Ernesto to return. While he and his brother waited in Ernesto's garret, Severo's son appeared with word that Ernesto was to fight a duel with the Viscount Nebreda, who had openly aired his malicious gossip in Ernesto's presence at a café. Don Julian immediately left to find Nebreda to force him to a duel in defense of his own honor.

The boy, left behind, was searching the apartment when Ernesto returned. In the angry conversation that followed, Ernesto told the boy that he and all society, with their slanders, were no better than Galeoto, who had been the go-between for Lancelot and Guinevere in their infamous affair, as told in Dante's story of Paolo and Francesca.

After the boy had gone Teodora came to Ernesto's quarters to see him. She had just learned that Ernesto was leaving Spain the following day and had come to tell him goodbye. Learning of the duel that Ernesto was to fight with Nebreda, she was disturbed that he should possibly humiliate her husband by dueling in his place, when Ernesto was the one, according to gossip, who had laid Don Julian's honor open to question.

While they argued, Severo's son returned to tell them that Don Julian had found Nebreda, fought with him, and had been wounded severely. He added that Don Julian had first returned to Ernesto's quarters to see him, but that a servant had told Don Julian he could not

disturb Ernesto, who was with a lady. Severo and a servant appeared, carrying the wounded Don Julian. Teodora hid in the bedroom, but her presence was discovered when Don Julian asked to be placed on the bed.

After a dreadful scene Ernesto rushed out to find the Viscount Nebreda. He discovered him, fought a duel, and killed Nebreda. In the meantime Severo removed the wounded man to his home. After the duel Ernesto went to Don Julian's house to tell what he had done and to say goodbye to Don Julian and Teodora. Mercedes and her son refused to let him see the sick man. Ernesto told them how Teodora happened to be in his garret and added that she had been trying to prevent the duel between her husband and Nebreda.

After his departure Mercedes brutally questioned Teodora in an effort to make the young woman confess she was in love with Ernesto. She failed, but Teodora promised that Ernesto could never enter the house again. When Ernesto returned, he was ordered to leave, but he agreed to do so only after Teodora had repeated the request. As he was leaving, Severo laid hands on Teodora. Ernesto returned and compelled Severo on his knees to beg Teodora's pardon. He assured Severo that she was innocent of any infidelity.

Don Julian, hearing the commotion, left his sickroom. Infuriated, he slapped Ernesto's face and threatened to kill him in a duel. Severo and Mercedes helped Don Julian, his strength exhausted, back to his room, where he died a few minutes later. Severo, refusing to let Teodora enter her husband's room, claimed the house was his, and after his brother's death he tried to put Teodora out of it because of the scandal and shame that gossip had associated with her.

Teodora fainted. Ernesto picked her up and told Severo that he would take her away. He denounced Severo and society, who had forced him and Teodora into scandalous behavior. Society, he insisted, was no better than a pimp, a great Galeoto.

THE GREAT GATSBY

Type of work: Novel
Author: F. Scott Fitzgerald (1896-1940)
Type of plot: Social criticism
Time of plot: 1922
Locale: New York City and Long Island
First published: 1925

Principal characters:
NICK CARRAWAY, a young bond salesman
DAISY BUCHANAN, his cousin
TOM BUCHANAN, her husband
MYRTLE WILSON, Tom's mistress
JAY GATSBY, a racketeer of the Twenties

Critique:

The short life of F. Scott Fitzgerald was long enough for that brilliant young man to show what the United States meant in terms of the reckless Twenties. Prohibition and speak-easies, new automobiles, victory abroad, popular fads, new wealth—he understood and wrote about all these things. Despite its limitations of style and its imperfections in character development, The Great Gatsby belongs to that literature which endeavors honestly to present the American scene during those riotous years from the first World War to the depression. If F. Scott Fitzgerald's view of character was limited, it may be because his over-all comprehension of society was so positive. His acute sensibility was devoted to an understanding of the results of human action, rather than an understanding of the reasons for human action.

The Story:

Young Nick Carraway decided to forsake the hardware business of his family in the Middle West in order to sell bonds in New York City. He took a small house in West Egg on Long Island and there became involved in the lives of his neighbors. At a dinner party at the home of Tom Buchanan he renewed his acquaintance with Tom and Tom's wife, Daisy, a distant cousin, and he met an attractive young woman, Jordan Baker.

Almost at once he learned that Tom and Daisy were not happily married. It appeared that Daisy knew her husband was deliberately unfaithful.

Nick soon learned to despise the drive to the city through unkempt slums; particularly, he hated the ash heaps and the huge commercial signs. He was far more interested in the activities of his wealthy neighbors. Near his house lived Jay Gatsby, a mysterious man of great wealth. Gatsby entertained lavishly, but his past was unknown to his neighbors.

One day Tom Buchanan took Nick to call on his mistress, a dowdy, over-plump, married woman named Myrtle Wilson, whose husband, George Wilson, operated a second-rate auto repair shop. Myrtle, Tom, and Nick went to the apartment Tom kept, and there the three were joined by Myrtle's sister Catherine and Mr. and Mrs. McKee. The party settled down to an afternoon of drinking, Nick unsuccessfully doing his best to get away.

A few days later Nick attended another party, one given by Gatsby for a large number of people famous in speak-easy society. Food and liquor were dispensed lavishly. Most of the guests had never seen their host before.

At the party Nick met Gatsby for the first time. Gatsby, in his early thirties, looked like a healthy young roughneck.

He was offhand, casual, eager to entertain his guests as extravagantly as possible. Frequently he was called away by long-distance telephone calls. Some of the guests laughed and said that he was trying to impress them with his importance.

That summer Gatsby gave many parties. Nick went to all of them, enjoying each time the society of people from all walks of life who appeared to take advantage of Gatsby's bounty. From time to time Nick met Jordan Baker there, but he began to lose interest in her after he heard that she had cheated in an amateur golf match.

Gatsby took Nick to lunch one day and introduced him to a man named Wolfshiem, who seemed to be Gatsby's business partner. Wolfshiem hinted at some dubious business deals that betrayed Gatsby's racketeering activities and Nick began to identify the sources of some of Gatsby's wealth.

Jordan Baker told Nick the strange story of Daisy's wedding. Before the bridal dinner Daisy, who seldom drank, became wildly intoxicated and announced there would be no wedding, that she had changed her mind and intended to go back to an old flame, Jay Gatsby. Her friends and family, however, had argued with her until she finally married Tom Buchanan. At the time Gatsby was poor and unknown; Tom was rich and influential.

But Gatsby was still in love with Daisy, and he wanted Jordan and Nick to bring Daisy and him together again. It was arranged that Nick should invite Daisy to tea the same day he invited Gatsby. Gatsby awaited the invitation nervously.

On the eventful day it rained. Determined that Nick's house should be presentable, Gatsby sent a man to mow the wet grass; he also sent over flowers for decoration. The tea was a strained affair at first, both Gatsby and Daisy shy and awkward in their reunion. Afterward they went over to Gatsby's mansion, where he showed them his furniture, clothes, swimming pool, and gardens. Daisy promised to attend his next party.

When Daisy disapproved of his guests, Gatsby stopped entertaining. The house was shut up and the bar-crowd turned away.

Gatsby informed Nick of his origin. His true name was Gatz, and he had been born in the Middle West. His parents were poor. But when he was a boy he had become the protégé of a wealthy old gold miner and had accompanied him on his travels until the old man died. Then he changed his name to Gatsby and began to dream of acquiring wealth and position. In the war he had distinguished himself. After the war he had returned penniless to the States, too poor to marry Daisy, whom he had met during the war. Later he became a partner in a drug business. He had been lucky and had accumulated money rapidly. He told Nick that he had acquired the money for his Long Island residence after three years of hard work.

Gatsby gave a quiet party for Jordan, the Buchanans, and Nick. The group drove into the city and took a room in a hotel. The day was hot and the guests uncomfortable. On the way, Tom, driving Gatsby's new yellow car, stopped at Wilson's garage. Wilson complained because Tom had not helped him in a projected car deal. He said he needed money because he was selling out and taking his wife, whom he knew to be unfaithful, away from the city.

At the hotel Tom accused Gatsby of trying to steal his wife and also of being dishonest. He seemed to regard Gatsby's low origin with more disfavor than his interest in Daisy. During the argument, Daisy sided with both men by turns.

On the ride back to the suburbs Gatsby drove his own car, accompanied by Daisy, who temporarily would not speak to her husband.

Following them, Nick and Jordan and Tom stopped to investigate an accident in front of Wilson's garage. They discovered an ambulance picking up the dead body of Myrtle Wilson, struck by a hit-and-run driver in a yellow car. They tried in vain to help Wilson and then went on to Tom's house, convinced that Gatsby had struck Myrtle Wilson.

Nick learned the next day from Gatsby that Daisy had been driving when the woman was hit. However, Gatsby was willing to take the blame if the death should be traced to his car. Gatsby explained that Myrtle, thinking that Tom was in the yellow car, had run out of the house, and Daisy, an inexpert driver, had run her down and then collapsed. Gatsby had driven on.

In the meantime George Wilson, having traced the yellow car to Gatsby, appeared on the Gatsby estate. A few hours later both he and Gatsby were discovered dead. He had shot Gatsby and then killed himself.

Nick tried to make Gatsby's funeral respectable, but no one attended except Gatsby's father, who thought his son had been a great man. None of Gatsby's racketeering associates appeared. His bar-friends had also deserted him.

Shortly afterward Nick learned of Tom's part in Gatsby's death. Tom had visited Wilson and had let Wilson believe that Gatsby had been Myrtle's lover. Nick vowed that his friendship with Tom and Daisy was at an end. He decided to return to his people in the Middle West.

THE GREAT MEADOW

Type of work: Novel
Author: Elizabeth Madox Roberts (1886-1941)
Type of plot: Historical romance
Time of plot: 1775-1783
Locale: Western Virginia and Kentucky
First published: 1930

Principal characters:
DIONY HALL JARVIS, a pioneer wife
BERK JARVIS, her husband
EVAN MUIR, married to Diony after Berk Jarvis' supposed death
THOMAS HALL, Diony's father
ELVIRA JARVIS, Berk's mother

Critique:

Unlike most historical novels, *The Great Meadow* keeps formal history in the background. The novel is essentially a study of a woman's place and problems in the wilderness. Diony Hall is the central character, and her problems are those which beset many women in the days of the early settlements. The need for food, for leather and cloth, for the aid of a husband's carpentry and farming experience —all are problems she has to face. The novel does not add to our knowledge of the settlement of the Kentucky country, but it does present a picture of life in the wilderness quite different from that of most writers on the subject. The style is an unusual one for historical fiction. Miss Roberts attempted to give insight into Diony Hall's mind by means of images and symbols, as in poetry, and through a modified form of the stream-of-consciousness technique.

The Story:

Thomas Hall, well-educated son of a tidewater Virginia family, had settled in upper Albemarle County after having lost his fortune to a dishonest relative. In the upper country he had married a young Methodist woman who had come down into Virginia from Pennsylvania. After their marriage Mrs. Hall bore four children, two boys and two girls.

Of all the children, the oldest girl was by far her father's favorite. She had been named Dione, out of Greek mythology, but everyone called her Diony and spelled her name with a "y." Diony, with her father's help and the use of his small library, educated herself as best she could.

During the middle 1770's visitors occasionally stopped at the Hall house, really little more than a large cabin, as they passed from the Fincastle country or perhaps from even farther away in the cane meadows of Kentucky. Word came to the Halls in that manner of Boone, Henderson, and Harrod, and of the settlements those men had begun in the Kentucky country. The accounts of the back country held smaller charms for Diony than thoughts of visiting her rich relatives on the coasts of Virginia and Maryland; as a girl she believed a life of balls, great houses, carriages, and fancy clothes far more enticing than the rigors of the wilderness.

Among the Halls' neighbors was a family named Jarvis. Of the several boys of the Jarvis clan there was one who was over six feet tall, taller even than Diony's older brother. He was the first to succumb to travelers' tales of the Kentucky country. While he was gone he sent back word by a trapper that he hoped Diony would wait for his return before she accepted a husband. She had one suitor, a man from the tidewater, but Berk Jarvis so captured her imagination that she had her father send a letter ending the suit with the man of wealth and position who had been seeking her hand.

When Berk returned Diony quickly agreed to marry him and to go with him immediately into the wilderness, to the new settlement called Harrodsburg in the Kentucky country. Cloth was woven, garments were sewed, cattle were gathered together, kitchen utensils were selected, and seeds for a garden packed away. At last all was in readiness for the marriage and the wilderness trek to follow immediately. Thomas Hall had had the banns cried in the Anglican Church, according to the British law of the Virginia colony, but the couple and Diony's mother wanted the Methodist minister to perform the ceremony. He did, but many of the people, including Diony and Berk, had some misgivings as to the legality of the marriage, even though the argument of the newly signed Declaration of Independence was brought forth.

After the marriage Diony, Berk, his mother, and a number of other Virginians set out on the wilderness road across the Appalachian highlands to Kentucky. They followed the trail laid out by Daniel Boone. Without accident, but with great difficulty, the party reached Harrod's fort in the wilderness. Berk bought a claim on a farm at some distance from the fort. As the months passed, the lives of the newly married couple slowly took shape. Only one shadow appeared. One day, while Diony and her mother-in-law were out of the fort, they were surprised by Indians. Before Mrs. Jarvis was killed and scalped, she managed to save Diony's life. Berk swore that he would be avenged and kill the Indian who had taken his mother's scalp.

Diony recovered from injuries received when attacked by the Indians. One day, while Berk was purposely gone from the fort, she gave birth to a boy whom they named Tom. The baby was not many weeks old when Berk set out with a party of men to aid George Rogers Clark in his expeditions against the British in the Northwest Territory. Within a few weeks one of the party came back with an injury to his hand and the report of an Indian ambuscade. Berk had been taken by the Indians. Capture was at that time, even though the British gave a higher bounty for prisoners than for scalps, a certain death warrant for most prisoners.

In the weeks and months which passed after her husband's capture Diony stayed in the cabin in the settlement and provided for herself and the baby. Help was forthcoming from Evan Muir, the man who had returned with news of Berk's capture. In return for her nursing and cooking, Evan kept Diony and the child in meat and leather during the summer, fall, and winter. The following summer he farmed the Jarvis homestead claim on a share basis.

Gradually the people in the settlement began to feel sure that Berk was dead, and at last a report came in that he had been killed. Still Diony refused to believe that her husband would not return. Although Evan did not press his suit for marriage, the women of the village warned Diony that it was not fair for her to continue taking his labor on her behalf without giving him the rights of a husband. Diony finally yielded to their arguments and agreed to marry Evan. She soon discovered that she really loved the man and her passion for him was greater than it had been for Berk.

Diony and Evan moved to the Jarvis claim and lived in the house Berk had built there. For two years they lived happily and worked steadily to improve the place. In that time Diony gave birth to a child by Evan, another boy who was named Michael.

One night a call came from the edge of the clearing and Berk Jarvis walked up to the door. Neither Diony, Evan, nor Berk knew how to resolve the predicament of a wife with two legal husbands and a child by each of them. Berk and Evan began a fierce argument, but they were interrupted by visitors from the settlement. The people from the settlement said that the frontier law was that the wife had to choose which of the husbands she would keep; then the other one had to leave for good.

After the visitors left, Evan waited silently; he felt that all he had done for Diony, his labor of three years, would speak for itself. But Berk began a recital of his adventures among the Indians, telling how he had traveled as a prisoner-visitor as far as Sault Sainte Marie and had finally been able to escape and return. He described his tortures in the early weeks of his captivity: the floggings, the gantlet running, and the fear of being burned at the stake.

Late in the night Berk finished speaking. When he had, Diony said that she had made up her mind. She chose to have Berk remain, even though Evan had been a steadier husband. She told them both to leave the cabin that night, for she wanted to be alone for a time before she faced her new start on life with her first husband.

THE GREAT TESTAMENT

Type of work: Poetry
Author: François Villon (1431-after 1463)
First published: First edition undated; second edition, 1489

In 1461 ("the thirtieth year of my age, wherein I have drunk so deep of shame") François Villon, born Montcorbier, wrote *The Great Testament* and by so doing gave to future generations an unrivaled glimpse into Paris at the end of the Middle Ages and a picture of the complete degradation of a human personality. Also, he preserved for us, like flies caught in amber, a score of men and women of the fifteenth-century Paris underworld, who, but for him, would have been lost forever in the night of history.

By 1456, Villon had written *The Little Testament,* a poem of forty eight-line stanzas composed in the form of a mock will in which he could bequeath to friends and enemies gifts appropriate to each. In *The Great Testament* he employed the same device, extending the poem to a hundred and seventy-four stanzas interspersed with lais, rondeaux, and ballades, the most celebrated of the last being the "Ballad of Dead Ladies," familiar to us through Rossetti's translation with the famous refrain, "But where are the snows of yester-year?" The device of a testament enabled Villon to pay off old grudges by bequeathing, with mock solemnity, legacies that would illuminate the character of each recipient, as when he left to the Sieur de Grigny the ruined tower of Billy, Grigny being in all probability a coiner and the tower an excellent spot in which to ply his trade.

The months prior to the composition of the poem had been unhappy ones for Villon. Having been banished from Paris and having barely escaped hanging, he had fled southward, only to become further involved with the law. The summer of 1461 he spent as a prisoner, sentenced by Thibault d'Aussigny, Bishop of Orléans, to a dungeon in the castle at Meung-sur-Loire, a dungeon below the level of the moat, into which the prisoner was lowered in a basket. The diet was bread and water, and additional water was supplied in the form of the dreaded "Question"—a distressing circumstance for a poet who did not care for water as a beverage at the best of times. Release had come unexpectedly when the new king, Louis XI, passed that way and prisoners, in accordance with custom, were freed. Thus the eminently unattractive Spider King won a fervent admirer.

Such, however, was not the fate of the Bishop of Orléans. The poet holds him up to posterity as the example of the merciless prelate who can himself expect no mercy. Having thus disposed of the bishop, Villon next passes in review before us a strange collection of figures: pickpockets, thieves, coiners, harlots, and murderers whom he had known in the Parisian underworld, for it is fairly certain that the poet belonged to a well-organized and widely-spread gang of criminals. Much in the poem is purely conventional: the complaints against fortune; the figure of Death, who brings high and low to the same end; even the "Ballad of Dead Ladies" is on the well-worn theme of Time sweeping away all beauty. But interspersed are the vignettes of Parisian lowlife and of Villon himself living on the earnings of Fat Margot, "within this brothel where we keep our state."

The popularity of Villon's poetry is evidenced by thirty-four editions before 1542. During the neo-classic seventeenth and eighteenth centuries he was almost forgotten, to be resurrected as part of the medieval revival during the nineteenth century. His appeal to such diverse characters as Swinburne and Stevenson is understandable, for the *nostalgie de la boue* is a common phenomenon among members of a highly conventionalized society. These men, moreover, could live vicariously and in safety the life that Villon had lived in grim reality. Further, he provided a different view of the Middle Ages; his was not the world of *The Divine Comedy* or of the Arthurian romances; it was the world of the desperately poor and criminal classes and of the taverns and brothels that they frequented, and the prisons. It is the great realistic work of the late Middle Ages.

But Villon posed a difficult problem for the Victorian translators. The passage of four hundred years had wrought a great change in what might or might not be said in poetry. His frank obscenity graveled them; even Swinburne, in his rendering of the "Regretz de la belle Heaulmiere," took refuge behind six lines of asterisks. One might translate the charming "Ballad of Dead Ladies" or the touching "Ballad to the Virgin" that he wrote for his mother, but in many English editions the "Ballade de la grosse Margot" was omitted or discreetly altered. This attitude is to be regretted, for, as Stevenson remarked, in this ballade Villon outdid Zola in naturalism four hundred years before *Nana* was written; the poem gives us an unforgettable picture of a man who has touched the bottom of degradation and who knows that the cause of his abasement lies only within himself: "Filth we love and filth follows us." It is this very frankness that explains much of Villon's charm. While he made the conventional gesture of railing at Fortune, who creates some men rich and some poor, he clearly recognized where the real blame should fall. For whether one gains money by honest or by dishonest means, where does it go?

To taverns and to harlots all!

And as for his future, he had a shuddering foreboding that he would be one of those

Whose neck, in the bight of a rope of three,
Must prove how heavy my buttocks be.

Among the Victorians, there was considerable sentimentalizing over Villon that might have astonished that "povre petit escollier." Of Swinburne's typically hyperbolic statement

A harlot was thy nurse, a God thy sire,

the second phrase would surely have puzzled him; the first Villon would have understood very well.